The JDP and Making the Post-Kemalist Secularism in Turkey

Pinar Kandemir

The JDP and Making the Post-Kemalist Secularism in Turkey

palgrave
macmillan

Pinar Kandemir
Istanbul, Turkey

ISBN 978-3-031-07604-6   ISBN 978-3-031-07605-3   (eBook)
https://doi.org/10.1007/978-3-031-07605-3

© The Editor(s) (if applicable) and The Author(s), under exclusive license to Springer
Nature Switzerland AG 2022
This work is subject to copyright. All rights are solely and exclusively licensed by the
Publisher, whether the whole or part of the material is concerned, specifically the rights
of translation, reprinting, reuse of illustrations, recitation, broadcasting, reproduction on
microfilms or in any other physical way, and transmission or information storage and
retrieval, electronic adaptation, computer software, or by similar or dissimilar methodology
now known or hereafter developed.
The use of general descriptive names, registered names, trademarks, service marks, etc.
in this publication does not imply, even in the absence of a specific statement, that such
names are exempt from the relevant protective laws and regulations and therefore free for
general use.
The publisher, the authors, and the editors are safe to assume that the advice and information in this book are believed to be true and accurate at the date of publication. Neither
the publisher nor the authors or the editors give a warranty, expressed or implied, with
respect to the material contained herein or for any errors or omissions that may have been
made. The publisher remains neutral with regard to jurisdictional claims in published maps
and institutional affiliations.

Cover illustration: © Alex Linch shutterstock.com

This Palgrave Macmillan imprint is published by the registered company Springer Nature
Switzerland AG
The registered company address is: Gewerbestrasse 11, 6330 Cham, Switzerland

For my husband Erkan Kandemir and my dear children Hatice Beyza, Fatıma Zehra and Mehmet Akif.

CONTENTS

1	Introduction	1
2	Two Sides of the Same Secularism Story: Kemalists Versus Non-Kemalists in Modern Turkey	29
3	The Anatomy of the JDP and the Emergence of Post-Kemalist Secularism	59
4	JDP's Secularism and the Headscarf	111
5	The JDP's Secularism and Religious Education	143
6	JDP's Secularism and Turkey's Religious and Sectarian Minorities	177
	Conclusion	219
	Bibliography	229
	Index	271

ABBREVIATIONS

ANAP	Anavatan Partisi
AP	Adalet Partisi (Justice Party)
CYDD	Çağdaş Yaşamı Destekleme Derneği
DP	Demokrat Parti (Democrat Party)
ECHR	European Court of Human Right
EU	European Union
HDP	Halkların Kardeşliği Partisi
IHS	İmam-Hatip Okullar (Imam Hatip Schools)
JDP	Adalet ve Kalkınma Partisi (Justice and Development Party)
MGK	National Security Council
MHP	Milliyetçi Hareket Partisi (Nationalist Movement Party)
MIT	Turkish Intelligence Service
NGO	Non-Governmental Organisation
NOM	Milli Görüş Hareketi (National Outlook Movement)
RPP	Cumhuriyet Halk Partisi (Republican People's Party)
YOK	Council of Higher Education

CHAPTER 1

Introduction

One year after its establishment in August 2001, the Justice and Development Party (JDP), officially abbreviated to the AK Party, but generally referred to as the AKP elsewhere in the literature, came to power in Turkey's 2002 General Election. The JDP, a self-declared conservative, centre-right political party has successfully dominated the political arena ever since, breaking new ground in Turkish politics over the past two decades. Since its inception, the JDP has secured first place in every single election, remaining in power despite resistance from the representatives of the old regime, i.e. the Kemalist establishment, state bureaucracy (particularly the military and the judiciary), and the Republican People's Party (RPP).

Besides being the democratically elected longest-serving political party in Turkish Republican history, the importance of the JDP resides in its vision of a self-declared "new Turkey,"[1] which differs markedly from that defined under Kemalism, the traditional state ideology formulated and introduced in the early Republican years (1923–1950), and added to the constitution in 1937.

Under the guidance of six main principles (Republicanism, nationalism, populism, secularism, statism, and reformism), the Kemalist establishment dominated the centre of Turkish life, instilling Kemalist reforms in social, political, legal, cultural, and religious domains. Even after Turkey's

© The Author(s), under exclusive license to Springer Nature Switzerland AG 2022
P. Kandemir, *The JDP and Making the Post-Kemalist Secularism in Turkey*, https://doi.org/10.1007/978-3-031-07605-3_1

1

transition to a multi-party democracy in 1946 and the rise of the central-right Democrat Party (DP), which won the first democratic elections in 1950, the principles of Kemalism remained in force in a "multiplex fashion"[2]-changing tones, with the protection of the Kemalist establishment. Consequently, despite the democratisation and liberalisation steps taken under DP governments for 10 years, and followed by other centre-right parties such as the Anavatan Partisi (ANAP) in later decades, minimal changes to Kemalist secularism were recorded. Ultimately, all these attempts coming from alternative power blocs, whom I refer to as non-Kemalist(s) in this book, were blocked and criminalised by Kemalist establishment.

Eventually, the JDP founded and supported by a non-Kemalist coalition including conservatives, liberals, and Islamists in 2001, first matured and then forged a Post-Kemalist Turkey[3] following a Constitutional Referendum in 2010. This new aura in Turkish politics removed statism, authoritarian secularism, and Turkish ethnic nationalism and balanced civil-military relations from the centre of the politics. Thus, by providing an alternative political, economic, and social force to challenge the domination of the Kemalist hegemony in social and political sphere, the JDP has successfully institutionalised a different type of social contract opening a gateway of the centre to key peripheral elements. One of the most distinctive features of this reconfigured "social contract" is its novel formulation of secularism.[4]

Indeed, following its foundation in 2001, the JDP developed a unique approach to conceptualising the relationship between state and religion. In contrast to other mainstream parties and political positions both in the past and present, it offers an alternate vision and model to that of inherited Kemalist secularism, as first formulated by; Mustafa Kemal Ataturk, founder of Turkish Republic, but then refined by his close associates in the formative period of the Republic. This means that the JDP, a religion friendly, economically liberal centre-right conservative party, has successfully presented a new approach to secularism as an alternative to Kemalist secularism. This newly emerging situation during the first two decades of the twenty-first century created a new environment within the political and social sphere that enabled competing secularism(s) to exist simultaneously.

Thus, this book is an analytical study of secularism in contemporary Turkey by tracing its historical trajectory within the context of political transformation in a country that experienced a social and cultural rupture in its formative years. Its principal focus is on the policies and practices of the current ruling party, the Justice and Development Party (JDP), which has influenced the process of change, evolution, and transformation with regard to secularism and state policies toward religion.

To locate aforementioned historical discussion in a theoretical context, this book utilises the multiple modernities paradigm,[5] first developed by Shmuel Eisenstadt. The latter is a renowned scholar engaged in the debate surrounding modernity and its ability to transcend regional origins and formative contexts. The paradigm is based on the understanding that societies can construct and experience modernity according to their own cultural codes, traditions, and historical experiences, without necessarily duplicating the Western model.[6]

Therefore, contrary to the dominant literature on Turkish secularism, which uses modernity and secularism as synonyms, and presents Western secularism as a prerequisite for modernisation, this study explores, categorises, and defines Turkey's path to modernisation and its changing relationship with secularism by taking historical realities, political dynamics, cultural context and the sociological structure of the country into account, all of which mark the development and shaping of state-religion relations to varying degrees. While doing so, it takes inspiration from Post-Kemalist literature, which brought a fresh and critical view of Turkey's 150-year modernisation story in the 1990s by challenging the sacralisation of Kemalism.

Kemalist Secularism as the Elephant in the Dark Room

Secularism as a concept was adopted in the English language after its first use by George Jacob Holyoake in 1854. He used it to refer to "a series of principles intended for the guidance of those who find theology indefinite, or inadequate, or deem it unreliable."[7] However, subsequent discussions have repeatedly redefined it in different periods relative to varying social, economic, and political conditions. This has resulted in the existence of numerous definitions of secularism/secularisation and several suggested forms. However, in its simplest definition in the Oxford Dictionary, Secularism is "the principle of separation of state from religious institutions"[8]; that is, secular means, "not connected with religious or spiritual matters."[9]

Since this study does not intend to engage in a detailed discussion of the genealogies of secularism, Charles Taylors' summary of propositions related to secularisation in literature would be sufficient to exhibit an understanding of it according to three different approaches. Taylor notes that secularism was defined as "(1) a tendency to eliminate religion from government and public affairs, (2) a decline in spirituality, and (3) the general understanding that faith... is one human possibility among others."[10] Besides, evaluating Jose Casanova's work, which does not reject "examination of validity" of all these propositions "independently," "secularisation as the privatisation of religion as a precondition for modern liberal democratic politics" and "differentiation of the secular sphere" can be seen as additional to these discussions about how to define secularism.[11]

In light of these definitions, when one evaluates the character of Kemalist secularism, it would be easy to classify it as *unique*.[12] Recollect that when the Turkish Republic was founded in 1923, secularism was deliberately adopted as one of its main principles, to formulate a new identity rejecting pre-existing cultural and traditional codes and social norms. It was intended as a total rupture from the Ottoman Empire's Muslim identity and homogenisation of society in an ethnic and religious sense. To achieve this, it ended the *millet system* created by the Ottoman Empire to encourage different religious groups to implement their own legal and administrative systems.[13] Indeed, this strategy was effective in terms of creating a secular elite class to convey Kemalist principles and dominate the centre. Since then, the Republican, ultra-secular and pro-Western Kemalist elites not only retained political and economic power, but also maintained the cultural hegemony[14] in their hands.

Since its introduction, Kemalist secularism has entirely avoided separating religion and world affairs, aiming to combine national and religious identity "by keeping Islam in reserve."[15] Reflecting this, Binnaz Toprak who extensively studied state-religion relations defines Turkey as a semi-secular state, in which there is substantial state control of religion, rather than a separation of state and religion.[16] Therefore, Kemalist secularism fully regulates the realm of religion, choosing to either use or eliminate[17] the latter on impulse, and allowing religious practice only insofar that it suits the state agenda[18] and does not challenge the secular foundations of the Republic.

Thus, the state, which promoted and regulated Sunni Islam,[19] even presented a framework to demonstrate how Islam should be.[20] This was a radical step, designed to encourage a particular kind of piety via state tools, such as the Directorate of Religious Affairs (*Diyanet*) and compulsory religion course in the schools. Within this context, one can conclude that the most important aspect of Kemalist secularism is that it instrumentalises religion as a tool to control the non-Kemalist periphery. This subsequently created tension, framed as *centre-periphery polarity*, which survived until the emergence of a Post-Kemalist Turkey. To understand what I mean here, one should revisit Şerif Mardin's centre-periphery cleavage,[21] derived from Edward Shill's initial "Centre and Periphery" formulation.[22] According to this paradigm, as conveyer of social values, the state spreads its principles to the periphery using elites.[23] Thus, inTurkish case, the ruling elites of Turkey not only access economic privileges, but also have the cultural capital to implement hegemony over the "the backward, the uncultured and uneducated, the rural, the traditional, the particular, the lower class" (by their definitions) periphery.[24] This makes Kemalism an elitist ideology, as well as a Jacobin one, creating significant barriers between the centre and the periphery.

Ultimately, the Kemalist secularisation project was imposed upon society through top-down reforms and at times by repression.[25] When Turkish periphery showed no enthusiasm for the imposed secularism reforms introduced through education and other means, the centre, Kemalist establishment used force to homogenise[26] and secularise society undersingle party rule. In this regard, Kemalism imposed a fixed nationalist curriculum, military conscription, a statist economic model, single language, and homogenised cultural identity. While, the ruling elites—the *centre*, which constituted the bulk of the Turkish army, the Turkish bureaucracy, the RPP, and its supporters—was successfully exhibiting a secularised approach, the *periphery* were marginalised, and excluded.[27] This state of affairs was saliently described by Jose Casanova, who stated that Kemalism was "too secular for the Islamists, too Sunni for the Alevis, too Muslim for the non-Muslim minorities and too Turkish for the Kurds."[28]

Within this context, despite being subject to a change in tone from time to time, and by preventing the emergence of alternative power hubs, Kemalism survived as a hegemonic ideology concentrated in the centre. Any political movement that dared to oppose this hegemonic discourse and offer an alternative narrative was punished by the Kemalist establishment via an internal coup or the closure of the political party. Tens of political parties that were closed by the Constitutional Court[29] and coup d'états or military interventions serve as proof of this. Thus, the Kemalist concept of secularism, alongside nationalism and statism, has been a political taboo, deemed beyond reproach. This made it impossible, up until 2010, to be openly anti-Kemalist or to propose an alternative approach that diverges from the vision of Kemalist elites. In the final instance, all the political parties draw their validation from Atatürk's legitimacy, because the other option would be extremely radical.

The JDP and Emergence of Rival Modes of Seculasrisms in Turkey

Although Turkish history is replete with counter-arguments suggesting that secularism as developed in the Western world differed from that implemented by the Kemalists, none of the political movements voiced this argument succeeded in becoming alternatives to Kemalism. The JDP is the only exception to this. By exploiting Kemalism's ongoing crisis since the 1980s,[30] and adopting the rising trend towards political and economic liberalisation globally, it managed to formulate a new type of political proposal, not always drawing its legacy from the principles of Kemalism. Thus, the JDP effectively confronted most of the assumptions underpinning Kemalism by representing an anti-establishment standpoint.[31] As will be discussed in detail later in this book, this process resulted in a changing power balance, the removal of tension between the state and citizens outside of the Kemalist elite, the hybridisation of Kemalism and Islamism, and changing forms of piety, which might be seen as an outcome of Post-Kemalist secularisation.

Creating and then promoting an alternative proposal to Kemalism (specifically its secularism principle) has been a challenging journey for the JDP. It should be noted that the JDP experienced great resistance from the Kemalist establishment during this period. After facing the threat of a ban in 2008, multiple interferences from the military and judiciary, and constant defiance from the Kemalist elites, it took the JDP almost eight years, between 2002 and 2010, to partly resolve Kemalist domination over state institutions. Finally, with the constitutional referendum in 2010, a new era began in Turkey and a Post-Kemalist Turkey came into being step by step. As "a broadly-based political movement with a pragmatic ideology,"[32] the JDP initiated a direct change announcing it as a "New Turkey." Hence, while the predecessors of the JDP lost the battle against the Kemalist establishment by closure of their party or through coups, the JDP became the first survivor, continuing to exist after confronting Kemalism, and even able to establish a different mode of secularism at state and societal level during its struggle against the Kemalists. At this stage, one should understand that what makes the JDP successful, if not its courage, is having a reformist agenda, its steps towards democratisation, its EU membership initiatives, its efforts to revise civil-military relations, its growing popularity despite some increasingly radical steps and the new state-religion relations within the framework of its secularism proposal.

To understand what I mean by JDP's new secularism proposal, it is crucial to visit the Party's ideological formulation and Islam-secularism dichotomy in the relevant literature on the JDP. However, even before this, one should remember that according to those who apply this dichotomy in different cases as well as the JDP, the movements are clearly identifiable, as their Muslim identities are generally not considered secular, being positioned along Islamist political lines. Seemingly, this reductionist approach attempts to analyse secularism in Turkey through the Islam-secularism, by claiming that secularism decreases when religious identity, Islam in this context, becomes apparent, and increases when religious identity is repressed. By affirming the methodology of aggressive Kemalist secularism policies under the justification that it was a "one-way street"[33] in Turkey's path to modernisation and Westernisation, this assumption creates a misconception, namely that a Muslim is, by default, anti-secular. Thus, rather than, for instance, considering An-Naim's secularism perspective, suggesting that secularism is "a willingness to acknowledge and mediate a positive role for religion in public life, instead of attempting to suppress or control religion,"[34] in their work, as an alternative perspective to analyse some of the JDP's actions, any reforms related to Muslims (including lifting the headscarf ban) are labelled as an Islamisation step,[35] while other liberalisation reforms directed towards other religious groups were undermined by viewing them as the JDP's reluctant and pragmatic steps developed to become members of the EU. By seeing this as a symptom of Orientalism inspired by Eisenstadt's analysis on this discussion,[36] I do not evaluate any of the JDP's reforms as an evident of Islamism or Islamisation. Yet, as will be demonstrated in book, religion has always been alive at the Turkish *periphery*, in spite of efforts by the Kemalists to demolish it; the JDP's role has been to carry it from *periphery* to *centre*.

8   P. KANDEMIR

This does not mean I reject the gravity of the Islamism debate when discussing the JDP. However, it could be claimed that this approach often undermines authentic discussion about secularism, since this dichotomy precludes nuanced analysis. By applying the multiple modernities approach, I dismiss the validity of the aforementioned approach presented in the literature. In this regard, one of the contributions of this study, in addition to the previously mentioned ones, is that it provides a close examination of the secularism practices of the JDP without reducing the discussion to a false dichotomy. Beyond any labelling exercise, what is more significant for this book is how the JDP proposes and applies secularism, in particular whether it fulfils the requirements of this form of secularism with its practices.

Prior to discussing the relevant literature relating to whether the JDP is Islamist, new Islamist, Islam-sympathetic, post-Islamist, transformed Islamist, or moderate Islamist,[37] it is useful to review what Islamism is. There is an extensive literature that provides several definitions of this term. According to Denoeux, Islamism is "A form of instrumentalization of Islam by individuals, groups and organisations that pursue political objectives. It provides political responses to today's societal challenges by imagining a future, the foundations for which rest on appropriated, reinvented concepts borrowed from the Islamic tradition."[38] Bayat claims the motivation that informs this ideology is to establish "some kind of an Islamic Order; a religious state, Sharia law, and moral codes in Muslim societies and communities."[39] Ayoob writes, "Islamism, as far as its exponents and adherents are concerned, is above all a political ideology and not a theological construction. It is a product of modernity as much as a response to it."[40] Prominent scholar İsmail Kara likewise argues this point, stating the main purpose of Islamism is to formulate Islam as an ideology in a Western sense.[41] Haldun Gülalp goes further, claiming the emergence of contemporary political Islam should be defined "in the context of the global crisis of modernism and secular nationalism."[42]

Outside this circle, there are scholars who differentiate their perspective by explaining what type of Islamism the JDP can be identified with. Prominent scholar, Ümit Cizre, is among them and distinguishes the concepts of political Islamism and post-Islamism through her concept of "New Islamism" in her work "Secularism and Islamic Politics." According to Cizre, the JDP is a "pragmatic-conservative and Islam-sensitive party",[43] as well as "Islam friendly."[44] Jeffrey Haynes also uses similar terms when describing the JDP, referring to them as "an Islam-influenced government."[45] Küçükcan uses "Muslim Democrats" in his work,[46] notwithstanding Erdoğan's explicit rejection of this term. Çınar and Duran have referred to the JDP as "transformed Islamists."[47]

Yıldız is one of the many respected scholars who applies "new Islamists" appellation to the JDP, claiming "the New Islamism reflects a re-evaluation that sees the civilisational dialogue between the Islamic and Western worlds as essential, a radical contrast to the conflict-ridden cold war perspective that considered the clash of civilisations as something intrinsic to world politics."[48] Dağı also claims that the JDP "represents a new articulation of coexistence between Islam and the West" with its "pro-Western, liberal and democratic orientation,"[49] but he instead uses a term formulated by Asef Bayat: post-Islamism[50] that "refer primarily to a shift in the attitudes and strategies of Islamist militants in the Muslim world."[51] Similarly, although the panic over "a resurgent Islamism" came to the surface after the landslide victory of Islamist parties in the region, Bayat claimed the newly emergent movements (such as Hizb-al Nahda in Tunisia, Justice and Development in Morocco, and Justice and Development in Turkey) are post-Islamist rather than Islamist, and that they "self-consciously remain Islamic."[52]

It should be noted that for remarkable numbers of the scholars that I refer here, Islamism or any attributed definition to its tones, does not necessarily in conflict with secularism. In other words, even if they define the JDP as Islamist, this does not mean that it is directly anti-secularist. For instance, Dağı also claims the JDP has adopted some aspects of post-Islamism while embracing measures that allowed its leadership to manoeuvre within the existing political system.[53] In another article Dağı says they transformed, demanding a genuinely liberal democratic regime in Turkey rather than challenging modernity and modern political values and institutions.[54] Overall, according to Dağı, the JDP integrates universal concepts such as democracy, human rights, secularism with "Islamic morality, brotherhood, and solidarity," representing a new formulation in Turkish politics.[55]

Nevertheless, without constraining the JDP with an ideological label, the concept of conservative democracy provides a second lens through which to examine the JDP's approach to secularism. Axiarlis, who prefers to apply the concept of "conservative democracy", claims the JDP is a secular movement that "is not in practice or in rhetoric, opposed to the secular system, nor does it seek to usurp or in any way undermine the

10   P. KANDEMIR

principle of secularism."[56] Gülalp also outlines the same approach in his several works on the JDP, claiming it has a liberal attitude towards secularism.[57] Although there are limited works applying this argument, their overall point is that JDP is setting "a new social contract between the different sectors of Turkish society" and "it is indeed largely based on the synthesis between liberal desires for reform and conservative (religious) cultural sensitivities."[58] Rather than seeing this Islamisation, Hakan Yavuz describes it as process of normalisation.[59]

Thus since the beginning, the JDP constantly proposed its novel secularism approach while pushing other political parties to do so. This process of transformation run by the JDP has effectively formulated rival modes of secularism in harmony with the cultural and historical realities of Turkey. This leads us to the following summary relating to current mainstream forms of secularism(s) in Turkey: (1) the JDP's Post-Kemalist secularism, which encourages free visibility, representation, and circulation of religion in the social sphere, but imposes some limitations from the Kemalist secularism tradition such as controlling the content of religious education or continuation of the existence of Diyanet. (2) Kemalist secularism, which is aggressively anti-religion and restrictive against all religious representation in the public sphere; and (3) moderate Kemalist secularism, which has no problem with religious freedom for minority religious groups, but is still cautious when it comes to majority Sunni Muslims' visibility, especially in the context of relations between religion and politics. Although this book will focus mainly on the first form, it will still regularly reference other mainstream secularism approaches taken in contemporary Turkey.

In this context, the question relates to how the diversification of secularism and the removal of a one-size form under state guarantee have been possible in Turkey. In answer, I claim that a radical shift has been made possible with three main changes in Turkey that fully impact the political, social, and economic environment: (1) the rise of liberal economic policies since the 1990s, which peaked in the JDP years and ended absolute state control over the economy with complete economic liberalisation, and the consequent increasing political power at the national level of the lower-middle and middle-middle class (that occurred before the JDP came to power, preparing fertile ground for further democratisation); (2) the decline in the military's and judiciary's dominance over civil politics resulting from the JDP's continued success in democratic elections, which inevitably brought about political stability; and (3) and the EU accession process, which afforded political justification for the JDP to some extend in national and international level. These factors ended the guardianship of Kemalist establishment on secularism, creating a space for the JDP to make changes without risking a military coup or closure cases (despite several failed attempts at both).

Nevertheless, regardless of the changing political environment, Kemalist secularism has not vanished during the JDP years. As with many forms of emerging secularism(s), it continued to develop different tones during this period, albeit in a less belligerent configuration. However, today, in contemporary Turkey, Post-Kemalist secularism holds sway and has progressed through legal and constitutional changes. As will be discussed in details later, while Kemalist secularism still has its strong base within and without the RPP, some of former Kemalist seculars are becoming more moderate than previously, most of the time to attract voters. This shows there is no longer a single vision of a secularism understanding, under the guardianship of the Kemalist establishment, as in the pre-2010 period. Rather, multiple varieties of secularism(s) now co-exist as rivals with competing visions, although the JDP's Post-Kemalist secularism form dominates at present, since they hold power. To understand more how the multiple secularisms can emerge within a single country, it is very crucial to revisit modernism discussions in the context of secularism discussions.

RETHINKING THE MULTIPLE MODERNITIES PARADIGM IN THE CONTEXT OF TURKISH CASE

The modernisation theory that emerged at the end of the nineteenth century suggested a type of modernity that promoted particular principles, such as democracy, secularism, human rights, free markets, and industry within the context of Westernisation. It viewed modernisation as a singular process expanding linearly to reform and secularise non-Western communities. According to this approach, religion was expected to lose its importance within society, and individuals' level of piety was predicted to decrease. Thus, it was claimed the rise of modernity would result in the decline in religiosity.[60] However, with the revival of religion during the last century, the classical modernism theory supported by prominent scholars, including Durkheim, Comte, Marks, Weber, Nietzsche, and Freud, has proven contentious. Thus, two school of thought emerged regarding this issue[61]; while one school of thought argues that modernisation necessarily leads to secularism and results in the universal decline of religion,[62] which has been the primary wish of many scholars since the Enlightenment, according to Jeffrey K. Hadden,[63] for others, the revival of religion is proof that this approach, which dominated over the last 150 years was erroneous.[64] The US case and that of secular Muslim countries provide the evidence for this. At this stage, Peter Berger's seminal work, "Desecularisation" explains how even he acknowledged he had miscalculated in his early works in taking the decline of religion as guaranteed in the modern age.[65] Similar to many other scholars, he rejected the assumption that modernisation leads to the decline of religion as framed in Karel Dobbelaere's formulation on macro-secularisation (decreasing the importance of religion in society), meso-secularisation (decreasing level of religiosity in private beliefs), or micro-secularisation (decline of religion at the organisational level).[66]

One of the initial, and most consistent, objections to classical modernisation theory, which derives from a Eurocentric point of view and appoints the West as the yardstick, would be Eisenstadt's multiple modernities paradigm, which introduced a critical approach to the uniformity expected from modernism vis-à-vis lifestyle, political system, and state-religion relations. According to him, "the actual developments in modernizing societies have refuted the homogenizing and hegemonic assumptions of this Western program of modernity."[67] Thus, by differentiating themselves from the West, but retaining modernism, these patterns are "greatly influenced by specific cultural premises, traditions, and historical experiences."[68] Eisenstadt notes, the multiple modernities paradigm centres around three important aspects: social actions, social structure, and cultural orientations.[69] Therefore, it is not modernisation itself which Eisenstadt rejects; he rather rejects modernity that excludes culture and tradition.[70] Fourie concurs, stating "(…) the impact of modernity around the world is and always has been highly contingent on the cultural backgrounds of individual societies, its ideological and institutional manifestations are bound to vary greatly."[71]

From a similar point of view, Gusfield's argument that tradition is not necessarily on a collision course with modernity, and that modernity does not necessarily weaken tradition,[72] guides us to understand the importance of tradition and history on the path of modernisation in different contexts. Gusfield notes, "both tradition and modernity form the bases of ideologies and movements in which the polar opposites are converted into aspirations, but traditional forms may supply support for, as well as against, change."[73] This suggests the new is not necessarily a substitute for the old, and that it is possible for both to be co-exist and be mutually sustainable. It also claims that a society in which traditions are preserved can also be described as modern. Therefore, it is possible for secularism to conform to a new model of society, in which both the traditional and the modern are not in conflict but in harmony. In that case, this makes the "entire world modern,"[74] not equally as meant by Eisenstadt, but differently as suggested by Wagner.[75]

When one implements these approaches and introduces them alongside secularisation theory, it provides an excellent theoretical foundation from which to examine non-Western secularism experiences. By suggesting this, Burchardt and Wohlrab-Sahr noted, "[S]ecularity should be understood as the sometimes latent, sometimes explicit forms of distinction between religious and non-religious spheres and practices in society and that secularities should be analysed not so much in quantitative terms ('more' or 'less' of it) but in terms of its cultural underpinnings."[76] Indeed, this cultural difference shifts from one example to another, leading us to question whether all secularisms convey the same thing or not. Bilgrami asks: "Are there not, rather, subtle differences that can bedevil cross-cultural discussions of these matters?"[77] To respond this question, the multiple secularism paradigm opens up a new perspective, by supporting the idea that if there is not a single, uniform type of secularism, different forms can then be construed that are compatible with the cultural and traditional values of state and society.

Similarly, by noting that only secularised society can be taken under the following category, Jürgen Habermas also contradicts with classical antagonism between religion and secularism.[78] For him, post-secular societies recognise the cruciality and success of secularism in a post-Enlightenment world while they are not rejecting the value of religion.[79] This doesn't mean that Habermas rejects revival of religion globally, but he also does not agree with desecularisation theories.[80] Habermasian post-secularism theory argues that secularists and religious have a lot to learn from each other. According to Loobuyck, "this means that those holding religious and secularist worldviews should take each other's contributions to controversial public debates seriously."[81] But beside this, "where possible, the discourse of pious citizens should be translated into a secular language, and secular citizens must remain sensitive to the force of articulation inherent in religious languages."[82]

This school of thought also underlines the diversification of religiosity by noting that "resurgence is not taking place with much uniformity around the globe. Rather, it is taking many forms—not all of which fit into an easily codifiable definition of 'religion.'"[83] By highlighting the role of globalisation, Haynes notes that "the increase in various forms of spirituality and religiosity are manifested in various ways including 'new' religious and spiritual phenomena, including manifestations of 'New Age' spirituality; 'foreign', 'exotic' Eastern religions, including Hare Krishna; 'televangelism'; renewed interest in astrology; and 'new' sects, such as the Scientologist."[84] Although contradicting with Byrd's understanding, Fenn sees this diversification of religiosity as an outcome of secularisation rather than a post-secular condition,[85] Dustin Byrd still claims that "indeed, like an elastic band that is stretched at both ends, the more secular the contemporary world becomes, the more it creates the conditions for this new post-secular form of religion."[86]

When one reconsiders all these modernism discussions in the context of Turkish case, it is easy to see that features that are attributed to the West by Kemalist scholars constitute an essential understanding of the equation between modernism and secularism.[87] One of the most noteworthy and leading books on Kemalist secularism, *The Development of Secularism in Turkey*," written by prominent scholar Niyazi Berkes in 1964, exemplifies this trend. According to him, secularisation and modernisation are synonymous,[88] with secularism being a precondition of modernisation.[89] In Berkes' other reference work, he considers secularism as the most crucial outcome of modernism, while the decline of religion is assumed to be guaranteed as a result of secularisation process as most of scholars inspired by the classical modernisation approaches.

The first consistent objection to this assumption originated with Post-Kemalist scholars in Turkey, who were inspired by works rejecting classical modernisation and secularisation theories. In academia, these discussions find a place using the concepts of alternative modernities, local modernities, and "Modernisation in non-Western societies"[90] within the context of Turkish secularism history. Developed by prominent academics such as Şerif Mardin and Nilüfer Göle, Post-Kemalism discussions created a foundation enabling other academics to view Kemalist modernism through a different lens, especially after the 1990s. Before this time, there was one dominant view sacralising the Kemalist modernisation project, which equated modernisation with Westernisation, and initiated the institutionalisation of secularism, which "attempted to place the Turkish people, now purified from Islam and Islamic culture, into a Western-Christian international order via newly shaped Turkish nationalism."[91] Post-Kemalist literature brought a fresh perspective from which to challenge entrenched views.

In this regard, as one of the leading figures of the Post-Kemalist academic approach, Şerif Mardin was the first scholar to tackle Kemalism as an ideology within the context of modernism. Mardin criticises the Kemalist modernisation project, and its practices, by claiming that removing religion from the social and private lives of citizens destroys society's fabric.[92] This was actually one of the first counter arguments from a respected international academic against the Kemalist literature, which presented secularism or modernism in a singular form.

Utilising a similar approach, Göle also opposes "the homogenising practices and assimilatory strategies" of the classical modernisation approach adopted by Kemalists.[93] She criticises understanding of modernisation as a linear process that must take place similarly in every society and the imposition of Western values on non-Western societies. Specifically, Göle presents a non-Western definition of modernity, which claims that a universal language can be created by analysing local cases.[94] In this context, Göle's conceptualisation of an "extra modernity" can be refreshing. Extra modernity identifies the relationship constructed between the West and modernism, which has transformed into an indicative desire for and fetishisation of modernity.[95]

In view of these discussions on modernism and secularism, Çınar's further analysis is especially stimulating. According to her, people in these countries perceive secularism and subsequently "meet it, negotiate it, and appropriate it in their own fashion."[96] Once the domination of the Kemalists of the social and political sphere ended in 2010, this was able to happen in Turkey. Therefore, by applying this theoretical foundation and deepening it with tangible data from evaluative case studies in a historical context, the JDP case and its secularism approach can be analysed without falling into the trap of the Islam-secularism dichotomy. As I highlighted before, instead of making statements like "the JDP is not secular because it is Islamist," I offer a new analytical perspective, investigating the practices of this party from the prism of the concept of Post-Kemalist secularism and applying paradigms, such as multiple modernities and local and alternative modernities, which align with the arguments of Post-Kemalist academics analysing modernisation within the context of secularism.

Thus, by inspiring from post-Kemalism discussions[97] grounded in Eisenstadt's multiple modernities paradigm, this book introduces the most up-to-date contributions to the literature[98] on religion and politics in Turkey, filling a notable gap by claiming that diversified, distinctive, and hybridised visions of, and approaches to, secularism can co-exist within a single country without leading to radical social or political disruption—similar to that of the formative period of Turkish Republic. It also shows that tensions may emerge due to competing visions and interpretations of secularism because of social, political, ethnic, and ideological heterogeneity within the country, a heterogeneity that has long resisted an established hegemony of thought.

This book also proves that three localised models of secularism (Kemalist secularism, moderate Kemalist secularism, and Post-Kemalist secularism) have been competing with one another at a national level since 2010—the date that the constitutional referendum officially changed fundamental dynamics in Turkey. In response to the current social and political realities of Turkey, this dual process continues, as rival approaches to secularism compete to attain political dominance, wide-scale implementation, and public support.

Examining this argument, which is not captured by the current literature, and by applying and elucidating different historical cases, gives this book additional novelty to further provide an explanation of contemporary Turkish history through different lenses. On the other hand, this advantage imposes a limitation on this study. As political parties are living organisms, it is challenging to imagine what will happen to Turkish secularism(s) after this book is published. Turkey has witnessed great change, not only in secular terms but also religious ones over the last two decades. However, it still remains indefinite whether the emergence of multiple secularism(s) in Turkey will survive in governance practices or not. Nevertheless, there is one thing that I can confidently claim, by drawing inspiration from Jurgen Habermas' great work, "Notes on post-secular societies"; the near future will be "a complementary learning process" for religious and secular mentalities in Turkey, allowing them 'to balance shared citizenship and cultural differences.'[99] This complementary learning process was begun in earnest after 2010, and the current model of Kemalists and non-Kemalists embody it.

CONDUCTING RESEARCH ON THE TRANSFORMATION OF SECULARISM IN TURKEY

The historical research methodology is applied in this study to analyse Turkey's newly emerging secularism model. By gathering primary historical data, including official records from governmental and non-governmental institutions, and private materials such as autobiographies, memoirs, in addition to public survey data, this study also used the semi-structured interviews with high-level policymakers to provide an original contribution to the literature. Although the JDP remains in power and its Post-Kemalist secularism in Turkey is still developing, evaluating the last 18 years with a historical methodology can serve as guidance for today.

Therefore, by centralising secularism discussions, Turkish history is divided into two main periods: pre-2010 and post-2010. The former is referred to as the Kemalist era, while the changes made in Turkey after 2010 are described as Post-Kemalist Turkey. These two periods are compared to each other focusing on three aspects: education policy, the headscarf controversy, and religious and sectarian minorities as cases that crystallise the changing dynamics and patterns with regard to the transformation of secularism. Thus, at the beginning of each case chapter, the historical background to the topic is explained chronologically, allowing a comparison between the two different periods in Turkey.

I chose these three cases to illustrate how the JDP's secularism impacted and tackle on everyday problems in Turkey. The primary issue of concern was the headscarf controversy, as historically it has been the main point of divergence and dispute between Kemalist seculars and non-Kemalists in Turkey, with every social and political group holding an opinion and adopting a stance. The other discussion is the JDP's education policy, which presents a factual case that helps to grasp the contours of the JDP's new model. The third issue, also providing factual data, explains the changes in religious and sectarian minorities' conditions in Turkey to test whether the JDP's model is religion friendly only for the Sunni majority or also for other religious groups.

Interviews

This study brings an original contribution to the literature relating to the JDP, since it provides direct access to the memories of those who contributed to shaping the country's history. "Knowledge about the

18   P. KANDEMIR

past is transmitted by testimonies, either your own or those of other people,"[100] states Collingwood. The in-depth interview is a preferred technique for non-superficial correspondence, in order to learn the views and approaches of witnesses. The majority were recorded with the consent of the interviewees. Some of the interviews were not recorded to allow the interviewee to feel at ease, but each response was carefully noted. The snowball sampling technique was applied to create a network of interviewees.[101]

The semi-structured and in-depth interviews are predominantly conducted with politicians from the JDP. We can identify the majority of the interviewees as political elites. My definition of elite follows Harvey's conceptualisation, which refers to this category as "those who occupy senior management and board-level positions within organisations,"[102] differing from Zuckerman's ultra-elite[103] and Mcdowell's hybrid elite[104] definitions. Also, conducting additional interviews with policymakers, civil servants, academics, religious leaders, and journalists who are all relevant sources of information for the secularism debate in Turkey has been useful to develop a neutral approach.

More than 50 salient participants in the secularism debate were interviewed during my fieldwork and some of them gave their consent to be named in this dissertation. These include former Deputy Prime Minister, and one of the main founders of the JDP, Bülent Arınç; former Minister of Education Nabi Avcı, current Minister of Justice Abdulhamit Gül, current Parliament Speaker Mustafa Şentop, former Minister and current spokesperson of the JDP, Ömer Çelik; former Minister and Spokesperson, Mahir Ünal; one of the representatives of the centre-right within the JDP and former Minister of Justice, Cemil Çiçek; Erdoğan's close associate since the beginning of his political journey and his former senior advisor, Hüseyin Besli; and former Minister and current Deputy Chairman(second name in party hierarchy) of the JDP, Numan Kurtulmus; former MP and spokesperson Yasin Aktay, and Deputy Chairwoman and MP Özlem Zengin.

I received many off-the-record comments and information detailing the background to events, especially in interviews with high-level politicians. However, most of that information was not included in the thesis to maintain their confidentiality. During my interviews with JDP members, I noted a remarkable heterogeneity in terms of the perspective and interpretation. The interviews conducted with the representatives of the opposition parties (the most productive ones were Ilhan Kesici and Tuncay Özkan from RPP and Hisyar Özsoy from HDP), senior bureaucrats (the most productive one was then the National Education Undersecretary Professor Yusuf Tekin), religious/community leaders (the most productive ones were then the Armenian Deputy Patriarch Archbishop Aram Ateşyan and Yusuf Çetin, the Patriarchal Vicar of the Syriac Orthodox Church in İstanbul, Ankara and Izmir) or intellectuals from religious minority groups were equally appreciated.

Primary Documents

The most important benefit of using the interview technique is that data obtained from interviews offers original information and can deliver in-depth understanding. However, there is a number of drawbacks to this technique. The most significant one is the risk of the interviewee misleading the researcher due to the influence of subjectivity.[105] As a way to mitigate this risk, I sought to triangulate the data by drawing on diverse additional sources. The research utilises seven main primary sources: JDP's official publications, parliamentary discussions and parliamentary reports, autobiographies, and memoirs of politicians (Ahmet Davutoglu, Abdulkadir Aksu, Yalçın Akdoğan, Ibrahim Kalın, İsmail Safi, Bülent Arınç, and Hüseyin Besli are some of the authors whose publications are referred to in this book), local newspapers including Hürriyet (Mainstream, critical to government, Secular), Yenisafak (Conservative, Pro-government) and Cumhuriyet (Kemalist, secular and anti-Government), public surveys conducted by Konda (pro-RPP), Tesev (liberal), and Genar (pro-JDP) between 2002 and 2019, documents of ministries and state institutions including Ministry of Education and Diyanet, and periodical reports from the EU, UN, and the US State Department on Turkey.

STRUCTURE OF THE BOOK

Following Chapter 1, introduction which includes the conceptualisation of the study through the multiple modernities approach and identify the post-Kemalist and related literature, Chapter 2 of this book presents an in-depth historical analysis of crisis of Turkish modernism and secularism, with particular reference to Post-Kemalist literature. In this part, the historical journey of Kemalist secularism was analysed by focusing on the tension between the Kemalists and non-Kemalists within the context of the *centre* and the *periphery*. By bringing a critical approach to Kemalist secularism and the modernisation project, a rationale for the JDP's approach to state-religion relations was provided. In Chapter 3, the ideology of the JDP was discussed by applying a chronological historical explanation. This chapter is key to understanding the transformation in Turkey within the context of political and ideological rivalry within centre-right political parties, Kemalists, and Islamists. Chapter 4 of the book focuses on one of the most symbolic issues in the Turkish secularism debate: the headscarf controversy. After providing historical background to elucidate the Kemalist approach to the headscarf issue, this chapter gives a brief review of how the period after the coup of February 28, 1997, radically affected the approach of devoted Muslim politicians in Turkey. The ideological evaluation and changing narrative of alleged former-Islamist politicians with respect to headscarf issue are discussed in this context. Chapter 5 evaluates the transformation of the educational system in Turkey, which is particularly important, as education has always been employed as a tool to develop the secular mind in Turkey. Compulsory religious lessons, pre-school, primary school religious course, and *İmam Hatip Schools* (IHS) are discussed in this chapter to explain how the JDP's secularism approach is reflected by changes to the education sector. Chapter 6 discusses the repercussions of the transformation of secularism on the religious and sectarian minorities in Turkey by proving a historical background of the tension or coalition between these groups and the state.

NOTES

1. This term was first used by the JDP in 2010. Ak Parti, Accessed January 24, 2019. Available at: https://www.akparti.org.tr/galeriler/foto-galeri ler/hep-birlikte-yeni-Türkiye-25-agustos/.
2. I borrowed this term from Keyman, Fuat. "Assertive Secularism in Crises: Modernity, Democracy, and Islam in Turkey", *Comparative Secularism in a Global Age*, edited by Linell E. Cady and Elizabeth Shakman Hurd, 143–158, p. 143. New York: Palgrave Macmillan, 2010.
3. For a very insightful and insprirational analysis into the discussions about Post-Kemalism and the JDP, see Aslan, Ali. "Post-Kemalist Türkiye'de Siyaset." [Politics in Post-Kemalist Turkey]. *Ak Parti'nin 15 Yili: Siyaset* [JDP's 15 Years: The Politics], edited by Nebi Miş and Ali Aslan, 13–46. Istanbul: SETA Yayinlari, 2018, p. 26. Also see Keyman, "Assertive Secularism in Crises".

1 INTRODUCTION 21

4. I borrowed this phrase from Edip Asaf Bekaroğlu's inspring article, see full version: "Post-Laik Türkiye: AK Parti iktidarları ve Güncellenen Laiklik Sözleşmesi" [Post-Secular Turkey: The JDP Governments and Updating the Secular Contract], İnsan ve Toplum, 5.9 (2015): 103–122, p. 111.
5. Eisenstadt, Shmuel N. *Multiple Modernities*. New Jersey: Transaction Publishers, 2002, pp. 1–29.
6. Dalacoura, Katerina. "The Secular in Non-Western Societies." Social Science Research Council. February 11, 2014. Accessed January 4, 2019. Availabel at: https://tif.ssrc.org/2014/02/11/the-secular-in-non-western-societies/.
7. Holyoake, George Jacob. *Principles of Secularism*. London: Book Store, 1871, p. 11.
8. For a definition of secularism, see "secularism." *Oxford Dictionaries*. Accessed March 20, 2019. Available at: https://en.oxforddictionaries.com/definition/secularism.
9. Idem.
10. Taylor, Charles. *A Secular Age*, Cambridge MA: Belknap Press of Harvard University Press, 2007, p. 3.
11. Casanova, Jose. "Rethinking Secularization: A Global Comparative Perspective." *The Hedgehog Review* 8.1/2 (2006): 7–22, pp. 7–8.
12. Azak is another scholar noting the unique character of Turkish secularism. Azak, Umut. *Islam and Secularism in Turkey: Kemalism, Religion and the Nation State*. New York: I.B. Tauris, 2010, p. 8.
13. Küçükcan, Talip. "Sacralisation of the State and Secular Nationalism: Foundation of Civil Religion in Turkey." *The George Washington International Law Review*, 41.4 (2011): 963–983, p. 973.
14. This term was developed by the Marxist intellectual Antonio Gramsci. See: Gramsci, Antonio. *Selections from the Prison Notebooks*. Edited by Quintin Hoare and Geoffrey Nowell Smith, London: International Publishers Co, 1989.
15. Çelik, Nur Betül. "Kemalizm: Hegemonik Bir Söylem." [Kemalism: A Hegemonic Discourse] in *Modern Türkiye'de Siyasî Düşünce: Kemalism Vol: 2*, [Political Thinking in Modern Turkey: Kemalism], edited by Ahmet Insel, 75–91. İstanbul: İletişim, 2001.
16. Toprak, Binnaz. *Islam and Political development in Turkey*. Leiden: E.J Brill, 1981. Also see Berkes, Niyazi. *The Development of Secularism in Turkey*. New York: Routledge, 1998.
17. Köker, "Liberal Muhafazakârlık ve Türkiye", 224; Davison, Andrew. *Türkiye'de Sekülerizm ve Modernlik*. [Secularism and Revivalism in Turkey], translated by Tuncay Birkan. İstanbul: Iletisim, 2006, pp. 223–226.

22   P. KANDEMIR

18. Yavuz, M. Hakan and Öztürk, Ahmet Erdi. "Turkish Secularism and Islam Under the Reign of Erdoğan." *Southeast European and Black Sea Studies* 19.1 (2019): 1–9.
19. Keyder, Çağlar. *State and Class in Turkey: A study in Capitalist Development*. London and New York: Verso, 1987, p. 210.
20. Cady, Linell E. and Hurd, Elizabeth S. *Comparative Secularisms in a Global Age*. New York: Palgrave Macmillan, 2010, p. 16.
21. Mardin, Şerif. "Centre-Periphery Relations: A Key to Turkish Politics." *Daedalus* 102.1 (Winter 1973): 169–190, p. 187.
22. Shils, Edward. "Centre-Periphery." in *The Logic of Personal Knowledge: Essays Presented to M. Polanyi on his Seventieth Birthday, 11th March, 1961*, edited by Polanyi Festschrift Committee. New York: Routledge, 2016.
23. Idem.
24. Çınar, Alev. "Subversion and Subjugation in the Public Sphere: Secularism and the Islamic Headscarf." *Signs*, 33.4 (Summer 2008): 891–913, p. 897.
25. Çelik, "Kemalizm: Hegemonik Bir Söylem", 88.
26. This term was borrowed by Hasan Bülent Kahraman. He refers to Kemalist modernization as an oppressive and idealist project to homogenise society. Kahraman, Hasan B. "Bir zihniyet, kurum ve kimlik kurucusu olarak Batılılaşma." [Westernisation as a founder of mentality, institute and identity] in *Modern Türkiye'de Siyasî Düşünce: Modernleşme ve Batıcılık Vol: 3*, [Political Thinking in Modern Turkey: Modernisation and Westernisation], edited by Uygur Kocabaşoğlu, İstanbul: İletisim, 2002, p. 136.
27. Yavuz and Öztürk, "Turkish Secularism".
28. Fuat Keyman also refers to Casanova's framework. See: Keyman, Assertive secularism in Crises, 143. Casanova, Jose. "Civil Society and Religion: Retrospective Reflections on Catholicism and Prospective Reflections on Islam." *Social Research: An International Quarterly* 68.4 (2001): 1041–1080, p. 1064.
29. To see the list of political parties in Turkish history, and the one closed by Constitutional Court, see Turkish Parliament, Accessed June 19, 2019. Available at: https://www.tbmm.gov.tr/kutuphane/siyasi_partiler.html.
30. At this stage, we should remember Keyman's argument claiming that "Turkish secularism," which has been suffering from "a profound crisis" since the 1980s required reconstruction; yet, there was a demand for "democratic restructuring through institutional and discursive reform." See: Keyman, Assertive secularism, 143.
31. Hale, William and Ozbudun, Ergun. *Islamism, Democracy, and Liberalism in Turkey: The Case of the AKP*. New York: Routledge, 2009, p. 17.

1 INTRODUCTION 23

32. Öniş, Ziya. "The Political Economy of Islam and Democracy in Turkey: From the RP to the AKP." in *Democratization and Development*, edited by D. Jung, 103–128. New York: Palgrave Macmillan, 2006, p. 15.

33. This definition was borrowed by Keddie, "Secularism and Its Discontents". p. 17.

34. An-Na'im, Abdullahi Ahmed. "Islam and Secularism." In *Comparative Secularism in a Global Age*, edited by Linell E. Cady and Elizabeth Shakman Hurd, 217–228. New York: Palgrave Macmillan, 2010, p. 217.

35. In spite of the fact that Hakan Yavuz's perspective is extremely inspiring for my work, his attitude towards defining the JDP as Islamist also exhibits a similar trend. In his work, he claims there has been ongoing secularisation in Turkey in recent years "despite the JDP's Islamisation efforts." See, Yavuz, M. Hakan. "Understanding Turkish Secularism in the 21st Century: A Contextual Roadmap." *Southeast European and Black Sea Studies* 19.1 (2019): 1–24, p. 16. Also see, Ertit, Volkan. "God Is Dying in Turkey as Well: Application of Secularization Theory to a Non-Christian Society." *Open Theology* 4.1 (2018): 192–211. Also see Ertit, Volkan. *Sekülerleşme Teorisi: Sekülerleşen Türkiye'nin Analizi.* [Theory of Secularisation: Analysis of Secularising Turkey] İstanbul: Liberte, 2020.

36. Eisenstadt, N. S. "Concluding Remarks: Public Sphere, Civil Society, and Political Dynamics in Islamic Societies", in Miriam Hoexter, et al. (ed.), *The Public Sphere in Muslim Societies,* New York: State University of New York Press, 2002, pp. 139–161.

37. For a detailed analysis of this discussion see: Cizre, Ümit. *Secular and Islamic Politics in Turkey: The Making of the Justice and Development Party.* New York: Routledge, 2008.

38. Denoeux, Guilain. "The Forgotten Swamp: Navigating Political Islam." *Middle East Policy* 9.2 (2002): 56–81, p. 56.

39. Bayat, Asef. *Post-Islamism: The Changing Faces of Political Islam.* Oxford: Oxford University Press, 2013: p. 4.

40. Ayoob, Mohammed. "The Future of Political Islam: The Importance of External Variables" *International Affairs* 81.5 (2005): 951–961, p. 955.

41. Kara, İsmail. *Türkiye'de İslamcılık Düşüncesi, Vol. I.* [The idea of Islamism in Turkey]. İstanbul: Risale Yayınları, 1986, p. 48.

42. Gülalp, Haldun. "Using Islam as Political Ideology Turkey in Historical Perspective." *Cultural Dynamics* 14.1 (2002): 21–39, p. 23.

43. Cizre, *Secular and Islamic*, 1.

44. Cizre, *Secular and Islamic*, 3.

45. Haynes, Jeffrey. "Politics, Identity and Religious Nationalism in Turkey: From Atatürk to the AKP." *Australian Journal of International Affairs* 64.3 (2010): 312–327.

24   P. KANDEMIR

46. Küçükcan, Talip. "Are Muslim Democrats a Threat to Secularism and Freedom of Religion?" In *The Future of Religious Freedom: Global Challenges*, edited by Allen D. Hertzke, 269–288. Oxford: Oxford University Press, 2013.
47. Çınar, Menderes and Duran, Burhanettin. "The Specific Evaluation of Contemporary Political Islam in Turkey and Its Difference." in *Secular and Islamic Politics in Turkey: The Making of the Justice and Development Party*, edited by Umit Cizre, 17–41. New York: Routledge, 2008, pp. 17–40.
48. Yıldız, Ahmet. "Problematizing the Intellectual and Political Vestiges: From 'Welfare' to 'Justice and Development.'" In *Secular and Islamic Politics in Turkey: The Making of the Justice and Development Party*, edited by Umit Cizre, 41–62. New York: Routledge, 2008, p. 46.
49. Dağı, İhsan. "Transformation of Islamic Political Identity in Turkey: Rethinking the West and Westernization." *Turkish Studies* 6.1 (2005): 21–37, p. 34; Yıldız, "Problematizing the intellectual", 47.
50. Bayat, *Post-Islamism*, 2013.
51. Bayat, Asef. "What is Post-Islamism?" *ISIM Review* 16 (2005): 5. Accessed June 25, 2019. Available at: https://openaccess.leidenuniv.nl/bitstream/handle/1887/17030/ISIM_16_What_is_Post?sequence=1.
52. Bayat, *Post Islamism*, 4.
53. Dağı, İhsan. "Post Islamism a la Turca'." In *Post-Islamism: The Changing Faces of Political Islam*, edited by Asef Bayat, 71–108. Oxford: Oxford University Press, 2013, p. 71.
54. Dağı, İhsan. "Rethinking Human Rights, Democracy and the West: Post-Islamist Intellectuals in Turkey." *Critique: Critical Middle Eastern Studies* 13.2 (2004): 135–151, p. 139.
55. Dağı, "Post-Islamism", 73.
56. Idem, 34.
57. Gülalp, Haldun. "Islam and Democracy: Is Turkey an Exception or a Role Model?" in *The Sage Handbook of Islamic Studies*, edited by Akbar Ahmed and Tamara Sonn, 240–262. London: Sage Publications, 2010.
58. Çınar and Duran, "The Specific Evolution", 82. Also see, Bekaroğlu, "Post-Laik Türkiye?"
59. Yavuz, Hakan. *Secularism and Muslim Democracy in Turkey*. Cambridge: Cambridge University Press, 2009, pp. 116–117.
60. Davie, Grace. "Europe: The Exception That Proves the Rule?" in *The Desecularization of the World: Resurgent Religion in World Politics*, edited by Peter L. Berger, 65–83, Washington: Ethics and Public Policy Center, 1999.
61. For a detailed historical and theoretical analysis of this discussion, see Cady and Hurd, *Comparative Secularisms in a Global Age*. Calhoun, Craig, Juergensmeyer, Mark and Van Antwerpen, Jonathan. *Rethinking*

Secularism. Oxford: Oxford University Press, 2011. Taylor, *A Secular Age*.

62. Wilson, Bryan, R. *Religion in Secular Society: Fifty Years On*. Oxford: Oxford University Press, 2016. Shiner, Larry. "The Concept of Secularization in Empirical Research." *Journal for the Scientific Study of Religion* 6.2 (1967): 207–220.

63. Hadden, Jeffrey K. "Toward Desacralizing Secularization Theory." *Social Forces* 65.3 (1987): 587–611.

64. Berger, Peter. "Secularization Falsied." *First Things*, February 2008, Accessed March 20, 2020. Available at: https://www.firstthings.com/art icle/2008/02/secularization-falsified. *The Desecularization of the World: Resurgent Religion and World Politics*. Michigan: Eerdmans, 1999. Martin, David. "The Denomination." In *Sociology of Religion Vol: 2*, edited by Steve Bruce, London: Edward Elgar Publishing Limited, 1995.

65. Berger, Peter. *The Desecularization of the World: Resurgent Religion and World Politics*. Michigan: Eerdmans, 1999.

66. Dobbelaere, Karel. *Secularization: A Multidimensional Concept*. London: Sage Publications, 1981.

67. Eisenstadt, *Multiple Modernities*, 1.

68. Idem, 2.

69. Eisenstadt, *Comparative Civilizations*.

70. Preyer, Gerhard and Sussman, Michael. "Introduction on Shmuel N. Eisenstadt's Sociology: The Path to Multiple Modernities." In *Varieties of Multiple Modernities*, edited by Gerhard Preyer and Michael Sussman 1–29, Netherlands: Brill, 2015, p. 10.

71. Fourie, Elsje. "A Future for the Theory of Multiple Modernities: Insights from the New Modernization Theory." *Social Science Information* 51.1 (2012): 52–69.

72. Gusfield, Joseph R. "Tradition and Modernity: Misplaced Polarities in the Study of Social Change." *American Journal of Sociology* 72.4 (1967): 351–362. Accessed October 12, 2018. Available at: https://www.jstor.org/stable/2775860.

73. Idem.

74. Schmidt, Volker. "Modernity and Diversity: Reflections on the Controversy Between Modernization Theory and Multiple Modernists." *Social Science Information* 49.4 (2010): 511–538, p. 532.

75. Wagner, Peter. *Modernity as Experience and Interpretation*. Cambridge: Polity Press, 2008.

76. Burchardt, Marian and Wohlrab-Sahr, Monika. "Multiple Secularities: Religion and Modernity in the Global Age." *Introduction, International Sociology* 28.6 (2015): 605–61, p. 606.

77. Bilgrami, Akeel. *Beyond the Secular West*. New York: Columbia University Press, 2016.

26   P. KANDEMIR

78. Habermas, Jürgen, *Europe: The Faltering Project*. Malden, MA: Polity Press, 2009, p. 59.
79. Idem.
80. Habermas, Jurgen. "Notes on Post-Secular Societies." *New Perspectives Quarterly* 25.4 (2008): 17–29.
81. Loobuyck, Patrick. "Religious Education in Habermasian Post-Secular Societies". *Religious Education in Habermasian Post-Secular Societies*. Berlin, Boston: De Gruyter, 2015, 91–108, p. 93.
82. Idem.
83. Gorski, Philip S. et al., *The Post-Secular in Question*. NYU Press, 2012.
84. Haynes, Jeffrey. "Politics and Religion in a Global Age." *Religion and Politics: European and Global Perspectives*, edited by Johann P. Arnason and Ireneusz Paweł Karolewski, Edinburgh University Press, Edinburgh, 2014: 37–58, p. 41.
85. Fenn, Richard K. "The Secularization of Values: An Analytical Framework for the Study of Secularization." *Journal for the Scientific Study of Religion* 8.1 (1969): 112–124, p. 122.
86. Byrd, Dustin J. *Islam in a Post-Secular Society: Religion, Secularity and the Antagonism of Recalcitrant Faith*. Boston: Brill, 2017, p. 9–10.
87. Tunaya, Tarık Zafer. *Türkiye'nin Siyasi Hayatında Batılılaşma Hareketleri*. [The Westernisation Movements in Turkey's Political Life] İstanbul: Yenigun Matbaası, 1960. Lewis, Bernard. *The Emergence of Modern Turkey*. Oxford and New York: Oxford University Press, 1961. Berkes, *The development of secularism in Turkey*. Toprak, *Islam and Political Development*.
88. Etymologically, Medeniyet (civilisation) is Arabic, and modernité (modernism) is Latin. Both are ubiquitous words *in modern* Turkish, but were interestingly not used when translating the book's title into Turkish. The choice of the word *cagdaslasma* instead covers both civilisation *and modernisation*Berkes, *Türkiye'de Çağdaşlaşma*, 16. His other related work, Berkes, Niyazi. *Teokrasi ve Laiklik*. [Theocracy and Secularism] İstanbul: Yapi Kredi, 2016.
89. Berkes, *Teokrasi ve Laiklik*, 91.
90. Göle, Nilüfer. *Islam ve Modernlik Üzerine Melez Desenler.* [Hybrid Patterns: On Islam and Modernism] Istanbul: Metis, 2000b. *The Forbidden Modern: Civilization and Veiling*. Ann Arbor: University of Michigan Press, 1996.
91. Yıldız, Ahmet. "Kemalist Milliyetçilik." [Kemalist Nationalism] in *Modern Türkiye'de Siyasi Düşünce: Kemalizm Vol: 2* [Political Thinking in Modern Turkey: Kemalism], edited by Ahmet İnsel, 210–214. İstanbul: İletişim, 2002.
92. Mardin, Şerif. *Bediüzzaman Said Nursi Olayı-Modern Türkiye'de Din ve Toplumsal Değişim* [The Case of Bediuzzaman Said Nursi—The change

1 INTRODUCTION 27

of Religion and Society in Modern Turkey]. Istanbul: İletişim, 2013, pp. 282–285.

93. Göle, Nilüfer. "Batı Dışı Modernlik: Kavram Üzerine." [Non-Western Modernism: On The concept] in *Modern Türkiye'de Siyasi Düşünce: Modernleşme ve Batıcılık Vol: 3* [Political Thinking in Modern Turkey: Modernisation and Westernisation], edited by Uygur Kocabaşoğlu, 56–68. İstanbul: İletisim, 2002, p. 60. Göle, *İslam ve Modernlik Üzerine: Melez Desenler,* 36.

94. Göle, "Batı Dışı Modernlik".

95. Göle, "Batı Dışı Modernlik", 65.

96. Çınar, Alev. *Modernity, Islam, and Secularism in Turkey: Bodies, Places and Times.* Minneapolis: University of Minnesota Press, 2005, p. 2.

97. In addition to aforementioned ones, there are some leading scholars contributed to these issues with their works such as Yuksel Taskin, İsmet Akca, Ilhan Uzgel, Tanil Bora, Fuat Keyman, Cihan Tugal from left and Hakan Yavuz, Etyen Mahçupyan, Atilla Yayla, Ali Arslan, Ali Bayramoglu, and Ahmet Yıldız from liberal side. Yasin Aktay should also be mentioned here as differing from these two categories, since he is a self-declared Islamist. For a similar clasification see: Aslan, "Post-Kemalist Türkiye'de Siyaset", 26.

98. For an in-depth critical analysis of Post-Kemalist literature, see Aytürk, İlker. "Post-post Kemalizm: Yeni bir paradigmayı beklerken (Post-Post Kemalism: Waiting for a New Paradigm), *Birikim* 319.11 (2015): 34–48.

99. Habermas, Notes on Post-Secular Societies, 17–29.

100. Collingwood, Robin G. *The Idea of History.* Oxford: Oxford University Press: 2007, p. 3.

101. Hesse-Biber, Sharlene N. and Leavy Patricia. *The Practice of Qualitative Research.* London: Sage, 2006.

102. Harvey, William S. "Strategies for Conducting Elite Interviews."*Qualitative Research* 11.4 (2011): 431–441.

103. Zuckerman, Harriet. "Interviewing an Ultra-Elite." *Public Opinion Quarterly* 36.2 (1972): 159–175.

104. McDowell, Linda. "Elites in the City of London: Some Methodological Considerations." *Environment and Planning* 30.12 (1998): 2133–2146.

105. Cohen, Louis, Manion, Lawrance, and Morison, Keith. *Research Methods in Education.* 6th ed. London: Routledge, 2007. See also Dornyei, *Research Methods in Applied Linguistics,* 134–147.

CHAPTER 2

Two Sides of the Same Secularism Story: Kemalists Versus Non-Kemalists in Modern Turkey

The elevated status attributed to Kemalist secularism in the political and public sphere was developed by the Kemalist elites in the early Republican years, as they implemented top-down reforms to secularise Turkish society. Although the Kemalist establishment used all available state tools to achieve secularisation during the single-party era (1923–1946), as soon as political system was transformed from a single-party regime to a multi-party democracy in 1946, the majority of the public reacted to Kemalist oppression by supporting non-Kemalists and anti-Kemalists, and particularly centre-right political parties and Islamists have prospered in the subsequent free elections.

Throughout this period, the great majority of the Turkish population were either anonymously or directly opposed to Kemalist groups, as revealed by the results from the elections. Only once did the Kemalist RPP achieve enough votes to come to power alone in an election after 1923 and can be attributed to then young leader of the RPP, Bülent Ecevit's promise of a new perspective on state-religion relations, based on a "respect for religious beliefs."[1] Therefore, the political bloc that resisted the Kemalist *centre* and came to power solely through democratic elections counterintuitively comprised the *periphery*. As saliently analysed by Şerif Mardin, to unlock the complexities of Turkish political history, Kemalists held political and cultural sway as the hegemonic power at the *centre*[2]; thus, the Kemalist establishment continued to endure, claiming

© The Author(s), under exclusive license to Springer Nature   29
Switzerland AG 2022
P. Kandemir, *The JDP and Making the Post-Kemalist Secularism in Turkey*, https://doi.org/10.1007/978-3-031-07605-3_2

to be guardians of the regime and the country, drawing on support from the army, judiciary, bureaucracy, and the bourgeoisie.

To understand the reasons for the JDP's struggle against *status quo*, and the social support that has kept the party in power for the last 20 years, it is important to remember that the JDP was founded to represent the periphery,[3] including different ethnic, religious, and cultural identities and school of thought distinct from Kemalist secularism. Although the minor components of this political coalition (minorities, Turkish nationalists, liberals) have periodically changed, the major components have remained the same as the centre-right and Islamists groups since the beginning. Thus, the JDP, by uniting the non-Kemalist blocs, has become a de facto representative of centre-right conservative parties, Islamist movements, and liberals.[4] Therefore, it is crucial to examine the political journey of two of the most important centre-right parties, which the JDP inspired from, the Demokrat (Democrat) Parti (DP) and Anavatan (Motherland) Partisi (ANAP), and a so-called Islamist party, Milli Görü (National Outlook) Movement (NOM), to elucidate the JDP's objections and approach to Kemalist secularism. This is to say, despite the JDP's successes in terms of its transformation of secularism in Turkey, it has capitalised on the foundation afforded by its predecessors, e.g. Menderes' DP, Özal's ANAP, and Erbakan's NOM. Among the key contributions of this chapter to the literature consists of evaluating the ideological combination of these earlier political movements and exploring whether the JDP was inspired by them in its critique of *status quo* and its Kemalist secularism principle.

A Critical Analysis of Kemalist Secularism and Opposition Against It in a Subdued Society (1923–1946)

The Republic of Turkey was formed following the collapse of the Ottoman Empire after the War of Liberation (1919–1923) by Atatürk who influenced by many "myths, symbols, rituals, shared memories, and objectives"[5] derived from his experiences during the war. He founded the new nation state following a novel political approach based on six main principles, aiming to create a Western-style modern state. Although this political approach became the hegemonic ideology after the foundation of the Turkish Republic, there was no official definition of it. The most detailed framework of it was provided during the RPP's 1931 convention.[6] Under this formulation, this modernity project was structured according to six main principles, referred to as the "six arrows": Republicanism, nationalism, revolutionism, secularism, statism, and populism. In 1937, the six arrows were officially enshrined in the Turkish Constitution; thereby, defining the genealogy of Modern Turkish Republic. Crucially, Kemalism not only consisted of ideology based on Atatürk's perspective; it also incorporated the doctrine of RPP ideologues such as those of Ismet İnönü and Recep Peker, who, respectively, adopted the roles of President and Prime Minister during and after Atatürk's period.

One of the primary purposes of Kemalism was to secularise Turkish society and state institutions, as it equated being secular to being modern.[7] Notably, they were not alone in their desire to model the new state on a Western political, economic, and cultural hegemony; European-style modernisation had become popularised in many democratic, semi-democratic, and non-democratic countries during the previous 150 years.[8] In many Muslim countries, especially after the First World War, modernity had been transformed into "a national project," the aim of this being to "transform society" in accordance with the doctrines of Western civilisation employing state control.[9] Although Turkey was never directly colonised before or after the War of Liberation, it had adopted European cultural norms, as it is only "valid reference."[10] This embracing of Western cultural, societal, and political norms did not reflect the preferences of ordinary citizens, but was a conscious decision taken by Atatürk and his associates. According to Özyürek, Kemalism was "an elitist, centralist, statist, and positivist ideology that sees people as objects of the Westernising state."[11] The Kemalist's imposition of this elitist secularisation on the nation is central to much Post-Kemalist criticism.

Before revisiting the Kemalist secularism practices during the early Republican years, one should remember the discussions about secularism, along with the reforms in the military, governance, jurisdiction, and the economy, had been taking place during the Ottoman Era for at least a century before the Empire's collapse.[12] Ultimately, when these discussions turned to the secularisation policies of Ottoman reformists (Young Turks) during this period, several reforms are notable. First, the position of the *Ulama*, or religious scholars, had been weakened. Following the codification of Western Law in the modern Turkish Republic ranges from commercial law to extended family law.[13] Additionally, a new family law was introduced "which permitted women to initiate a divorce if their husbands committed adultery, violated the terms of the marriage contract, or engaged in polygamy without the first wife's consent."[14] This began a process of transformation from the established religious jurisdiction to a secular law upholding personal rights. In 1909 these reforms prompted protests by civilian movements in İstanbul demanding the restoration of *Sharia* law, in opposition to the rule of the Young Turks.[15] Concurrently, the first generation of Islamists were already framing "such ideas as freedom, constitutional rule, democracy, parliament and public opinion."[16]

When the Ottoman Empire collapsed, the new Republic instigated reforms with a different methodology and tone, with the result that Kemalist modernisation can be defined as an offspring of the "[W]estern and secular oriented."[17] Evidence of the "significant degree of institutional, ideological, and elite continuity between the Ottoman and the Republican periods"[18] is sourced from background information regarding those generations who initiated this modernisation project. It is well-known fact that Turkish modernisation was heavily influenced by "the ideas of the French Revolution and the rationalism and positivism"[19] present, as youths visited Paris for educational purposes. Ironically, it was the Ottoman Sultan Abdulhamid who sent and sponsored considered numbers of students to overseas higher education. After returning from Paris, the younger generation initiated their plan to introduce French ideologies into the Ottoman system.[20] These reformists believed Westernisation was the only way to revive and rescue the ailing Ottoman Empire.

While "the Ottoman reformists wanted to save what was left from the empire and considered modernisation a tool with which to do this," the Kemalist elite, after years of war, wanted to eradicate all remnants of the empire.[21] Kemalism sought to destroy the Ottoman-Islamic tradition, and the effects of religion upon social life.[22] Therefore, three main objectives informed the secularisation of the new Republic: First, "to undermine traditional strongholds of Islam when secularising the state, education, and law"[23]; second, to replace Islamic symbols with symbols of European civilisation; and third, to organise social life in a secular way to remove "the impact of popular Islam in everyday life".[24] Mardin describes this approach using a single term: "Enlightened despotism."[25]

Thus, the Kemalist secularism emerged as a political project, attempting to create a new version of Islam, which could be regulated and controlled by the state.[26] Especially during the period of early Kemalist modernisation, the Kemalist elites "attempted to place Turkish people, now purified from Islam and Islamic culture, into western-Christian international order via newly shaped Turkish nationalism."[27] To achieve this goal, several reforms were undertaken to secularise the state and the public: Abolition of the Ottoman Caliphate, which had been "the institutional ruler of Islam all over the world since the sixteenth century"[28]; abolition of Shari'a law and the *medrese* (religious school) system; adoption of laws unifying education and implementing the closure of religious schools; transfer of the management of all *vakıf*s to the Prime Minister (1924); abolition of the Ministry of Religious Affairs and Pious Foundations (1924); closure of religious shrines (*turbes*) and dervish lodges (*tekkes*) (1925); adoption of Swiss civil law; removal of an article from the constitution declaring Islam as the state religion (1928); "Turkification" of the call to prayer (1932); adoption of the Latin alphabet (1928), thereby completely disconnecting from cultural and literary texts of the past.[29]

The Kemalist state's drastic secularisation programme was not confined to institutional changes. To ensure a "complete transformation of society," the Kemalists made reforms with significant societal implications.[30] This was especially harsh in the area of reforms related to clothing, which traumatised society more than anything else. In 1925, wearing a hat in the Western style became compulsory for every man living in Turkish territory, and the wearing of the fez was banned, along with any other kind of religious dress.[31] Another traumatic step taken by the Kemalists was to change the Arabic call to prayer from to "pure Turkish" (1932)—"Turkification" of the call to prayer; aided by the Turkish Language Association founded by Atatürk, this was one of the most significant acts of Kemalist secularisation to amend and control the content of religion.[32] By making these radical state interventions concerning lifestyle, language, music, and clothing, Kemalism aimed to build a new "civil religion",[33] rendering Kemalism entirely Jacobin.[34]

As Kemalism sought to create a monopoly via the control of religion, the principle of secularism emerged as a political project, creating a regulated version of the state (Sunni) Islam. Therefore, rather than seeking to eliminate religion entirely, the state chose to keep it under close control by making it less visible. Controlling religion "by keeping Islam in reserve" became the principal strategy and chief characteristic of Kemalist secularism.[35] Establishment of the Directorate of Religious Affairs, to operate

34 P. KANDEMIR

under the supervision of the Office of the Prime Minister (1924), was considered the most significant step towards maintaining dominance over religious life.[36]

Secularism was successfully institutionalised during this period through the application of the aforementioned authoritarian reforms.[37] Thus, in a country founded upon the sacralisation of secularism, with a population largely devoted to Islam, it became inevitable that these two dynamics would create tension. Consequently, while dictating secularism from the top-down was an essential facet of Kemalist secularism, not only in political but also in cultural terms, Kemalism encountered "passive resistance in family and community life"[38] within the Republic from the outset. The representation of this resistance in the political sphere has always been centre-right, Islamist, and liberal political movements.

Although the official transition to a multi-party democracy happened in 1946, there were unsuccessful attempts to achieve this earlier in the century. Two parties, *Terakki Perver Cumhuriyet Fırkası* (Progressive People's Party)and *Serbest Cumhuriyet Fırkası* (Free Republican Party), were founded in different periods when Atatürk was still alive; however, he immediately shut each of them down as they gained unexpected popularity. While the first one closed down after seven months of surveillance by accused of being responsible for a reactionary Islamist uprising in the south of Turkey, known as the 1925 Sheik Said Rebellion,[39] second one shut down by its leader Fethi Okyar, Atatürk's close associate, to not undermine the authority of Atatürk.[40] Following initial failed attempts to establish a political opposition to Kemalism, resistance to any type of alternative proposal became stricter and harsher.

In 1930, another anti-secular incident occurred in the western part of Turkey in Izmir. This was a pro-Caliphate rebellion and is known as the Menemen Incident that a small group of fundamentalists rebelled by carrying a green flag symbolising the Islamic state. They informed people, "whoever wears the hat is an infidel," in reference to Atatürk's hat reform, adding "the Caliph will be back soon." A local garrison sought to stop their call for the restoration of an Islamic rule and the Caliphate; however, the group beheaded one of its soldiers, Kubilay, who then became a martyr of the revolution.[41] Many people who took part in the revolt were executed by military courts instituted by the government. The Menemen Incident was later used as vital propaganda when justifying the top-down implementation of Kemalist reforms.[42] After this event, Kemalism gradually crystallised throughout the 1930s.[43] The Kemalist elites became

2 TWO SIDES OF THE SAME SECULARISM STORY ... 35

aware that the general public was reluctant to adopt secularism without modifications, but that did not prevent them from consolidating the ideology.

CHALLENGING KEMALIST SECULARISM WITH THE INVENTION OF ATATURKIST SECULARISM: THE MENDERES CASE (1946–1960)

Neither the beginning nor the end of the DP was an easy experience in Turkish politics. Before the DP was founded, the Turkish opposition had been silent for almost 15 years under İsmet İnönü's single-party regime between 1938 and 1946. When President İnönü, the leader of the RPP, announced that Turkey would become a multi-party democracy, four members of the RPP founded the DP in 1946, with his permission.[44] DP founders, Celal Bayar, Adnan Menderes, Fuat Köprülü, and Refik Koraltan were prominent politicians who had built their expertise from within the RPP.[45]

As an inclusive movement, intending to satisfy a displeased public with its new political discourse, the DP positioned itself as a representative of popular will: *Milli irade*. The motto of the Democrats was: "Enough! The people have the word!". This slogan referred to the single-party regime and the RPP's top-down reforms. Thus, analysing rhetoric within its historical context is as important as criticising the DP's populist tendency.[46] Certainly, in a period of oppression under state authority, highlighting the people's voice and will was essential if the DP were to rise as an effective opposition.

With regard to their approach to Kemalist ideology, the Democrats developed a new concept, rather than adopting the term of Kemalism: *Atatürkçülük* (*Ataturkism*). Notably, when they came to power, Atatürk continued to be the main icon of politics; the Eternal Chief, National Chief, Commander in Chief, and Teacher in Chief. However, the principles set by Kemalism were opened to revision and were also reviewed during *Ataturkism* debates. Thus, although they created slightly different ideological stand against RPP's Kemalism narrative, they still managed to justify it by referring to it as *Ataturkism*.

Ataturkism resulted in a new interpretation of the secularism principle of Kemalism. In the DP's Programme, they highlighted recognition of "freedom of faith, like other freedoms, as a fundamental right of humanity."[47] Although President Bayar and Prime Minister Menderes made careful and selected remarks about secularism, seeing it as a red line for the regime, they also constantly highlighted that authentic secularism actually differed from how it was put into practice by the RPP. According to Celal Bayar, the most effective and well-respected figure engaged in creating the DP's identity concurred with Menderes, "secularism [did] not [pose] any hostility against religion."[48] As one might observe, they opposed the anti-religious character of Kemalist secularism and state control over religion; however, they proposed no alternative model, simply offering to change and soften the method.[49]

Following the transition to a multi-party period and democratic elections, the RPP also acknowledged the necessity of revising its secularist approach to achieve a compromise that would attract ordinary citizens. When they realised that Kemalist reforms provoked a reaction against the RPP, they diluted their discourse.[50] This included making several changes to their harshest policies by establishing IHSs, allowing religion as an elective course, and by reopening tekke and *sawiya* (Islamic monasteries). Thus, there is scope to claim that the revision of Kemalist principles was not only brought about by DP politicians, but also that the RPP made notable contributions between 1946 and 1950.[51]

During the years from 1950 to 1960 when the DP governed Turkey, they initiated several reforms to promote religious freedom and remove the pressures on religion. As Mardin states, "the RPP represented the bureaucratic centre, whereas the DP represented the democratic periphery"[52] in this period. One of the most momentous changes was the removal of the ban on the Arabic *ezan* (call to prayer).[53] Subsequently, religious broadcasting on public radio emerged, nineteen Iman-Hatip schools were opened, and religious instruction was added to the curriculum of primary schools.[54] Crucially, *Köy Enstituleri (Village Institutes) in villages and Halk Evleri (People's Houses) in cities*, which had been founded by the RPP to promote the ideals of Kemalism, were closed down in 1951. When we consider this was the only bridge between Kemalist elites and the periphery, the substantial failure of Kemalism with regard to ordinary citizens becomes more understandable.

All these moves were immediately interpreted as a counterattack against Kemalism by the Kemalists establishment.[55] Indeed, although they undeniably created an atmosphere for "Islamic resurgence" as noted by Feroz Ahmad,[56] this was not the ultimate goal of DP politicians. The DP was a liberal movement in regards to its economy and a political approach. Its founders were very aware of the cornerstones of the regime, and at every turn they pledged loyalty to Atatürk to legitimise their approach and not cross any red lines. Although the DP proposed a revision in Kemalist secularism practices, it tended to have a Kemalist reaction to the majority of demands related to state-religion issues. One should remember that Menderes and other DP members had grown up in a party formed by Atatürk's political characteristics, the RPP. Yet, there were several incidents of Menderes exhibiting very Kemalist reactions, such as the closure of the *Millet Partisi* (Nation Party), because it was considered to be reactionary and Islamist.[57] It must also be remembered that the DP invented the "Law on Protection of Atatürk,"[58] underlining that while it did take foundational steps towards the removal of Kemalist implementations, they maintained more than they changed.

The DP remained in power for almost 10 years via democratic elections. When the military staged a coup against the DP government in 1960, one of the reasons they cited was the party's alleged anti-secular policy. One year after the *coup*, in 1961, Prime Minister Menderes, Foreign Minister Zorlu, and Finance Minister Polatkan were sentenced to death by coup plotters. The DP was shut down and DP politicians banned from politics. İnönü was reappointed as President by the putschists and remained in power until the next democratic election.

Although the army claimed the protection of Kemalism to be the rationale behind the coup, the actual reason was more about power sharing. During the Atatürk era, the military had been central to politics. When the DP was founded in 1946 and elected to power in 1950, the power balance suddenly shifted, as the proportion of Kemalist elites began to dramatically reduce. Ultimately, they had supported and guided this coup aiming not to lose their privileges. Essentially, after the army tasted absolute power, they endeavoured to keep it—no matter the cost.

The DP and its leader, Adnan Menderes hold great importance in the Turkish memory. By referring to Menderes as a martyr for democracy, Turkey's centre-right movements always claimed to be his natural successor. Being the first party to voice objections to Kemalism, especially towards its interpretation of secularism, the DP cultivated the seeds of the non-Kemalist approach in Turkish politics, placing secularism at the heart of its resistance. When the JDP was founded, Menderes and the DP again provided a reference point for its founders' political stance.[59] Thus, understanding the DP, its background, ideology, and practices are crucial for analysing the JDP and its secularism approach.

OPENING THE CENTRE FOR PIOUS MUSLIMS: THE ÖZAL CASE (1983–1993)

Following the 1960 coup, civil-military relations became increasingly complicated. The army became the de facto primary actor in Turkish politics, and coups became the tradition for the restoration of (Kemalist) order in Turkey, occurring every 10 to 15 years. Exactly ten years after the 1960 coup, the Turkish military made another intervention into politics. On March 12, 1971, the General Chief of Staff gave an ultimatum and pushed the government to resign.[60] During this period, the main issue was concern over the rise of the radical left, rather than Islamism.

The resultant military intervention was one of the turning points in RPP history. Young politician Bülent Ecevit was the Secretary General of the RPP, while İnönü was still leader of the party. During this critical period, by adjusting the RPP's role in promoting Kemalist secularism, Ecevit began to search for a new narrative to communicate with the religious segments of society and gain their support. To do this, he conceived a new phrase to define secularism: "Respecting all religious beliefs".[61] That proved to be valuable and allowed Ecevit to become the only RPP leader ever to take the RPP to victory in a democratic election, from its founding in 1923[62] to the present day. This demonstrates that the only time the RPP ever won an election was when it stood against the military and criticised Kemalist secularism.

Another military intervention occurred on September 12, 1980. According to the official declaration made by the Turkish Army, this action opposed an increase in anarchism, terrorism, and Kurdish separatism. The threat of Islamic fundamentalism was also contributory factors to the coup d'état. General Kenan Evren, who led the 1980 coup, was quite different from the generals who had led previous coups or interventions. While the previous coup plotters were adopting an anti-Islam stand, Evren, in contrast, promoted a new perspective: using religion as an antidote to fundamentalist ideologies. For him, Sunni Islam was the only antidote to communism under the cold war atmosphere.[63] Although this strategic outlook had not been previously tested, it is complementary to Kemalist secularism; ostensibly, Kemalist secularism promoted the state's control over religion.

This new approach to Kemalist secularism was later referred to as Turkish-Islam synthesis. The creation of a new combination of Turkishness and Muslim identity explains the fulcrum of the 1980 coup d'état.

According to Yavuz, the generals turned over a new page in Turkey's secularism history with their reforms, expanding the scope of acceptance for religious life in Turkey by opening new Quran courses, making religious courses in the public-schools compulsory for the first time, and employing more imams.[64]

The military opted to hold the first general election after the coup in 1983. A new political actor, Özal's ANAP, came to power by winning the 1983 elections albeit several political limitations such as bans on both right- and left-wing political parties. Turgut Özal then became a role model for many centre-right politicians, and his personality amazed people due to "the increasing personalisation of political representation by individual leaders."[65] By calling Özal's stance, "new right," Ahmet Yıldız defines him as a nationalist, social democrat, conservative, and liberal, while underlining populism as his most important characteristic which "can best be understood in the context of the New Right framework."[66] When Özal was elected as Prime Minister, US President Reagan, the UK Prime Minister Thatcher, and Germany's Chancellor Kohl were already demonstrating a new political alternative. Meanwhile, President Gorbachev was changing not only Russia, but also all Turkey's northern neighbours with the introduction of policies of *perestroika* (restructuring) and *glasnost* (openness).[67]

Despite the high pressure from the coup plotters, Özal formulated an alternative political stance relative to Turkish politics.[68] Özal's "limited state" ideology was certainly not original; the Democrat Party's proposal to position the state as the nation's servant and to prioritise the citizen above the state, inspired Özal's vision. In this regard, contrary to Yıldız's arguments, the combining of economic liberalisation (free-market economy and entrepreneurship) with political liberalism (freedom of speech, thought, and religion) was a political stance[69] shared by Özal and Menderes.

Nevertheless, Turgut Özal offered a fresh start for Turkish democracy. He was a Kurdish pious Sunni politician who was personally conservative. Özal was also the first Prime Minister in Turkish history to perform the *Hajj*, and his quote "Will I leave *namaz* (praying) since I became President?" inspired important discussions concerning whether attending the *Cuma* (Friday) prayer as President was contrary to the Kemalist secularism. He also hosted an *iftar* (dinner after fasting) in the Presidential Residence during Ramadan, starting a tradition in this respect. Visiting religious leaders and mosques during official visits to other countries also prove that Özal differed from his predecessors. The public visibility of Islam was heightened during Özal's period, and he "indirectly facilitated the rise of Islamic movements with his liberal policies."[70] The privatisation of education and the media under his rule also opened up opportunities for new groups to express themselves freely. Thus, Turgut Özal was recognised as a key figure in meeting the challenge against Kemalism.

On the other hand, while Özal was personally pious, Özal's ANAP was a purely centrist bloc. It was a coalition, similar to Menderes' Democrat Party, comprising liberal, social democrat, nationalist, and Islamist politicians.[71] In addition to this, Özal's wife, Semra Özal, was a very visible public figure with good relations with the upper cadres of the society. Her liberal lifestyle attracted considerable scrutiny; she danced and drank in public places, acting in stark contrast with Özal's conservative behaviour. Her behaviour incidentally provided him with the requisite cover to avoid being labelled an Islamist.

Indeed, Özal was the second most important politician after Menderes in terms of effectively diminishing the tension between pious Muslims and the state.[72] Özal viewed religion as an important basis for national unity and solidarity, and took the opportunity to forge good relationships with all previously oppressed religious groups who had been subjugated by the Kemalists.[73] The monopoly of Kemalist intellectuals in universities, economic affairs, and the bureaucracy likewise began to be broken for the first time during this period. Overall, the transformation inspired by Özal created an atmosphere that afforded the space for non-Kemalist actors to exist in the political and economic *centre*. The new liberal policies introduced during Özal's term resulted in an erosion of the state's monopoly over economic and social life, despite his reputation as an "economic wizard."[74] Özal unleashed the liberalisation period in Turkey, using "free-market principles, removing state controls, and encouraging foreign trade."[75] Özal permitted private enterprises to open up new television and radio channels and private universities. According to Ahmad, during this period, "the government became an active partner of the private sector in the search for foreign markets and diplomacy became the hand maiden of trade."[76]

While this created new opportunities for foreign investment, small- and medium-sized entrepreneurs also took advantage of liberalisation. According to Demir, "starting with this period, small- and medium-scale enterprises (SMEs) at local levels have formed a new business community by improving their business practices, learning technology, and searching new markets. Even without direct support from the government, the advantages brought about by openness have triggered a process of production and capital accumulation in Anatolia."[77] Şevket Pamuk describes this change as a transition from Import Substitution Industrialisation to Export Oriented Industrialisation. He also argues that third (Kocaeli, Kayseri, Konya, Antep Adana) and fourth (Corum, Denizli, Maras, Diyarbakir) generation cities became the principal supporters of the conservative parties during Turkey's transition to a capitalist system.[78] Under a liberal economic system, they increased their economic power, not only changing the power balance in the Turkish economy, but also later sponsoring the JDP, thereby overturning the political balance.

Further change began to occur at this time with the establishment of a "number of associations; foundations, newspapers, periodicals, publishing houses, radios, TV networks, Qur'an courses, student dormitories, university preparation courses, an Islamist trade union (HAK-IS), and Islamist businessmen's association (MUSIAD) and holding companies."[79] Civil initiatives became a vital part of social and political life. The most crucial moment in this regard was the establishment of the Independent Industrialists and Businessmen Association (MUSIAD) in 1990, which united conservative business people. It was the first of its kind. Until that moment, the Turkish Industry and Business Association (TUSIAD), founded in 1971, was the only non-governmental organisation for private enterprise. The emergence of MUSIAD as an alternative to TUSIAD played a critical role in disrupting the economic hegemony of the Kemalist elites.[80] Although the attendant economic improvement did not initially help the new class to rise socially, due to the enduring cultural hegemony of the Kemalists, it offered them a new start.

As it happened in 1950s, the possibility of power sharing with the periphery alarmed the Kemalist bloc, who had been entirely in control since the foundation of the Republic. Rather than sharing power with democratically chosen politicians, the Kemalist establishment preferred to intervene in Turkish politics as a non-registered actor.[81] Additionally, it should be remembered that with the existence of the civil society sector following the neo-liberal policies of Özal in 1990s,[82] the state's monopoly over Kemalism also decreased as it was also promoted by civil society. It was the first-time civilians voluntarily started to promote Kemalism without any visible state intervention. The most striking point here was the motivation behind the "voluntary and active participation of the masses in the sacralisation of the image of Atatürk as the embodiment of the secular regime."[83]

This period of liberalisation created a new environment in Turkish politics. The political atmosphere changed rapidly, and a new open market permitting all ideologies facilitated a liberal political environment.[84] By abolishing Articles 141–142 and 163 of Turkish Criminal Code in 1991, Özal took a revolutionary step towards ensuring "freedom of thought" in Turkey. As framed by Cemil Çiçek, those articles criminalising socialist and Islamic views were always used as a whip by the Kemalist state.[85] By the lift of this bans on thoughts, Özal finally reached his "tripod of values": freedom of thought and association, freedom of religion and conscience and freedom of enterprise.[86] In the last instance, the liberation of the economy and social life was arguably the foundation for the changes that would take place in the 2000s.

When Özal unexpectedly died in 1993 from a heart attack, the Turkish people used three words on their banners at his funeral: Civilian, pious, democrat. Rather than being buried in a state cemetery, Özal had requested he be buried next to Adnan Menderes, reflecting where he saw himself on the political spectrum. Like Menderes, Özal's approach to the relationship between religion and state differentiated him from other politicians in Turkish history until the beginning of the Erdoğan era.

The sudden death of Özal paved the way for Prime Minister Demirel, one of the important political leaders of the central right tradition to become president. Demirel was loyal to the Kemalist establishment in a pragmatist sense, which indeed led him to follow liberal economic policies when he was in the governance but limited him in the sense of stepping away from the Kemalist line, meant he did not belong in the same ideological category as Menderes and Özal. Similar to when Mesut Yılmaz replaced Özal as the General Chairman of the ANAP following Özal's presidency, Tansu Çiller replaced Demirel in the other centre-right party, the Dogru Yol Partisi (DYP),[87] during this period. The change of leadership in these two centre-right political parties was critical, as these developments determined the future direction of Turkish politics. The two leaders were clearly less conservative than their predecessors, Özal and Demirel.[88] Both Yılmaz and Çiller were secular political figures, with far from humble backgrounds. This situation created an opportunity for Erbakan's Welfare to capture the attention of the more pious segments of society. Erbakan's NOM had been in politics since the 1970s, but the change in the atmosphere rendered the party more visible and attractive to voters.

The Rise of Political Islamism as an Alternative to Centre-Right Politics: The Erbakan Case (1970–2002)

Alongside dynamism at the centre-right of the political spectrum during Republican history, there has been a visible resurgence of Islamic identity in the social and political sphere since the emergence of the multi-party democracy. After this time, three different faces of Islamism developed in parallel to each other employing disparate methodologies.[89] The first group involved in intellectual activities and principally focused on theoretical discussions, choosing to stay away from the grind of daily politics. They formed the rhetoric of Islamists and their intellectual foundation. This group includes two of the most significant poets in Islamic narratives: Necip Fazıl Kısakürek and Sezai Karakoç. Kısakürek in particular is an important figure, as he heavily influenced Erdoğan and the other founders of the JDP. Erdoğan frequently recites his poetry during the party meetings. As for the second group in the Islamist entities, such as *Nurcus* and *Süleymancıs* became visible at this time. They formed an understanding of Islam that referred not only to religious norms, but also to embracing social norms, placing considerable attention on the transformation of society at the periphery. The process of socio-cultural transformation was attempted through the use of education and similar tools. Finally, the last group, Islamism, was represented in the political sphere by Erbakan's NOM movement.[90]

As the leader of NOM, Necmettin Erbakan (1926–2011) first entered Turkish politics in the 1970. Although he tried to join central right Adalet Partisi (Justice Party) as being an MP candidate in the beginning, with the veto of its leader Süleyman Demirel, he changed his route. Thus, he offered a third way, establishing an approach that extended beyond right- or left-wing politics: Adil Düzen. However, despite common definitions of the party as Islamist or pro-Islamist,[91] the founder defined his political movement with unique wording: *Milli Görüş* or the National Outlook Movement in English. As Yıldız noted, NOM "played a key role in the re-politicisation of Islam by enlarging the channels of political representation."[92]

Erbakan founded several political parties under different names, but all accorded with NOM ideology. The parties founded with links to NOM included *Milli Nizam*, the National Order Party (1970–1971),

Milli Selamet, National Salvation (1972–1980), the *Welfare Party* (1983–1998), *Fazilet*, the Virtue Party (1998–2001) and *Saadet*, the *Felicity Party* after 2001. Exemplifying the dominance of the secular Kemalist establishment, all the political parties that arose from the NOM tradition were closed down either by the Constitutional Courts, or immediately following military coups. Many of the politicians currently serving for the JDP had their first political experiences within one of these political parties under the leadership of Erbakan.

After almost every closure, a party with another name emerged sharing the same ideology: *Adil Düzen*. *Adil Düzen* (Just Order) was the main motto associated with this fixed political identity. As noted by Yavuz, it was claimed that *Adil Düzen* stood for "justice, a secure social and economic environment, protection of state property, an end to nepotism and corruption, cooperation between state and nature, protection of the unity of the state, and an end to undue Western influence over Turkey."[93] As also observed by Yıldız, the main source for the *Adil Düzen* rhetoric was Islamic ethical norms, which included "social solidarity, the prevention of wasteful expenditures, justice in taxation, equal treatment of all in the allocation of state credits, the abolition of interest."[94]

At the centre of this ideology, there was an intention for economic integration with the Islamic world, rather than alignment with Western-oriented perspectives. However, this was not meant as a rejection of technology or industry.[95] Although *Adil Düzen* had never been considered "real-politik projects," it was important to define the "enemy" or a particular target; *Adil Düzen* designated capitalism the enemy, offering Muslims an alternative model.[96]

However, while criticising Western values, such as secularism and modernity, and being the representative of the Political Islam in Turkey, on contrary to the similar movements in the Muslim World they still preferred to remain within the democratic system and attend elections. In this context, the Turkish Islamists always presented a moderate and non-violent model as "a counter-cultural model of modernity" to the West.[97] This was indeed a rational and pragmatic choice that enabled them to survive in an aggressively secular regime, and their alternative proposal conveyed the NOM to third place in Turkish politics during the 1970s for the first time.

When Ecevit's RPP won without a sufficient margin to form a government in the 1973 elections, Erbakan's party-MSP joined him in forming a coalition government, which made Erbakan Vice Prime Minister. It was the first time in modern Turkey that an Islamist party had become part of the governance structure. Paradoxically, they were the coalition partners of the representatives of Kemalist secularism in Turkey. During this period in the governance, Erbakan's party managed to reopen secondary sections of IHS, and graduates were allowed to enter all departments at the universities.[98]

As soon as the 1980 coup occurred, Erbakan's MSP was closed by the army as were the other political parties. Later this period, politics became relatively normalised, Erbakan founded the Welfare Party in 1983, three years after the coup. Receiving 4.4% of the votes in 1983, it steadily increased its support winning 19% of the votes in the 1994 elections.[99] Gülalp claims that the victory was particularly a consequence of "efficient organisation and internal discipline"[100] within the party, while Çınar notes that the mid-1990s was a time when Islamic movements began to rise in popularity following the Iranian Revolution in the Muslim world.[101]

Finally, NOM attained incredible success in the 1994 election. Yet, this development generated "shock and disbelief" in secular circles.[102] They were very conscious that Erbakan was not a Kemalist, nor an Ataturkist. On the other hand, officially, by defining themselves as Ataturkist, Erbakan aimed to justify itself in the eyes of the Kemalist bureaucratic elites. As stated previously, existential concerns, such as being closed down by the Constitutional Court, were the main reason behind this discursive formulation. According to Yıldız, it was "not mere hypocrisy but a conclusion derived from the interpretation of Kemalism from the vantage point of the NOM *(Milli Görüş)*."[103] Indeed, this move towards Ataturkism should not be analysed as a simple step to convince the Military only; it was also designed to show they were serious about becoming a mass party.[104]

At this stage, I should also note that since the very beginning Islamism as an ideological brand was rejected by NOM politicians, as they never adopted the term. Ex-NOM senior politicians and the current JDP's deputy Numan Kurtulmus explain this as follows:

> The West has been using this term- Islamism, for many years. I would like to say that this is something wrong. *Milli Görüş*, have never made such a claim. We care about Islamic values, we try to apply Islamic values in our lives, we try to eliminate the pressures on Islamic thought and life. We make every effort to ensure the honour and dignity of Islamic societies.

46   P. KANDEMIR

> But in a society where 99% of them are Muslims, in order to develop our basic social claims completely with our people, we do not say that we are Islamists and others are far away by pulling a group into it. This is a Western term. It is an expression used to attribute those who care about Islamic value and thought.[105]

Yet one should understand that to date, there has never been any political party in Turkish political history that has identified or defined itself as Islamist. This does not mean that there is no Islamist Party, but this means that they do/could not accept they were Islamists. As aforementioned, the Constitutional Court has closed several political parties by blaming them of being Islamist- most of them were founded by Necmettin Erbakan under NOM. The Islamist attribution to them was preferred by the Kemalists or the Constitutional Court most of the time if not the academic works.

At this stage, it is crucial to note that as the strongest political Islamist movement in Turkey, NOM never promoted violence as a political tool, either in theory or practice.[106] In another words, Turkish Islamism has never fought against the state.[107] According to Çınar and Duran, the "state-dominant" political culture of Islamists in Turkey[108] was the main reason for the non-violent character of Turkish Islamism.[109] As Sunni Islam views the existence of the state as indispensable, it is understandable why the Islamists never initiated an armed struggle against the state,[110] even during the 28th February coup that they faced several injustices and political persecutions.

The Criminalisation of Piousness: The 28th February Coup

In the municipal elections of March 27, 1994, the national elections of December 24, 1995, and the local elections of June 2, 1996, the Welfare Party experienced great success in terms of election results. Erbakan, as the leader of the largest party in parliament after the 1995 election, formed a coalition with the DYP leader Çiller, "despite the opposition of the secularist Turkish armed forces and big business."[111]

As soon as the Welfare Party became one of the main political powers in Turkey, considerable alarm was palpable among the Kemalist establishment. The Kemalists began a smear campaign, accusing the Welfare Party of not obeying the secularist principle of Kemalism.[112] They stressed "the need to suppress it with authoritarian measures as in the single party period."[113] The University Rectors' declaration against the Welfare Party was one such complaint. The media had been extremely insulting and aggressive towards the RP, and danger signals referring reactionary Islam dominated secular media headlines such as Hürriyet and Cumhuriyet.[114] Through this campaign, some non-Kemalists bloc admitted to, "feeling themselves threatened in their way of life by the Islamists, many former liberals and even socialists among Turkey's intellectuals reacted by reconverting to classic Kemalism in the early 1990s."[115]

The role of Kemalist NGOs as guardians of Kemalist principles, notwithstanding the military and bureaucracy, began to increase during this time. As Azak stated, "these organisations [were] marked by their identification with the state."[116] While not only justifying the existence of the army in politics but also inviting them to further interfere, these Kemalist organisations had struck a constructive partnership with the army. Kemalist women's movements, trade unions, and employers' federations were unified against Welfare Party as a "front for secularism."[117]

Beyond the abundance of propaganda dispersed by Kemalist groups, the Welfare Party politicians' actions and discourse were used as a tool to increase fear. One of the most striking events was "Jerusalem Night" on February 2, 1997. The event had been organised by the mayor of Sincan (a province in Ankara). The Iranian ambassador had been invited to attend the event, and his anti-Western speech, which was calling for an Islamic state, was not surprisingly in all the newspapers the following day.[118] The day after, fifteen tanks, the intimidating symbol of a coup, appeared in the streets of Sincan.[119] By displaying their tanks, the army communicated directly to the Welfare Party and Erbakan that there was potentially a coup coming.[120]

Another crisis surfaced when Erbakan invited the leaders of the Islamic *tariqa*s to an *iftar* on January 11, 1997. Images of *tariqa* leaders in religious clothing were published everywhere as proof of Islamism.[121] Subsequently, Erbakan's visits to Egypt, Libya, and Nigeria, and his meeting with Gaddafi, were heavily criticised by the media and the opposition parties. There were also some marginal speeches from Welfare Party politicians, which were later used to prove the Welfare Party is an anti-secular party. These included, for instance, his promise to build a mosque in Taksim Square in the centre of İstanbul. This was taken as a sign of his "Islamic agenda." The mosque was never built by the Welfare Party, but was referred to repeatedly as evidence of his Islamist intentions.[122] Incidentally, the JDP began constructing a mosque in 2017 in

48   P. KANDEMIR

central Taksim next to the Greek Orthodox Church and the Armenian Catholic Church.[123] Taksim Mosque was completed and opened on May 28, 2021, by the attendance of President Erdoğan. RPP's İstanbul Mayor Ekrem İmamoğlu also one of those attending the opening ceremony.

While the Welfare Party maintained its coalition despite growing criticism from the Kemalist establishment, on February 28, 1997, a significant incident took place which concluded with a post-modern coup. At the end of a nine-hour meeting, the National Security Council (MGK) declared that secularism is the guarantee of democracy in Turkey.[124] Following the aforementioned meeting, a long "officially advised" list of demands from the military was presented. Although Erbakan declared he would not accept the list as it had been drafted on March 4, 1997, he officially signed the military's eighteen demands without any amendments on March 13, 1997.

In May 1997, a closure case was opened against the Welfare Party by the "fanatically secularist" Chief Public Prosecutor Vural Savas.[125] He argued that the reason for this closure demand was that the Welfare Party had "become the focal point of criminal activity."[126] Consequently, the Constitutional Courts closed down the RP, and Erbakan resigned as Prime Minister on June 18, 1997, due to relentless military pressure. On January 16, 1998, the Constitutional Court banned his Party, and Erbakan received a lifelong political ban. In the following period, as will be discussed later in this book, Erdoğan, the then Mayor of İstanbul, and rising star at the time, was also sentenced to ten months in prison.

During the events of 1997, the direct involvement of the army in discussions about secularism and Islam afforded the necessary conditions for the *securityness of secularism*. As Bilgin emphasised, "the centrality of secularism to Turkey's politics and the security of such centrality" placed pressure on all the alternative movements that opposed Kemalism.[127] Although the army claimed they were safeguarding the interests of the common people with their actions, they were in fact closing those parties the common people had voted for in democratic elections. Even beyond this, the army's reaction to the events of February 28th included threatens to civilians: "We are ready to use weapons if necessary."[128] While evaluating civil-military relations, it is important to remember here that Minister of Justice Abdulhamit Gül said, "Authoritarian secularism has been used in Turkish politics as a tool that disconnected the periphery from the centre and that created a space and opportunity to speak on behalf of the nation by tutelage (not by proxy)."[129]

Following the February 28 coup, a programme of massive oppression of pious Muslims was introduced; from media sector to professors, civilians to bureaucrats, every group in the Kemalist bloc was involved in what became a purge. Furthermore, it should be noted here that in addition to the social and political pressures placed on conservative Muslims, economic pressures were also considerable. The coup affected those business people who were members of MUSIAD remarkable.[130] The military declared an embargo on those companies owned by conservative Muslims, termed "Green capital"[131] by the secularists. They were blocked by the state from accessing bank credit. Their companies and products were added to the blacklist, and their sales prevented.[132] It is also striking that TUSIAD was one a major supporter of the February coup 28,[133] a sign that secularism was not the only red line they were trying to protect; they were also seeking to retain their economic and social privileges in the face of the peripheral conservative class.

Indeed, there was an on-going change in their social foundations also as a result of liberalisation in the 1990s, which affected Turkish society considerably. This new situation "led to the formation of a new class of pious-conservative businessmen with their summer resorts, fitness and beauty centres, popular culture and entertainment products, private schools, fashion shows, and professional association."[134] Ultimately, when the group's lifestyle began to change, their political demands also shifted accordingly. Consequently, the way the conservative segment of society, and associated politicians voiced their criticisms also evolved. They started to use human rights discourse and liberal language when criticising Kemalism. This prompted a shift towards the narrative of the centre-right parties,[135] although their religious tone was relatively higher. Thus, by "being [in] favour of a free market economy and speedy and comprehensive privatisation," changes in its discourse towards universal values, the NOM led to the initiation of a new phase in Turkish Islamism.[136] Individuals were still inspired by religion, but it did not inform their politics. Consequently, this was the beginning of emergence of the post-Islamism in Turkey, which will later be represented by *Saadet Party*.

Therefore, although Islamist parties did not make common people more pious, the democratic system liberalised them dramatically.[137] Certainly, while NOM possesses an unchangeable essence,[138] a new interpretation of its new stance was introduced by Saadet in contemporary politics who often criticises the JDP as having "neo-liberal and capitalist policies."[139] Considering this novel situation, Yavuz agrees it should be

50   P. KANDEMIR

understood that there are Islamism(s) in Turkey today, not Islamism as one bloc.[140] This deserves more detailed discussions beyond the short references made in this book.

CONCLUSION

In spite of the argument that presents secularism as "an inevitable and universal phenomenon closely tied to modernisation in general," it is predominantly a Western experience[141] turned from a local value into a universal one. When we ponder why secularism has never been successful in the Muslim world, we find the reasons in its roots and its methodology. What I mean by this is simple: secularism was brought to non-Western societies as a by-product of Western Colonialism to secularise and Westernise them,[142] and it was implemented via top-down reforms which mostly failed in terms of legitimisation or final result. As an example of this, Reza Shah's term in Iran from 1921 until 1941 was an imitation of the Kemalist model. He forced Iranians to obey a dress code and adopt a secular education system. The implementation of modernisation was more harsh and "sudden" in Iran than Turkey and concluded in a contra religious revolution. A similar step was taken in Tunisia, after the 1956 Tunisian Independence—Habib Bourguiba also established a secular regime.[143]

To summarise, the most important event in the evolution of non-Kemalist political practice was the 1950s electoral win of the Democrat Party (DP); yet this administration only survived 10 years. Later, with the emergence of Islamism at the centre of mainstream politics in the 1970s, the representatives of the non-Kemalist bloc were separated into two main groups: the centre-right and conservative parties, and the Islamist political movement. The conservative centre-right parties had always been the real power, as they competed with the Kemalist RPP, while the Islamists had formed the minority component of the non-Kemalist bloc until their remarkable success in the 1994 local election, which brought them the opportunity to govern the İstanbul Municipality.

One should remember here that, until this time, the principal conflict zone in Turkish politics lay in the differences affecting various dichotomies, from left to right, autocrat to democrat, anti-religious to religious and statist to liberal. While the Kemalists always represented the first approach, the non-Kemalist bloc provided the second as an alternative. Despite the JDP's foundation in 2001 resulting in the re-unification of the centre-right and Islamists as a mainstream non-Kemalist alternative, this dichotomy dominated the political arena until recently. It is important to highlight that the re-unification of the non-Kemalist group under the JDP in 2001 brought about the hybridisation of Islamism as well as Kemalism.

Accordingly, the JDP should be assessed in terms of its centre-right conservative tradition as much as the Islamist tradition. The JDP's ideological formulation was inspired not only by centre-right DP and ANAP tradition, but also by *Milli Görüş*, where many of its politicians gained their first political experience. Additionally, although the JDP has its ideological roots in these three political movements, it should nevertheless be considered the first of its type, as it succeeded in being the most effective voice against the Kemalism in general and Kemalist secularism in particular. Before joining the JDP, the non-Kemalist political movements, including the DP, ANAP, and *Milli Görüş*, sought to resist Kemalism via indirect routes. They never announced it as this and always employed Atatürk's name as a validation. The invention of Ataturkism by the DP exemplifies this strategy. The parties were aware that the state was watching them, and that they would be penalised for not playing by the Kemalist principles.[144] As will be discussed in the following chapter, the JDP out-manoeuvred their rules and went above and beyond the three non-Kemalist parties not only engaging in a direct battle against Kemalism, but also ultimately defeating it. This feat could not have been possible without building on the original work done by three political parties: Menderes' DP, Ozal's ANAP and Erbakan's Welfare.

NOTES

1. Ecevit, Bülent. *Bu Düzen Değişmelidir* [This Order Should Change]. Ankara: Tekin Yayinevi, 1973.
2. Mardin, "Center-Periphery Relations".
3. Recep Tayyip Erdoğan's speech at 1st Ordinary Grand Congress of the Justice and Development Party held in Ankara, on October 12, 2003. Accessed January 2017. https://acikerisim.tbmm.gov.tr/xmlui/bitstr eam/handle/11543/964/200403930.pdf?sequence=1&isAllowed=y.
4. Liberals continued to support the JDP up until 2015 when security policies were raised and patriotist discourse infused with party terminology.
5. Küçükcan, "Sacralisation", 963–983.

52   P. KANDEMIR

6. Köker, Levent. *Modernleşme, Kemalizm ve Demokrasi* [Modernisation, Kemalism and Democracy]. İstanbul: İletişim Yayınları, 2016, pp. 133–135.
7. Göle, Nilüfer. "Secularism and Islamism in Turkey: The Making of Elites and Counter-Elites." *Middle East Journal* 51.1 (1997): 46–58. Also see Berkes, *The Development of Secularism in Turkey*.
8. Berger, Peter, Davie, Grace and Fokas, Effie. *Religious America, Secular Europe? A Theme and Variations*. London: Ashgate Publishing Limited, 2008.
9. Çınar, *Modernity, Islam, and Secularism*, 26.
10. Idem, 15.
11. Özyürek, Esra. *Nostaljia for the Modern*. Durham and London: Duke University Press, 2006, p. 14.
12. Zurcher, Erik Jan. "Kemalist Düşüncenin Osmanlı Kaynakları" [The Ottoman Sources of the Kemalist Thinking]. In *Modern Türkiye'de Siyasi Duşunce: Kemalism Vol: 2* [Political Thinking in Modern Turkey: Kemalism], edited by Ahmet Insel, 44–56. İstanbul: İletişim, 2001, pp. 44–45.
13. Bozkurt, Gülnihal. *Batı Hukukunun Türkiye'de Benimsenmesi: Osmanlı Devleti'nden Türkiye Cumhuriyeti"ne Resepsiyon Sureci (1839–1939)* [The Familiarisation of Western Law in Turkey: Reception Process from Ottoman State to Turkish Republic]. Ankara: Turk Tarih Kurumu Yayınları, 1996.
14. Altunışık, Meliha Benli and Tur, Özlem. *Turkey: Challenges of Continuity and Change*. London and New York: Routledge Curzon, 2005, p. 12.
15. Idem.
16. Gülalp, "Using Islam as Political Ideology", 25. This is the reason why they called as occidental Islamist by Mardin. See: Mardin, Şerif. *Türkiye'de Din ve Siyaset* [Religion and Politics in Turkey]. İstanbul: İletişim, 1997, p. 21.
17. Küçükcan, "Sacralisation", 963.
18. Altunışık and Tür, *Turkey: Challenges of Continuity and Change*, 1.
19. Idem, 6.
20. Keddie, "Secularism and İts Discontents", 22–23.
21. Altunışık and Tür, *Turkey: Challenges of Continuity and Change*, 1.
22. Tuncay, Mete. *Türkiye Cumhuriyetinde Tek Parti Yönetiminin Kurulması 1923–1931* [The Foundation of Single Party rule in Turkish Republic 1923–1931]. 3th ed. İstanbul: Türkiye Ekonomik ve Toplumsal Tarih Vakfı, 1999, p. 230. For a similar view, see Mardin, Şerif. "Religion and Secularism in Turkey." In *Atatürk: Founder of a Nation State*, edited by Ali Kazancıgil and Ergun Ozbudun. Hamden: CT: Archon, 1981.
23. Küçükcan, "Sacralisation", 964.

2 TWO SIDES OF THE SAME SECULARISM STORY ...   53

24. Idem.
25. This term was borrowed from Mardin, *Türkiye'de Din ve Siyaset*, 42.
26. Tuncay, *Türkiye Cumhuriyetinde Tek Parti*; Köker, *Modernleşme, Kemalizm ve Demokrasi*, 133–135. Göle, "Secularism and Islamism in Turkey"; Kuru, Ahmet T. *Secularism and State Policies Toward Religion: The United States, France, and Turkey*. Cambridge: Cambridge University Press, 2009.
27. Yıldız, "Kemalist Milliyetcilik", 223–224.
28. Çınar, *Modernity, Islam, and Secularism*, 16.
29. Tuncay, *Türkiye Cumhuriyetinde Tek Parti*, 230.
30. Azak, *Islam*, 9.
31. In spite of common thinking, the fez was not a traditional Ottoman clothing, yet it was introduced by Sultan Mahmut II as one of his reforms in the late Ottoman period. See: Altunışık and Tur, *Turkey: Challenges of Continuity and Change*, 22.
32. Çınar, *Modernity, Islam, and Secularism*, 17.
33. By referring Turkey as one of the examples, Haynes considers "civil religions" as "an attempted strategy to try to avoid social conflicts and promote national coordination and cohesion". See, Haynes, Jeffrey. ed. *Religion and Politics in Europe, the Middle East and North Africa*. Vol. 64. Routledge, 2009, p. 4.
34. "Giriş" [Introduction]. in *Modern Türkiye'de Siyasi Dusunce: Kemalizm Vol. 2* [Political Thinking in Modern Turkey: Kemalism Vol. 2], edited by Tanıl Bora and Murat Gultekin, 17–28. İstanbul: İletişim Yayınları, 2002, p. 22.
35. Çelik, "Kemalizm: Hegemonik Bir Söylem"; Atay, Tayfun. "Cumhuriyet Türkiyesi'nde bir sorun olarak dine bakış" [Perspectives on Religion as a Problem in Republican Turkey]. *Birikim* 105–106 (1998): 100–106.
36. Çınar, *Modernity, Islam, and Secularism*, 16.
37. To understand authoritarian character of Kemalist reform, see Beris, Hamit Emrah. *Tek Parti Döneminde Devletçilik* [Statism in the Single Party Era]. İstanbul: Liberte, 2009, p. 50; İnsel, Ahmet. "Cumhuriyet Döneminde Otoritarizmin Sürekliliği." *Birikim* 125–126 (1999): 143–166. Çelik, "Kemalism: Hegemonik Bir Söylem", 75.
38. Berger, "Secularization Falsied."
39. Zurcher, Erik Jan. *Political Opposition in the Early Turkish Republic: The Progressive Republican Party 1924–1925*. Leiden: Brill, 1991.
40. Ahmad, Feroz. *The Making of Modern Turkey*. London: Routledge, 2003, p. 60.
41. Azak, *Islam*, 43.
42. Idem.
43. Demirel, Ahmet. "İsmet İnönü." In *Modern Türkiye'de Siyasi Dusunce: Kemalizm Vol. 2* [Political Thinking in Modern Turkey: Kemalism Vol.

54   P. KANDEMIR

2], edited by Tanil Bora and Murat Gultekin, 124–137. İstanbul: İletişim Yayınları, 2002, p. 128.

44. As soon as the Turkish political system transferred to a multi-party democracy, several political parties were founded, almost all with anti-Kemalist motives. Some examples of these political parties include: Milli Kalkınma Partisi (1946), Sosyal Adalet Partisi (1946), Ciftci ve Koylu Partisi (1946), and Arıtma Koruma Partisi (1947). None were defined as Islamist by Şerif Mardin. See: Mardin, *Türkiye'de Din ve Siyaset*, 29.

45. For detailed analysis of DP, see: Agaoglu, Ahmet. *İki Parti Arasındaki Farklar* [Differences Between Two Parties]. Ankara: Arbas Matbaası, 1947; Eroğul, Cem. *Demokrat Parti* [Democrat Party]. Ankara: İmge, 1998.

46. For an analysis of the relationship between democracy and populism in the DP's understanding: Sunar, İlkay. "Demokrat Parti ve Populizm" [Democrat Party and Populism]. In *Cumhuriyet Donemi Türkiye Ansiklopedisi(8)*. İstanbul: İletişim Yayınları, 1983.

47. Tunaya, Tarık Zafer. *Türkiye'de Siyasi Partiler (1859–1952)* [Political Parties in Turkey (1859–1952)]. İstanbul: Arba Yayınları, 1952, pp. 663–664.

48. Bayar, Celal. *Başvekilim Adnan Menderes* [My Prime Minister Adnan Menderes]. İstanbul: Baha Matbaası, 1969, p. 109.

49. Azak, *Islam*, 88.

50. Zurcher, *Modernlesen Türkiye'nin Tarihi*, 222.

51. Uzun, Hakan. "İktidarını Sürdürmek İsteyen Bir Partinin Kimlik Arayışı: Cumhuriyet Halk Parti'sinin 1947 Olağan Kurultayı" [Identity Search of a Party Wishing to Maintain Its Power: 1947 Ordinary General Assembly of the Republican People's Party]. *Çağdaş Türkiye Tarihi Araştırmaları Dergisi* 12.25 (2012): 101–139, p. 130.

52. Mardin, Centre-Periphery Relations, 186.

53. One thing must be noted: President Bayar did not support this reform but he believed it was a mandatory precaution at the time. See: Bayar, *Başvekilim Adnan Menderes*, 111.

54. Kuru, *Secularism and State Policies*, 226.

55. Bayar, *Başvekilim Adnan Menderes*, 65.

56. Ahmad, *The Making of Modern Turkey*, 219.

57. This party had not been a political rival for the Democrat Party, and it was quite small in the sense of popular support.

58. Zurcher, *Modernleen Türkiye'nin Tarihi*, 233.

59. "AKP Lideri Erdoğan: DP "nin devamıyız"" [AKP leader Erdoğan: We Are the Successor of DP]. *Hürriyet*, May 16, 2003. Accessed March 13, 2013. http://hurarsiv.hurriyet.com.tr/goster/ShowNew.aspx?id=147213.

60. Zurcher, *Modernleşen Türkiye'nin Tarihi*, 258.

2 TWO SIDES OF THE SAME SECULARISM STORY ...   55

61. Çolak, Mustafa. *Bülent Ecevit-Karaoğlan.* İstanbul: İletişim Yayınları, 2010.
62. The RPP won the 1973 election by getting 33.5% of the vote.
63. White, Jenny B. "Islam and Politics in Contemporary Turkey". In *Turkey,* edited by Resat Kasaba, 357–380, Cambridge: Cambridge University Press, 2008, p. 363.
64. Yavuz, Hakan. "Political Islam and the Welfare Party in Turkey." *Comparative Politics* 30.1 (1997): 63–82, p. 67.
65. Cizre, Ümit. "Ideology, Context and Interest: The Turkish Military." In *Turkey,* edited by Resat Kasaba, 301–332. Cambridge: Cambridge University Press, 2008a, p. 316.
66. Yıldız, Ahmet. "Muhafazakarlık-Liberalizm Sarkacında 'İnformel' Bir Demokrat: Turgut Özal'dan kalan" [An "Informal" Democrat on a Pendulum of Liberalism and Conservatism: The Legacy of Turgut Ozal]. *Muhafazakar Düşünce,* no. 55 (2018): 39–57, p. 39.
67. Idem, 40.
68. Idem.
69. Idem.
70. Kuru, *Secularism and State Policies,* 230.
71. White, "Islam and Politics", 363.
72. Yıldız, "Liberalizm-Muhafazakarlık sarkacında", 52–53. Also revisit Turam's discussion on this: Turam, Berna. *Secular State and Religious Society: Two Forces in Play in Turkey.* New York: Palgrave Macmillan, 2012.
73. Yıldız, "Liberalizm-Muhafazakarlık sarkacında", 52.
74. Mackenzie, Kenneth. "Turkey in Transition." *The World Today* 42.6 (1986): 101–104, 101.
75. White, "Islam and Politics", 364.
76. Ahmad, *The making of Modern Turkey,* 206.
77. Demir, Ömer, Acar, Mustafa and Toprak, Metin. "Anatolian Tigers or Islamic Capital: Prospects and Challenges." *Middle Eastern Studies* 40.6 (2004): 159.
78. Pamuk, Sevket. "Globalization, İndustrialization and Changing Politics in Turkey." *New Perspectives on Turkey* 38 (2008): 267–273.
79. Hale and Özbudun, *Islamism, Democracy,* 16.
80. For a detailed analysis, see Bölükbaşı, "Milli Görüş'ten Muhafazakâr Demokrasiye", 166–187.
81. This definition was borrowed from Cemil Çiçek, former deputy Prime Minister and once one of the leading names in the JDP. Interview with Cemil Çiçek, Former Deputy Prime Minister, Ankara, on May 28, 2019.
82. Keyman, Fuat. *Türkiye'de Sivil Toplumun Serüveni: Imkansızlıklar içinde bir Vaha.* [The Adventure of Civil Society in Turkey: An Oasis in the İmpossibilities]. Ankara: Sivil Toplum Geliştirme Merkezi Yayını, 2006, pp. 26–28.

56 P. KANDEMIR

83. Azak, *Islam*, 13.
84. Ataman, Muhittin. "Özal Leadership and Restructuring of Turkish Ethnic Policy in the 1980s." *Middle Eastern Studies* 38.4 (2002): 123–142. Also see Öniş, Ziya. "Turgut Özal and His Economic Legacy: Turkish Neo-Liberalism in Critical Perspective." *Middle Eastern Studies* 40.4 (2004): 113–134.
85. Interview with Cemil Çiçek, Former Deputy Prime Minister, Ankara, on May 28, 2019.
86. Heper, Metin and Sayarı, Sabri. *Political Leaders and Democracy in Turkey*. London: Lexington Books, 2002, pp. 173–176.
87. Doğru Yol (True Path) Partisi was founded after Demirel's AP was closed by the army in the 1980 Coup D'état.
88. Kuru, *Secularism and State Policies*, 231.
89. This formulation was borrowed from Akdoğan, Yalçın. "Adalet ve Kalkınma Partisi" [Justice and Development Party]. in *Modern Türkiye'de Siyasi Düşünce: islamcılık Vol. 6* [Political Thinking in Modern Turkey: Islamism Vol. 6], edited by Yasin Aktay, Murat Gultekingil, and Tanıl Bora. İstanbul: Iletişim Yayınları, 2005, p. 621.
90. Erbakan, Necmettin. *Milli Görüş* [National Vision]. İstanbul: Dergah Yayınları, 1975.
91. For a definition of Islamist, see: Keddie, "Secularism and Its Discontents." 14–30; White, "Islam and Politics". For the definition of "Pro-Islamist" see Gülalp, Haldun. "Islamist Party Poised for National Power in Turkey." *Middle East Report* 194.195 (1995): 54–56.
92. Yıldız, Ahmet. "Politico-Religious Discourse of Political Islam in Turkey: The Parties of National Outlook." *The Muslim World* 93.2 (2003):187–209, p. 187.
93. Yavuz, "Political Islam", 73.
94. Idem, 191.
95. White, "Islam and Politics", 362.
96. Yılmaz, Nuh. "İslamcılık, AKP ve Siyaset" [Islamism, AKP and Politics]. in *Modern Türkiye'de Siyasi Düşünce: İslamcılık Vol. 6* [Political Thinking in Modern Turkey: Islamism Vol. 6], edited by Yasin Aktay, Murat Gültekingil, and Tanıl Bora, 604–620. İstanbul: İletişim Yayınları, 2005, p. 608.
97. Göle, "Secularism and Islamism in Turkey", 46–58.
98. Kuru, *Secularism and State Policies*, 227.
99. Gülalp, "Islamist Party Poised", 54.
100. Idem.
101. Çınar, *Modernity, Islam, and Secularism*, 6.
102. Gülalp, "Islamist Party Poised", 54.
103. Yıldız "Politico-Religious Discourse", 191.

2 TWO SIDES OF THE SAME SECULARISM STORY ... 57

104. Çakır, Ruşen. "İslamcılar ve Atatürk: Atatürk yaşasaydı Refahçı olur muydu?" [Islamists and Atatürk: If Atatürk Had Lived, Would He Have Supported the Welfare Party?]. *Milliyet*, November 29, 1994. Print.
105. Interview with Numan Kurtulmus, Deputy Chairman of the JDP and Minister of Culture, Ankara, on April 8, 2019.
106. Yıldız, "Politico-Religious", 200.
107. Although Turkish Hizbullah (a very weak, marginal and small religious group who has never win any political or social power) used violence, it was not against the state; but against its internal members.
108. The result of a research conducted by Sabanci University proves that there is a high obedience to state authority within Turkish people. Çarkoğlu and Kalaycioglu, *Türkiye'de dindarlik*, 19.
109. Çınar and Duran, "The Specific Evolution", 25.
110. Duran, "Cumhuriyet Dönemi İslamcılığı", 129–156.
111. Yavuz, "Political Islam", 73.
112. "Rektörler Endişeli" [Rectors Are Concerned]. *Sabah*, December 10, 1996. Print.
113. Azak, *Islam*, 176.
114. For an in-depth analysis of February 28 coup, see Bayramoğlu, Ali. *28 Subat: Bir Müdahalenin Güncesi* [28 February: A Diary of an İntervention]. İstanbul: İletişim Yayınları, 2007. Birand, Mehmet Ali. *Son Darbe 28 Şubat* [The Last Coup February 28]. İstanbul: Doğan Kitap, 2012.
115. Zurcher, *Modernleşen Türkiye'nin Tarihi*, 290.
116. Azak, *Islam*, 176.
117. Zurcher, *Modernleşen Türkiye'nin Tarihi*, 301.
118. "Bu ne rezalet" [What a Disgrace]. *Sabah*, February 2, 1997. Print.
119. "Sincan'da tanklı protesto" [Tank Protest in Sincan]. *Cumhuriyet*, February 4, 1997. Print.
120. "Ordudan dört uyarı" [Four Warnings from the Army]. *Cumhuriyet*, February 4, 1997. Print.
121. Ergin, Sedat. "Tarikat İftarı Bardağı Taşırdı" [Iftaar with Religious Cults Was the Limit], August 23, 1997. Accessed June 23, 2019. https://www.hurriyet.com.tr/tarikat-iftari-bardagi-tasirdi-39260952.
122. White, "Islam and Politics", 367.
123. "Taksim Camii'nin Temelleri Atıldı" [Taksim Camii's Foundations Are Found]. *Hürriyet*, February 17, 2017. Accessed Accessed June 23, 2019. https://www.hurriyet.com.tr/gundem/taksim-camiinin-temeli-ati ldi-40368952.
124. "Muhtıra gibi tavsiye" [Advice Like a Memorandum]. *Cumhuriyet*, March 1, 1997. Print.
125. Zurcher, *Modernlesen Türkiye'nin Tarihi*, 300.
126. Idem.

127. Bilgin, Pinar. "The Securityness of Secularism: The Case of Turkey". *Security Dialogue* 39.6 (2008): 593–614.
128. "Gerekirse silah bile kullanırız" [If İt İs Necessary, We Can Even Use Gun]. *Hürriyet*, July 12, 1997. Print.
129. Interview with Abdulhamit Gül, Minister of Justice of the Republic of Turkey, Ankara, on April 9, 2019.
130. Dağı, "Post-Islamism", 82.
131. Green is known as the color of Islam; that is the reason why the companies owned by Conservative Muslim businessmen were labeled as Green Capital by the army and Kemalist bureaucrats. Afterwards, it became a term that is commonly used in daily life by society.
132. "28 şubat, MUSİAD'a Anadolu Kaplanları'na yapıldı!" [28 February was for MUSIAD, Anatolian Tigers]. *Haberturk*, April 28, 2012. Accessed June 23, 2018. Available at: https://www.haberturk.com/ekonomi/ makro-ekonomi/haber/737930-28-subat-musiada-anadolu-kaplanlar ina-yapildi.
133. For one of their statements criminalising the RP, see, "TÜSİAD: Refah Türkiye'nin partisi olmayı başaramadı" [TUSIAD: Welfare Party Couldn't Manage to Become a Party of Turkey]. *Hürriyet*, January 23, 1998. Accessed June 23, 2018. Available at: http://www.hurriyet.com. tr/ekonomi/tusiad-Welfare-Party-Türkiyenin-partisi-olmayi-basaramadi-39003540.
134. Demir et al. "Anatolian Tigers or Islamic Capital", 180.
135. Yıldız, "Politico-Religious", 199.
136. Dagi, "Post-Islamism", 84.
137. Yavuz, M. Hakan. *Erbakan'dan Erdoğan'a Laiklik, Demokrasi, Kürt Sorunu ve İslam* [Secularism, Democracy, Kurdish Issue and Islam from Erbakan to Erdoğan]. İstanbul: Kitap, 2011, p. 67.
138. Yılmaz, "Islamcilik, AKP ve Siyaset", 604–620.
139. Another self-declared Islamist İhsan Eliaçık defines it as "new Islamism" in an early interview. His movement is currently known as "anti-capitalist Muslims". For an interview about the philosophy of this movement see "Yeni Islamcilik", *Tempo*, December 13, 2006. Accessed June 23, 2019. Available Online: http://www.ihsaneliacik.com/2006/ 12/soylesi-tempo.html.
140. Yavuz, "Understanding Turkish Secularism".
141. Gülalp, Haldun. "Enlightenment by Fiat: Secularisation and Democracy in Turkey." *Middle Eastern Studies* 41.3 (2005): 351–372, p. 351.
142. Zakariyya, Fouad. *Myth and Reality in the Contemporary Islamist Movement*. London: Pluto Press, 2005, pp. 14–16.
143. See: Keddie, "Secularism and İts Discontents", 23–24.
144. Refering Foucault, Michel. *Discipline and Punish: The Birth of the Prison*. Vintage, 2012.

CHAPTER 3

The Anatomy of the JDP and the Emergence of Post-Kemalist Secularism

There were three main periods, marked by various ups and downs that led Turkey's conservative politicians to successfully integrate into the political system while retaining the visibility of non-Kemalist identities. These were, the Menderes' DP era, which occurred after the transition to the multi-party system (1950–1960); the Özal's ANAP era, when the seeds of a liberal economy were planted in Turkey (1983–1993); and the JDP's Erdoğan era after 2002. Although it must be noted that Erbakan's short experience in governance cannot be considered successful, as it was precipitately disrupted by the Kemalists with and their February 28 coup, it still inspired Turkey's current President Erdoğan politically that they also brought a different approach to Kemalism in general. However, when compared to aforementioned leaders, Erdoğan has gone one step further towards re-imagining Turkey, directly declaring its dissimilarities with Kemalism between 2001 and 2010 and ultimately entering into confrontation with the latter from 2010 onwards.

This part of the book proposes a framework defining the newly emerging Post-Kemalist secularism that has been designed and implemented by the JDP. Therefore, this part presents an expanded discussion about the JDP's conservative democracy ideology, its secularism approach, and political journey since 2001. By comparing Kemalist and Post-Kemalist secularism in this context, the main discussion focuses on

---

© The Author(s), under exclusive license to Springer Nature
Switzerland AG 2022
P. Kandemir, *The JDP and Making the Post-Kemalist Secularism in Turkey*, https://doi.org/10.1007/978-3-031-07605-3_3

59

the tension, struggle, and competition within the Kemalist, non-Kemalist, and anti-Kemalist circles.

By providing a theoretical discussion, this chapter claims that the JDP did not challenge or reject the princible of secularism; rather, it struggled against *Kemalist* secularism, which exclude existence of religion in the public sphere. Since 2002, the JDP prepared an environment for a fluid interchange between religion and secularism.[1] It avoids the established understanding that people must choose one or the other. This new dynamic has been made possible by eliminating the standard approach that religion friendly movements and secularism are two contrary and incompatible approaches. To explain this transformation in political and public sphere, this chapter will provide a historical discussion by classifying the first part as the years of rhetoric until 2010 while the second part will afforded a discussion focusing on the post-2010 period that the JDP started to take concurate steps towards the New Turkey.

FORMATION OF THE JUSTICE AND DEVELOPMENT PARTY (2001–2004)

The Justice and Development Party (JDP) was founded on 14 August 2001. The Party chose a yellow and black light bulb as their logo, and its leader Recep Tayyip Erdoğan announced at the first conference organised to introduce the party to the public that the light bulb represented a constant light.[2] The publicity for the party from the start employed both secular and Islamic symbols. Attendees, serving as founders and members of the JDP, stood in silence to remember Atatürk while the Turkish National Anthem was played.[3] One day after the meeting, the founders of the party also visited Atatürk's Mausoleum,[4] a symbolic ritual for Kemalists, later joining in Friday prayers together.[5] By attending two symbolic ceremonies, the JDP communicated their intention to stay in the centre and address different segments of society by operating as a centre-right coalition as it will be discussed in details in this chapter.

Before start discussing the JDP's political identity, it should be highlighted that it is indeed a compilation of Erdoğan's lifetime experiences. Thus, the only way to evaluate the JDP's 19-year journey is to carefully analyse Erdoğan's journey[6]; undoubtedly, the JDP's identity and Erdoğan's ideological viewpoints and political experiences have been exceedingly integrated since the beginning. Erdoğan comes from a humble background. His father was a sailor, and he was born and raised in *Kasımpasa*, a modest neighbourhood of İstanbul. Yavuz states, it is "a cosmopolitan and economically lower-middle-class district of İstanbul" with "a strong conservative moral ethos with a deep sense of solidarity among its poor dwellers," where Erdoğan's "personality was first shaped."[7] He graduated from an IHS and then participated actively in the social movements of his time. Subsequently, Erdoğan progressively served as the head of the youth branch of the Welfare Party in the Beyoglu district in 1976, the district head of the party in Beyoglu in 1984, the provincial head of the party in 1985, and the mayor of the İstanbul Metropolitan Municipality in 1994.

Hüseyin Besli, the writer of Erdoğan's biography, and his companion since his early days in politics, states that the Islamist youths of the era did not engage in left–right conflicts, but instead focused on intellectual activities such as reading Hasan al Banna, Mawdudi, and Sayyid Qutb. Erdoğan was reportedly fonder of reading works by Mehmet Akif Ersoy, the writer of the Turkish national anthem, and the well-known conservative poet Necip Fazıl Kısakürek, displaying a preference for local rather than foreign figures.[8] In turn, his ideological roots were Turkish Islamist, nationalist, and conservative intellectuals, positioning him slightly differently to his peers who highly inspired from Iranian Revolution.

Although all these details regarding Erdoğan's background could suggest that he was a classical Islamist throughout his Welfare Party experience, Besli states that Erdoğan criticised the *NOM* even when he was just 24 years old. Erdoğan did not find the party's political actions rational, since he thought that their messages did not appeal adequately to all the groups in Turkish society. For instance, he criticised the removal of shoes when entering the party's building, as one does when entering a mosque. He felt that this meant the party resembled a religious community rather than a political entity.[9]

As a result of this approach, when Erdoğan became a mayoral candidate for NOM for the Beyoglu province in 1994, he began calling for reforms within the party. During his campaign, for the first time in *Milli Görüş*'s history,[10] women worked very actively within the party. In later periods, after Erdoğan became provincial chairman, he arranged for women to be seated in the front rows at political meetings, whereas previously they had not even been allowed to enter the hall. These actions were harshly criticised by the traditionalist within the party at the time. During the mayoral election, when Erdoğan requested votes from people drinking in a tavern in an RPP neighbourhood near the *Hacıhusrev* castle, the upper cadre of the Welfare Party reacted harshly.[11]

In those years, Erdoğan moved the RP's provincial building from *Fatih*, a district that hosts the highest number of ultra-pious Muslims, to the vicinity of the British consulate in *Sishane*, a decision that affords valuable insight into Erdoğan's political vision.[12] The move signified that Erdoğan was targeting support from a wider audience, which necessitated that he leaves the party's comfort zone. In hindsight, Erdoğan's election campaign for *Beyoglu* as the Mayoral candidate was a pilot project for his entire political career.[13] This is also because he later developed the same strategy and applied it in election campaigns all over Turkey, forging connections with different segments of society to acquire them as voters.

When Erdoğan was elected as Mayor of İstanbul in 1994, his election campaign strategy was certainly an important factor. Subsequently, when he became mayor of İstanbul, Erdoğan began to travel all over Anatolia making him very popular. One of these visits, on 12 December 1997, was to the city of Siirt, which was populated mostly by Arabs and Kurds. During his speech, he read a poem by Ziya Gökalp, the pioneer of sociological studies, Turkish nationalist and one of the figures who influenced Atatürk. Due to this action, Erdoğan was sentenced to ten months in prison, accused of being anti-secular for reciting the following lines from Gökalp's poem. After being sentenced for the crime of "provoking hatred and enmity," almost every newspaper and even the mainstream media in Turkey reported that Erdoğan would no longer have a political life, stating that he would not even be able to become a *Muhtar* (neighbourhood representative).[14]

In hindsight, however, Erdoğan's imprisonment in 1999 increased his popularity among various ethnic and religious groups in Turkey. Ahmet Kaya, the most popular Kurdish singer ever, performed a concert for Erdoğan the day before his imprisonment. On the day he was scheduled to be imprisoned, Erdoğan visited the tomb of *Eyüp Sultan*, a figure of symbolic importance to Muslims in Turkey. Later, he joined the Friday prayer in the *Fatih* Mosque, located in a neighbourhood with a strong religious community in İstanbul. He was welcomed by thousands of people, in both *Eyüp* and *Fatih,* as well as in *Pınarhisar*, where the prison was located.[15]

During his four-month incarceration, Erdoğan began working for the new party.[16] Parallel to this, a group of Erdoğan's fellows within *Fazilet*, the party founded following the closure of RP, also started to call for reform of the *Fazilet*'s political methodology, discourse, and ideological approach. Abdullah Gül, one of three important leaders who co-founded the new party with Erdoğan and Bülent Arınç, and who later served as Prime Minister, Foreign Minister, and President, described the difficulty critics faced with rising in a movement in which *biat* (obedience) was one of the "central virtues."[17] Regardless of the external and internal barriers, the Reformist wing openly took an oppositional stance in the party congress of 2000. Their colleagues accused them of "plotting to split the party by inserting *nifak* (functionalism)."[18] In this congress, Abdullah Gül served as candidate on behalf of the Reformist group, as Erdoğan was subject to a court decision banning him from politics. When they lost by a narrow margin, the leaders chose to establish their own party.[19] During this period, the Constitutional Court closed the *Fazilet* Party on 22 June 2001 on the grounds that it was an extension of a prohibited party, and for committing anti-secular actions.[20] Following the closure of *Fazilet*, the *NOM* separated into two. The leader of the traditionalist group was Erbakan, and the Reformist group united under the leadership of Erdoğan.[21]

Following the establishment of the JDP on 14 August 2001, six general elections, five local elections, two referendums, and two presidential elections have taken place in Turkey. The JDP took first place in all these elections. All the elections resulted in the JDP gaining a sufficient majority to form a government on its own without entering into any coalitions except for the June 2015 elections. At that juncture, Erdoğan left the role of party leader to become President, and Ahmet Davutoglu became both Prime Minister and Party leader. When a coalition could not be formed in the June 2015 elections, another election be held in November. The JDP was then able to establish the government alone with 49% of the votes. Moreover, with all of referendums and presidential elections during this period resulting in victory for the JDP,[22] it is even more remarkable to note that none of the results fell below that of the first election result in November 2002 (34.4%). The JDP has been able to remain in power through democratic elections for the longest period in the Turkish Republic's history. This makes it to be defined as a dominant party by several scholars.[23]

To understand the JDP's long running election success, it is important to evaluate what the JDP offers ideologically. As it will be detailed in the following part, the JDP embodies an extended ideological opening in Turkey, in terms of both structure and perception; although it remains a fairly hybrid continuity of centre-right tradition and NOM ideology. Ideologically, it is in fact a well-formulated blend of both. By including reputable names ranging from liberals to Islamists, *Alevis* to Turkish and Kurdish nationalists, and non-Muslim minorities, the JDP had firmly established itself as a centre-right coalition.[24] There have always been centre-right, liberal, and even social-democrat politicians[25] at the heart of the policy making process, shaping the JDP's policies on social issues.[26] Ömer Çelik highlights that although the main founders of the party came from the *Milli Görüş*, it is clear that "Perspective of *Milli Görüş* is not sufficient enough"[27] to entirely describe the JDP. He rather describes it as "a natural link in Turkey's democratisation adventure."[28]

However, when we look at the JDP's formal ideological stand, we see that they were clearly rejecting *Milli Görüş*'s ideological roots in their new ideological formation. To fully understand why politicians from NOM chose to cut ties with their former ideology, and "even refrained from using the Muslim democrat label,"[29] required them to revisit the limitations placed on politics under the dominance of the Kemalist establishment. Firstly, the JDP's founders had witnessed the risks of being affiliated with Islamism. Had the JDP been called Islamist at that time in Turkey, it would have immediately been closed down by the Constitutional Court. Secondly, being Islamist, or retaining anything close to such an identity, did not accord with the JDP's objective of inclusivity.[30] The maximum vote share an Islamist party could receive in Turkey was 21%, as experienced by the RP. However, being a centre-right movement practically guaranteed the JDP almost half the votes if they campaigned effectively. As previously mentioned, by forging "more ties with the mentality of the ANAP of the 1980s than the Welfare Party of the time",[31] they managed to attain greater popularity than any NOM party had previously. To reach this aim, the JDP preferred to apply a new political term: Conservative Democracy. Now, it is essential to understand what they meant by this and how the conservative democracy brand influences secularism discussion.

The JDP's Ideological Formation and Emergence of the Conservative Democracy Brand

In spite of the considerable number of prominent works defining the JDP with different terms almost all related to Islamism,[32] such as being an Islamist, New Islamist, Islam-sympathetic, and post-Islamist movement,[33] according to the party's official programme, the JDP is "a conservative democratic mass party that situates itself at the centre of the political spectrum."[34] Before start discussing what the JDP means with this brand new term—conservative democracy, one should understand that it is a concept uniquely articulated in Turkey,[35] even while it also draws on some Western philosophical tenets. While definitions abound regarding the nature of conservatism, I adhere to the definition proposed by the late Finnish historian Pekka Suvanto, who refers to this political stream as "a movement acting within a dynamic society in need of adapting itself to new types of solutions."[36] In his conclusion, Suvanto lists several conservative tenets and values: hostility to revolution; "personal liberty;" "the right of ownership;" "private enterprise;" "a view of life based on Christianity;" a belief in the inalterability of human nature; the firm belief that change ought to occur within the framework of tradition and "historical continuity"; and antipathy towards what emerges from the abandonment of tradition."[37]

It could further be claimed that conservatives tend to be fixated on the imagined past holding a deep-seated reverence for tradition. However, arguably this does not mean that they necessarily oppose change, but rather they are against radical and dramatic change. Therefore, when browsing the conservative literature, concepts like "reform" and "restoration" are generally valued highly. The works acknowledge the need to preserve identity and traditions but accept change as a necessity to improve day-to-day societal conditions. As British statesman and political philosopher Edmund Burke stated, "a state without the means of some change is without the means of its conservation."[38]

Erdoğan defined this notion at the "International Symposium on Conservative Democracy" organised by the JDP in 2004; stating that a conservative democracy delivers "a modernity that does not exclude tradition, a universality that accepts locality, a rationality that does not deny the meaning, a non-fundamentalist change."[39] This approach is indeed very similar to the one proposal by Eisenstadt within the context of multiple modernities paradigm. As also highlighted by Gusfield as well as Eisenstadt, tradition does not necessarily on a collision course with modernity.[40] This approach repeats itself while evaluating the relationship between modernity and culture, modernity and history and modernity and religion in JDP's conservative democracy formulation.

66   P. KANDEMIR

Similarly, JDP officials have offered the following key words to define this brand: "a gradualist approach to change; an understanding of politics as an art of compromise rather than conflict; recognition of the national will as a source of political legitimacy; a conception of the state as arbitrator; and support for pluralism and the rule of law."[41] In several documents, this new identity has also been presented as "a new understanding of politics free from the politicisation of religion, populism and corruption."[42]

Summarising a similar approach Yalçın Akdoğan, a JDP politician, describes the JDP's position:

> First, it is against revolutionary transformation, which would damage social institutions; second, it prioritises the building of consensus in the political sphere; third, the JDP puts societal values at the centre of its policies by localising its authority on a legal and justifiable basis; fourth, the JDP does not apply any authoritarian policies; fifth, pluralistic democracy remains at the core of the party's identity; and lastly, the JDP rejects any kind of radical discourse or polarisation.[43]

As understood from this outset, conservative democracy, a completely novel concept in Turkish politics at the time, has been the main pillar of the JDP's branding strategy, differentiating it from NOM tradition specifically and Islamism in general. It primarily opened up a space for the JDP to invest in a new political narrative. Firstly, while NOM applied terms such as "heavy industrialisation, material and spiritual development, national planning, national civilisation, the glorious past, justice, national consciousness, and national morality," the JDP discovered new, fresh, and attractive concepts, such as "globalisation, a realist foreign policy, international competition, free market economy, privatisation, foreign investment, reform of the bureaucracy, strengthening of local administrations, democracy, human rights, liberties, civil society, universal standards and civilizational dialogue."[44]

In addition to their liberal economic approach and welfare state proposal, the JDP applied new narrative included particular keywords like "democracy, human rights, the rule of law, limited government, pluralism, tolerance and respect for diversity."[45] These key concepts were not only emphasised within the speeches of the JDP's leaders, but also in the party programme; i.e. the "Development and Democracy Programme," election hand-outs and other types of written documents. As a tangible example indicates all these, during the 2002 election campaign, the principal theme of the JDP's political discourse was "the universality of human rights, the Copenhagen criteria, freedom of thought and expression, and freedom of economic enterprise."[46] Hale and Özbudun defined this further, stating, "while the old Islamists categorically rejected such notions as democracy, human rights, modernity, and progress as inherently Western and alien to Islam, now the same people speak in terms of liberalism, democracy and human rights and see the EU as a saviour."[47] One example of this is elucidated by the JDP's narrative concerning the headscarf issue. While previously the wearing of a headscarf was viewed as "an Islamic obligation," it became a matter of human rights and part of the right to an education in revamped JDP rhetoric.[48]

Thus, the JDP aimed to offer a common and inclusive framework to be applied by different ideological groups.[49] Prominent Turkish scholar Ahmet Çiğdem supports this argument by citing Turkish conservatism as a component of almost all the mainstream ideologies in Turkey. Examining the principal ideologies of the Republican era, Islamism, Turkism, and Westernisation, he argues that while they appear to pursue different paths, they ultimately follow the same course. His conclusion is that the label of conservatism cannot be assigned to any of these ideologies, as it exists in small amounts in each.[50] Additionally, surveys demonstrate that this term is highly applied by ordinary citizens in Turkey who define themselves both conservative and religious with a great margin.[51] Despite small fluctuations in numbers in different surveys, the pattern of results is clear overall. At this juncture, it should be remembered that the concept of conservatism has a broad meaning in Turkey that includes history, tradition and religion within.

Beyond the popularity of this term within the Turkish society, there is little doubt that the JDP had many aims with regard to adopting conservative democracy as an ideological brand. One of its goals was to "reconnect with pious Muslims in Turkey," as put by respected scholar and former JDP politician Yasin Aktay.[52] While the JDP has tried to avoid any term related to Islamism, it aspires to attract pious Muslims and conservatives, as potential voter bases. Notably, conservatism not only refers to "the preservation of certain values and acquisitions"[53] or "a change based on an evolutionary, gradual, and natural societal transformation"[54] in a Turkish context, but also to religiosity, as explained by veteran JDP politician Mahir Ünal.[55] Thus, the word "conservative" expresses the JDP's desire to communicate with this group[56] who "provides core electoral foundations"[57] for this movement.

The second goal was to send a clear message to the Kemalist establishment. From the outset, the Kemalists fixated closely on the JDP, blaming it for being Islamist but making *taqiyyah*.[58] Adopting a conservative democracy identity was an important way in which the JDP was able to avoid generating a polarisation with the Kemalist establishment. Yet, one should not forget that any act that could potentially raise concerns within the Kemalist establishment regarding secularism could have resulted in the closure of the JDP. At the time of the foundation of the party, Erdoğan had only recently been released from prison, and his political ban was still in place when the JDP was founded. These conditions led JDP politicians to repeatedly explain why they did not represent a threat to the secular Republic. This was also viewed as the only way for them to escape the "paradox of a deep sense of insecurity despite a huge electoral support."[59] Thus, aversion to polarisation, as exemplified by the JDP's use of alternative narrative, facilitated the main conditions that prevented it from being banned directly during the party's period of emergence.

Another goal was to introduce them to the West with a concept that was already recognisable. As mentioned previously, the JDP took the West very seriously with further integration with the West being a central objective. Accordingly, the Western countries constructed a close relationship with the JDP especially during its early days. The West was an important ally, as it applied JDP's Post-Kemalist Turkey narrative "outside Islamic circles."[60] As a political party that promised increased integration with the West during its first election campaign, the JDP successfully differentiated itself from NOM vis-à-vis unconditional support from the EU.[61] This diverged from the main characteristic of an anti-Western stance, as was prevalent in Turkish variants of Islamism.

At this point, it should be also highlighted that despite being a mass movement attracting votes from various segments of society, there is a recognisable profile for the overall votes being polled for the JDP at each and every election since 2002. JDP voters define themselves in reference to conservatism, nationalism, and the centre-right, while RPP voters use Kemalism/Ataturkism, secularism, social democracy, and patriotism.[62] Additionally, the level of religiosity of JDP voters is above average. While the percentage is 72 for Turkey overall, it is 87 for the JDP.[63] This means JDP voters are generally pious. As an example of this, according to Konda's survey, 88% of those people who fast in Ramadan voted for the JDP.[64] In terms of headscarf preferences, 13% of JDP support comes from women who do not wear headscarves and men whose wives are not veiled. This profile includes 32% of Turkish voters overall. Konda's 2018 survey found that 98% of JDP voters are Sunni Muslims[65]; for the RPP, this is 76%.[66]

Another important data that the public pools indicates, the majority of JDP voters do not vote according to ideological motivations. For example, a small number of JDP voters referred to the JDP's secularist policies or "religious freedoms" as a source of motivation when deciding to vote for the JDP.[67] Indeed, Turkish voters in general prioritise economic concerns over political ones in their voting behaviour.[68] JDP voters also tend to refer to the JDP's economic and social reforms when seeking to explain why they support the JDP; frequently offering macroeconomic stability, infrastructure, better welfare state or freedom for investment as an example.[69]

When we reconsider aforementioned data, JDP's constant reference on the service-focused politics, which highlights governments' actions, becomes more understandable. Naci Bostancı, the JDP's Deputy Chief in the Parliament, found it unnecessary to invent various abstract definitions for the party's ideological stance. Although he conceded that the term conservative, played a worthwhile role in their narrative, he believes additional terms such as "developmentalism" are useful for defining the JDP.[70] He mainly suggests applying specific terminology to accurately convey the JDP's service-focused politics, such as developing infrastructure or improving Turkey's social state.[71] Ömer Çelik, the deputy chairman and the current spokesperson of the JDP, presents a similar view with a different focus. He explains the JDP was the only party central to Turkish politics, which was capable of presenting "a democratic proposal;"[72] nevertheless, this led service-based and project-focused politics to become the focal point of the JDP's narrative.[73] The principal objective of this strategy was to explain that the JDP would carry out reforms to enhance the quality of life for its citizens, rather than prioritising ideological discussions.[74] Within this context, as will be discussed below; JDP politicians did not view secularism as an ideological discussion; rather, it was viewed as a factor affecting the daily life of ordinary citizens, and as an asset guaranteeing equal coexistence in the social and political sphere,[75] rather than a tool of indoctrination designed to control the periphery.

70 P. KANDEMIR

Inspired by Mardin's framework, which locates the DP as a *peripheral* force, we should recollect Erdoğan promised in his speech to the first Party Convention in 2003 where he declared the role of the party is "to bring the values and demands of the 'social centre' to the political *centre*"[76] Remembering Erdoğan's words, Numan Kurtulmus repeated the same line in my interview with him: "The JDP is neither centre-right nor centre-left party." He claims that, it rather offers a new *centre* in Turkish politics. He states,

> When you evaluate some social reforms that the JDP had done, you see that they cannot be done by even left-wing parties in Turkey. Similarly, when you look at the reforms that the JDP has made in the past in terms of reviving the free market, you see that no liberal party or the centre-right party has succeeded what the JDP has succeeded. Now there are parties to the left and right of this new centre created by the JDP.[77]

All these discussions indicates that although the DP and ANAP also represent the *periphery*, the JDP's bid in this context is better formulated, partly as a result of inspiration drawn from NOM. As one might remember from the introductory chapter, NOM identified with *Adil Düzen*. According to Hüseyin Besli, when the JDP began its repositioning from the periphery to the centre, it upgraded to a further level in international discussion by identifying itself as the voice of weaker countries, countering the international world order. Besli states,

> When Erdoğan said that "The world is bigger than 5", he made one of the biggest political manoeuvres of the 21st century. By leading a debate on this, Erdoğan moved the centre-periphery discussion to an international level. He positioned himself in the periphery against the international centre.[78]

This proves the JDP did not fully relinquish its identification with NOM, rather its blended elements of NOM with the centre-right DP and ANAP and thus expanded its support by formulating itself as a representative of the conservative democratic periphery opposing the anti-religious and anti-democratic Kemalist centre.

Finally, while making this discussion on the JDP's ideological stand, I should highlight that during this process of 19 years of governance, while the JDP's political narrative has retained its essence, its tone has changed. As put by Cemil Çiçek, "Parties are also living organisms.

What is happening in the world and in the country changes both society and political parties. Nobody can preserve their position and discourse from 40 years ago."[79] Walzer saliently puts it, identities are in fact historically constituted "mixed" structures, and political identities contain various elements and tend to change.[80] This means that while the JDP continues to use the "conservative democracy" brand to define itself officially, at present, it is best not to perceive this as a static expression that elucidates its ideological journey since 2002.[81] It is indeed the party's flexible ideology that has helped it achieve long-term success. Thus, by embracing and uniting different ideological, ethnic, and religious and sectarian segments of society under various titles, the JDP has brought together peripheral elements by proposing a non-Kemalist narrative. This coalition later became the very founder of the New Turkey.

The JDP's Post-Kemalist Secularism

As stated previously, the multiple modernities paradigm and the Habermasian post-secular perspective contradict in many ways the classical modernisation/secularisation theories. The first is to recognize the freedom to religion as a necessity of pluralism. The second is not to put scientific knowledge in a race with religion and not see these two as an alternative to each other. The third is that pious people respect the secular character of the state and the constitution.[82] Despite the inadequacies and malfunctions in practice time to time, the programme of the JDP has been formulated to meet all these conditions. Nevertheless, it should be noted that it is not twin brother of other Post-Kemalist examples. Yet, the paradigm of multiple modernities claims that different countries, different movements, and even different individuals have established their understandings of modernity through their own approach.[83] This has become a viable approach to secularism today. By referring similar arguments, Erdogan and other senior JDP politicians noted, they did not copy their secularism understanding from the West.[84]

In the party programme, the JDP's approach to religion is as follows under the title of "Basic Rights and Liberties": "Our party considers religion as one of the most important institutions of humanity, and secularism as a pre-requisite of democracy, and an assurance of the freedom of religion and conscience. It also rejects the interpretation and distortion of secularism as enmity against religion."[85] Another article there outlining

72   P. KANDEMIR

the political programme highlights the importance of freedom of religious expression: "Basically, secularism is a principle which allows people of all religions, and beliefs to comfortably practice their religions, to be able to express their religious convictions and live accordingly, but which also allows people without beliefs to organise their lives along these lines. From this point of view, secularism is a principle of freedom and social peace."[86] Secularism essentially means freedom of religious expression for the JDP. All the JDP politicians I interviewed constantly defined it this way. Criticising the anti-religious approach of Kemalist secularism "which disrupted social peace since the beginning, but particularly during 90s",[87] the JDP highlights that adhering to religion is an acceptable choice.[88] For the JDP's politicians, this is the main difference between Kemalist secularism and the JDP's Post-Kemalist secularism.[89] This argument reminds us Taylor's approach see the faith "… is one human possibility among others."[90] Therefore, the JDP largely presents secularism as "an emancipatory guarantee for different beliefs and lifestyles."[91]

Erdoğan believes it is only possible to bring freedom of practice to all religious groups by applying this type of secularism. He repeatedly highlighted this nature of secularism during his visits to Muslim world following the Arab Uprisings.[92] He recommended that secularism be added to Egypt's upcoming constitution, elaborating on its positive meaning, as he understands it. He said: "(…) If you present or apply secularism as anti-religion, of course, you will face objections. Whereas secularism is the state's equal distance to all beliefs, all groups, including atheists; with secularism, all faith groups are under the guarantee of the state."[93] He continued to advance this approach with the following words in Tunisia following his statement in Egypt: "(…) A person cannot be secular. The state is secular; thus, a Muslim can successfully rule a secular state. We need to know that the secular state stays in the same distance to every faith group. Whether Muslim, Christian, Jewish, or atheist… It is the guarantee of all."[94] Erdoğan visited Libya immediately after Tunisia as a part of the same official road trip and repeated his call.[95] As understood from Erdoğan's approach, he believes that secularism provides freedom to all in terms of believing and practising, and argues that this model should be disseminated to other Muslim countries. In my interview with them both Ömer Çelik and Mahir Ünal mentioned that this step was a tangible proof of Erdoğan's belief in secularism.[96] From the vantage point of the argument of this book, Erdogan's secularism approach is proved once again to be fallen under post-secularism. As might be remembered, post-seculars does not reject value of religion and they also admits significance of secularism.

Despite all the evidence showing that the JDP's approach to secularism differs from the Kemalist one, there is a question that should not be overlooked. Are there any similarities between these two secularism(s)? JDP's secularism is not in absolute conflict with Kemalist secularism. There remain some characteristics of Kemalist secularism that abound in contemporary Turkey. *Diyanet* and compulsory religious courses are chief examples of this argument.[97] In this case, it would not have been realistic for a political movement claiming to be conservative to come up with a completely revolutionary and completely disconnected practice from this issue. It should not be forgotten that conservatives are not very willing to destroy the practices that have been filtered from the years of experience of the society. Although, these two practices were started by particular political elites, the society approves their contunity on contrary to other secularism policies. This will be detailed with public opinion pools in the upcoming part.

Additionally, the JDP was unconcerned by the role of the Directorate of Religious Affairs, which was originally established as a control mechanism of religion in the public sphere by Kemalist, but "taken as a bridge between state and society proving religious services as others by the JDP."[98] Thus, as a religion-friendly political movement, the JDP even maximised the influence of this institution. Throughout the JDP period, the head of *Diyanet* began to accompany the President on official visits, and it was raised from level 51 to level 10 in state protocol.[99]

As a reaction to Diyanet's rising visibility, Diyanet in particular and the long-standing state promotion of the Hanafi jurisprudence in general has become more prominent in these international reports, which turns into a demand: "Allow for the independent and peaceful practice of Islam outside of the *Diyanet.*"[100] EU's Turkey Progress report noted that, "The work of the Religious Affairs Presidency (Diyanet) increased in all spheres of public life and its budget for 2020 was increased substantially."[101] Indeed, it is possible to see the same determination in all reports prepared by the EU since 2016.

As noted above, the JDP's secularism approach does not contradict with the continuity of Diyanet, my interviews with JDP politicians indicates. Also, on contrary to my argument, "its existence does not necessarily donate similarity with the Kemalist secularism due to its

74   P. KANDEMIR

changing role and image."[102] Similarly, during my interview with him, JDP's Mahir Unal also said that Diyanet should be reconsidered independently of its original purpose (refers the one formulated during the early Republican years).[103] When asked whether the Presidency of Religious Affairs contradicted the JDP's understanding of secularism, Speaker of The Grand National Assembly of Turkey and JDP MP Şentop replied:

> First of all, religious services are also a need of society. Like other social needs, the needs of religious life must be met. There can be two simple models of meeting this. Either these needs can be met by the State itself, or a legal basis is prepared for non-governmental organizations to meet these needs. The arrangement of religious life by civil institutions is an Ottoman practice and has continued for centuries. With the Republic, this business was nationalized, so to speak. In other words, since the desire for the organization of religious life to be left to civil institutions is limited, it has started to be governed by the State.[104]

He added,

> It is natural that a nation that has lived with deep-rooted religious institutions for centuries needs the continuity of these institutions. However, the ideological understanding of secularism did not take an innocent approach to both Diyanet and compulsory religion lessons. It is possible to simply say this: Diyanet was planned to fulfill the purpose of the State to control and rule religious life. Compulsory religion lessons are also intended to teach a religion whose content will be determined by the State. The experiences of our nation over the centuries have enabled us to find the right channel for the Diyanet and compulsory religion classes, even if the planned and the desired are different.[105]

Minister of Justice Abdulhamit Gül also emphasised the difference between the presence of the Ministry of Religious Affairs in a country of authoritarian secularism and a country with a liberal understanding of secularism. He said:

> The Presidency of Religious Affairs, as an autonomous religious authority in a country where the overwhelming majority of its people is Muslim, is exactly the institutional guarantee of the separation of religious-state affairs. It is the duty of the State not to interfere with religion, but to ensure that every citizen has the means to preserve his faith and to fulfill his beliefs. In fact, it is only a problem in the context of authoritarian and militant

secularism, not liberal secularism. If the former, an erroneous interpretation of secularism, is adopted, institutions such as the Diyanet may well turn into a State's means of keeping religion under control.[106]

While making this discussion, one should not skip the Turkish people's perception of, and expectations for, the *Diyanet*. According to Konda's survey, 84.1% of Turkish people believe the *Diyanet* should be included in the constitution[107] and 72% agree that it does not contradict secularist objectives.[108] It should be mentioned here that while 66% approve the *Diyanet*'s services, the great majority of Turkish society believes it should provide services to all religious groups.[109] The RPP does not demand the removal of *Diyanet*; rather, their election declarations propose a change in the structure of *Diyanet* to represent all sects possible.[110] When I asked the RPP deputy İlhan Kesici whether *Diyanet*'s existence contradicted secularism or not, he outlined the legacy behind the establishment of *Diyanet*. He noted that it originated with budget negotiations that took place on 21 February 1925. This led to the Presidency of Religious Affairs wabeings opened and its remit determined as "the service of the state to religion." For him, tackling religious misinterpretation is another goal. He added, "The continuation of *Diyanet* is essential. Otherwise, different sects become religion. Then, these sects hijack that religion."[111] However, this does not mean that the RPP fully approves JDP's perception and policies towards Diyanet. For instance, RPP MP Özkan claims that this creates a hegemonic pressure by using a religious functionary.[112]

By defending a different approach, the pro-Kurdish HDP is the only political party promise to shut down *Diyanet* in the election declaration.[113] HDP MP Hişyar Özsoy stated "the HDP advocates that religious affairs should be autonomous from the state, administratively and financially. So, we believe that the religious community should work without orders from the government." He added,

> The interesting thing is that the political tradition, which the JDP also originated from, had the same understanding (on *Diyanet*) that the HDP advocates do today; they were concerned with removing religious affairs from the tutelage or monopoly of the state and putting them into the service of the people in an autonomous, democratized and socialized way. But when the JDP came to power, it started to use the field of religion more than the Kemalists in the framework of its political interests. The JDP also follows the Kemalist model as much as the RPP.[114]

76 P. KANDEMIR

Basically, when we evaluate the continuity of Diyanet during the JDP era within the context of post-secularism discussions, this situation does not present a reverse situation due to two reasons. First, post-secularism does not exclude secularism and does not position secularism as anti-religion. Second, exactly because of this very situation, the JDP's model of secularism has been described as "post-Kemalist" by this book. It is not an absolute break from previous periods' secularism, but continuity to a certain extent due to such elements.

Equally important, the JDP also shares similarities with Kemalist secularism regarding compulsory courses pertaining to religion. Despite the demands of Alevis and the liberals, the JDP knowingly and wilfully stayed limited with revising the curriculum of this course but did not remove mandatory religious course, from the public schools. At this very stage, it should be noted that such as Diyanet, compulsory religious course also supported by the great margin of Turkish society.[115] As will be dissussed in details in the education chapter, in spite of the contunity of the lesson in the schools, the JDP reformed its content by adding other religions and sects to the cirriculum. Additionally, one might also easily claim that while the Kemalist secularism was using these tools to regulate a redefined version of Sunni Islam and even sometimes for anti-religious indoctrination, the JDP applied them with a religious friendly approach to rapprochement of religion and state. This indicates a fundamental difference between Kemalist secularism and the JDP's new model. Additionally, the JDP's Post-Kemalist secularism relates to the encouragement for all to receive a religious education, not only Muslim citizens. This also poses a difference between Kemalist secularism and JDP's Post-Kemalist secularism.

In the final instance, all these discussions indicated that "The JDP is not in practice or in rhetoric, opposed to the secular system, nor does it seek to usurp or in any way undermine the principle of secularism" as noted by Axiarlis.[116] According to the results of anthropological field work, JDP supporters who believe Turkey is secular offer two arguments: First, there is no *Sharia* law, and second, different religious and non-religious groups live together peacefully. Some of the JDP's supporters even claim that Turkey is more secular than ever as a result of reforms assuring religious freedom.[117] Another group of JDP supporters argue that Turkey is secular because *Diyanet* remains there to control religion, and there is still no special permission required to go to *Cuma* prayer(not a positive attribution).[118] When their thoughts on secularism were questioned, the results showed they either supported secularism, attributing a similar meaning to secularism as their party. According to Konda's 2016 surveys, 46% of JDP voters supported secularist principles being included in the constitution; 41% of JDP voters supported the state maintaining equal distance from all religious groups; and 14% of JDP voters did not support secularism remaining in place as a constitutional rule.[119] This does not necessarily mean they oppose secularism. As an example of this, TESEV conducted six different surveys asking, "Do you want a *Sharia* state?" and reached a similar conclusion. The results of this survey are as follows (no/yes percentages): 1995 (61.8/19.9). 1996 (58.1/26.7). 1998 (59.9/19.8). 1999 (67.9/21.0). 2002 (74.1/16.4) 2006 (76.2/8.9).[120] All the data suggests this is a new era in terms of pious Muslims' approach to secularism. However, one should not forget at this stage, as mentioned by Ünal, what is meant by secularism has differed over time. He stated, "What we mean by secularism today is talking about something that is the subject of the state and politics, which are equidistant to all beliefs."[121] Remarkably, the percentage of people who define themselves as secular has risen throughout the JDP years, and continues to increase. For instance, a 2014 survey reveals the percentage of people defining themselves as secular at the time was 65.8, while 22.8% gave no response, and just 11.5% defined themselves as anti-laic.[122] When we consider how and why the pious Muslims of Turkey turned positive towards secularism, we see the changing practices of secularism as the main factor behind.

JDP's Bilgin claims that "democratic and modern" secularism has been adopted. Therefore, he says, by carrying out democratic reforms, the state abandoned the use of secularism as a means of oppression, ending authoritarian secularist practices.[123] Similarly, Özlem Zengin states that Kemalist authoritarian secularism has removed during the JDP period because the state respects its citizens, allowing them to believe in, learn, and live their religion. She also asserts that alongside this freedom, the concept of secularism remains valuable for all the country's citizens.[124] This argument generates an important conclusion: Both the JDP politicians' approaches to secularism and the aforementioned survey results demonstrate constructive changes in the perspective of Muslims regarding the concept of secularism. Nonetheless, the JDP's Post-Kemalist secularism remains flexible; it is not a fixed concept and pragmatically adapts to the public's demands through careful evaluation of the results of public surveys.[125] JDP's Vedat Bilgin argues the JDP has no desire to make society more religious; he adds "What they don't understand is this; they think the society is an object to be edited or editable, if it would be the reality, they would establish the 'positive society' they wanted with their anti-democratic interventions."[126]

The new situation in secularism discussions and the JDP's reforms is transforming its own audience, but also other political groups. This might be considered as a complementary learning process in Habermasian sense. Although the RPP MP Tuncay Özkan explains that formerly there was a period in Turkey when pious Muslims were silenced and Kemalists liberated, and now the situation is reversed. However, in my opinion, this is not a silencing period in regards to defending or not defending/ challenging or not challenging secularism. Rather, the JDP has succeeded in encouraging these two groups to communicate.[127] It is notable that while all these developments were occurring after 2010, both the opposition and the government presented their arguments implementing democratic maturity, with the exception of rare incidents. In contemporary Turkey, Kemalist secularism is no longer safeguarded as the state's official ideology, and there is no monolithic secular understanding. However, while secularism in its new mode is open to revisions and no longer untouchable, it remains protected by the constitution as a founding principle of the state.

THE JDP's STRUGGLE AGAINST THE STATUS QUO (2004–2010)

One cannot separate variations in secularist policies from internal and external developments in Turkey, which have undoubtedly had direct repercussions on the political, economic, and social environment. Certainly, European Union candidateship approval in 2004, the Republican Rallies in 2007, the closure case against the JDP in 2008, Constitutional Referendum in 2010, the Gezi Protests in 2013, the Syrian Civil War especially after 2015, and the July 15 coup attempt in 2016 have significantly impacted the JDP's style of politics and its narrative which are the milestones of Turkish politics. To analyse change in JDP politics especially after 2011 by skipping domestic and external developments as most of literature does would simply resulted with ignoring the *zeitgeist*.

Immediately after the JDP was elected, Turkey's EU integration process became a fundamental driving force in domestic and international politics.[128] In addition, to the anticipated political and economic benefits, the JDP told voters it needed to adopt EU processes to guide reforms, thereby opening an "institutional channel for [driving] Turkey towards democratisation."[129] The series of reforms pertaining to "civil-military relations, the judiciary, parliamentary procedure, minority rights, national security, macroeconomic management and the public sector"[130] were legitimately presented as mandatory steps in the EU accession process. Henceforth, the EU was drawn on as a significant instrumental power against the oppression of Kemalist cadre within the bureaucracy, military, politics, social and business life helping transform the system into a more democratic form from the beginning of the JDP's period of governance. This reform process was deemed successful enough by the EU to initiate accession negotiations with Turkey in December 2004.[131]

As will be discussed in the following three chapters, the JDP took no steps to agitate the establishment on religious issues during this period. Despite this, the Kemalists sought to criminalise the JDP as anti-Kemalist by referring its historical references. Indeed, the Kemalist newspapers from that time afford a wealth of examples.[132] Although the Kemalists' arguments were primarily sourced from prejudice and shared only by a small group within society,[133] there were still several incidents that triggered the Kemalists' prompting concerns "The regime is under threat."[134] One example was the assault against the Council of State in 2006, which was considered one of the bastions of secularism in Turkey.

Following a relatively calm period between 2002 and 2007, the JDP nominated Abdullah Gül as its candidate for the Presidency in 2007, despite huge pressure from the status quo. Yet, he was a pious Muslim coming from the NOM tradition, and his wife wore a headscarf.[135] This step of the JDP was reacted with a harsh response of Kemalists. In this sense, the pre-presidential election protests in 2007, called the "Republican Rallies" (Cumhuriyet Mitingleri), remain the most substantial reaction from Kemalists during the JDP era; highlighting issues of secularism and headscarf debates.[136] The organising committee for these protests called upon their followers to stage demonstrations.

The Republican Rallies were organised by Kemalist NGOs such as The Atatürk Thought Association (Atatürkçü Düşünce Dernegi); Association of Republican Women (Cumhuriyet Kadınları Dernegi); The Readers of Ankara Cumhuriyet Daily (Ankara Cumhuriyet Okurları) and The Association for Supporting Contemporary Life (Cagdas Yasamı Destekleme Dernegi). According to Bülent Arınç, the most important figure engaged in secularist discussions at the time along with Erdoğan and Abdullah

80   P. KANDEMIR

Gül, those who attended these meetings were families of army officials, RPP members and the Kemalist Halk Evleri.[137] Meanwhile the Labour Party and the Social Democratic People's Party announced their corporate participation in the protests, and the RPP and the Democratic Left Party (DLP) sent out a special call for participation, but did not engage at the corporate level. Throughout April and May, Republican Rallies were held in key metropolitan cities, primarily Izmir, İstanbul and Ankara. Various civil society organisations, presidents, and party leaders, such as Deniz Baykal, Zeki Sezer, Yaşar Okuyan, and Mümtaz Soysal, attended the protests.

The main slogan to appear was "Look out for your Republic" (Cumhuriyetinize sahip çıkın); other slogans included "Çankaya's way is closed to sharia" (Çankaya yolları şeriata kapalı), "Turkey is secular and will remain secular (Türkiye laiktir, laik kalacak), and "We are the soldiers of Atatürk" (Atatürk'ün askerleriyiz). Arınç claimed the RPP had been politically pragmatic at this time. They identified the RPP's decision to not organise additional election rallies in cities where they organised Republican Rallies was given as proof of this.[138] He added, "Baykal (the then the RPP leader) said that they got what they wanted."[139]

Following these rallies, the Turkish military released an e-memorandum on 27 April 2007, which was published at night on the official website of the General Staff.[140] This was especially concerning, as the 1971 military declaration by the army that resulted in the resignation of the then government placed intense emphasis on the secularism issue. In this instance, the declaration reaffirmed that the military and the JDP had a different understanding of secularism; it stated the next president to be elected "should be secular not in the words but in the core."[141] By meaning a possible coup, the Head of General Staff stated, "Society has received the message."[142] While messages from abroad criticised the e-memorandum of April 27, Kemalist public figures and politicians readily applauded it.

The JDP did not remain silent and released a robust statement rejecting the move. Cemil Çiçek, spokesperson for the government at this time, said in my interview with him that they prepared the statement with the senior management of the party at night and got approval from the then PM Erdoğan in the morning.[143] The government's response was extremely harsh as a first in Turkish politics:

3 THE ANATOMY OF THE JDP AND THE EMERGENCE ... 81

> It is not possible for the General Staff, which is a subsidiary of the Prime Ministry, to use a statement against the Government in any matter under the democratic state of law. The General Staff is an institution whose duties are assigned by the Constitution and related laws are at the disposal of the Government. According to our Constitution, the Chief of General Staff is responsible to the Prime Minister for his duties.[144]

The statement was a milestone in Turkish political history in terms of civil-military relations, as the civilian government was asserting the role of the military relative to Turkish politics for the first time.

When the JDP responded to the 27 April e-memorandum severely, the Kemalist establishment sought another way to stop the JDP, later called the Decision of 367 also a first in Turkish Republican history. According to the Turkish constitution, to elect a President to Parliament 367 votes were required in the first two rounds and 276 in the third round. However, amid of the continuing tension on presidential elections, the Cumhuriyet newspaper published an op-ed, written by the former Head of the Advocate General of the Court of Cassation, Sabih Kanadoglu (who was well-known to the public for his commitment to Kemalism), in which he claimed the presence of 367 MPs in the parliamentary chamber is a necessary precondition to hold an election. The JDP's number of MPs was 354 at the time, and they were planning to make their candidate President in the third round. Following this claim, the leader of the RPP Deniz Baykal announced they would not attend the election meeting in parliament that the election would be invalid. As soon as Abdullah Gül received 357 votes in parliament, the RPP took the issue to Constitutional Court demanding the election's cancellation, by claiming that it had been held without the attendance of 367 MPs.[145]

The Constitutional Court decided that 367 MPs was necessary to hold an election in parliament.[146] Nevertheless, in spite of the Kemalist establishment's vigorous efforts to prevent the election, the MHP declared that they would attend the election, although not support the JDP's candidate. This made the election valid. Following this decision, the JDP's candidate Abdullah Gül was elected Turkish President on 20 August taking 339 votes in the third round.

This step of status quo brought the apparent question of who governs the state and who takes decisions for the state to the forefront. At that time, tutelage had been the main concept the JDP had applied to explain this contradiction. By regarding this decision, Mahir Ünal comments,

"We call it tutelage to those who are out of the will of the nation but have the right to make decisions about the state."[147] In reference to Carl Schmitt, he adds, "Sovereign is he who decides on the exception. Exception was decided by the status quo at that time and 367 decision was an exception."[148]

After this period, the JDP became more practical and valiant in it is stand. Although RPP's Tuncay Özkan says, "I fully believe that Republican Rallies affect the JDP's view of secular lifestyle. You have to measure this; but my observation is that they adopt a healthier process management,"[149] these events emboldened the JDP to push against "the representatives of the tutelage within the state."[150] Thus, when the aggressive and threatening attitude of the establishment combined with the rising confidence of the JDP due to public support, transformation of the JDP's policies from passive to active began. Bülent Arınç defines this situation stating, "They thought that we will be afraid, but we did not. They thought, our votes will decrease; they only helped to rise our popularity."[151] Thus, the JDP's election victory in 2007 played an important role in its growing confidence to counter the Kemalist establishment.[152] Another development of 2007 was the referendum, which resulted in a 68.9% yes vote, confirming 21 changes in the constitution.[153]

The response of Kemalist bloc within the state to the JDP's shakeup was a closure case opened by the Chief Public Prosecutor Abdurrahman Yalçınkaya on 14 March 2008, referring to Articles 68, 69, and 101 of the Constitution requesting the dissolution of the JDP. 17 cases and indictments were filed by Yalçınkaya, who claimed the JDP was violating the secularist principles of the constitution.[154] Indeed, this was the harshest response from the Kemalist establishment to that point. Here, one should remember the fact that Yalçınkaya was assigned by President Ahmet Necdet Sezer in 2007 prior to leaving the Presidency. Behind the decision by Sezer to assign Yalçınkaya, who received only 95 votes compared to the other candidate, Ersan Ülker, with 146 votes, afforded a transparent motivation for supporting Kemalism. Indeed, Yalçınkaya fulfilled expectations by opening the closure case one year following his assignment.

In the indictment file, prepared in reference to the JDP's 6-years of governance, Public Prosecutor Yalçınkaya presented three important factors. The JDP's attempt to lift the ban on the headscarf that had applied at universities, its desire to lift the age limit for taking Qur'an courses, and its aim to lift the obstacles faced by IHS students in university entrance exams.[155] Interestingly, when the Constitutional Court put forward the claims, it also recognised demands from the public to resolve those issues. However, the prosecutor claimed the problem lay in the exploitation of religion by the JDP, which allegedly opposed secularism.[156] The indictment of the closure case detailed speeches and referenced the actions of Prime Minister Recep Tayyip Erdoğan, President of the Assembly Bülent Arınç, the Minister of Foreign Affairs Abdullah Gül, the Minister of National Education Hüseyin Çelik, and other deputies, claiming they were anti-secularist. Therefore, in addition to the closure of the party, a five-year political ban was demanded for 71 JDP politicians, including Erdoğan.

The JDP rejected all the accusations and significant points were made in its preliminary and main defence, which drew attention to its respective differences in understanding of secularism. The indictment of the closure case stated, "The values of the Republic were made disputable by creating artificial problems such as redefining secularism."[157] In this context, the JDP claimed the main reason behind the closure case was the differences between the states' understanding of secularism and that of the party. According to the JDP, the state perceives "secularism" as a one-dimensional concept, "a civilized way of life" and "philosophy of life" individuals should adopt. The JDP likened this to the strict "progressive" approach of the nineteenth-century positivism. Meanwhile, it defined its own conceptualisation of secularism as "an approach fully compatible with the libertarian sense of secularism of contemporary democratic societies."[158] Moreover, the JDP asserted: "The understanding of secularism that is advocated by our Party never poses a threat to the fundamental rights and freedoms of others. On the contrary, this understanding anticipates that all individuals with different beliefs and ways of life would live together in a peaceful way."[159] Therefore, the JDP claimed the case was not a legal matter but one of political one.[160]

Ultimately, the Constitutional Court announced its decision in front of journalists live on every single TV channel in Turkey. The President of the Constitutional Court, Haşim Kılıç, at a press conference on 30 July 2008, stated that six members of the court had voted in favour of the closure, while five members had rejected it. Haşim Kılıç also voted not to close the JDP, but required that it be punished with a legal warning and removal of the treasury aid (usually made available to all political parties) for one year.[161] This judgement was what the majority of Turkish society had expected.[162]

The closure case was the strongest attempt by the status quo to prevent the JDP's ascent. After this affair, it was anticipated that the JDP would become more cautious; however, the reverse happened. As an extra experience over Decision of 367 crisis, the JDP realised that no matter what it did, it would be unable to create a mutual understanding with the establishment via dialogue.[163] Consequently, it began to openly oppose the status quo, especially with regard to non-democratic secularism practices. Thus, after the JDP won its first struggle against the status quo by making Abdullah Gül President in 2007, it continued avidly to strive to implement reforms.[164]

At this stage, one should question the main motivation behind the Kemalists' resistance. Although the Kemalists claims, their resistance intended to protect secularism, non-Kemalists believe that it was more about power sharing. JDP deputy Numan Kurtulmus explicated,

> For [the] privileged minority who benefit from the blessings of the system, there was the fear of losing this cake in their hands. So, they covered it very nicely over a secularism discussion. I would like to express that this is a very important factor. They had everything in their hands, they were running the system, they were managing the economy, they were making the decisions as they wish, and they were preventing any kind of questioning towards their acts.[165]

However, indeed, after being beaten by the JDP, they lost ground in the *centre* and were appointed owners of it.

Whatever the motivation is, it is important to note that since the very beginning it remained challenging for the JDP to implement reforms and make changes to the status quo, because Kemalists dominated the state machinery. Indeed, the Ergenekon case of 2007, which had the announced purpose of cleaning the deep state,[166] might have been considered the JDP's first proper attempt to discontinue the tutelage within state institutions. In his fieldwork Dexter Wilkins summarised what is understood by a deep state in Turkey:

> The deep state is a presumed clandestine network of military officers and their civilian allies who, for decades, suppressed and sometimes murdered dissidents, Communists, reporters, Islamists, Christian missionaries, and members of minority groups—anyone thought to pose a threat to the secular order, established in 1923 by Atatürk. The deep state, historians

say, has functioned as a kind of shadow government, disseminating propaganda to whip up public fear or destabilizing civilian governments not to its liking.

In spite of the hot debates on the controversy of this case as will be discussed soon, the reality is that this process has been milestone in reformulating the civil-military relations in Turkey.

While discussing the changing power balance within the state, one should remember the role of the *Gülen* Organisation, a global network turned from an *Islamic cemaat* into a political and radical ideological group aiming to control the state via illegal tools and methodology.[167] This group was classified as a terrorist organisation—Fethullah Terrorist Organisation, (FETO) by the Turkish state since 2016. Considerable numbers of this group were tried in the context of Turkey's Anti-Terror law after the July 15 Coup attempt, and FETO term was officially used in the indictments in this trial.

By summarising the historical data derived from the "2017 Final Report of the Special Committee set up by the Grand National Assembly to inquire into the attempted coup of July 15, 2016," Berktay and Kandemir noted that there are three phases in the evaluation of this terrorist network:

> It is a very worldly end that their spiritual leadership has pursued single-mindedly over three main phases. (1) Roughly from around 1966 to 1980 was when they were just establishing their doctrine, strategy and organisational identity, and taking the very first steps, in utmost secrecy, in infiltrating the state apparatus. (2) Paradoxically, it was a military coup in 1980 that, in its opportunistic search for a "tolerable, usable" Islam, provided them with their greatest opportunity, which they seized in quite aggressive fashion -- though even then, their sole tactical objective was simply to keep accumulating more and more power. (3) From around 1997 onward, they were increasingly overt, at times even arrogant in their ambition to achieve full control over state and society. It was this "final" drive that was cut short when they gambled everything on their military takeover attempt of 15th July 2016, and were defeated by the democratic resistance of the people.[168]

When the JDP came to power in 2002, this group ultimately supported the JDP such as the other non-Kemalist groups in its reforms. Indeed, they were the only non-Kemalist group to have penetrated the state after the 1990s and managed a strong network in the education, business, and media sectors. When the gate of the state institutions and private sector was opened to non-Kemalists during the Özal era, followers of this group were the first one taking advantage of it. Particularly after the 1990s, education became an important sector for them, as they recruited qualified manpower. Until 2012, there had been a close relationship with the JDP and FETO. JDP does not describe this as an alliance, though. Mahir Unal highlighted this point during my interview with him by saying, "I do not accept an alliance has been formed with them. Within the framework of democratisation affords, all civil initiative groups defending democracy acted together. This (de facto coalition) seemed like a civil initiative group at the time."[169]

Indeed, with the support of a broad non-Kemalist coalition, the JDP entered into struggle against the status quo and deep state as part of the Ergenekon case.[170] As noted above, an alleged ultranationalist and secularist illegal group, *Ergenekon* was defined as the deep state of Turkey, which had already been present in everyday discussions in Turkey since the 1990s.[171] The case first started in 2007, and was expanded and deepened after 2008 and completed in 2013. During this process, almost 300 people were arrested and accused of plotting "to bomb mosques, assassinate prominent figures, or start wars to stir chaos and prepare the grounds for a military coup."[172] The prior files for this case had targeted military officials who were preparing for a coup against the JDP. However, later on, followers of FETO within the state institutions, especially in the police forces and judiciary were able to take full control. According to Unal, "FETO diluted this process."[173] Later, it was proven that some of the evidence had been fabricated by the members of this group, including police officers and prosecutors. During this process, FETO elevated their followers to positions neutralised by the state elites.[174]

JDP's current spokesperson Ömer Çelik portrays this process, "While the JDP government was successfully carrying out its struggle for democratisation against the status quo, this time it faced threats from FETO that wanted to exploit the expanding democratic space to establish their own tutelage."[175] One lasting effect of those developments, however, was that it led the JDP to reconsider the relationship between religious groups and the state."[176]

Returning to the main discussion, it is significant to understand that the disruption of the Kemalists monopoly within the state was not only a result of the Ergenekon Case.[177] As Erdi and Yavuz noted, "initially opposing the singular and restrictive political imaginary of the established *raison d'état*, the JDP created an appeal not only among conservative groups, but also within those who had been marginalised by the Kemalist order."[178] This explains the aforementioned harmony between different ideological groups under the JDP umbrella. The strength of this harmony enabled the JDP to pacify the Kemalist establishment and alter the power balance. However, although this coalition endured until 2010, and assisted the JDP to structure a Post-Kemalist Turkey, the broad coalition subsequently began to sputter and then collapse,[179] with liberals replaced in the coalition by Turkish nationalists after 2015.

Foundation of Post-Kemalist Turkey and Post-Kemalist Secularism: 2010 and Onwards

As stated earlier, although there have been improvements at the narrative level between 2002 and 2010, there has been no remarkable development in the context of legal and political reform. The fundamental changes fulfilled by the JDP, which we call the reformation of the state, started to take place with the 2010 Constitutional Referendum in spite of the previous crucial but minor steps. When I asked JDP's Ünal why the JDP had waited years to initiate reforms on freedom of religion, he responded by stating, "Change would never happen without creating its own environment. You have to determine your priority to get success in politics. Our priorities were to end tutelage, democratises the state of mind and set the will of the nation sovereign at the first stage. Because when they were realized, others would already happen spontaneously as a legitimate right and demand."[180] Indeed, the JDP's 2010 Constitutional Referendum was intended to create an environment that would ultimately be conducive to democratic change. This was later followed by 2013 Democratisation Package.

Thus, 2010 constitutional referendum campaign was merged with discussions about the JDP's "Democratic Initiative" also named as the "National Unity and Brotherhood Project."[181] This process was actually started with the announcement of Erdogan in 2009. After the official announcement, the JDP began to prepare legal foundations upon which to implement reforms. The initiative was targeted to bring long-term solutions to manage Turkey's problems, especially Kurdish issue. Although public support for this kind of radical step was relatively low according to the public pools at the time,[182] by "getting advantage of

88 P. KANDEMIR

Erdogan's unlimited credit in the eyes of ordinary Turkish people,"[183] the JDP nevertheless initiated it. The 2010 constitutional referendum was indeed a significant step in this process. Rather than simply being an ordinary change in the constitution, it marked a new beginning for Turkey.

Within the context of this discussion, herein I consider the starting point of the new Turkey to date to the 2010 Referendum, which brought about the necessary changes to the constitution to transition into a Post-Kemalist period. The purpose of this change was to "raise democratic standards and further erode the powers of the country's once omnipotent generals".[184] The 26 proposed changes affected multiple areas, including civil-military relations, economic and social rights, human rights, and judicial reforms. The primary motivation was the institutionalisation of democracy,[185] with the JDP's motto during the referendum campaign being "From the law of superior to rule of law."[186] In a booklet prepared by the JDP to explain these chief motivations, Erdoğan states, "On the 30th anniversary of the 12 September 1980 coup, after 30 years, again, on the 12th of September, our people will realize the most comprehensive and most democratic change in the 1982 constitution."[187] Indeed, in the referendum, 57.88% voted in favour of this change.[188]

As mentioned above, these amendments in the constitution have not only introduced massive changes in the judicial system to make it independent, but it also lifted the virtual immunity of the coup leaders, widen the democratic rights and civil liberties, reformulated civil-military relations and narrowed the power of military. This and other modifications in terms of reorganisation of judiciary and institutionalisation of democratic rights had been a milestone in Turkey's democratisation path. While opponents claimed that this is "a power grab" and referred JDP's "Islamic roots", EU's Enlargement Commissioner Stefan Fule stated, "this is a step in the right direction" to fullfil EU entry criteria.[189] As a counterargument to this, it was written in Western media that "Yet the AKP's attempts to increase its power *vis-à-vis* bureaucratic institutions (which are also, let it be recalled, motivated by self-interest) also contribute to the consolidation of civil rule, expand the scope of popular politics, and generate opportunities that are exploited by historically marginalised political actors."[190]

The first and biggest move by the JDP following this constitutional change was the announcement of a Democratisation Package in

September 2013.[191] This package was the outcome of the aforementioned Democratic Opening, which began in 2009. It again included reforms regarding different segments of society, from Kurds to Alevis, and non-Muslim minorities to religious Muslims and Rumanias. Numerous radical steps took place, all of which challenged Kemalism in various ways. The removal of headscarf bans in public sectors (with the exception of armed and security forces and members of the judiciary), lowering the national threshold to 5% from 10, the right to education in one's mother tongue (for Kurdish society), political campaigning in different languages (for Kurdish society), and returning the rights of minorities to establish a university in the name of Hacı Bektaşi Veli (for Alevis) were some of the changes proposed.[192] The Democratisation Package thrilled all the groups formerly oppressed by Kemalists.

While the JDP was presenting these radical moves in 2013, another situation was emerging that would culminate in the Gezi riots and greatly damage the reputation of the JDP's government abroad.[193] The riots started with a small protest against the İstanbul Municipality's plan to restructure a historical building to be located in a park in Taksim, one of the most central locations in İstanbul, and led to the biggest riots in Turkish history. While the protestors initially asked for the cancellation of this aforementioned project, mass civil unrest resulted, leading to the cancellation of all the government's mega projects, including Istanbul Airport-the biggest airport in Europe (completed in 2018), Yavuz Sultan Selim Koprusu-a third bridge in İstanbul (completed in 2016), and Ataturk Kultur Merkezi-a Cultural Centre and Opera House in Taksim (completed in 2021). The protestors also demanded Erdoğan's government to resign. In addition to this, there were some changes implemented by the JDP government bothered them such as alcohol provision.[194] Significantly, some of the main reforms in education and with respect to the headscarf were implemented during this period in the democratisation packages, as briefly mentioned above but will be discussed in the next three chapters. Although the headscarf freedom or educational reforms were not mostly referred to during these protests, they could be described as revealing accumulated anger, as there were hard-core discussions in the political arena at that time because society was very polarised. Additionally, not only the rhetoric of Gezi Protestors included references to Kemalism and Kemalist secularism, but also their graffitis, posters or banners frequently denigrated JDP's moves that challenged Kemalist secularism. By revisiting Habermas' post-secular society discussions,[195] one can even claim that this anxiety was an expected reaction a group of people shocked with the new secularism interpretation contradicting with classical (Kemalist) approach.

Gezi brought together Kemalist civilians who were unhappy with the JDP government's reforms. The protests expanded as violence against the initial protestors brought more people out, including socialists, environmentalists, liberals, LGBT groups, worker's unions, and Alevis. Kurds did not attend the protests and pro-Kurdish HDP did not support the protests publicly, they preferred to stay neutral. Although the huge crowd in these protests was on the headline of the international media, in reality, 62.3% of society opposed the protests, and 53.4% claimed it had been organised by illegal groups.[196]

During this period, democracy replaced secularism as the dominant topic raised in political discussions in Turkey. However, although it was in the centre of Gezi protestors' narrative, public surveys indicates that less than 3% of Turkish society believed democratisation was the biggest problem in Turkey at the time.[197] It is important to remember that it was a time when the Democratic Opening was on track- the most inclusive democratisation step in Turkish Republican history. Indeed, Gezi Protests and the way the government deal with it by applying police voiolence inflicted irreparable wounds on the JDP's image inside and outside of Turkey. Although democratic reforms continued in practice with legal changes, the political climate has changed to an extend after this time and JDP's reformist nature was distrupted with security-focused narrative.

Of course, this shift in the narrative from democratisation to securitisation was not only happened with the Gezi atmosphere. Yet, following the Gezi Protests, several political earthquakes occurred between 2012 and 2016. But most importantly, a coup attempt happened in 2016 when Turkey was already in a fragile security environment due to the ongoing Syrian Civil War: July 15th coup attempt.[198] While it was totally change Turkey's political and social climate, it had been one of the biggest break in Turkey's history.[199] According to tangible proofs, "at a strictly legal level, mounting evidence - in the form of original documents, video footage, e-mails and witness testimonies - has been pointing incontrovertibly to Fethullah Gülen and the Gülenists network as having decided, planned, ordered and carried out the failed coup."[200] Accordingly, while Kemal Batmaz, a well-known Gulenist civilian who works at Kaynak Holding, the biggest commercial company of FETO, was recorded by security cameras at Akinci Air Base, which served as the command centre of the coup, while giving orders high ranking military officers all through July 15–16, another FETO member Adil Oksuz who works at a university as a theology professor was trapped just near the same place.[201]

As noted by Berktay and Kandemir, "15th-16th July clearly demonstrated that (through the army) the Gulenists were well and truly armed and ruthlessly capable of extreme violence."[202] At night-time, the Turkish Parliament was air bombed with F16 fighter jets live on TV as members of parliament from the JDP, RPP, MHP, and HDP made statements against the coup. Meanwhile, the coup plotters bombed several official buildings, including the presidential complex, the National Intelligence HQ, the Police Aviation HQ, the Police Special Operation Centre, the Gendarmerie HQ and TURKSAT (Turkey's main cable television and sole satellite communications operator). The coup plotters raided almost all the TV channels, including the public broadcaster TRT's İstanbul and Ankara main offices and Digiturk (the biggest DTH TV platform). They also raided the hotel that Erdoğan was staying in with his family for a holiday just before he left to travel to İstanbul airport upon hearing about the coup.[203]

This coup attempt resulted in the death of 249 Turkish citizens, and injured hundreds of people, who resisted the coup on the streets. From every segments of the society, thousands of people were in the street to stop the coup. 106 deputies from three political parties—JDP, RPP, and MHP came together in the parliament after figuring out a coup happening to show a resistance. Erdoğan's close friend and campaign manager since the foundation of the JDP, Erol Olcok, was one of the victims, along with his 16-year-old son. They were killed alongside 37 other civilians on the Bosphorus Bridge. Professor İlhan Varank, a prominent academic and brother of the Industry and Technology Minister, was shot dead while protesting against the putschists in İstanbul.[204]

The Turkish government's response to the coup attempt was to apply heightened security measures, including declaring a State of Emergency. The 2016 coup deeply affected the political atmosphere in Turkey, which was already tense following ongoing terrorist attacks by Daesh and the PKK, as well as ongoing conflicts in neighbouring Syrian and Iraq, and the influx of refugees. But more importantly, the JDP's general rhetoric shifted as levels of patriotism in the public sphere indisputably amplified. While the JDP had previously exhibited more liberal democratic inclinations, the following three years witnessed the development of a more nationalistic discourse and heightened security policies. JDP's broad coalition with liberals was collapsed after this time and it was replaced with a new one initiated with pro-Turkish MHP.

However, during my interview with him HDP's Hişyar Özsoy claimed that the JDP's broad coalition collapsed before this date in 2011, and it altered its narrative with a new one after this time: "The JDP became the representative of status quo if not the status quo itself. When the more democratic and liberal tendencies within the JDP were largely eliminated, there was not much left for democracy."[205] He also adds that JDP's conservatism has changed over time as well. In his view, "Conservatism both in the country and within the JDP has seriously eroded when facts such as the articulation of global capitalism, access to financial resources, and new and luxurious consumption cultures are joined together."[206]

Following the collapse of previous coalition, the JDP inevitably started to consider new coalitions, especially as a result of "post-traumatic syndrome"[207] due to the Gezi riots, the coup d'état in Egypt, the Syrian Civil War and the July 15 Coup attempt. There have been growing security concerns present in the narrative of patriotism. At this stage, while democratisation rather than secularism has become the main source of tension, Erdoğan's leadership style has also moved to the centre of the discussion. This was not particularly surprising, because as mentioned previously, Erdoğan's story was also the JDP's story and his fate had been the JDP's fate since the beginning.

It should even be noted that the fact Erdoğan is leader is more important than the party to voters. The majority of JDP supporters vote for the JDP because they trust Erdoğan's leadership and personality.[208] They explain their attachment to the JDP in reference to him.[209] Moreover, despite engaging a religion friendly narrative, Erdoğan never positioned himself as a spiritual leader, contrary to Erbakan.[210] In this sense, Erdoğan's success is based on political realism in addition to his leadership.[211] This realism and self-renewal capacity of Erdoğan's personality constitutes the basic dynamic of internal differentiation within the JDP's ideology. According to Aktay, the total energy of the movement, as led by Erdoğan has a certain charisma in terms of how Weber describes it. People have assigned meaning to both the JDP and Erdoğan, as emerged in the hard-economic crisis described above. However, an important point here is that the JDP's and Erdoğan's popularity is not limited to that election and that period of holding power. He now has greater support was possible 17 years ago. Nevertheless, Aktay claims that after so many years, Weber's concept of the routinisation of charisma is valid for the JDP, although not for Erdoğan. According to him, Erdoğan's charisma increases daily, while the JDP's appeal is static.[212] Simon Waldman, however, contends that Erdoğan's charisma and leadership has also become routine in recent years. For him, "the waning charisma of Erdoğan" makes even his mega projects appear ordinary to voters; thus, the people are likely to show only limited interest in his projects.[213] However, this assumption was falsified when Erdogan's popularity has even risen to 52.59 in the 2018 election compared to 2014 presidential elections when he has taken 51.79% of the votes.

However, more crucial than this, with his rising charisma and transforming power, Erdogan did not stay limited with changing the ideological positioning of his own supporters and party on different issues but most particularly secularism; but he also highly impacted the ideological stand of the other political parties. While defining post-secular societies, Loobuyck takes attention to this kind of happenings by saying religious and secularist worldviews should take eachother's contributions to controvertial public debates seriously; this obviously happened in Turkey. Consequently, there was a notable softening of the RPP narrative from its former anti-libertarian attitude towards acceptance of religious freedom.[214] However, this should be understood in the context of the RPP as a party that has opened a prayer room at its headquarters, allows members and even politicians to wear headscarf (one and only example of this is Sevgi Kılıç so far), cooperates with Islamists in elections (Saadet), and has transferred Mehmet Bekaroğlu, known for his Islamism, to its party. Thus, regardless of the reason and motivation behind, arguably a raproachment started between Kemalist seculars and pious Muslims in Turkey.

In the 2014 presidential elections, the RPP nominated Ekmelettin İhsanoglu due to his conservative identity. Also, in the 2019 elections, it held meetings with Abdullah Gül, co-founder of the JDP and former President, to nominate him as a candidate. One should underscore the radical nature of this step by remembering that Gül's presidency was opposed by the RPP in 2007 because his wife wore a headscarf and he was deemed anti-secular. Likewise, in the 2019 local elections, the RPP's candidate for Ankara, Mansur Yavaş, used "Tamam İnşallah" (If God allows, it is done) banners, which had been used by Erdoğan in the 1994 elections. The RPP's candidate for İstanbul, Ekrem İmamoglu, also came to the forefront revealing his conservative identity; he had a mother who wore a headscarf, and himself recited the Quran. The two candidates, both of whom emphasised their conservative identities, achieved the first victory for the RPP in the Metropolitan Municipalities of İstanbul and Ankara for 35 and 25 years respectively. Whether the RPP's transformation to be sincere or not, it brought a considerable success in terms of RPP's reputation. According to Ünal, this is borne out by the RPP's policy of not stating anything new but instead remaining silent, suggesting adaptations are largely political positioning in response to the public.[215] The JDP's spokesperson Çelik also states that the current level of consciousness in society with regard to secularism, human rights, rule of law, and democracy has compelled the RPP to remain neutral.[216] Another senior polician of the JDP also noted, "These political manoeuvres of RPP should not deduce that Kemalists see pious Muslims of this country as their equals. They still adopt a pros-pertist style while establishing relations with them; they talk about 'showing tolerance' or 'the necessity of enduring' (while talking about the IHSs or veiled women.) Even this is a proof that they still see themselves as the absolute and sole owner of this country."[217]

In a nutshell, there are two main legacies of Erdoğan and the JDP, both of which have changed Turkey forever. The first relates to civil-military relations, as the JDP has made civil governance appear trustworthier than the army for the first time in Turkish history.[218] This has disrupted the army's strategy to securitise secularism, which had risen since the 1990s. Therefore, the military's "self-selected guardian role"[219] came to the end. By removing the Kemalist establishment's monopoly over the state, the JDP has paved the way for non-Kemalists, creating a new centre.[220]

Secondly, there had been a change at the social level in addition to political one. The JDP changed the nature of its relationship between the state and citizens, allowing secular citizens and religious citizens to be visible in the public and their identities equally respected. Parliament Speaker Professor Mustafa Şentop, defining the JDP period as "normalization," said "As the old understanding of power and tutelary administration and operation were eliminated, the ideological tools used by it (secularism) became ineffective and dysfunctional over time."[221] He added, "the JDP's efforts to make the State" the state of the nation, and to "bring the nation to the State and integrate them, are valuable in this respect."[222]

Although the RPP's Özkan accepts that a change happened in the perspective, he says it has happened "in spite of the Islamisation affords of the JDP";

> We are now in a very different place as regards the attitude of the individual towards the state and attitudes between individuals. Secularism is the backbone of this. (…) Society tried to be Islamised using state apparatus (by the JDP). Unnecessary mosques were built, extravagance emerged, but since a greater consensus has arisen, I think all this will be tolerated by society. The important thing is to compromise. Their fears collided with our fears; they changed, we changed too.[223]

By considering these practical and perceptional changes in political and social sphere, it is crucial to understand that the JDP sees the transformation in social and political level as "a mentality revolution." The Minister of Justice, Abdulhamit Gül, answered the question of whether the reforms on institutionalising secularism in the JDP are permanent by probing the "legal, and therefore political, legitimacy" of the previous restrictions. He stated, "Legal regulations are certainly important as a fundamental reform tool, but the success of the JDP in the liberation of our country is closely related to a mentality revolution and social-political transformation that transcends legal regulations."[224]

Şentop also thinks that the assurance of new social practices in Turkey is not legislative changes but rather the very notion of "large-scale social transformations in society."[225] He stated that, at the end of the 1980's, they believed that legal regulations would change the prohibition. Yet, the amendments were canceled by the Council of State, then the legal changes were canceled by the Constitutional Court, and in 2008, the transformation started automatically without any legal change.[226]

Indeed, there have been numerous positive developments as an outcome of this change in political environment including the emergence of new middle class, new freedoms of religious expression, and the integration of a democratic and universal approach that is hybrid, pragmatic, and pluralist.[227] Etyen Mahçupyan saliently analysis it, "With the JDP coming to power in 2002, the Islamic group, fostered by globalization and post-modern criticism, was able to create its own bourgeoisie and middle class. However, instead of creating a form of secularization that diminishes the religious community, modernization has expanded the community on the one hand and changed the meaning of religiousness

96 P. KANDEMIR

on the other."[228] As discussed in different chapters, this concluded with the integration of the Muslims of Turkey to the other communities within society. Mahçupyan also claims, while this was happening, "Religiosity has adapted to the needs of everyday life, the reciprocity between morality and religiosity has been disturbed, whereas Islamic and secular communities have been hybridised, everyone has become more or less "religious".[229] However, there is no concrete data providing this inference as will be detailed in following three chapters. However, from my perspective, it is conservative cultural sensitivities on rise, not the religiosity.

Conclusion

As a hybrid and updated version of the centre-right DP, ANAP, and Islamist NOM, the JDP represents an alternative ideological stance in Turkish politics. Its approach to secularism, democracy, economy, and social rights adheres to a new model. Beyond this, having remained in power since 2002 by winning every election, the JDP's model has proven to be successful. Yet, during the Republican history, Erdoğan managed to be the only leader takes the votes of different spectrums of society including Kurdish nationalists, Turkish nationalists, Armenian Turkish citizens, liberals, and anti-capitalist Islamists concomitantly by creating a broad coalition. Thus, the JDP's history reveals the successful evolution of religion-state relations in Turkey, rather than a revolution. This state of affairs indicates its conservative character of ideological positioning.

Since the JDP can be considered the first political movement to challenge Kemalism directly, it managed to move its vision beyond rhetoric into practice, resulting in the successful institutionalisation of its new model. This explains why I define the JDP years as Post-Kemalist Turkey. My findings demonstrate that Post-Kemalist Turkey should be holistically evaluated in terms of its social policies, economic policies, civil-military relations, and discussions about democracy and foreign policy; these in tandem encapsulate what Post-Kemalist Turkey can offer in terms of secularism.

Putting its rhetoric into practice especially after 2010 onwards was only made possible by subduing Kemalist groups within the state; sometimes by force, such as in the Ergenekon trials, and sometimes with public support, such as in the 2007 and 2010 constitutional referendums. By changing the power balance within the state and moving those with non-Kemalist identities such as Kurds, non-Muslim minorities, devoted

Muslims, Islamists, and liberals to the centre, the JDP ended the tension between the Kemalist state and its non-Kemalist citizens. While changing state approach towards secularism did not Islamise Turkey, it ended with diversification of secularism.

Finally, it is remarkable that while secularism was one of the most hotly debated topics in Turkey when the JDP came to power in 2001, at the time of writing it had become a non-issue and it lost its centrality in Turkish politics. In other words, although Kemalist secularism constituted a hegemonic ideology for a long period of time, it is no longer a taboo subject believed to be inviolable and sacrosanct. Especially after 2010 constitutional referandum, the fundamentals of Kemalist secularism have been addressed individually and consequently revised or even eliminated in response to the needs and demands of the majority of the public. The JDP has been a major catalyst behind this process, as a result of both referendums and legal changes in Parliament. Overall, these outcomes together demonstrate the JDP has ultimately won the battle against the Kemalist elites, thereby delivering on its democratic mandate.

NOTES

1. Yavuz, "Understanding Turkish."
2. "Adalet ve Kalkınma Partisi kuruldu" [Justice and Development Party is established], *Hürriyet*, August 14, 2001. Accessed January 2019. http://www.hurriyet.com.tr/gundem/adalet-ve-Kalkınma-partisi-kuruldu-10017.
3. "Ak Parti Böyle Kuruldu" [JDP is established like this], *YouTube*, January 19, 2014. Accessed January 2019. https://www.youtube.com/watch?v=7_lUFxtPcEE.
4. Idem.
5. "Adalet ve Kalkınma Partisi kuruldu", *Hürriyet*.
6. This term was borrowed from the title on *Time's* cover.
7. Yavuz, Hakan. *Secularism and Muslim Democracy in Turkey*. Cambridge: Cambridge University Press, 2009, p. 123.
8. Besli, Hüseyin and Özbay, Ömer. *Bir liderin doğuşu: Recep Tayyip Erdoğan* [The Birth of a Leader]. İstanbul: Yeni Türkiye Yayınları, 2014.
9. Besli and Özbay, *Bir liderin*, 42.
10. Idem, 44–45.
11. Idem, 117–122.
12. Idem, 57.
13. Erol Olcok, Erdoğan's campaigner since the beginning and close friend who accompanied him almost since the beginning, was shot to death

by coup plotters with his 16-year-old son during the July 15th coup attempt.

14. "Siyasi Hayatı Bitti" [His Political Life İs over], *Hürriyet*, November 1, 1998. Accessed January 2019. http://www.hurriyet.com.tr/gundem/siy asi-hayati-bitti-39045560.

15. "Duygulandıran Pinarhisar mektupları" [Emotional Letters from Pinarhisar], *Yenisafak*, September 3, 2013. Accessed January 2019. http://yenisafak.com.tr/politika-haber/duygulandiran-pinarhisar-mek tuplari-03.09.2013-560650.

16. Besli and Özbay, *Bir liderin*, 235.

17. Idem, 254.

18. Dağı, "Post-Islamism," 85.

19. Hale and Özbudun, *Islamism, Democracy*, 19.

20. "Constitutional Court Decision No 2001/2." *Anayasa*, June 22, 2001. Accessed January 12, 2019. http://www.kararlaryeni.anayasa.gov.tr/ Karar/Content/0a6f1734-1ab5-49f7-aea8-77764a0fb3b7?excludeGe rekce=False&wordsOnly=False.

21. Erdoğan was quite popular even before the JDP; according to a public poll conducted by TESEV in 1999, the response to the question asking, "Who should be the leader of *Fazilet*?" proved this claim. While only 4% supported Erbakan, 53.4% pointed directly at Erdoğan. If the no answer rate of 32.7% is also considered, this was a quite reasonable rate. Çarkoğlu and Toprak, *Değişen Türkiye'de Din*, 60.

22. In 2010, the Presidential System was established through a referendum that resulted in a 58% "yes" vote. In the presidential elections of 2014 and 2018, Erdoğan was elected with 51.79 and 52.38% of the vote, respectively. While the participation rate was 74% during the first election, the turnout increased to 84% in the second election.

23. See some of them; Çarkoğlu, Ali. "Turkey's 2011 General Elections: Towards a Dominant Party System?" *Insight Turkey* 13.3 (2011): 43–62; Keyman, Fuat. "The JDP: Dominant Party, New Turkey and Polarization." *Insight Turkey* 16.2 (2014): 19–31; Gumuscu, Sebnem. "The Emerging Predominant Party System in Turkey." *Government and Opposition* 48.2 (2013): 223–244.

24. Hale and Özbudun, *Islamism, Democracy*.

25. Dağı presents a similar view. See: *Dağı*, "The Justice," 88–106.

26. Some of the most important examples of this would be Süleyman Soylu, Abdulkadir Aksu, and Cemil Çiçek, who hold the most important positions in the party.

27. Interview with Ömer Çelik, Minister of European Union Affairs and former Minister of Culture and Tourism, Ankara, May 3, 2018.

28. Idem.

29. Hale and Özbudun, *Islamism, Democracy*, 20.

3 THE ANATOMY OF THE JDP AND THE EMERGENCE ... 99

30. Interview with Bülent Arınç, Former Minister and one of the founders of the JDP, Ankara, on April 12, 2019.
31. Aydın, Ertan and Dalmis, Ibrahim. "The Social Bases of the Justice and Development Party." In *Secular and Islamic Politics in Turkey: The Making of the Justice and Development Party*, edited by Umit Cizre, 201–223, 209. New York: Routledge, 2008.
32. For some of the most detailed ones, see: Cizre, *Secular and Islamic*; Bayat, *Post-Islamism*; Dağı, "Post Islamism a la Turca."
33. For a detailed analysis of this discussion, see: Cizre, *Secular and Islamic*, 3; Cayır, Kenan. "The Emergence of Turkey's Contemporary 'Muslim Democrats'" İn *Secular and Islamic: The Making of the Justice and Development Party*, edited by Umit Cizre, 34, 62–80. New York: Routledge, 2008; Yıldız, "Problematizing the İntellectual," 45.
34. "Party Programme." *AK Parti*. Accessed June 21, 2018. http://www.akparti.org.tr/english/akparti/parti-programme#bolum.
35. See for instance the speech of then vice-chairman of the AKP: Mir Mehmet Fırat Dengir, speech at Uluslararası Muhafazakarlık ve Demokrasi Sempozyumu [International Symposium on Conservatism and Democracy] (İstanbul, January 15, 2004), Ak Parti. Accessed January 23, 2019. http://www.akparti.org.tr/media/272223/uluslarar asi-muhafazakarlik-ve-demokrasi-sempozyumu.pdf.
36. Suvanto, Pekka. *Conservatism from the French Revolution to the 1990s*, translated by Roderick Fletcher, Ipswich: The Ipswich Book Company Ltd., 1997, p. 3.
37. Idem, 179–182.
38. Burke, Edmund. *Reflections on the Revolution in France*. Indianapolis: Bobbs-Merrill, 1955, p. 24.
39. Erdoğan, speech at "Uluslararası Muhafazakarlık ve Demokrasi Sempozyumu" [International Symposium on Conservatism and Democracy] (İstanbul, January 15, 2004), *Ak Parti*. Accessed January 23, 2019. http://www.akparti.org.tr/media/272223/uluslararasi-muh afazakarlik-ve-demokrasi-sempozyumu.pdf.
40. Gusfield, "Tradition and Modernity'.
41. Yıldız, "Problematizing the intellectual", 44.
42. Duran, Burhanettin. "The Justice and Development Party's New Politics: Steering Toward Conservative Democracy, a Revised Islamic Agenda or Management of New Crises?" In *Secular and Islamic Politics in Turkey: The Making of the Justice and Development Party*, edited by Ümit Cizre, 80–107, 82. New York: Routledge, 2008.
43. Akdoğan, Yalçın. *AK Parti ve Muhafazakâr Demokrasi* [JDP and Conservative Democracy]. İstanbul: Alfa, 2004.
44. Yıldız, "Problematizing the intellectual", 51.
45. Hale and Özbudun, *Islamism, Democracy*, 20.

100   P. KANDEMIR

46. Yavuz, "Understanding Turkish secularism", 28.
47. Hale and Özbudun, *Islamism, Democracy*, 28.
48. Dağı, "Post-Islamism", 88.
49. Interview with Bülent Arınç, Ankara, on April 12, 2019.
50. Çiğdem, Ahmet. "Muhafazakarlık Üzerine" [On Conservatism]. *Toplum ve Bilim Dergisi* 74 (1997): 32–51, p. 45.
51. Erdem, Tarhan. "*Yeni Türkiyeyi Anlamak*" [Understanding New Turkey]. *Konda Araştırma ve Danışmanlık*, November 3, 2007. Also see, Konda. "Toplumdaki Ayıp, Günah ve Suç Algı ve Tanımları" [Definitions of Shame, Sin and Crime within the Society]. *Konda Barometresi*, May 2012.
52. Interievw with Yasin Aktay, a former MP and spokesperson of the JDP, Ankara, on December 12, 2018.
53. Hale and Özbudun, *Islamism, Democracy*, 24.
54. Idem.
55. Interview with Mahir Ünal, current JDP group deputy in TBMM MP, also former spokesperson to the JDP and former minister, Ankara, on June 4, 2018.
56. Interview with Yasin Aktay, Ankara, December 12, 2018.
57. Haynes, "Politics, identity and religious nationalism," p. 313.
58. Britannica defines this Arabic word as follows: "taqiyya, in Islam, the practice of concealing one's belief and foregoing ordinary religious duties when under threat of death or injury." Stefon, Matt. "taqiyyah" *Encyclopedia Britannica*. Accessed June 23, 2019. https://www.britannica.com/topic/taqiyyah.
59. *Dağı*, "The Justice," 88–106.
60. Dağı, "Post-Islamism," 87.
61. Yılmaz, "İslamcılık, AKP ve Siyaset", 610.
62. Konda, "Siyasal Kimlikler" [Political Identities]. *Konda Barometresi*, July 2010.
63. Uncu, "Seçmen Kümeleri: Ak Parti Seçmenleri", 21.
64. Konda, "Ramazan Pratikleri" [Ramadan Practices], *Konda Barometresi*, June 2017.
65. Uncu, "Seçmen Kümeleri: Ak Parti Seçmenleri", 23.
66. "7 Haziran Sandık ve Secmen Analizi" [7 June: Ballot and Voter Analysis], *Konda Araştırma ve Danışmanlık*, June 18, 2015.
67. Çelik, Ayşe Betül, Balta, Evren and Paker, Murat. "Yeni Türkiye'nin Yurttaşları: 15 Temmuz Darbe Girişimi Sonrası Siyasi Tutumlar, Değerler ve Duygular" [Citizens of New Turkey: Attitudes, Morals and Emotions After July 15 Coup Attempt], *Konda Araştırma ve Danışmanlık*, May 2017.
68. "Seçim 07: Siyasal Eğilimler Araştırmaları." *Konda Araştırma ve Danışmanlık*, July 18, 2007.

3 THE ANATOMY OF THE JDP AND THE EMERGENCE ...   101

69. Çelik et al., "Yeni Türkiye'nin Yurttaşları."
70. Interview with Naci Bostancı, Deputy Chief of JDP and Ankara MP, Ankara, on April 28, 2019.
71. Idem.
72. Interview with Ömer Çelik, Ankara, on May 3, 2018.
73. Yıldız, "Problematizing the intellectual," 44.
74. For the details of the election campaigns of the JDP see, "1 Kasım 2015 Seçim Beyannamesi Broşürleri" [Declaration Brochures for 1 November 2015 Election], *AK Parti.* Accessed June 23, 2018. https://www.akparti.org.tr/parti/dosya-arsivi/.
75. This is a common view shared by JDP politicians which I conducted interview with.
76. Recep Tayyip Erdoğan's speech at 1st Ordinary Grand Congress of the Justice and Development Party held in Ankara, on October 12, 2003. Accessed January 2017. https://acikerisim.tbmm.gov.tr/xmlui/bitstream/handle/11543/964/200403930.pdf?sequence=1&isAllowed=y.
77. Interview with Numan Kurtulmus, Deputy Chairman of the JDP and Minister of Culture, Ankara, on April 8, 2019.
78. Interview with Hüseyin Besli, Former İstanbul MP of JDP, İstanbul, May 3, 2019.
79. Interview with Cemil Çiçek, Former Deputy Prime Minister, Ankara, on May 28, 2019.
80. Walzer, Michael. "Yeni Kabile Varlığı" [Existence of New Clan]. *Birikim* 45/46 (1993): 60–66.
81. Interview with Hüseyin Besli, İstanbul, May 3, 2019.
82. Loobuyck, Religious Education, 93. Also see Habermas, Notes on Post-secular societies.
83. Eisenstadt, Shmuel N. *Comparative Civilizations and Multiple Modernities.* Netherlands: Brill, 2003, p. 536.
84. Interview with Ömer Çelik, Ankara, on May 3, 2018; Interview with Mahir Ünal, Ankara, on June 4, 2018.
85. "Party Programme," *AK Parti.* Accessed June 21, 2018. http://www.akparti.org.tr/english/akparti/parti-programme#bolum_.
86. Idem.
87. Interview with Respondent 1, senior JDP Politician. Ankara.
88. "Yarınlar ülkemiz icin bu noktadan çok daha iyi olacak" [Tomorrow İs Going to Be Much Better for Our Country Than Today], *Yeni Safak,* April 29, 2017. Accessed January 2019. https://www.yenisafak.com/gundem/yarinlar-ulkemiz-icin-bu-noktadan-cok-daha-iyi-olacak-2650890.
89. Interview with Mahir Ünal, Ankara, on June 4, 2018.
90. Taylor, *A Secular Age,* p. 3.
91. Dağı, "Post-Islamism", 100.

102 P. KANDEMIR

92. This fundamental transformation in Turkey was treated as a case study in the literature when examining the compatibility of Islam and democracy, as well as Islam and secularism. At the macro level, following the Arab uprisings, several Middle Eastern nations faced similar discussions concerning the illegitimacy of oppressive state models and the need to open the public sphere and include all social and political movements. As a result, the JDP started to be seen as inspirational in relation to the confluence of Islam and democracy by a different group of academics. Ramadan, Tariq. *The Arab Awakening: Islam and the New Middle East*. London: Penguin, 2012; Taşpınar, Ömer. "Turkey: The New Model?" *Brookings*, April 25, 2012, Accessed July 14, 2017. https://www.brookings.edu/research/turkey-the-new-model/; Atasoy, "The Turkish Example," 86.

93. "Erdoğan 'laiklik' ile ilgili ne demisti?" [What Did Erdoğan Say About Secularism], *CNN Turk*, April 27, 2016. Accessed January 12, 2019. https://www.cnnturk.com/video/yasam/Erdoğan-laiklik-ile-ilgili-ne-demisti.

94. Idem.

95. "Kişi laik olmaz, devlet laik olur" [People Cannot Be Secular, States Can], *Cumhuriyet*, September 16, 2011. Accessed January 12, 2019. http://www.cumhuriyet.com.tr/haber/diger/282650/_Kisi_laik_olmaz__devlet_laik_olur_.html.

96. Interview with Mahir Ünal, Ankara, on June 4, 2018; Interview with Ömer Çelik, Ankara, on May 3, 2018.

97. Bekaroğlu, "Post-Laik Türkiye?"

98. Interview with Respondent 1, senior JDP Politician. Ankara.

99. "Protokole reis ayarı" [Chief Adjustment in the Protocol], *Sabah*, May 14, 2012. Accessed January 12, 2019. https://www.sabah.com.tr/gundem/2012/05/14/devlet-protokolunde-sivillesme-donemi.

100. Check the reports 2009, 2010, 2011: "TURKEY Annual Reports." *U.S. Commission on International Religious Freedom*. https://www.uscirf.gov/countries/turkey.

101. EUROPA, "Turkey 2019 Report," 2019.

102. Interview with Respondent 1, senior JDP Politician. Ankara.

103. Original purpose refers "control over religion," here. Interview with Mahir Ünal, Ankara, on June 4, 2018.

104. Interview with Mustafa Şentop, Speaker of The Grand National Assembly of Turkey and Tekirdağ MP for JDP, Ankara, on April 19, 2019.

105. Idem.

106. Interview with Abdulhamit Gül, Minister of Justice of the Republic of Turkey, Ankara, on April 9, 2019.

107. "Diyanet İşleri Başkanlığı Araştırması: Algılar, Memnuniyet, Beklentiler" [Research on Directorate of Religious Affairs: Perceptions, Satisfaction and Expectations], *Konda Araştırma ve Danışmanlık*, November, 2014.

3 THE ANATOMY OF THE JDP AND THE EMERGENCE ... 103

108. Idem.
109. "Anayasaya Dair Tanım ve Beklentiler" [Expectations and Definitions on Constitution], *Konda Araştırma ve Danışmanlık*, September, 2012.
110. RPP's election declarations (2002 and onwards) are available online in the official website. "CHP Secim Bildirgeleri" [Election Manifesto Elections], *CHP*, 2019. Accessed June 20, 2019. https://www.chp.org.tr/yayinlar/secim-bildirgeleri.
111. Interview with Ilhan Kesici, RPP MP, Ankara, on April 7, 2020.
112. Interview with Tuncay Özkan, RPP MP and former journalist for the Cumhuriyet newspaper and the head organizer of Republican Rallies, Ankara, on April 27, 2019.
113. Available online in their official website: "HDP Secim Bildirgeleri" [Election Manifesto Elections], *HDP*, 2019. Accessed June 20, 2019. https://hdp.org.tr/tr/secim-arsivi/11963.
114. Interview with Hişyar Özsoy, HDP MP, Ankara, on April 13, 2019.
115. According to TESEV's survey 82.1% of the society supports compulsory religion course in the state schools. See: Çarkoğlu and Toprak, *Değişen Türkiye'de Din*.
116. Axiarlis, *Political Islam and the Secular State in Turkey*, 34.
117. Çelik et al., "Yeni Türkiye'nin Yurttaşları", 43.
118. Idem.
119. Uncu, "Seçmen Kümeleri: Ak Parti Seçmenleri", 36.
120. Mahçupyan, *Türkiye'ye iceriden bakış*.
121. Interview with Mahir Ünal, Ankara, on June 4, 2018.
122. Konda, "Otoriterlik ve Siyasi Kimlikler", 5.
123. Interview with Vedat Bilgin, current Minister, former JDP MP and deputy chairman, Ankara, on March 27, 2019.
124. Interview with Özlem Zengin, JDP MP and former JDP deputy group chairwoman in TBMM, Ankara, on August 25, 2015.
125. Interview with Mustafa Şen, JDP Deputy Chairman, İstanbul, on August 24, 2015.
126. Interview with Vedat Bilgin, Ankara on March 27, 2019. Same point was highlighted by Mahir Ünal also.
127. Interview with Tuncay Özkan, Ankara, on April 27, 2019.
128. Usul, "The Justice and Development Party and the European Union", 181.
129. Kosebalaban, Hasan. "The Impact of Globalization on Islamic Political Identity: The Case of Turkey." *World Affairs* 168 (2005): 27–37, p. 31.
130. Cizre, *Secular and Islamic*, 1–2.
131. Grigoriadis, Ioannis. *Trials of Europeanization: Turkish Political Culture and the European Union*, Basingstoke: Palgrave Macmillan, 2009.
132. One of the examples of this was ultra-Kemalist newspaper Cumhuriyet's headline implying preparation for a coup. "Genç Subaylar Tedirgin" [Young Soldiers Are Anxious], *Cumhuriyet*, May 23, 2003. Print.

104   P. KANDEMIR

133. See: "Partiler 22 Temmuz yarısına nereden baslıyor?" [Where Do Parties Start July 22 Race?]. İstanbul: GENAR, 2007. For similar results: "Türkiye Toplum Siyaset Araştırması" [Turkey Society Politics Research]. İstanbul: GENAR, 2009.
134. Genar's 2007 survey shows that 38% of Turkish society believes that there is a threat to the Kemalist regime. See: "Partiler 22 Temmuz yarışına nereden başlıyor?" GENAR, 2007.
135. Genar's 2007 survey shows that 27.7% of society stated that a first lady with a headscarf would bother them. See: "Partiler 22 Temmuz yarisina nereden basliyor?" GENAR, 2007.
136. "Huge rally for Turkish secularism." *BBC News*, April 29, 2007. Accessed July 25, 2018. http://news.bbc.co.uk/2/hi/6604643.stm.
137. Interview with Bülent Arınç, Ankara, April 12, 2019.
138. Idem.
139. Idem.
140. This statement was removed from the website in 2011.
141. 27 April 2007, No: ba-08/07. This e-memorandum was later removed from the website.
142. "Türk Toplumu mesajımı aldı" [Turkish Society Received My Message], *Hürriyet*, April 20, 2007. Accessed June 13, 2019. http://www.hurriyet.com.tr/gundem/turk-toplumu-mesajimi-aldi-6366872.
143. Interview with Cemil Çiçek, Ankara, on May 28, 2019.
144. "Hükümet genelkurmay açıklamasını değerlendirdi" [The Government Assessed General Staff's Statement], *Hürriyet*, April 28, 2007.
145. "Anayasa Mahkemesi Kararı No: 2007/54" [The Decision of the Constitutional Court Nr: 2008/2], *Resmi Gazete*, June 27, 2007. Accessed July 23, 2018. https://www.resmigazete.gov.tr/eskiler/2007/06/200 70627-17.htm.
146. "Anayasa Mahkemesi 367 şart dedi" [Constitutional Court Stated That 367 Is Necessary], *Hürriyet*, May 2, 2007.
147. Interview with Mahir Ünal, Ankara, on June 4, 2018.
148. Idem.
149. Interview with Tuncay Özkan, Ankara, on April 27, 2019.
150. Interview with Respondent 1, Ankara.
151. Interview with Bülent Arınç, Ankara, April 12, 2019.
152. "Seçim 2007: Türkiye geneli seçim sonuçları" [Election 2007: General Turkey Results], Hürriyet, July 22, 2007. Accessed June 23, 2020. http://secim2007.hurriyet.com.tr/partidetay.aspx?pid=8.
153. "Türkiye Cumhuriyeti Anayasasının Bazı Maddelerinde Degisiklik Yapılması Hakkında Kanun" [Law on Making Changes at Some of the Articles of the Constitution of Turkish Republic], *Resmi Gazete* [Official Gazette], June 16, 2007. Accessed June 23, 2019. https://www.resmigazete.gov.tr/eskiler/2007/06/20070616-1.htm.

3 THE ANATOMY OF THE JDP AND THE EMERGENCE ...   105

154. See the official website includes the full text of the bill of indictment: "Anayasa Mahkemesi Karar Sayısı: 2008/2" [Consitutional Court Decision No: 2008/2], *Anayasa* [Consitution], July 30, 2008. Accessed April 29, 2018. http://kararlaryeni.anayasa.gov.tr/Karar/Content/566 4600f-6ce5-4b3b-885f-6a936d14abe2?higllightText=basortu%3Bbaso rtu&excludeGerekce=False&wordsOnly=False.

155. Idem.

156. Arslan, Zühtü. *Başörtüsü, Ak Parti ve Laiklik: Anayasa Mahkemesinden İki Karar Bir Gerekce* [Headscarf, JDP and Secularism: Two Decisions and a Justification from Constitutional Court]. İstanbul: Seta Analiz, 2009, p. 17.

157. See the official website includes full text of the bill of indictment and JDPs response to it: "Anayasa Mahkemesi Kararı No: 2008/2" [The Decision of the Constitutional Court Nr: 2008/2]. *Resmi Gazete*, October 24, 2008. Accessed July 23, 2018. http://www.resmigazete. gov.tr/eskiler/2008/10/20081024-10.htm.

158. Idem.

159. Idem.

160. Idem.

161. "'AKP Kapatılmadı" [JDP İs Not Closed], *Hürriyet*, July 30, 2008. Accessed July 23, 2018. https://www.hurriyet.com.tr/gundem/akp-kap atilmadi-9546038.

162. According to Genar's survey, while 43.2% of society believes the JDP was at the centre of anti-secular activities, only 22.2% of society considers the closure case to be about secularism. In the same survey, 66% of society claimed to be against the closure case. See: GENAR, "Türkiye Toplum Siyaset Araştırması", 2008.

163. Interview with Bülent Arınç, Ankara, on April 12, 2019.

164. Idem.

165. Interview with Numan Kurtulmus, Ankara, on April 8, 2019.

166. Filkins, Dexter. "The Deep State: The Prime Minister İs Revered as a Moderate, But How Far Will He Go to Stay in Power?" *New Yorker*, March 5, 2012. Accessed June 14, 2019. https://www.newyorker.com/ magazine/2012/03/12/the-deep-state.

167. Yavuz, Hakan. "The Three Stages of the Gulen Movement: From Pietistic Weeping Movement to Power-Obsessed Structure" in *Turkey's July 15th Coup: What Happened and Why*, edited by M. Hakan Yavuz and Bayram Balci, 20–45. Chicago: University of Utah Press, 2018; For a literature review on the academic Works on Gulen Movement see: Watmough, Simon and Öztürk, Ahmet Erdi. "The Future of the Gülen Movement in Transnational Political Exile: Introduction to the Special Issue." *Politics, Religion & Ideology* 19.1 (2018): 1–10.

106 P. KANDEMIR

168. Berktay, Halil and Kandemir, Pınar. *History and Memory: TRT World in the Face of the July 15 Coup*. İstanbul: TRT World Research Centre, 2017, p. 61. Accessed June 23, 2019. https://researchcentre.trtworld. com/wp-content/uploads/2021/03/HistoryAndMemoryTRTWorld InTheFaceOfTheJuly15Coup-English1.pdf.
169. Interview with Mahir Ünal, Ankara, on June 4, 2018.
170. Yıldız, Güney. "Ergenekon: The Court Case That Changed Turkey." *BBC*, August 5, 2013. Accessed July 24, 2019. https://www.bbc.com/news/world-europe-23581891.
171. See some detailed articles on Ergenekon Case: Kaya, Serdar. "The Rise and Decline of the Turkish "Deep State": The Ergenekon Case." *Insight Turkey* 11.4 (2009): 99–113; Cizre, Umit and Walker, Joshua. "Conceiving the New Turkey After Ergenekon." *The International Spectator* 45.1 (2010): 89–98.
172. Arsu, Şebnem. "Ex-Chief of Turkish Army İs Arrested in Widening Case Alleging Coup Plot." *The New York Times*, January 5, 2012. Accessed January 12, 2020. https://www.nytimes.com/2012/01/06/world/eur ope/turkey-arrests-ex-chief-of-military-gen-ilker-basbug.html.
173. Interview with Mahir Ünal, Ankara, on June 4, 2018.
174. For a detailed analysis of this, see Khan, Mujeeb R. "The July 15th Coup: A Critical Institutional Framework for Analysis." İn *Turkey's July 15th Coup: What Happened and Why*, edited by M. Hakan Yavuz and Bayram Balci, 46–77. Chicago: University of Utah Press, 2018.
175. Interview with Ömer Çelik, Ankara, on May 3, 2018.
176. Idem.
177. Genar's 2009 public survey shows that at the time 71.1% of Turkish society believes that Ergenekon case aims to clean out the deep state, 28.5% of the society takes it as an operation to silence opposition. "Türkiye Toplum ve Siyaset Araştırması: 3. Ceyrek" [Research on Turkey, Society and Politics: Third Quarter]. İstanbul: GENAR, 2009.
178. Yavuz and Ozturk, "Turkish secularism", 1–9.
179. According to Genar's survey JDP still gets vote from Ataturkist, democrat, pious, conservative, Islamists, laic, liberal, nationalist, conservative democrat, liberal in 2011 election. "Türkiye Toplum ve Siyaset Araştırması" [Research on Turkey, Society and Politics]. İstanbul: GENAR, 2011.
180. Interview with Mahir Ünal, Ankara, on June 4, 2018.
181. AK Parti, *Sorularıyla ve Cevaplarıyla Demokratik Açılım Süreci, Milli Birlik ve Kardeşlik Projesi* [Democrating Initiative Process, National Unity and Brotherhood with Questions and Answers]. Ankara: AK Parti Tanıtım ve Medya Baskanlığı, 2010.
182. "Türkiye Gündem Araştırması: Demokratik Açılım" [Research on Turkey's Agenda: Democratic Initiative]. İstanbul: GENAR, 2009.

3 THE ANATOMY OF THE JDP AND THE EMERGENCE ... 107

183. Interview with Respondent 1.
184. "Erdoğan pulls it off." *The Economist*, September 13, 2010. Accessed June 23, 2019. https://www.economist.com/newsbook/2010/09/13/Erdoğan-pulls-it-off.
185. Ete, Hatem. "Turkey's Constitutional Referendum of 2010." *SETAV*, February 15, 2011. Accessed June 23, 2019. https://www.setav.org/en/turkeys-constitutional-referendum-of-2010/.
186. "Erdoğan'dan önemli açıklamalar" [Important Announcements from Erdoğan], *Hurriyet*, August 6, 2010. Accessed January 23, 2020. https://www.hurriyet.com.tr/gundem/Erdoğandan-onemli-aciklamalar-15502847.
187. JDP, *Anayasa Değisiklik Paketi ile ilgili Sorular ve Cevaplar*. July 2010. Accessed January 23, 2020. http://www.akparti.org.tr/media/272664/2010-anayasa-degisikligi-paketi-ile-ilgili-sorular-ve-cevaplar.pdf. For the results of the referendum see: "12 Eylul'e yargı yolu: 2010 anayasa referandumu" [Judgment to 12 September 2010 Constitutional Referendum], *Yeni Safak*, September 12, 2010. Accessed January 12, 2020. https://www.yenisafak.com/secim-referandum-2010.
188. For the full changes see: "Türkiye Cumhuriyeti Anayasasının Bazı Maddelerinde Degisiklik Yapılması Hakkında Kanun" [Law on Making Changes at Some of the Articles of the Constitution of Turkish Republic], *Resmi Gazete* [Official Gazette], May 13, 2010. Accessed June 23, 2019. https://www.resmigazete.gov.tr/eskiler/2010/05/201 00513-1.htm.
189. "Turkey votes for constitutional reform". *DW*, September 12, 2010. Accessed January 12, 2020. https://www.dw.com/en/turkey-votes-for-constitutional-reform/a-5994895.
190. "Turkey's referendum: a democratic dynamic", Open Democracy, September 15, 2010. Accessed January 12, 2020. https://www.opendemocracy.net/en/turkeys-referendum-power-democracy-nexus/.
191. For full manuscript: "Demokratiklesme Paketi" [Democratisation Package], *Ak Parti Halkla İliskiler Baskanlığı*, November 7, 2013. Accessed January 20, 2020. https://docplayer.biz.tr/35489780-Dem okratiklesme-paketi.html.
192. "Temel hak ve Hürriyetlerin gelistirilmesi amaciyla cesitli kanunlarda degisiklik yapilmasina dair kanun" [Law on Making Changes at Some of the Laws to İmprove the Fundamental Rights and Liberties], *Resmi Gazete* [Official Gazette], March 13, 2014. Accessed June 23, 2019. https://www.resmigazete.gov.tr/eskiler/2014/03/20140313-15.htm.
193. See EU Progress Reports published after this date towards Turkish democracy. See "Turkey 2020 Report Brussels, October 10, 2020." Accessed February 2, 2021, p. 10. https://ec.europa.eu/neighbour hood-enlargement/sites/near/files/turkey_report_2020.pdf.

108 P. KANDEMIR

194. In 2011 and 2013, the JDP put some restrictions on the advertisement of alcohol. The sale of alcohol was banned between 10:00 pm and 6:00 am. See details, "Bazi kanunlar ile 375 sayili kanun hükmünde kararnamede değişiklik yapilmasi hakkinda kanun." *Resmi Gazete* [Official Gazette], June 11, 2013. Accessed June 23, 2019. https://www.res migazete.gov.tr/eskiler/2013/06/20130611.pdf.
195. Habermas, Europe, 63.
196. "Türkiye Sosyal, Ekonomik ve Politik Analiz 9" [Turkey Social, Economic and Politic Analysis 9]. İstanbul: GENAR, June 2013.
197. "Türkiye Sosyal, Ekonomik ve Politik Analiz 4" [Turkey Social, Economic and Politic Analysis 4]. İstanbul: GENAR, April 2012.; "Türkiye Sosyal, Ekonomik ve Politik Analiz 6" [Turkey Social, Economic and Politic Analysis 6]. İstanbul: GENAR, October 2012.
198. For one of the most detailed academic works unpacking historical and ideological discussions on this issue: Yavuz, M. Hakan and Balci, Bayram. *Turkey's July 15th Coup: What Happened and Why.* Chicago: University of Utah Press, 2018; Also see Yavuz, M. Hakan and Koç, Rasim. "The Turkish Coup Attempt: The Gülen Movement vs. the State." *Middle East Policy* 23.4 (2016): 136–148; Jacoby, Tim. "A Historical Perspective on the July 2016 Coup Attempt in Turkey." *Insight Turkey* 18.3 (2016): 119–138.
199. See the full text of hearing report, which contains the reasoned decision accusing Fethullah Gulen and other FETO members coup plotters of behind July 15 coup attempt. Accesed 23 February 2021. https://drive. google.com/file/d/11-ASzelt3x_nPL2XZBgWMxnJ2usCKlJ6/view.
200. Berktay and Kandemir, History and Memory, 72.
201. For the photos, see Berktay and Kandemir, History and Memory.
202. Idem.
203. Berktay and Kandemir, History and Memory.
204. Idem.
205. Interview with Hişyar Özsoy, HDP MP, Ankara, on April 13, 2019.
206. Idem.
207. Interview with Ertan Aydın, former MP and political scientist, Ankara, on April 29, 2019.
208. Uncu. "Secmen Kumeleri: Ak Parti Secmenleri," 26.
209. Çelik et al. "Yeni Türkiye' nin Yurttaşları," 15.
210. Interview with Ravza Kavakcı, JDP MP, Ankara, on February 24, 2015.
211. Akdoğan, Yalçın. "AK Parti ve Erdoğan'ın liderliği" [JDP and Erdoğan's Leadership]. İn *Kuruluşundan Bugüne AK Parti: Toplum* [JDP Since Its Establishment: The Society], edited by İsmail Çaglar and Ali Aslan, 105–114. İstanbul: SETA Yayinlari, 2018.
212. Interview with Yasin Aktay. For more detail, see Aktay, Yasin. *Karizma Zamanları: Türkiye Siyasetine Karizma Sosyolojisi Açısından Bir Yaklaşım*

3 THE ANATOMY OF THE JDP AND THE EMERGENCE ... 109

[Time of Charisma: An Approach to Turkish Politics with Charisma Sociology], 8–9. İstanbul: Tezkire, 2015.
213. Waldman, Simon A. "Elections in Turkey: The Waning Charisma of Recep Tayyip Erdoğan." *Simon A. Waldman*, June 19, 2018. Accessed January 11, 2020. http://www.simonwaldman.org/blog/elections-in-turkey-the-waning-charisma-of-recep-tayyip-Erdoğan.
214. Interview with Vedat Bilgin, Ankara on March 27, 2019. Same point was highlighted by Mahir Ünal as well.
215. Interview with Mahir Ünal, Ankara, on June 4, 2018.
216. Interview with Ömer Çelik, Ankara, on May 3, 2018.
217. Interview with Respondent 1.
218. Several surveys have proven that while the army was the most trusted institution in Turkey, this started to change after 2009. The presidency supplanted the army. While it was perceived as 82% reliable in a 2009 survey, this has declined to the 70s. See: "Türkiye Toplum ve Siyaset Araştırması 3. Ceyrek" [Research on Turkey, Society and Politics, Third Quarter]. İstanbul: GENAR, 2009. "Türkiye Sosyal, Ekonomik ve Politik Analiz 6" [Turkey Social, Economic and Politic Analysis 6]. İstanbul: GENAR, October 2012; "Türkiye Sosyal, Ekonomik ve Politik Analiz 7" [Turkey Social, Economic and Politic Analysis 7]. İstanbul: GENAR, January 2013.
219. This definition was borrowed by Haynes. Haynes, "Politics, İdentity and Religious Nationalism," p. 312.
220. Interview with Numan Kurtulmus, Ankara, on April 8, 2019.
221. Interview with Mustafa Şentop, Ankara, on April 19, 2019.
222. Idem.
223. Interview, Tuncay Özkan, Ankara, on April 27, 2019.
224. Interview with Abdulhamit Gül, Ankara, on April 9, 2019.
225. Interview with Mustafa Şentop, Ankara, on April 19, 2019.
226. Idem.
227. Mahçupyan, *Türkiye'ye içeriden bakış*.
228. Idem.
229. Idem, 4.

CHAPTER 4

JDP's Secularism and the Headscarf

Conservative cultural codes, particularly the headscarf, a visible sign of piousness,[1] has historically been identified by Kemalists as a symbol of an uneducated, rural, and backward identity.[2] Until recently, "while unveiled women enjoyed the benefits of a modern female identity," veiled women in Turkey were oppressed, stigmatised, and accused of representing or supporting Islamism. As Göle stated, in Turkey, "no other symbol than the veil reconstructs with such force the 'otherness' of Islam to the West."[3] As a result of the tension caused by debates on this issue, women's bodies became a political battlefield between Kemalists and non-Kemalists or anti-Kemalists.[4]

The headscarf controversy in Turkey began in the early Republican years, increased in the 1980s, reached its highest level in the 1990s and the early 2000s, and seemingly ended in 2013 with the announcement of headscarf freedom in the Democratisation Package prepared by the JDP government. In this regard, the removal of the headscarf ban represented a shift from Kemalist secularism to Post-Kemalist secularism in Turkey.

Kemalist secularism claimed the right to intervene in the private spheres of religious groups, from their lifestyles to their relationships with religion. Thus, whereas state elites imposed restrictions on veiled women for the sake of protecting secularism, the pious segment of society retaliated against Kemalist secularism by either voting for opposing parties or protesting it directly. The repercussions of this tension on state-society

---

© The Author(s), under exclusive license to Springer Nature   111
Switzerland AG 2022
P. Kandemir, *The JDP and Making the Post-Kemalist Secularism in Turkey*, https://doi.org/10.1007/978-3-031-07605-3_4

relations had been extremely negative. Although there had always been limited support for the headscarf ban in the public,[5] its formal implementation caused the majority of Turkish society to perceive secularism as a front for pervasive state intervention in their personal lives.

Thus, until 2000s, headscarf was discussed merely in the context of secularism rather than violation of human rights and democracy.[6] The state under the hegemony of Kemalist establishment have perceived wearing a headscarf as a sign of Islamist political sentiments if not see those veiled women belong to uneducated low class. In turn, the veiled women in Turkey has always supported non-Kemalist political particies, from DP to ANAP, NOM parties to JDP. Nevertheless, although it is true that a great majority of veiled women were (and still are) supporting conservative or centre-right parties,[7] it must be noted that these parties were the only one in political sphere defending their right to wear the headscarf at the time.

Finally, in this part of the book, I reject the false dichotomy, which suggests a woman is either veiled or adopt pro-secular views. I also reject the argument that the JDP removed the headscarf ban due to Islamist motivations or Kemalist criticised this move due to the secular concerns only. A careful analysis of the Democratisation Package in 2013 indicates that there is a range of solutions proposed in this reform package from Kurdish issue to Headscarf problem, which later progressed simultaneously.

Kemalist Secularism Versus the Headscarf: A Historical Dispute

In Turkey, debates around the headscarf arose regarding the visibility of religion in the public sphere and its position as an ostensible threat to Kemalist modernisation.[8] Yet, it relied mostly on visual aids; in this regard, Western-style clothing became a symbol of the early Republican years,[9] to differentiate young Turkey from the Ottoman Empire. In this sense, women's rights reforms[10] were one of the main aspects of this differentiation and were indeed regularly applied in order to promote Kemalism as the bastion of modernism. One of the main Kemalist reforms implemented in this period was the introduction of women's suffrage to the nation; "the new law declared polygyny and marriage by proxy illegal, and granted women equal rights with men regarding divorce, custody of children, and inheritance."[11] Although these steps were supported individually by public women figures who had experienced the last modernisation discussions in the Ottoman Empire, this pseudo-feminist Kemalist strategy was limited.[12]

Thus, in the young Republic, "women became bearers of Westernisation and carriers of secularism, and actresses gave testimony to the dramatic shift of civilization."[13] As can easily be discerned from the pictures of that period, there was no place for the headscarf in the construction of the new modern woman. Photographs of Atatürk with women wearing Western-style clothes were often used to demonstrate the modernity of women during the Atatürk era. On the other hand, a famous picture of Atatürk's wife, Latife Hanım, wearing a black burqa in 1923 was not frequently used, and its exposure to the public was limited. Instead, photos of her wearing a headscarf that covered some parts of her head and hair were common.[14] In fact, photographs of women in Western looking clothes from that period and women's clothes with headscarves belonging to this period are brought side by side and are frequently used as a negative trend referring taking Turkey back by many Kemalist secularists these days.

Over time, Kemalist secularism became stricter, and as illustrated by Atatürk's official photo album in Anıtkabir's (Atatürk's Mausoleum) webpage,[15] changes in clothing became even more visible. One most famous photo in the collection, taken in a ball in 1929 hosted by Atatürk, shows Atatürk posing with women with uncovered hair. Photographs from the following years also depict Atatürk with women wearing hats. The photographs of Atatürk's funeral show that not wearing a headscarf became the new normal in the Kemalist republic.[16] Therefore, it could be argued that images of women in Western-style clothes "became central to the iconography of the regime", especially after the 1930s.[17] As Arat highlighted, women were instrumentalised during the Kemalist era to conceal the increasingly authoritarian nature of the single-party regime. She argued that it was both a symbolic act and a functional move for the regime to promote their project of modernity.[18]

In fact, although men's headgear was abolished as it was deemed to represent being Ottoman during the early Republican years, the headscarf was never banned at the national level.[19] However, it was alienated and otherised by the new authority as a symbol of backwardness associated with the lower class.[20] According to Merve Kavakcı—Turkey's first veiled MP, whereas a Western-looking woman who never wore a headscarf represented "knowledge, confidence, aptness, open-mindedness, and progressiveness" in the Kemalist worldview, a religious woman was an embodiment of "illiteracy, self-consciousness, backwardness, narrow-mindedness, ineptness, and ignorance."[21] This notion sits within the dichotomist framework of the "modern, liberated Republican woman" and "religious headscarved woman" by Hülya Arık.[22] This was indeed one of the main norms set by the Kemalists as an unchangeable notion of modernism since the early Republican years.

At this stage, it is useful to remember that Kemalism managed to succeed this by creating its own upper cadres and empowering them by providing privileges via its statism principle. Particular number of individuals had an eternal attachment to Kemalism and voluntarily fulfilled the principles of Kemalism took advantage of these policies; therefore, in the early Republican years, education, language lessons, employment, and even visibility in the public arena were only possible for women who belonged to this privileged class. Conversely, women with headscarves as well as pious people were discarded to the periphery in a kind of "dichotomist understanding of public and private spheres;"[23] it was not problematic as long as they stayed in their villages or obeyed the Kemalist dress code when moving in central Kemalist circles.

Since the headscarf was not visible in the *centre*, Kemalist elites still regarded it as a symbol of the periphery, and thus were not taking any concrete steps to prevent its usage. This situation continued for a long period of time and could not be suddenly changed even by the non-Kemalist parties such as DP. As a result, no reference was made to the headscarf either in the first official constitution of the Republic or the constitutions after the 1960 coup d'état. An exceptional case was sparked when the number of students who wore headscarves increased at universities during the 1960s. In 1964, Gülşen Ataseven—who was graduating first place at the Faculty of Medicine of İstanbul University—was not allowed to speak at the graduation ceremony due to her headscarf; instead, the male student graduating second place gave the speech. However, although "there were noticeable incidents of harassment and animosity at public buildings, hospitals and cultural centres,"[24] no concrete regulations were put in place. The first regulation came after the 1980 coup, when wearing a headscarf in universities and public buildings was disallowed. From this point onwards, the headscarf became a crucial part of the political debate.

Three years after the 1980 coup, the presence of Turgut Özal in the Turkish government led to the softening of some legislative practices after 1983 election. As discussed in the historical background chapter, the authority of Kemalist secularism waned during the Özal era, and the pressure of the state on pious Muslims as well as the other oppressed groups partially lessened. In 1984, Özal asked the Council of Higher Education (YÖK) to loosen the ban on the headscarf at universities. On 10 May 1984, YÖK announced that female students would be able to enter universities if they wore a türban instead of a headscarf. Therefore, for the first time in the history of the Turkish Republic, the distinction between a headscarf and a türban was made, with the latter, different from the older generation's style, being associated with a political statement.[25]

However, Kenan Evren, the General of the 1980 coup and the President from that time, requested that YÖK forbade the wearing of a headscarf or türban at universities completely.[26] Thus, on 8 January 1987, YÖK reintroduced a series of regulations that completely banned the headscarf at universities. As an objection, on 16 November 1988, Özal argued that clothing choice would not harm Atatürk's principles and issued a law that received a sufficient number of votes to allow university students to continue to dress, as they wanted. Subsequently, President Evren used his right to veto and sent the law back to parliament without approval. On 10 December 1988, the assembly—which had the right to re-vote against the President's decision—accepted the law again with very few changes. In response, as a counter-strategy, the law was sent to the Constitutional Court by President Evren and cancelled on 7 March 1989, after the court deemed it incompatible with the Constitution.[27] At this stage, since the headscarf was accepted as an element that risked national security, all the steps that were taken to scrap the ban were blocked first by the Kemalist bureaucracy, which included the military, and later by the efforts of the judiciary, the Constitutional Court. Tok described this approach as the securitisation of the headscarf issue.[28]

During the 1990s, the headscarf ban became a main focus of NOM parties in their narrative. However, beyond being a discussion point, the issue became a platform to unite women within the non-Kemalist circles, mostly under NOM parties. Referring to women activists within the RP, Yesim Arat claimed, "Women's organisation and activism in the Welfare Party was an unprecedented phenomenon. No other party in Turkey could boast a similar membership of women."[29] Thus the visibility of veiled women increased as soon as NOM raised its political status. Moreover, the wives of majority of the NOM politicians were also veiled, which created another problem for the establishment. After NOM's victory in

116   P. KANDEMIR

the 1995 general election, it was the first time that the Prime Minister's wife wore a headscarf in Turkish history.

Accordingly, the headscarf became one of the main symbols of this process, which eventually reached to its pick with a coup on 28 February 1997. At the National Security Council meeting that day, one of the ultimatums issued to the government was on clothing—specifically the headscarf. Directly after this time, wearing a headscarf at schools and universities was strictly prohibited. On 31 March 1997, the government issued a general code on the use of the headscarf in every city. Starting from June, students with headscarves, even those with only a week to graduation, were not allowed to take their exams, particularly the university entrance exam, and were dismissed from classes. By November 26, even the students of theology faculties were not able to go attend wearing a headscarf. On September 10, the Ministry of National Education prohibited gender-segregated schools. On 10 December 1999, university protests against the February 28 coup d'état were forbidden.[30] All these regulations were implemented quickly.

The first ban began with a circular published by Istanbul University. The circular, which was issued by the president of the university, was not based on any legal grounds; however, it later became a de facto rule.[31] During this time, universities were encouraged by Kemalist bureaucrats to prohibit students with headscarves from entering universities, to request photographs without a headscarf for college enrolments, and to ban students with headscarves from attending graduation ceremonies through the circulars that they published.[32] The headscarf ban continued with numerous developments: Students with headscarves weren't allowed to take university entrance exams; veiled experts and scholars weren't allowed to make speeches in conferences; legal dealings or court proceedings did not go ahead when participants wore headscarves in their identity card photographs; and students with headscarves were not awarded prizes in graduation or award ceremonies, were not allowed to attend school trips, and were not able to benefit from school-based health services.[33]

Furthermore, female students, who were depicted by Kemalists as deceived and misled, were forced to remove their headscarves with psychological pressure. Rooms known as "persuasion rooms" (ikna odaları) were established in universities by Kemalist academics to pressure students already studying or newly enrolled immediately after February 28 coup to remove their headscarves. These rooms caused great indignation in the public. Gülşen Demirkol Özer interviewed thirty female students who had experienced the persuasion rooms, and found that students were told they would be accepted to schools, receive a student ID, and be allowed to graduate if and only they removed their headscarf.[34]

During this period, many students removed their headscarves[35] and the ones refusing to take off their headscarves abandoned their education. For instance, JDP MP Fatma Benli was a student at the time and refused to take off her headscarf. Although she completed her MA, she was not permitted to attend her thesis defence meeting due to her headscarf. She said that she deeply felt humiliated during this period.[36] Thus, while some refuse to take off their headscarf at all costs, some others wore wigs in the rooms that were set up at the outer door of campuses, where the police were waiting to enter their universities. Usually veiled students, who might wear a short black toupee and a long skirt or long trench coat on school campus no matter what the season is, struggled to complete their education under other students' occasionally curious, sometimes condemning, and typically pitying glances.[37] These kinds of corporal and psychological punishments against veiled girls who rejected becoming "good daughters"[38] of the Kemalist state were very common during this time. Turkey's first headscarf-wearing MP, Merve Kavakcı, classified these girls as black Turks.[39] Using the frame of "public gaze" as "a constitutive element of the public sphere", Çınar discussed whether the public sphere should be a place of freedom or oppression.[40] It is clear that this "public gaze" made the public sphere a space in which veiled women were oppressed.[41] During the same period of time, the prohibition of veiled students from entering university buildings initiated a debate about the status of the headscarf in public spaces. Public discussions were conducted regarding whether veiled women should be allowed to enter courts,[42] restaurants, hospitals, and even grocery stores in government institutions.[43]

One of the areas in which the ban was felt most significantly was in politics. Women who wore a headscarf and voluntarily worked in political parties—even for the Welfare Party—were unable to reach the higher positions of minister, deputy, mayor, and so forth, until 1999. The first attempt to do so occurred with Merve Kavakcı, who was elected a deputy of the FP, one of the parties under the NOM tradition that was established after the closure of the RP. Her election entitled her to enter parliament. However, the investiture, held on 2 May 1999, was highly controversial. In this ceremony, the then-Prime Minister, Bülent Ecevit, blamed Merve

Kavakcı of "revolting the state"[44] and effectively obstructed her instatement in the Grand National Assembly—the parliament. Merve Kavakcı was evicted to cheers from deputies in the DSP—a party with the same ideogical background as the RPP with even more modetate secular policy approach. Ecevit's statement of "Please bring this woman into line"[45] has become a notorious moment in political memory. According to Shively, the Kemalist against her was so harsh because: "Kavakcı embodied the secularists' greatest fears: her body carried what was for many a sign of the type of militant Islam that seeks political power and dominance."[46]

Due to the character assassination that Kavakcı faced during this time, her circumstances became a publicly witnessed political battle between Kemalists and *periphery*. It was not "a sacred battle" from the NOM side as claimed by Shievely[47]: because, Kavakcı later expressed in a newspaper interview that while even the deputies in her own party neglected her, Erdoğan—who was in jail at the time—called her to express his support. Kavakcı was obliged to go into exile following a cabinet decision immediately after this incident, and she later moved to the US. As discussed later in this book, she returned to Turkey long after the JDP came to power and was appointed Turkey's Ambassador to Malaysia in 2017.

The headscarf ban was not limited with universities and politics. In fact, judges and soldiers whose wives wore headscarves were also investigated. Most of these investigations resulted in dismissal from professions and the deprivation of rights. From 1990 to 2011, 1635 staffers of the Turkish Army were dismissed from their jobs after being accused of involvement in Islamic reactionary activities. The number of veiled teachers fired between 1997 and 2001 was 3527. Due to the pressure, in total, 11,000 teachers resigned from their jobs. Seventy-one district governors were also laid off in this period. Thousands of people were blacklisted by the state and given disciplinary penalties due to their clothes and conservative behaviours such as practising the five daily prayers.[48]

According to Supreme Military Council decisions, it was forbidden to enter military hospitals, army houses, army canteens and restaurants, and hospital service vehicles with a headscarf. Inspections were carried out in soldiers' houses to determine whether their wives wore headscarves. Additionally, photographs of their wives were requested under the pretext of administrative procedures. Some soldiers also received signed written orders with the obligation to wear modern outfits.[49] According to witness statements, soldiers were ordered to ask their wives to remove their headscarves, and if their wife refused, they were ordered to seek a divorce;

some soldiers did file for divorce in response.[50] In addition, when families wanted to attend the oath ceremony of soldiers doing compulsory military service, the Turkish army did not allow the veiled mothers, wives, or relatives of these soldiers to enter the military buildings to watch. It is important to highlight here that Turkish army is compulsory for all male citizens.

All of this caused significant trauma for women with headscarves and their families. According to the findings of a study conducted in 2007, 70.8% of the respondents who removed their headscarves due to state pressure in this era felt that their identity was disordered, and 63.2% felt humiliated. 46.9% of the respondents stated that they were embarrassed whenever they removed their headscarf and 46.5% said they felt sinful.[51] Only 3.8% of the respondents said that they did not feel any psychological distress. It is important to note that the same research also indicated that 63.9% of the respondents felt degraded by the attitude of the media, and 54.1% said that they were treated like criminals.[52]

These debates in Turkey entered the agenda of the international courts through applications to the European Court of Human Rights (ECHR) In 2002, Leyla Şahin (who was not allowed to enter her school due to her headscarf but later studied medicine in Vienna and became a JDP MP in 2015), and Tekin (who received disciplinary punishment for wearing a headscarf) applied to the ECHR. Although admissibility concerns were considered regarding the court's intervention, the ECHR decided in 2004 that the intervention was "acceptable in a democratic society", referring to the decision of the Constitutional Court.[53] While this decision discouraged veiled girls, it also destroyed their trust in the law. Yet, it is notable that a study found that 76.2% of female students did not try any legal solutions, 62.8% of which stated that this was because they did not trust the judiciary.[54] Thus, the 28 February coup "directly resulted [in the] pacification of women" and "profoundly [affected] women's roles and mobility in Turkish society"[55] for a long period of time. Faced with a binary choice to either leave their careers and education or remove their headscarf, women suffered considerable trauma during this period. The women who received scholarships from NGOs and went to study in Europe were more fortunate; they graduated and duly came back to Turkey to wait the lifting of the headscarf ban to enter employment.[56] President Erdoğan's two daughters were among this group of women— which also included the family members of JDP politicians—who went abroad to study freely with their headscarf.

CONTINUATION OF THE BAN UNDER THE JDP'S GOVERNANCE (2002–2010)

Although the JDP's approach to the headscarf freedom was always the same, its methodological strategy the solution changed over time.[57] JDP politicians were aware that hasty and imprecise attempts to remove the headscarf ban could lead to the closure of the party or a military intervention, as had happened before several times. Due to this concern, they waited for the formation of a suitable political climate[58] and social consensus.

However, this also means that the JDP's election victory in 2002 did not practically change anything regarding the restrictions and ban on the headscarf despite the fact that Erdogan constantly gave hope to those asking for reforms and recommended patience,[59] However, during the transition period from ban to freedom, the JDP initiate to create a different political and social atmosphere. First, the JDP proposed the headscarf issue as a human rights problem that even seculars should talk about carefully and could not harshly resist from being politically correct, and secondly by diminishing Kemalist hegemony within the state, the JDP made them to not block attempted resolutions.

Since its foundation, in contrast to NOM's religious rhetoric on the headscarf, Erdoğan gave statements framing this ban within a human rights context. While doing this, Erdoğan and his party also criticised the Kemalist establishment for not opening the doors for dialogue or negotiations. Erdoğan's policy to raise the issue as a problem in most of his speeches in Turkey and abroad was disruptive for Kemalists. His strategy of highlighting the issue in these visits abroad suggests that Erdoğan expected support from the European countries. However, a significant number of Erdoğan's statements on the headscarf were later used as evidence in a closure case file to prove the anti-secularism stance of the JDP. On the other hand, Kemalists wanted Erdoğan to remain silent and postpone the demands of JDP voters for the sake of not raising tensions in the country. This approach was demonstrated in an interview with Erdoğan held by Ertuğrul Özkök, then editor-in-chief of *Hürriyet* newspaper and a journalist famous for his Kemalist stand, who asked: "Wouldn't you still postpone these subjects of tension?" Erdoğan—who was already frustrating Kemalists at the time—responded: "Look, we have been in power for three years. We have stated that we want to solve such problems with consensus. But nobody helped us. On the contrary, they did exactly the opposite. They tried to hit us on these issues."[60]

Although Erdoğan and JDP politicians referred to future plans to remove the headscarf ban with social consensus and not generate tensions, the harassment of women who wore headscarves became more public each day during the transition period. This proved that although the JDP was leading the goverment, it still had not seised power. At this stage, President Ahmet Necdet Sezer was the main obstacle for the JDP. As the President, Sezer (2000–2007) not only held the power to veto laws, he was also one of the main signs that Kemalists are keeping the ideological hegemony over the state. This was giving him an incentive to sacralise secularism. Even the fact that a hard-core Kemalist like Sezer was sitting in the highest office of the state, this created a psychological barrier for the JDP.

Yet, his behaviours encouraged the other Kemalists to otherise the veiled women. He never invited Prime Minister Erdoğan and ministers or deputies from the JDP with their wives to the official events so as to prevent the headscarf from entering state buildings.[61] He also made the radical decision to not invite the first lady of Afghanistan to the presidential office during the Afghan President's visit in 2006.[62] By doing so, he implemented a kind of de facto rule, as there was no legal arrangement preventing veiled woman from entering the state building. During this period, discrimination did not stay confined to ignoring and pacifying the veiled wives of JDP politicians who were consistently humiliated by the Kemalist-owned media.[63] Sezer's radical and aggressive attitude towards Muslims, particularly veiled women, had instigated a trend. It is very crucial to remember that the first time President Gül's wife, Hayrunnisa Gül, attended a state ceremony was in 2010, eight years later then the JDP was elected.[64] Until this point, the de facto norm set by the former President Sezer had been maintained.

Other discriminatory incidents continued to occur in the JDP period, with veiled patients being rejected for treatment at hospitals, TV guests not shown on-screen unless they removed their headscarf, and professors who were removed from their posts because they entered the university with their veiled mother in the car.[65] One of those was the Tevhide Kutuk case in 2007. Tevhide, who came first in a competition in Adana, was expelled from the stage where she was receiving her award because of her headscarf. She was later called by then-Prime Minister Erdoğan and consoled and promised on the phone, "These injustices will end."[66]

During these years, in a country where discrimination against women was frequently observed, veiled women faced additional pressures and exclusion in everyday life. They experienced discrimination in various places ranging from markets and hospitals to restaurants and courtrooms. Even the streets, public transport, shops, libraries, and holiday resorts[67] were dangerous areas for veiled women where they were made to feel uncomfortable and where they were harassed and insulted by Kemalists strangers.[68] Furthermore, it was not only the Kemalist state that oppressed veiled women, Kemalists civilians also carried out similar harassment and discrimination in both the public space and private companies.[69]

The reaction of veiled women against this alienation was to create their own *ghettos*. As a result, they refrained from going to these shared spaces and found their own environments where they felt safe. For this reason, women with headscarves classified the areas that they visited as "safe" or "unsafe," even during the rule of the JDP. They found cafes and restaurants with similar or tolerant clientele, instead of places where they were maltreated.[70]

During this period, some significant changes occurred in regards to mobilising Kemalists' reactions. One of these was the Republican Rallies. The headscarf played a significant role as a formulated horror object to mobilise people who joined these demonstrations. Although the Kemalists claimed that "people participated in those protests to express their concern about secular lifestyle and the republican regime," [71] they were also displaying their support for the headscarf ban and the restrictions on any kind of religious expression in public life. A good example of this phenomenon is the *Cumhuriyet* commercials published on TV, radios, the internet, billboards, and in newspapers during this time, which sought to alert people to act to protect secularism and played a notable role in spreading fear. The commercials directly targeted Islam and highlighted the supposed risk of the destruction of secular life by asking "Are you aware of the danger?" and mentioning the election date alongside the supposed danger of regressing 100 years and losing all the progress made by the Kemalist Republic. In one commercial, Arabic letter appeared to refer to Atatürk's language reform, with the primary question ("Are you aware of the danger?") asked at the end to meant to the threat posed by the JDP government towards secularism. A different commercial featured a woman wearing a black burqa and a male voiceover saying: "Of course I decide what I want to do." This referred to the idea that it was not women's choice to wear a veil, but rather men were making the decision on their behalf. Then the same question and the same slogans were repeated: "Are you aware of the danger? Look over your republic."[72]

Discussions, which peaked to its top during the 2008 Presidential elections, continued after the JDP's candidate Gül replaced the Kemalist president Sezer. This change was shocking in Kemalist circles because the new President's wife—Hayrunnisa Gül—wore a headscarf, which marked a first in Turkish Republican history. When one remembers the discussions during this time, it might be easier to understand that the headscarf played a major role in the resistance of the Kemalist establishment to Gül's candidateship to the Presidency. Nevertheless, the Prime Minister Erdoğan's wife—Emine Erdoğan—had already given hope to veiled women in Turkey regarding the future, and the representation of the headscarf at the highest level, with the first lady, represented another step towards the removal of the ban.

In the same year, another crucial development happened when the president of the Council for Higher Education (YÖK), Erdoğan Teziç, who was very well-known for his support of the headscarf ban in universities, completed his term. YÖK was the overarching institution of academies, universities, educational institutions[73] in Turkey, and the headscarf ban was mostly organised with its authority. With this change, Kemalists lost another important figurehead. As was expected, following the change in the chairmanship of the Higher Education Council (YÖK) in 2007, the students with headscarves were allowed to enter universities. The ban was lifted with an order that was sent to university presidents by the chairman of the YÖK without taking any legal steps. Since it was not a legal ban based on any legal document or legislation, its lifting did not need to be legally facilitated.

After loosening the restrictions in practical ways, the JDP wanted to guarantee the freedom with legal changes in 2008, so they brought the issue to the Turkish Parliament and obtained the support of the MHP—then the second biggest opposition party. The first legal step towards lifting the ban was taken as soon as the support of the majority (80% of the assembly) was gained. With the announcement of the MHP's support, the JDP initiated a process to change two articles of the Constitution with an amendment. Article 10, which referred to the principle of equality, was revised by adding the definition "benefiting from all kinds of public service," and hence the state's responsibility to provide public services fairly was now guaranteed by the Constitution. Meanwhile, Article 42

124 P. KANDEMIR

received the addition: "No one can be deprived of the right to get a higher education by a reason that is not stated in the law. The boundaries to use this right are determined by the law."[74] During the voting in the parliament, 411 out of 518 deputies supported these amendments. It is useful to note that the JDP had 340 seats in parliament at the time, and 338 of their deputies participated in the session that day. Thus, the JDP and the MHP fully supported the amendment, and some of the deputies of the Kurdish nationalist DTP (HDP today)[75] and some independent deputies also voted in favour.

However, the RPP, along with the other Kemalist party, the DSP, took this reform to the Constitutional Court to appeal for its cancellation and the amendment was cancelled in June 2008. The first sentence of the published reason summarises the stance taken by the Constitutional Court regarding this issue: "Secularism is the most important [of] Atatürk principles."[76] The text also claimed that if the headscarf were allowed at schools, it would "lead to differences and conflicts due to religious beliefs and opinions."[77] Furthermore, it stated "an arrangement that allows for covering for religious purposes leads to an exposition of religion by the use of clothes as symbols."[78]

Several critics contested the legal grounds of this document; in fact, the Constitutional Court contradicted itself by cancelling the amendment. According to Article 48 of the Constitution, the Constitutional Court only has the right to procedural audit. Thus, although it only has the right to supervise the format of a motion, in this case it intervened in the content of a law prepared by the parliament. This prompted the claim that the court's practice was unauthorised.[79] This and many other instances in this era were regarded as judicial interventions. Rather than instigating a direct coup, the Kemalist establishment used another bastion of Kemalism—the judiciary.

As with other Kemalist efforts, the Constitutional Court's decision was backed by the Kemalist media with headlines. "411 hands (raised) for the chaos"[80] is one of the examples to explain how the Kemalist media has seen this reform and tried to manipulate the public against it. Simultaneously, many of Erdoğan's previous statements on the headscarf were linked to anti-secularism and used as headlines to agitate the public, leading to a large public debate on the topic. It is important to note that on contrary, a considerable majority of the Turkish public was always against the ban.[81] However, as mentioned before "since the Kemalism is an elitist and Jacobin ideology applies arbitrary changes with their own reason rather than approving and appreciating democratic processes, this was not a surprising move for the JDP."[82]

As a follow up to the Constitutional Court's cancellation of the headscarf regulation,[83] a closure case was opened against the JDP. Regarding the headscarf issue, the case indictment stated,

The *türban* is a religious and political symbol that the defendant party uses as a libertarian discourse in the course of the counter-revolution to transform society in the fields of education, culture, economics and social life at its decisive struggle against the Republican reforms and especially the principle of secularism.[84]

It also blamed the JDP for perceiving the issue as "a compulsory part of the freedom of belief," which was against the Kemalist secularism understanding they maintained.[85] In the defence file, the JDP responded to the claims with the following words:

The State has to respect individuals' personal preferences as long as it does not harm others. When a mature student, who is old enough to study at university, wants to cover her hair because of her individual preferences, preventing it will mean interference in her freedom and autonomy. The secular state must see adult people as autonomous individuals who can decide what is right or wrong for them and thus express their preferences.[86]

When the JDP was not closed at the end of this case, the party started to take concrete steps towards a solution, although tensions in politics and among the public remained at the highest level.

HEADSCARF FREEDOM AS A SIGN OF POST-KEMALIST SECULARISM

Although it is a remarkable development that the ban on headscarf has been lifted in universities, professions such as lawyers, police officers, judges, military service, teachers, and parliamentarians were prohibited for those with headcarves in 2013. As an important step, in the June 12th elections, the JDP nominated a politician with a headscarf for the first time to be included in Antalya's list of deputies.[87] She was put in a position from which it was impossible to be chosen, but it was nevertheless a trial for the JDP to gauge the reactions. It was also a message from the

JDP to Kemalists to prepare them for subsequent steps. Following this, in October 2013, four MPs from the JDP announced that they would not remove their headscarf after returning from the Hajj Pilgrimage. Two days before their entrance to parliament, the RPP announced that they would not remain silent regarding this action since they thought the MPs' decision was against official procedure.[88] However, this announcement did not change the behaviour of the four MPs, and they entered the parliament wearing headscarves on 31 October. Although the RPP did not react in the way they had threatened to two days before, Dilek Akagün Yılmaz (an RPP MP) protested against the headscarf by wearing a t-shirt featuring a portrait of Atatürk.[89] On the other hand, another RPP MP, Sezgin Tanrıkulu, stated just after this occasion that they had no problem with the "türban and faith."[90] JDP's four deputies' civil disobedience was a breaking point in Turkish politics due to its symbolic meaning.

Just these days, the JDP was taking a legal step to abolish the ban on headscarves altogether. In 2013, the JDP made a final move to solve the headscarf issue in Turkey with one more reform proposal included in the Democratisation Package. Rather than solely focusing on the headscarf ban, the package proposed solutions to various chronic problems in Turkey. Thus, with the constitutional changes in 2013, the ban on the headscarf for public sector employees was also removed. As a follow up, an additional regulation was implemented three years later for occupations requiring official uniforms (soldiers, police officers, judges and prosecutors), which were not liberated by the Democratisation Package and did not yet allow the headscarf. After this date, officers received the right to practise while wearing a headscarf.[91]

This triggered a change towards the headscarf in political area as well as the social one. The total number of deputies wearing a headscarf in parliament in 2013 was four, which raised to twenty-one in the elections held on 7 June 2015, and twenty in the elections held on 1 November 2015. In 2015 election, Ravza Kavakcı was chosen as a JDP MP. As aforementioned, Kavakcı surname has a symbolic meaning in the journey of the headscarf controversy in Turkey. Ravza's older sister, Merve Kavakcı, was a former deputy who had been removed from parliament with insults due to her headscarf and later disenfranchised and expatriated in 1997. When Ravza Kavakcı was elected as an MP, she wore the same headscarf as her sister to make her parliamentary oath. In my interview with her, she explained how her family had suffered from the headscarf ban. Both her sister and her mother—who studied at Saint George's High

School, a Christian school in İstanbul and worked as a teacher of German Language and Literature at the University of Atatürk in Erzurum—had been dismissed from their positions in the past due to their headscarves.[92]

As made clear by the discussions, which happened within different political parties and the speeches of politicians, made while these radical changes were occurring, the RPP remained relatively passive compared with the previous periods. The JDP deputy Özlem Zengin stated that a woman deputy of the RPP and another deputy from the MHP congratulated her after she had taken her parliamentary oath. According to her, the Kemalists had seen that the uplifting of the ban had no negative influence on their own lives, so their fears had diminished, and they had become neutral on this issue. This shows that the RPP deputies had also diversified in their strict stand against the headscarf.[93]

Thus, under these new conditions, the RPP stopped raising the topic, as did the Kemalist media. On contrary, they initiated in senior level to prove that they are not against the headscarf. For instance, the RPP 2018 presidential candidate Muharrem İnce even stated that his sister had been wearing the headscarf for forty years, and promised in his rallies that the problem was solved and the file closed.[94] Similarly, the chairman of the RPP, Kemal Kılıçdaroğlu, announced several times after this period "the headscarf ban was removed with his very own support."[95] In the 2019 local elections, the RPP İstanbul and Ankara Mayoral candidates, İmamoğlu and Yavaş, also adopted a welcoming approach towards the headscarf.

I believe there were three reasons behind this change. Firstly, supporting the headscarf ban was marginalised under the JDP's rule. Since its inception, the JDP had emphasised the fact that the headscarf ban was against human rights and was not compatible with universal values such as democracy. As a part of this discourse, the JDP claimed that they were working on making Turkey a member of the European Union, and the accepting freedom of the headscarf was a necessary step of this modernist understanding. EU's officials' support at least in regards to narrative had been effective during the process.[96] Thus, the JDP politicians found a constructive strategy to expose the RPP and the Kemalists as against basic human rights and the EU standarts that the Kemalists have always admired to. Finally, the RPP realised that they were losing their rapport with the majority of society due to their anti-religious narrative.[97] To gain credibility in periphery, the RPP began to revise and modernise its rhetoric regarding the headscarf. Indeed, in my interview with RPP

MP Özkan stated that he no longer has a problem with the headscarf and his position has changed, like that of his party.[98] Although it is notable that most JDP politicians believe, such statements made by RPP politicians regarding the headscarf are not sincere but are merely an effort to be pragmatic and politically correct,[99] Özkan's statement is nevertheless extremely significant.[100] It is especially remarkable when one considers that in research conducted in 2012, politicians that represented Kemalism in Turkey stated that it was not possible to lift the headscarf ban.[101] And lastly, the JDP had successfully managed to subdue the Kemalist establishment-the biggest threat to the civilian politics, after eighteen years in governance.

Nevertheless, it is still hard to claim that there had been an ablolute change within the Kemalist circle. A survey conducted in 2017 revealed that among RPP voters, 43.9% supported an abolition of the ban whereas 56.1% wanted the ban to continue.[102] Also, another survey conducted by Genar indicates that the rate of survey participants who claimed a woman with a headscarf could be humiliated was 9.7%, and the rate of those who claimed that they should be considered second-class citizens was 14.9%.[103] Additionally, as the level of education rose, the support for freedom to wear a headscarf, even in daily life, decreased.[104] This indicates that since Kemalists resistence to the headscarf did and might never fully fade away. While fundamental anti-headscarf Kemalists still keep their position as it is, half of RPP votes are more moderate than ever. It is necessary to note at this moment that this moderate view does not mean approval of headscarf by some Kemalists though. In fact, there are those within the JDP circle who see this approach as a superior arrogance of Kemalists who constantly highlighting that they are showing tolerance to the disadvantaged veiled women.[105]

This attributed picture shows itself in the public sphere in citizen-to-citizen relations. Although Tuncay Özkan claims that "we are now in a very different place in the attitude of the individual towards the state and the individual towards the individual,"[106] several incidents still occur, especially in terms of the Kemalists' reactions to veiled women. For example, after the RPP's victory in local elections in İstanbul and Ankara in 2019, the discussion regarding harassment against veiled women and humiliation over the headscarf was raised again. While the RPP's İstanbul candidate's wife (Dilek İmamoğlu) was framed as a modern, Republican, real Turkish woman, the JDP candidate Binali Yildirim's wife (Semiha Yıldırım) was attacked on social media and humiliated by Kemalists for representing backwardness due to her headscarf, despite the fact that she was a retired respected teacher.[107] Additionally, pious Muslims from high income groups, in several cases veiled women, are often accused of being pro-government, gaining unfair profits, solecism and being dishonest in character assassination campaigns, apparent in pro-RPP and Kemalist media.[108] The derogatory phrases used in such cases show that the issue is not just about secularism. As discussed in other chapters, there is an implicit, hidden anger against the people perceived to have shared the privileges of the Kemalist elites.[109]

At this stage, it is important to remember that the rising middle class exemplified a fear of Kemalist elites, with the headscarf acting as one of the visible signs of this rise. It is a well-known fact that the headscarf is not compatible with Kemalist notions of the idealised "modern woman;" it is only tolerable for Kemalists when women in rural areas or housemaids wore it. Evidently, it only became a negative symbol when worn by educated, wealthy women in fashionable and expensive clothes. This highlights the ongoing class struggle in Turkey, and how the headscarf dispute was a manifestation of the politics and power in the country.[110]

As Armenian-Turkish intellectual Mahçupyan stated, when "the Islamic segment started to enter high income groups, to receive better education, to learn a foreign language and to make the biggest investment for its children," a new bourgeoisie and middle class emerged with direct contact with the global world.[111] Today, although the percentage of veiled women is not rising significantly in Turkey, they have become more visible in social life due to the economic transformation.[112] As expected, the issue of self-confidence has also played a critical role, since the wife and daughters of the leader of the country wear headscarves. In the last instance, if today the headscarf is more publicly visible in Turkey, that is not because of the Islamisation of Turkish society—it is, in fact, a sign of the liberalisation that has enabled veiled women to enter the public sphere, workforce, civil society, academia, media, and politics.

Therefore, the changing forms of piety, and the consequent liberalisation[113] might be considered outcomes of the shifting political balance in Turkey, and should not be ignored.[114] According to Zengin, many people have underestimated the transformation in the lives of veiled women, and the transformation did not actually begin with the resolution of the headscarf issue. Indeed, she claimed that the real transformation occurred during the process towards the solution, when the conservatives integrated liberalism into their political strategies.[115] That is, women who

130   P. KANDEMIR

wore headscarves were politicised during this process in both positive and negative interactions with other groups, including liberals, leftists, and non-Muslim minorities who supported the removal of the headscarf ban. In my interview with Fatma Benli, she highlighted the anonymous resistance by the professors who organised courses outside of university buildings to encourage veiled students to attend; or non-Muslim minorities translated documents by the girls into English voluntarily to then apply for the European Court of Human Rights. For her, this was the first rapprochement between veiled women and other groups; and it affected the perspectives of both parties.[116]

Back to the discussion, although some analysts have argued that this is a temporary change, some have claimed that this is the beginning of the "secularisation" of Turkey's devout Muslims.[117] Inspired by Eisenstadt's multiple modernities, Kaya refers this issue in his work, "The analysis of Islamist women has shown that they do not purely turn towards traditional Islam as a source of identity; rather, they have developed a new identity under conditions of modernity."[118] From the prism of multiple secularism paradigm, this change does not constitute a sign of secularisation in Turkey: but it is a tangible proof that there are multiple modernities simultaneously happening in the face of different segments of the society.

As I mentioned several times in this book, multiple modernities not only showcases that there are different modernities, but it also reveals that there are many paths to modernity to follow and diversify, and that there will be disparate results where it has been reached. Hence, in the light of the work of Eisenstadt on the multiple modernity paradigm one can go a step further and say that the diversification of modernisation paths within Turkey during the JDP era created a new situation, and it did not result in homogenisation either. Rather, it resulted in the emergence of different modernisation experiences even for people who belong to the same community; veiled women can be counted as a salient example of this. Yet, the modernism understanding of a veiled woman who experienced the headscarf ban and a veiled woman who was born in 2002 after the JDP came to power are not the same. Therefore, because their historical experiences are different from each other, their relationship with modernism and secularism is different. As noted by Kaya, "there have been multiple ways to modernity and that those multiple ways have given rise to multiple consequences."[119]

A diversification within the sociological orientations of Turkey's conservatives emerged during this period and headscarf freedom was on of the dimensions triggered this change. This concluded with the breaking of the ideological ghettos and hybridisation of the different social segments that seemed the same before, in an ideological sense. Not only veiled women, but also Muslims of Turkey in general are the best example of this. This also brings us to another outcome: The changing understanding of modernity in Turkey. Yet, as Nabi Avci said.

> The relationship that Muslims established with modernity differed during the JDP period. First of all, conservatives entered many areas where they had been hitherto neglected. With the economic development of the country, Muslims, like everyone else, adapted to the system. They have become able to meet their everyday demands from halal food to halal tourism within a system defined as modern.[120]

For him—as for many others, "Even re-discussing what modernity is - enabling that discussion - and listening to those who want to say something other than the imposed definition of modernity is an important change in itself."[121]

Thus while all these were happening, the tension between secularism term and veil has also came to an end. For me, it is the breaking point when the veiled women have seen another interpretation of secularism rather than the Kemalist one. Yet, they were oppressed under the name of secularism, treated differently not only by state institutions but also by the Kemalist RPP and Kemalist individuals. However, the JDP proposed a new approach under the same term with a different understanding, which is not against the freedom of wearing headscarf. This obviously brought about a new interpretation of secularism among devout Muslims, and generated newfound harmony between this concept and Muslims in Turkey.[122] At this point, we should remember Erdoğan's frequent use of the notion of secularism in a positive sense has had a great positive repercussion on women with headscarf, which is as if they re-established and reconciled with the concept in this period. Even in its closure case defence, the JDP conceptualised this as the "socialisation of secularism"[123] (*laikliği toplumsallaştırmak* in Turkish). As a result, conservatives who once thought the headscarf and secularism could not exist together began to believe that they could, especially after the reforms exhibited that a new formulation of secularism was possible.[124] In a nutshell, rapprochement between veiled women and secularism was concluded with a crucial outcome, diversification and hybridisation of veiled women in regards to their socio-political arrangments. JDP's Deputy Chairperson and Konya MP Leyla Şahin Usta said in my interview with her that "Conservatives' preferences have become heterogeneous; yet, obstacles have been removed and opportunities have been equalized."[125]

In this regard, wearing a headscarf previously indicated automatic support for the JDP or the Islamist Saadet.[126] Nowadays, although public surveys have indicated that the majority of veiled women still vote for the JDP, the perspective of the garment as inherently anti-secular has changed to some extent. In contemporary Turkey, there are deputies who wear a headscarf in parliament from three of the four political parties: the JDP, the MHP, and the HDP. Universities, military buildings, and presidential compounds are no longer forbidden spaces for veiled women, nor are neighbourhoods like Cihangir, Cadde Bostan, or Nisantasi where only Kemalists used to shop, relax, and spend time in İstanbul. It is also possible to see veiled women in every sector in contemporary Turkey. This has brought about a decline of the alienation of the headscarf in society, thereby pushing the argument of the headscarf as anti-secularist almost out of circulation. A perspective most notable illustrated by the diversification of veiled women. These changes prove that post-Kemalist secularism has been successful in setting a new narrative regarding the headscarf controversy in Turkey. It also indicates that as a result of diversification in the political attitude of veiled women, it is no more a symbol of anti-secularism or a distinct political-ideological stand. While multiple secularism(s) have a variety of approach(es) towards veiled women, veiled women have also changed their stances towards secularism. They also do not consider it as anti-religionism anymore.

Conclusion

Considering the symbolic meaning that the headscarf held in Turkey's secularist history, the removal of the ban demonstrated the emergence of Post-Kemalist secularism. As a result of the JDP's Post-Kemalist approach, three major developments arose from the headscarf controversy. First, the headscarf was neutralised in the eyes of the state and the citizens; its political power was removed, and it became a religious symbol rather than a political tool. Secondly, a rapprochement started between the state and veiled women for the first time in Turkish history; thus, the wall between the state, which previously coded veiled women as their enemies, and veiled women who saw the state as a mechanism that was oppressive and hindering their freedom, was lifted. Thirdly, not only life style but also the ideological stand of veiled women diversified as a result of the political normalisation of the garment and changing economic conditions. Let me clarify these points one by one.

Today in contemporary Turkey, the headscarf is regarded as a human rights issue and as an element of the freedom of religious expression, in contrast to the initial Kemalist view which was assuming that banning it was about freeing women from tradition and religion. Once the main political battlefield for Kemalists and non-Kemalists, today the headscarf is no longer a source of tension.[127] This does not mean that it has been wholly accepted by Kemalists; it is still an issue for some, and there is a "marginal minority of society" which does not accept a veiled woman as equal and "maintains a strict attitude towards headscarves."[128] Whereas the state was the biggest mechanism for the oppression of veiled women before, today it is the entity that keeps their freedom guaranteed. In the final instance, veiled women are considered equal in the legal system. Until the 2010s, all the legal or illegal implementations to regulate women who wore a headscarf were made via the authority of the state; today, it is the state that provides equal opportunities for them; the outcome of this shift in the perspective of veiled women towards the state and vice versa.

However, it should be highlighted that today's current situation results from a long historical process; it did not reach this state in one day. If Eisenstadt's multiple modernities paradigm holds that "all modernization should be seen in the light of its historical context,[129] then the current approaches of both the JDP and Kemalists towards headscarf freedom should be evaluated without neglecting the historical background that I discussed in the first part of this chapter.

After its various struggles, the JDP sees this normalisation in modernism and secularism understanding as a victory, while Kemalists are now on the path of acceptance. Thus, rather than taking this as a shift in secularism, this change towards headscarf freedom can be considered as a self-correction[130] of the modernism in Turkey. What that means is, as put by Eisenstadt, modernism is a dynamic process, and "as Nilufer Gole observed, one of the most important characteristics of modernity is simply its potential capacity for continual self-correction."[131] While headscarf

134   P. KANDEMIR

was previously considered to be challenging modernity in the eyes of state elites, Kemalist politicians and civilians, and even to an extent the Turkish upper-class including intellectuals, today it is not. They are self-correcting themselves in terms of their modernity understanding. This is not only because there has been a shift from periphery to the centre, but simultaneously because the mentality of a majority of Turkish society including moderate Kemalists is changing. This can only be taken as the outcome of the emergence of multiple modernities in Turkey. The groups that belong to different modernity understandings are inevitably learning from each other in post-secular Turkey, and respecting one's beliefs, including vis-à-vis the headscarf, is an example of this. As saliently contextualised by Habermas, this situation can be only defined as a complementary learning process.[132]

NOTES

1. According to a 2017 survey, 73% of Turkish women veils motivated by their religious beliefs while 13.7% veil for tradition. "Gündelik yaşamda din, laiklik ve türban araştırması." [Survey on religion, secularism and headscarf in daily life] *Konda Araştırma ve Danışmanlık*, September 9, 2007, p. 23.
2. Sandikci, Özlem and Ger, Guliz. "Veiling in Style: How Does a Stigmatized Practice Become Fashionable?" *Journal of Consumer Research* 37.1 (2010): 15–36, p. 18.
3. Göle, *The Forbidden Modern*.
4. Arik, Hulya. "Speaking of Women? Exploring Violence against Women through Political Discourses: A Case Study of Headscarf Debates in Turkey." *e-cadernos ces* 16 (2012): 10–31. June 1, 2012, Accessed on January 13, 2020. http://eces.revues.org/1009.
5. While only half of the Alevis support freedom of covering, 60% of the Kemalists support headscarf freedom. See: "Anayasaya Dair Tanım ve Beklentiler" [Expectations and Definitions on Constitution]. *Konda Araştırma ve Danışmanlık*, September, 2012.
6. See some works carried the discussion to the human rights context, Kadioglu, Ayse. "Women's Subordination in Turkey: Is Islam Really the Villain?" *Middle East Journal* 48.4 (1994): 645–660, p. 651.; Çınar, Alev, "Bodies, Places and Time: Islamic Visibilities in the Public Sphere and the Contestations of Secular Modernity in Turkey." *PhD thesis*, University of Pennsylvania, 1998.

4 JDP'S SECULARISM AND THE HEADSCARF 135

7. A great extent of veiled women supports JDP. See: Konda, "'Siyasal ve Toplumsal Araştırmalar Dizisi 4. Ara Rapor" [Series on political and social research: 4th Mid-Report] *Konda Barometresi* July 2011.
8. For one of the most compelling work on this discussion see Gole, *The Forbidden Modern*, 173–190.; Çınar, Modernity, Islam and Secularism.
9. Özbudun, Sibel. Kadınlar, *İslam, AKP ve Ötesi*. [Women, Islam, AKP and Beyond] Ankara: Utopya Yayınevi, 2016.
10. Arat, Yesim. "The Project of Modernity and Women in Turkey." In *Rethinking Modernity and National Identity in Turkey*, edited by Sibel Bozdogan and Resat Kasaba, Seattle: University of Washington Press, 1997, p. 101.
11. Kadioglu, "Women's Subordination", 632. Also see Toprak, Zafer. "Halk Fırkası'ndan once Kurulan Parti: Kadinlar Halk Firkasi." [The Party Founded Before the Populist Party: Populist Party of Women]. *Tarih ve Toplum* 9.51 (1988): 30–31.
12. Arat, *Rethinking Islam and Liberal Democracy*, 17.
13. Gole, The Forbidden Modern, 14.
14. For a photograph archive of Atatürk's life see: "Resimlerle Atatürk." [Atatürk by photos]. *Anıtkabir [Atatürk's Mausoleum Official Website]* July 2011. Accessed March 30, 2018. http://www.anitkabir.org/Ata türk/resimlerle-Atatürk.html.
15. Idem.
16. Idem.
17. Kandiyoti, Deniz. "Gendering the Modern: On Missing Dimensions in the Study of Turkish Modernity." In *Rethinking Modernity and National Identity in Turkey*, edited by Sibel Bozdogan and Resat Kasaba. Washington: University of Washington Press, 1997. p 125.
18. Arat, Yesim. *Rethinking Islam and Liberal Democracy*.
19. Kadioglu, "Women's Subordination," 651.
20. For a very deep and historical analysis of Kemalism's approach to woman in nation building process see: Kandiyoti, Deniz. "Identity and İts Discontents: Woman and the Nation." *American Journal of Political Science* 20.3 (1991): 429–443.
21. Kavakci, Merve. "Questioning Turkey's Role Model Status: A Critical Examination of Social and Political Implications of the Headscarf Ban in Turkey." *PhD Thesis*, Howard University, 2007, p. 69.
22. Arik, "Speaking of Women?," 11.
23. Idem.
24. Kavakci, "Questioning Turkey's Role Model Status", 222.
25. "Türban" is a Turkish word used by seculars to define the headscarf. However, it generally means a headscarf worn for political reasons. In Turkey, when conservatives use the term "başörtüsü", secularists use "Türban". In English, it is generally translated as veil and headscarf.

26. "Anayasa Mahkemesi Karar Sayısı: 1989/12." [Constitutional Court Decision No: 1989/12]. *Anayasa* [Constitution], 1989. Accessed April 29, 2018. http://kararlaryeni.anayasa.gov.tr/Karar/Content/152e95a6-8e5c-4e9e-ae1a-197acdaefe66?higllightText=basortu%3Bbaso rtu&excludeGerekce=False&wordsOnly=False.
27. Akyüz, İsmail. "Türkiye'de Uygulanan Din Politikaları İcin Bir Tipoloji Denemesi." [A Typology Essay for Religious Policies Applied in Turkey] *Siyaset, Ekonomi ve Yonetim Araştırmaları Dergisi [Research Journal of Politics, Economics and Management]* 5.1 (2017): 143–164. p. 156.
28. Tok, Gul Ceylan, "The securitization of the headscarf issue in Turkey: "The Good and Bad Daughters.
   of the Republic." *The International Studies Association of Ritsumeikan University: Ritsumeikan Annual Review of International Studies* 8 (2009): 113–137, p. 113.
29. Arat, "Rethinking Islam and Liberal Democracy", 8.
30. "Bir daha asla, 17 yıl sonra 28 şubat", [Never Again, 28 February after 17 years]. *Eğitim Bir Sen*, February 28, 2014, p. 29. Accessed on March 23, 2018. https://www.ebs.org.tr/ebs_files/files/yayinlarimiz/28_subat_rapor_web.pdf.
31. Genç, Özge and İlhan, Ebru. *Başörtüsü Yasağına İlişkin Değerlendirme ve Öneriler. [Evaluations and suggestions in regard to headscarf ban].* İstanbul: Tesev Yayınları, 2012, p. 13.
32. Interview with one of the former rectors at the time, İstanbul, July 20, 2017.
33. Genç and İlhan, *Başörtüsü Yasağına*, 14.
34. Demirkol, Gülşen. *Psikolojik bir işkence metodu olarak İkna Odaları.* [Persuasion Room: A Psychological Torture Method]. İstanbul: Beyan Yayınları, 2005.
35. Interview with Fatma Benli, JDP MP, Ankara, on May 8, 2018.
36. Idem.
37. In addition to the narrated experiences, my observations from the years of my undergraduate education in Marmara University were conveyed.
38. Tok, "the securitization of the headscarf issue in Turkey,".
39. Kavakci Islam, Merve. *Headscarf Politics in Turkey: A Postcolonial Reading.* New York: Palgrave Macmillan, 2010.
40. Çınar, "Bodies, Places and Time," 1998.
41. For several examples that the veiled women faced discrimination and harassment in their daily lives under the dominant image of Atatürk, see Özyürek, *Nostalgia for the Modern*, 99.
42. Tok, "The securitization of the headscarf issue in Turkey," 114.
43. For a detailed report on this see "Türkiye'de Dini Ayrimcilik Raporu" [Report on Religious Discrimination in Turkey] *Mazlumder* (2010). Accessed July 27, 2018. http://İstanbul.mazlumder.org/fotograf/yayinr esimleri/dokuman/Türkiyede_dini_eyrimcilik_raporu.pdf.

4 JDP'S SECULARISM AND THE HEADSCARF 137

44. "Ecevit: Kavakci'nin TBMM'de yeri yok" [Ecevit: Kavakci Has No Place in the parliament] *Hurriyet*, May 8, 1999. Accessed June 23, 2019. https://www.hurriyet.com.tr/gundem/ecevit-kavakcinin-tbm mde-yeri-yok-39078219.
45. Yeni Safak. "Utanc goruntuleri: Bülent Ecevit meclisten Merve Kavakcı'yi boyle kovdu." [Images of shame: This İs How Bülent Ecevit Dismiss from the Parliament] *YouTube*, February 28, 2017. Accessed June 23, 2019. https://www.youtube.com/watch?v=gvT2QMpjQeQ& feature=youtu.be.
46. Shively, Kim. "Religious Bodies and the Secular State: The Merve Kavakci Affair." *Journal of Middle East Women's Studies* 1.3 (2005): 46–72, 61.
47. Idem, 65.
48. Mazlumder, "Türkiye'de Dini Ayrımcılık Raporu.".
49. Idem, 171–172.
50. For the statement from Ali Cosar, who was a soldier in this period, see Mazlumder, "Türkiye'de Dini Ayrımcılık Raporu", 165–166.
51. HAZAR, *Türkiye'nin Örtülü Gerçeği*, 33.
52. Idem.
53. "Information Note on the Court's case-law 80- Leyla Şahin v. Turkey [GC] - 44,774/98." *European Court of Human Rights* (2005) Accessed February 4, 2019. https://hudoc.echr.coe.int/app/conversion/pdf/?lib rary=ECHR&id=002-3628&filename=002-3628.pdf&TID=thkbhnilzk.
54. HAZAR, *Türkiye'nin Ortulu Gercegi*, 27–30.
55. Shively, "Religious Bodies and the Secular State," 48.
56. Interview with Mustafa Şen, Ankara, on August 24, 2015.
57. For a very detailed chronology of the headscarf ban and its removal, see Benli, Fatma. "1964–2011 Türkiye ve Dunyada Başörtüsü Yasagı Kronolojisi" [Chronology of Headscarf Ban in Turkey and World: 1964–2011] *Mazlumder* 2011. Accessed July 27, 2018. http://www.mazlumder.org/fotograf/yayinresimleri/dokuman/ Türkiyede-dunyada-basortusu-yasagi-kronolojisi.pdf.
58. Interview with Mahir Ünal, Ankara, on June 4, 2018. and Interview with Bülent Arınç, Ankara, on April 12, 2019.
59. Karaalioğlu, Mustafa. "Başbakan Referanduma gider mi?" [Will the Prime Minister Hold a Referendum?]. *Yenisafak*, June 7, 2005. Accessed June 5, 2018. https://www.yenisafak.com/arsiv/2005/haziran/07/ mkaraalioglu.html.
60. For Ertuğrul Özkök's interview with Erdogan, see: Özkök, Ertuğrul. "Imam Hatiplere arka bahcemiz diyenlerle biz yolumuzu ayirdik." *Hurriyet*.
61. Bila, Fikret. "Resepsiyon sorunu 10 yasına bastı." [Reception Problem Exists for 10 Years] *Milliyet*, October 29, 2012. Accessed on June

138   P. KANDEMIR

29, 2019. http://www.milliyet.com.tr/yazarlar/fikret-bila/resepsiyon-sorunu-10-yasina-basti-1618500.

62. "Sezer'in Sınır Aşan Başörtüsü Yasağı." [Sezer's Borderless Headscarf Ban] *Yeni Safak*, January 7, 2006. Accessed July 4, 2019. https://www.yenisafak.com/gundem/sezerin-sinir-asan-basortu-yasagi-2718691.

63. Toruk, İbrahim. "Türkiye'de Başörtüsü Sorunu ve Yazılı Medyada Sunumu." [The Headscarf Problem in Turkey and Its Presentation in the Press] *Turkiyat Araştırmaları Dergisi*, 30 (2011): 483–514. Available Online https://dergipark.org.tr/tr/download/article-file/257725.

64. "Köşk'ten kırmızı halı açıklaması." ["Red Carpet" Announcement from the Presidential House] *Hurriyet*, October 21, 2010. Accessed July 30, 2018.http://www.hurriyet.com.tr/gundem/koskten-kirmizi-hali-aci klamasi-16102964.

65. For details of these examples see the report of Mazlumder based on the news: Benli, "1964–2011 Türkiye ve Dunyada Basortusu Başörtüsü Yasağı Kronolojisi.".

66. See: Güngör, Behçet. "Erdoğan'dan Tevhide'ye destek telefonu." [Support Call from Erdoğan to Tevhide]. *Yenisafak*. November 29, 2007. Accessed June 6, 2018. https://www.yenisafak.com/gundem/Erdoğandan-tevhideye-destek-telefonu-84646.

67. For examples of these kind of implementations, see Benli, "1964–2011 Türkiye ve Dünyada Başörtüsü Yasağı Kronolojisi".

68. Genç and İlhan, Başörtüsü Yasağına, 23.

69. A survey conducted in 2007 showed that 33% of participants did not have a job, as they could not find employment while they continued to wear a headscarf. HAZAR, *Türkiye'nin Ortulu Gercegi*, 27–30.

70. Genç and İlhan, Başörtüsü Yasağına, 24.

71. Özkök, Ertuğrul. "Cumhuriyet mitingleri dosyasını acıyorum." [I open the files of Demonstrations for the Republic]. *Hurriyet*, April 2, 2009. Accessed July 17, 2018. http://www.hurriyet.com.tr/cumhuriyet-miting leri-dosyasini-aciyorum-11345082.

72. "Cumhuriyet Gazetesi-Tehlike'nin Farkında mısınız?" [Cumhuriyet Newspaper-Are You Aware of Danger?] *Hurriyet*, August 8, 2013. Accessed on October 21, 2021. https://www.hurriyet.com.tr/video/cumhuriyet-gazetesi-tehlikenin-farkinda-misiniz-36012324.

73. "History of the Council of Higher Education" *Council of Higher Education*. Accessed on June 23, 2019. https://www.yok.gov.tr/en/instituti onal/history.

74. Arslan, *Başörtüsü, Ak Parti ve Laiklik*, 5.

75. HDP was founded after DTP was closed by the Constitutional Court.

76. "Anayasa Mahkemesi Kararı sayı: 27,032" [Constitutional Court's Decision no: 27032]. *Resmi Gazete [Official Gazette]*, October 22, 2008.

4 JDP'S SECULARISM AND THE HEADSCARF **139**

Accessed July 24, 2018. http://www.resmigazete.gov.tr/eskiler/2008/10/20081022-15.htm.

77. Idem.
78. Idem.
79. Arslan, *Başörtüsü, Ak Parti ve Laiklik*, 7–12.
80. "411 el kaosa kalktı." [411 hands for the chaos] *Hurriyet*, February 10, 2008. Print.
81. When asked about their opinions regarding the abolition or continuation of the headscarf ban in universities, 78% of the society thinks that the ban should be lifted. In the 2003 study, those who said that the ban on the headscarf should be lifted were 75.5%. See: "Gündelik yaşamda din, laiklik ve türban araştırması." *Konda Araştırma ve Danışmanlık*, p. 23.
82. Interview with Respondent 1.
83. "Anayasa Mahkemesi Kararı No: 2008/2" [The Decision of the Constitutional Court Nr: 2008/2]. *Resmi Gazete* October 24, 2008. Accessed July 23, 2018. http://www.resmigazete.gov.tr/eskiler/2008/10/200 81024-10.htm.
84. Idem.
85. Idem.
86. Idem.
87. Genç and İlhan, *Basörtüsü Yasağına*, 18.
88. "CHP'den türbanlı milletvekili kararı" [Hijabi Parliament Member Decision from RPP]. *Hurriyet*, October 28, 2013. Accessed June 23, 2019. http://www.hurriyet.com.tr/gundem/RPPden-türbanli-milletvekili-karari-24997255.
89. "Türbanlı milletvekilleri Genel Kurulda" [Hijabi Parliament Members Are in General Assembly]. November 1, 2013. Accessed July 3, 2019. http://www.hurriyet.com.tr/gundem/türbanli-milletvekilleri-genel-kurulda-25017264.
90. Idem.
91. "İşte "Demokratikleşme Paketi" nin tam metni." [Here İs the Full Script of the Democratisation Package]. *Yenisafak*, September 30, 2013. Accessed July 23, 2018. https://www.yenisafak.com/gundem/iste-demokratiklesme-paketinin-tam-metni-569627.
92. Interview with Ravza Kavakcı, Ankara, on February 24, 2015.
93. Interview with Özlem Zengin, Ankara, on August 25, 2015.
94. "Muharrem İnce: Endustri 4,0 diyen bir cumhurbaskanı olacak" [Muharrem İnce: There Will Be a President Who Says Industry 4.0] *Hurriyet*, May 11, 2018. Accessed July 13, 2019. http://www.hurriyet.com.tr/gundem/muharrem-ince-Erdoğanin-selamini-iletiyorum-40833468.
95. "Kılıçdaroğlu: Başörtüsü sorunu vardi biz cozduk." [Kılıçdaroğlu: There Was a Headscarf İssue, We Solved İt]. *Ihlas News Agency*, March 6,

2014. Accessed July 23, 2018. http://www.iha.com.tr/haber-kemal-Kılıçdaroğlu-basortusu-sorunu-vardi-biz-cozduk-338040/; "Kılıcdaroglu radyo yayınına katıldı." [Kılıçdaroğlu Joined the Radio Broadcast]. *Anadolu Agency*, June 18, 2018. Accessed July 23, 2018. https://www.aa.com.tr/tr/politika/Kılıçdaroğlu-radyo-yayinina-katildi/1178221.

96. Nevertheless, we should remember that as stated by human rights activist and former JDP MP Benli, irrespective of how the JDP viewed the EU criteria and its accession process as impacting the headscarf issue, the EU had not done its respective part and the EHRC's decision on the Leyla Sahin case in 2004 was incompatible with democracy and human rights. As their current decisions on similar applications are also a violation, it might be thought that the decision taken back then was political. Interview with Fatma Benli, Ankara, on May 8, 2018.

97. One of the surveys shows the support level of the society, see: Konda, "Gündelik yaşamda din, laiklik ve türban araştırması", 45.

98. Interview, Tuncay Özkan, Ankara, on April 27, 2019.

99. I hear this quite often during my interviews with the JDP politicians.

100. Interview, Tuncay Özkan, Ankara, on April 27, 2019.

101. Genç and İlhan, *Basörtüsü Yasağına*, 2012.

102. Konda, "Basını örtme ve türban Araştırması." [Survey on Wearing Headscarf and Veil] *Konda Barometresi*, November 2010, p. 15.

103. "Simgesel Külturel Sınıflar Analizi" [Analysis of Symbolic Cultural Classes]. İstanbul: GENAR, 2009.

104. "Anayasaya Dair Tanım ve Beklentiler" [Expectations and Definitions on Constitution]. *Konda Araştırma ve Danışmanlık*, September, 2012, p. 67.

105. This outcome derived from my interview data with the JDP politicians.

106. Interview, Tuncay Özkan, Ankara, on April 27, 2019.

107. "Binali Yıldırım'ın eşi Semiha Yıldırım: Dilek İmamoglu'na cok teşekkur ediyorum." [Binali Yıldırım's Wife Semiha Yıldırım: I thank Dilek İmamoglu] *Cumhuriyet*, June 12, 2019. Accessed January 1, 2020. http://www.cumhuriyet.com.tr/video/binali-yildirimin-esi-semiha-yildirim-dilek-İmamoğluna-cok-tesekkur-ediyorum-1435181.

108. See a documentary prepared by Kemalist Cumhuriyet newspaper as a good example of this narrative, "Beraber yurudunuz siz bu yollarda: AKP'nin 20 yilda zengin ettikleri [You Walked Together: Who the JDP Has Made Rich in 20 years]. *Cumhuriyet*, August 25, 2021. Accessed: August 25, 2021. https://www.cumhuriyet.com.tr/haber/beraber-yur udunuz-siz-bu-yollarda-i-akpnin-20-yilda-zengin-ettikleri-1863307.

109. Interview with Ertan Aydın, Ankara, April 29, 2019.

110. Cinar, "Bodies, Places and Time", 1.

111. Mahçupyan, *Türkiye'ye içeriden bakış*, 11.

4 JDP'S SECULARISM AND THE HEADSCARF   141

112. Genç and İlhan, *Basörtüsü Yasağına*, 23. One of the Most İmportant Research Studies on This Topic Is: Çarkoğlu and Toprak, *Religion, Society and Politics in a Changing Turkey.*
113. Arik, "Speaking of Women?," 15. Also see Gokariksel, Banu and Mitchell, Katharyne. "Veiling, Secularism, and the Neoliberal Subject: National Narratives and Supranational Desires in Turkey and France." *Global Networks* 5.2 (2005): 147–165; Komecoglu, Ugur. "New Sociabilities: Islamic Cafes in İstanbul." In *Islam in Public: Turkey, Iran and Europe*, edited by Nilüfer Göle and Ludwig Amman, 163–188. İstanbul: İstanbul Bilgi University Press, 2006.
114. Interview with Vedat Bilgin, Ankara on March 27, 2019.
115. Interview with Özlem Zengin, Ankara, on August 25, 2015.
116. Interview with Fatma Benli, Ankara, on May 8, 2018.
117. Akdoğan, Ali and Sungur, Erol. "Post-Modern Ortamda dindarin degisen giyim anlayisi: Başörtüsü ve Tesettur ornegi uzerinden kimlik tartismasi." [Changing Dressing Style of Pious People in Postmodern Atmospheric: Debates on İdentity on the Basis of Headscarf and Modest Dress]. *Erzincan Universitesi Sosyal Bilimler Enstitusu Dergisi* 9.1 (2016): 67–78, p. 76.
118. Kaya, İbrahim. *Social Theory and Later Modernities.* Liverpool: Liverpool University Press, 2004, pp. 142–143.
119. Idem, p. 141.
120. Interview with Nabi Avcı, Former Ministry of Education and Former Minister of Culture and Tourism, Current Eskişehir MP, Ankara, on December 14, 2018.
121. Idem.
122. Interview with Fatma Benli, Ankara, on May 8, 2018.
123. See original text of the JDP defence text: "Anayasa Mahkemesi Kararı No: 2008/2" [The Decision of the Constitutional Court Nr: 2008/2]. *Resmi Gazete*, October 24, 2008. Accessed July 23, 2018. http://www.resmigazete.gov.tr/eskiler/2008/10/20081024-10.htm.
124. Interview with Özlem Zengin, Ankara, on August 25, 2015.; Interview with Ravza Kavakcı, Ankara, on February 24, 2015.
125. Interview with Leyla Şahin Usta, Deputy Chairperson of JDP, Konya MP of JDP, Ankara, on December 14, 2018.
126. According to a survey conducted in 2007, the rate of those who did not vote for the JDP but cover their heads was 14 per cent. Those who do not cover their heads among RPP voters are 59.3% and the rate is 32.4% among MHP voters. Konda, "Gündelik yaşamda din, laiklik ve türban araştırması," *Konda Araştırma ve Danışmanlık*, 19.
127. Interview with Tuncay Özkan, Ankara, April 27, 2019.
128. Interview with Mustafa Şentop, Ankara, on April 19, 2019.

129. Fourie, Elsje, "Does Modernity Still Matter? Evaluating the Concept of Multiple Modernities and Its Alternatives." *Bath Papers in International Development and Wellbeing*, No. 10 (2010).
130. This term was borrowed by Nilüfer Göle. See Göle, *The Forbidden Modern*.
131. Eisenstadt, *Comparative Civilizations*, p. 546.
132. Habermas, Notes on Post-Secular Societies.

CHAPTER 5

The JDP's Secularism and Religious Education

Althusser once observed that schools are the most crucial institutions for reproducing the dominant ideology.[1] Indeed, education has been a key indoctrination apparatus for *status quo* to promote its secularism and nationalism principles. In this regard, understanding the history of secularism in Turkey is only possible through an in-depth analysis of religious education policies in Turkey. Yet, changes that have taken place in religious education often reflect the political preferences of the establishment, rather than the wider needs of the public.

Since the early Republican years, education has been one of the main tools used to construct "the ideal citizen" who is ethnically Turk, religiously Muslim, and politically Kemalist.[2] To achieve this, secular education strictly controlled by the state has been carefully implemented. Framing the borders of religiosity and defining religious identity was possible by controlling the content of the curriculum and the duration of exposure to this content.[3] Therefore, as part of this strategy, religious education has paradoxically been an integral part of Kemalist secularism project.

Accordingly, this part of the book articulates the role of education in creating "the ideal citizen" in the context of Turkey's secularisation history. In this regard, if we categorise the transformations that have affected religious education, it is possible to split Republican history into four periods: The period between 1924 and 1946, which began with the

© The Author(s), under exclusive license to Springer Nature Switzerland AG 2022
P. Kandemir, *The JDP and Making the Post-Kemalist Secularism in Turkey*, https://doi.org/10.1007/978-3-031-07605-3_5

143

establishment of the Republic and was defined as the Single-Party era during which religion was gradually excluded from formal education; the period of transition to a multi-party era from 1946 until the 1980 coup, during which pressure on religious education was partly removed; the period between the 1980 coup and 28 February 1997, which marks the date of the post-modern military coup, after which religious education was taken under the full control of the state; and finally the period from 1997 to the end of 2002 when religious education and training was totally obstructed.

As an outcome of the strictly secular state policies implemented since the early Republican years, contemporary Turkey's most important education-oriented issues include problems with negative treatment towards IHSs, the headscarf ban in schools, and a lack of religious education rights for pre-school children. After spending the first two government periods assessing the situation, laying out essential groundwork to implement reforms on religious education, and determining their compatibility with the secular system, the JDP undertook significant steps in the field of education to solve these problems in its third administrative period, after 2010. Initially, the JDP moved to annihilate the Kemalist policy of criminalising pre-school religious education. Then, by removing restrictions on IHSs students' entrance to universities, reopening elementary IHSs, and enhancing their overall status, the JDP lift the ban and criminalisation of religious education in Turkey.

Kemalists' objections countering JDP's reforms related to concerns about power sharing and class conflict (preserving Kemalist elites' privilege by being the only educated class in Turkey and keep the centre under their control) as well as maintaining secularism. IHSs are at the crux of this argument; however, in contrast to the Kemalists' approach, the JDP contends that IHSs are not representatives of Islamism and obscurantism, but are instead modern institutions that do not challenge secularism. Mehmet Ali Gökaçtı's excellent work on IHSs also states the view that IHSs are a product of modernity born out of Turkey's unique secularism experience. They are the sole representative example of institutional religious education in contemporary Turkey. However, (he claims) modernist historiography fails to evaluate this within Turkey's historical realities.[4]

In regards to JDP's education policies, there is a common argument that claims the reforms made reveal Islamisation policy. According to this approach, religious education challenges secularisation; and the revival of religiosity could result in the Islamisation of Turkey by creating a *sheria* state.[5] Some English language articles in particular are overwhelmingly critical of Muslim-related reforms, but approve reforms benefitting religious minorities; this includes reforms in education field. Since "different from the secularist, laicistic perspective, the post-secular perspective seems to be much more open to religious education courses on regular school curricula",[6] it is inevitable to refer these discussions to prove that liberalisation in religious education is an outcome of JDP's Post-Kemalist secularism, rather than Islamisation.

KEMALIST SECULARISM AND RELIGIOUS EDUCATION

The current educational system dates to the final decades of the Ottoman Empire. During the Tanzimat Era, the Ministry of Education was founded in 1847 and the public education system was reformed. While religious education became a component of the curriculum under the new system, control was taken from the hands of the *ulema*. After the foundation of the Turkish Republic, this process continued with a different methodology and tone.

The Tevhid-i Tedrisat law, issued on 3 March 1924, brought together all educational institutions under the Ministry of Education, resulting in the closure of 479 madrasas and establishing the foundation of the education policies to be implemented by the Kemalist Republic.[7] Under the new secular education system, primary schools, which were attended for six years during the Ottoman period were reorganised as five yearly, and religious education was included in the curriculum for two hours a week,[8] except for first graders (senior, junior, etc.), with the name of Kur'an-ı Kerim ve Din Dersleri (Quran and Religion Courses).[9] Also, İmam Hatip courses were opened to replace *medreses*.[10] Thus, "existing pluralist modes of education" were replaced with "a secular, centralist, and nationalist educational system."[11] In this sense, putting the management of religious education under non-religious leadership, namely the Ministry of Education, could be considered a key step in the path to secularisation.[12]

Directly after the introduction of the Tevhid-i Tedrisat law, religious education policies began to change rapidly. Content on religion, which had been taught under different names and over different periods in elementary, junior high, and high school, was slowly removed from the curriculum between 1924 and 1930.[13] In 1930, it was announced that religious education in primary schools would only be taught to 5th

146   P. KANDEMIR

graders with their parents' approval, for half an hour a week.[14] However, importantly, rather than teaching religion, the state was indoctrinating children with religion/dogma-free thinking in these courses.[15] Additionally, İmam Hatip courses were completely closed during this period, making it an interregnum for religious education. According to some scholars, this explains why the first educated generation of the Republic was quite detached from religion.[16]

After this period, Quran Courses, founded in 1932 became the only religious education offerings. While there were 9 Quran Courses with 232 students in 1932–1933, this increased to 127 with 8706 students in 1949–1950.[17] However, as highlighted by Gökaçtı, when one considers these courses were only teaching pupils how to read and memorise the Quran in Arabic lettering, it would be wrong to claim they were conveying religious teachings. Additionally, Gökaçtı demonstrates the education capacity of teachers was not sufficient enough to train others.[18]

With the emergence of a multi-party system in 1946, religious education issue became a matter of political debate and competition between the political parties. As the DP voiced criticism of the RPP due to its aggressive policies preventing religious education, the Kemalists loosened their ties more. Mardin additionally states this was an outcome of internal disputes within the RPP arising from concerns about new generations.[19] One outcome of this political battle was that it led to the official decision at the RPP's 1948 Congress that religious education be restored. It took a year to prepare religious education books, and in 1949 a course on religion started being taught to 4th and 5th grade pupils in primary schools for 2 hours a week, conditional on parental approval.[20] A report was also published after the congress of 1948, recommending establishment of new schools inspired by İmam Hatip courses, later called İmam-Hatip Schools (IHSs), to be affiliated with the Ministry of National Education.[21] The then-Prime Minister Şemsettin Günaltay, who was a Professor of Theology, was instrumental in this political move.[22]

The transformation in religious education accelerated after the election victory of the central right DP in 1950. Immediately after the start of their governence, religious courses began to be taught in elementary schools, and "religious instruction became mandatory unless parents requested an exemption."[23] According to Jenkins, the number of families choosing to exercise this option was very few.[24] In 1956, this process was followed by the introduction of religious courses in secondary schools. Additionally, ten-month-long İmam-Hatip courses were transferred to IHSs in big cities in 1951, resulting in the number of IHSs rising from ten in 1949 to eighteen in 1958.[25] The Faculty of Theology was re-established as a university-affiliated institution.[26] With regard to religious education in the private sector, the DP also lifted restrictions on Qur'an courses: and in 1960, when they were overthrowned by a military *coup*, the number of courses had increased from 127(1949) to 301.[27]

After the 1971 military declaration, the popularity of IHSs continued.[28] While the IHSs were known to focus on religious education until this time, they were later accepted as equivalent to regular high schools providing general education as much as a religious one. This was the main reason behind the rise of the popularity of IHSs. Thus, the number of students in IHSs increased drastically from as few as 900 in 1955 to 200,000 by 1981. With new amendments, IHSs graduates were provided with the opportunity to study at other departments at universities, in addition to the Faculty of Theology.[29] For the first time in 1976, upon the request of a parent who wanted to enrol her daughter in an IHS, the state council permitted female students to register for IHSs. At that time (NOM leader) Erbakan's party was part of the coalition government.

With regard to the state's religious education strategy, a new era began with the emergence of Turkish-Islam synthesis after the 1980 coup d'état.[30] There were two main motivations that informed this shift in the strategy: (i) to gain the hearts and minds of pious/conservative Muslim citizens to legitimise the junta, and (ii) to take control of leftist radicalisation within young Turkish and Kurdish groups and co-opt it by supporting a nationalist and conservative agenda remedially. As the initial step of this strategy, elective religious courses in schools turned into compulsory courses from the 4th grade to the final semester of high school in accordance with the Constitution.[31] The course was named to *Din Kültürü ve Ahlak Bilgisi* (Religious Culture and Ethics Knowledge).[32]

After the coup, no further changes were made regarding the IHS. However, no new schools were opened either. After the military coup, a debate about the dress code for female students who studied at IHSs had been emerged. Thus, with the order of Kenan Evren, the then-president and commander of the military coup, female students were allowed to wear a headscarf only to Qur'an lectures.[33] Nevertheless, in this period, the number of students who were enrolled in IHSs went from 48,895 in 1974–1975 to 200,300 in the academic year 1980–1981.[34]

148   P. KANDEMIR

A further development in religious education at this period involved releasing an official order to all mosques in 1980. *Diyanet* asked Imams to open up religious courses in the mosques so that everyone can attend. During the summertime, millions of children started to join these courses in local mosques to gain a religious education.[35] However, this did not prevent a rise in the number of Quran courses being offered, which rose to 3047 in 1983 from 2610 in 1980.[36] Lastly, at this time, increasing the religious content of state radio and television was another reform implemented to meet the strategy of Turkish-Islam synthesis.

This process and approach persisted after civil politics regained control from the military junta with the election victory of centre-right, liberal ANAP. A change in 1983 paved the way for IHSs graduates to enrol at university departments of their choice. While previously IHSs were only training religious servants, they were later chosen by pious families for their children's mainstream high school education. Additionally, the other major innovation of Özal was to implement reforms to improve the quality of IHS. During the Özal period, *Anatolian IHSs* offering English language education were opened.[37] While the number of IHSs doubled to 605, the number of students also increased from 200,000 to 500,000 between 1980 and 1998, accounting for 13% of all high school students at the time.[38]

As the rise of popularity in Welfare Party during 1990s, the state's strategy with regard to religious education began to change, as did other secularism practices. In this regard, this decade can be considered the harshest in Turkey's history of modernisation after the single-party era, which concluded in 1946. More than ever, IHSs and Quran courses became the symbols of Islamism in the eyes of Kemalists. That is the reason why they suddenly became a primary target for Kemalists to eliminate. Especially after the rise of the Welfare Party in politics in the 1994 election, the Kemalist establishment inflamed discussions about religious education. This period witnessed numerous examples in the media and in politicians' speeches, humiliating, criminalising, and defaming any type of religious education. Another dichotomy was formulated during these years vis-à-vis religious education and secularism.

On 28 February 1997, following a nine-hour meeting of the National Security Council, eighteen decisions were declared, three directly connected to the education system. One of the decisions was to require eight years of uninterrupted education "in order to protect the young brains of the generation from the effects of various forces, raise their awareness on ideals and aims of loving the republic, Atatürk, motherland and nation, and finally elevate the Turkish nation to the level of contemporary civilization."[39] This involved a move to close elementary IHSs that students were attending after their five years at primary school. The other decision was to reduce the number of IHS, "the number of which were higher than needed" and close the Qur'an courses, which they believe "run by fundamentalist groups."[40] These decisions recollected the anti-religion spirit of Kemalist secularism as it had manifest in the earlier single-party era. They were backed by newly emerging Kemalist NGOs devoted to protecting secularism.[41]

To understand the significance of these decisions on the life of citizens, it is best to start at the level of damage these decisions created with regard to religious education in Turkey. The 5 + 3 option proved important for conservative families; yet, the families sent their children to IHSs after five years of primary education; 8 years uninterrupted education demolished the elementary part of IHSs. The eight-year uninterrupted compulsory education requirement was enacted on 16 August 1997, and was voted in by 277 members of parliament. Subsequently, the secondary grades at the IHSs were closed, and religious education was banned until the age of 12 (there was no age limit previously). Moreover, Culture of Religion and Knowledge of Ethics courses in public schools were reduced to one hour per week.[42]

Additionally, during this period, under the instruction of the military, a decision was taken by the Council of Higher Education to apply a co-efficient system to university entrance exams, making it almost impossible for IHSs graduates to study anything except theology departments. This system was implemented from 1999 onwards, and while usually total exam score was calculated by multiplying every correct answer by 0.5 for a normal high school graduate, the ratio was 0.2 for an IHS graduate.[43] Note here that IHSs do not only offer religious education such as the Quran, Arabic language, religious commentary, and Islamic jurisprudence, they also include and even prioritise the curriculum of the Ministry of Education taught in other public schools, i.e. mathematics, physics, literature, and music.[44]

As a consequence of the above changes, IHSs received a major blow resulting in falling student numbers. The number of IHS students was over 500 thousand for the academic year 1996–1997, but had dropped to 64,534 by 2002–2003. The number of schools also fell, from 601 to 452.[45] In addition, IHS graduates were prevented from working in state institutions, such as "the army, the police force, and nonreligious jobs such as medical doctors/physicians, lawyers, engineers, and so forth."[46] Following the February 28 coup, several IHS graduates left Turkey to study abroad with the help of civil society organisations. Thus, the horizontal growth observed during Özal's time ended on 28 February 1997.[47]

The steps taken to limit or ban religious education during these years meant that religious education in general and Quran Courses and IHSs in particular were increasingly criminalised by the Kemalists establishment during this period. IHSs became one of the most controversial topics associated with Turkey's secularism, along with the headscarf debate that resulted from state policies introduced by the Kemalist establishment. Ergo, this resulted in a barrier between state and society in the following years.[48] Even the JDP's election victory in 2002 did not change anything. In fact, it took the JDP almost a decade to make gains.

THE JDP'S RELIGIOUS EDUCATION APPROACH VERSUS KEMALIST SECULARISM

After coming to power in 2002, one of the JDP's main targets became to improve the education capacity in Turkey by implementing a comprehensive education reform package.[49] Indeed, the budget of the Ministry of National Education dramatically increased, rising from 7.5 billion TL in 2002 to 76.3 billion TL in 2016.[50] Furthermore, the number of teachers increased twofold, whereas the curriculum for courses was completely renewed under the European Union's guidance[51] with Western support.[52]

While the reform process was limited with religious education in three different kinds—Pre-school religious education in Quran Courses, compulsory religious courses in schools, and IHSs, during which it relied on support from the EU for legitimacy, meaningful changes to religious education in Turkey did not take place until after the constitutional referendum in 2010. This chapter will particularly focus on these three issues.

Before start discussing them, demilitarisation of public education should also be noted. Yet, as the reforms related to these three sectors mostly took place from 2010 onwards, the JDP focused more on content and curriculum discussions. In this context, one of the most important reforms initiated by the JDP involved the removal of militarist discourse from school textbooks.[53] This was viewed as a significant step, as the Kemalists were indoctrinating ordinary citizens to prepare them to be "ideal citizens." Formulating a new rhetoric via schoolbooks was critical to the foundation of Post-Kemalist Turkey. These changes were legitimised under the European Union membership process, which made them more acceptable to Kemalists. Parallel to this reform, some other symbolic Kemalist ceremonies, such as the one-minute of silence and recitation of the nationalist oath were removed from the daily activities in schools. Accordingly, the mandatory "National Security Course" given by military officers in high schools was also removed from the curriculum.[54] Another change in primary schools, requiring parents' approval was the introduction of a casual dress code instead of a uniform. Thus, the JDP initiated to revise the approach not only in regard to historical events, but also removed the army's dominance over social and political life. These reforms helped for the reformulation of civil-military relations in the public sphere[55]; but of course, they were not strong enough to transform the Kemalist domination in the education sector. Additionally, these changes did not conclude with replacement of Kemalist ideology in the schools with the conservative nationalism; one might maybe call it as a change towards liberalisation but definetly not conservatism. In fact, despite the growing patriotist rhetoric of the JDP in recent years, even the JDP's close relationship with the nationalist MHP could not affect this situation. For example, although the MHP was insistent about readopting "student oath",[56] one of the symbols of Kemalist regime, imposing Turkish ethnicity starting from 1933 and abolished with Democratisation Package in 2013, the JDP pushed back strongly in 2018.[57]

While the JDP was in the process of removing Kemalist dominance over the education system and curriculum, this changes also contributed to the rehabilitation of the relationship between the state and citizens. The JDP utilised a diversified approach by removing militarist and discriminatory discourse from school books, added 23 new elective courses to the curricula—including a Kurdish lesson for the first time in Turkish history,[58] changed the content of compulsory religious education by transforming it into a course on the religions rather than a course that teaches Islamic practices, introduced 4+4+4 compulsory education, and reopened the elementary parts of IHSs, which were closed after the 28 February coup,[59] removed co-efficient system in university entrance exam and re-liberated the pre-school religious education in the Quran courses.

Finally, the JDP managed to open a space for an alternative teachers' union, Eğitim-Birsen, to counterbalance the Kemalist Eğitim-sen, the biggest teacher's union in Turkey previously.[60] It has experienced extreme growth during the JDP period, reaching 433,787 members, a rise from 18,000 in the 16 years between 2003 and 2019.[61] The chief demands of Eğitim-Birsen, particularly in their report on the education system vision for 2023, the 100th year anniversary of the Turkish Republic, include an education system that is "human centred, non-ideological, promotes critical understanding, combines local and universal values, [and] rejects discrimination."[62]

The National Education Undersecretary, Yusuf Tekin, explained the rationale mind behind these reforms by stating that the priority was to harmonise all educational materials, especially the curriculum, with national moral values and democratic principles, to turn schools not only into pedagogically oriented spaces but also to allow them to function as public spaces contributing to the positive development of state-citizen relations.[63] For him, their education model is "Constructivist," acknowledging that it is different from that in previous eras.[64] However, Hasan Under, a critic of the JDP, claims the JDP's stand was rather a political choice, "because its antirealist and relativist theses are useful in undermining the hegemony and the privileged position of science and positivism, which have buttressed modernist discourse and policies opposed by Islamism from the beginning."[65] This dichotomy echoes Kemalist secularism, and the JDP's argument was therefore naturally divergent. It rejected the idea of seeing religious education as an alternative to science, much like the majority of Turkish society.[66] In fact, the JDP's investment in science and technology, not only in schools but overall, reveals the JDP's commitment to support them equally rather than viewing them as opposing forces. One should understand that the JDP's reforms in education should be analysed with a holistic approach, rather than all the steps superficially being regarded as Islamisation. Overall, the JDP succeeded in transforming the education system in general and religious education in particular after its 18 years in governance. The evaluation of these changes affords us valuable insight into understanding Post-Kemalist secularism.

Post-Kemalist Secularism and Pre-School Religious Education

"Qur'an courses" are the main source of pre-school religious education in Turkey. The Directorate of Religious Affairs runs Qur'an courses across Turkey. They do not constitute an alternative to public schools, but are intended to dispense religious education. The education given via these "Qur'an courses" is practice-oriented, as institutions teach children how to read the Qur'an in Arabic letters. In these courses, the Arabic prayers, surahs, and verses, which are required for worship, are also taught and memorised. The courses are offered in boarding schools or in daytime schools. While gender-segregated courses exist, mixed education courses are also available although they are rare.

Qur'an courses were especially targeted in the aftermath of the February coup era, and the age limit for religious education was subject to considerable state control. The introduction of 8 years of uninterrupted education was a major source of controversy, as previously families had tended to send their children to begin their religious education at a young age before starting public school. This practice was officially banned by the state, and it became illegal to send children to the institutions offering religious education before they turned 12. Additionally, it was marginalised and also banned to provide any religion related education in the private kindergartens.

While the JDP followed a strategy of not taking steps that would alarm the Kemalist establishment in the beginning, it did successfully remove some restrictions in following years. In 2011, the JDP removed the age limit imposed on religious education, and law no. 28257 (7 April 2012) covering this aspect was adopted. After this time, religious education outside of the schools was once more permitted, and the Diyanet prepared a new programme with a religious friendly approach.[67] These changes led to an increase in the number of courses and enrolees. While the number of Quran courses taken between 2000 and 2001 was 3,368, this figure increased almost five-fold in 2015.[68]

When we examine the programme prepared for the pre-school age group in Quran Courses, i.e. 4 to 6 year olds, the subjects of the lesson were as follows: love and compassion, respect, duty and responsibility, justice, helping and sharing, patience, trustworthiness and truthfulness, goodness, praying and apology in the lens of Islam.[69] The second part of the programme related to Quranic education, in which Arabic letters are taught.[70] There is even a special website for children created by

154   P. KANDEMIR

the Directorate of Religious Affairs. On this website, there are special pages described thus, "I am learning my religion," "my prophet," "my worship," "I am aware of the world." There are also online games on the page entitled "My game world" which aim to help children obtain religious education through computer games.[71]

Despite the removal of the bans on early religious education and the ending of obstructions to Quran Courses developing their quality, proportionality of demand did not rise during the JDP era, and this has been substantiated in public surveys. Indeed, the percentage of people stating that they would prefer sport, foreign languages, or summer schools rose, and uptake of Quran courses slightly declined.[72] From my understanding, rather than being a sign of decline of religiosity within the society, this seems to be a consequence of the rising number of nurseries offering child-friendly religious courses before children begin their compulsory education and rising opportunites to get religious courses in public schools.

Finally, the criminalisation of pre-school religious education as central to anti-secularism is still not over but it continues within the Kemalist circles of the society, academia, and politics. JDP's efforts to propose this as a matter of freedom of religion did not help to change this mentality. Most of the Kemalists are still defending the closure of the Quran Courses and institutions belonging to religious communities and continues to label pre-school religious education as radical.[73] Although, there are some weak voices challenging with this view time to time, RPP's general approach indicates that they did not take any step to go beyond their previous secularism approach in the context of religious education. Nevertheless, for JDP's Mahir Unal, this kind views proposed and defended by "an elitist class indoctrinated by secular mind and education for years and years" are not mainstream even within the RPP's supporters. For him, "Kemalism is 'an enlightened cultural revolution originated from the West and these are the reflections of this understanding in today's political language."[74]

This indicates that while Kemalists followed an anti-religion path and sought to prevent and restrict religious education as discussed, and centre-right parties opened the way for freedom of religious education, the JDP went one step further by developing it. Of course, it is important to highlight that this liberalisation was not limited to Sunni Islam. Different religious groups in theory and in practice are provided accorded the same rights. For the first time in Turkish Republican history, the Syriac Ortodox community was allowed to open a nursery providing religious education.[75] This shows the JDP wished there to be no boundaries preventing religiosity within society, rather it was encouraged, in a manner typical of conservative movements in general.

Post-Kemalist Secularism and Compulsory Religion Course in Public Schools

Subsequent to compulsory ethical education being introduced in 1974, religion course became compulsory in Turkey's public schools following the 1980 coup d'état. This course entitled "Culture of Religion and Knowledge of Ethics" is taught in the 3rd and 4th grades of primary schools and in the first four years of secondary schools for 2 hours a week. The course is not dispensed to Turkey's non-Muslim citizens.[76]

In the guidebook, multiple references were made to the value that Atatürk placed on freedom of religion, conscience and thought, the principles of secularism, the importance of solidarity for the sake of a country's sovereignty and national integrity, his personality and characteristics, and his ideas concerning humanity and universality, views on Islam, and love of homeland and the nation.[77]

Kaymakcan notes that there are three main legitimate reasons for compulsory religion course in Turkey: The population is almost entirely Muslim, the religiosity rate is quite high compared to Europe, and there is a near consensus on compulsory religious education at the political and societal level except for *Alevis*.[78] These three reasons are highly correlated. Indeed, according to public poll, there is significant support for the existence and continuity of this course within Turkish society. While the rate of people supporting the removal of the course from the curriculum is only 3.6, 50.1% prefer that it to be mandatory, and 46.3% would prefer it to be optional.[79]

During the JDP years, compulsory religion course continued to be provided as part of the curriculum. However, this issue was opened to the discussion several times and concrete steps were taken by the JDP governments to revise the ongoing practices. One of the most important reforms was to revise curriculum of this already-existing compulsory Religion and Ethics Course to a more pluralistic format. To do this, in 2007, the government formed a committee to prepare a detailed report to create a strategy in compulsory religion course; and as a result of the final proposal of this committee, the JDP decided to not remove it but rather convert it into an ethics and culture course by separating the Islamic education content.[80] Following the change in the content and structure of the course, two additional courses were added to curriculum for high school students as elective alternatives, the life of Prophet Muhammed and the Quran course in 2012.[81] This step was interpreted and criticised as a policy of Islamisation by many sections, especially the Kemalists. However, the JDP was expressing that "there was a need for such an elective course providing an understanding of Islam due to the fact that they changed the compulsory course from being a course that provides Islamic education to an ethics and history of religion and sects course."[82]

When it comes to the content of this course, claiming to have a "supra-sectarian" (not based on any sect, not entering into sectarian discussions) and an "inter-faith" approach when teaching the basic facts of religion and the root values of Islam, the priorities detailed in this lesson were listed by the Ministry of National Education as follows: Respect for humanity, respect for dignity, respect for freedom, respect for moral values, and respect for cultural heritage.[83] When the syllabus is analysed, it is apparent that basic discussions are being held in the 4th, 5th, and 6th grades, when more detailed topics such as fasting, zakat, Hajj, and animal sacrifice are taught in the 7th grade. Similarly, when we examine the 8th grade curriculum, it is seen that students are introduced to other religions under the heading, "religions and universal organisations."[84]

It is noteworthy to mention that various lawsuits have been filed against the Ministry before and after the revision of the content. For instance, in 2005, the "Alevi Bektashi Federation (*Alevi Bektasi Federasyonu*, ABF) submitted a petition to the European Parliament including 1 million signatures asking for dissolution of the compulsory course on culture of religion and knowledge of ethics in Turkey."[85] The decision by the European Court of Human Rights (ECHR) on 9 October 2007, and the state council on 3 March 2008, found it illegal to conduct the class without taking into consideration the pluralistic composition of society. As noted above, although JDP responded this discussion by changing the content and practice of this course, Bülent Arınç framed this step as addressing the issue internally, but failing to resolve the problem.[86] Ultimately, similar decision was taken by ECHR in 2014 for a different case by "taking into account the significant changes that had since been made to the curriculum."[87]

As put by Arınç, by diversifying the content, the JDP has already taken an important step, but not one that has yet prevented additional discussions. In this context, with continuing discussions relating to the existence of compulsory religion course, multiple voices have arisen from the different political parties. While the RPP has promised to remove compulsory religion course in their election declarations since 2007,[88] the pro-Kurdish HDP also makes the same promise.[89] Pro-Turkish MHP advocates the necessity of keeping it mandatory in the schools.

Overall, when we consider the course was not introduced by the JDP but it became mandatory in 1980 and kept the same by all the governments since then, it cannot be taken as an indication of either increasing Islamisation or decreasing secularisation. But beyond this, when one revisit Habermasian post-secular perspective, it can be easily seen that not only learning about religion, but also learning from religion cannot be considered as contradictory with secularism. On the other hand, "while teaching about religion and learning from religion can be understood as a post-secular duty of all schools" within the context of post-secularism,[90] Loobuyck takes Turkey as a controversy and does not consider this course in Turkey under this category. He says that "when confessional religious education is organized in public schools, it should be done in such a way that different religions can offer their religious educations, and nobody is obliged to follow a confessional course"[91] I think, since the curriculum of this course has changed and it includes other religions and sects in current form and other religious groups are provided right to offer religious courses in their schools, his analysis becomes controversial. Nevertheless, as will be discussed in the next chapter, Alevis' situation is still the main battle in this discussion.

Post-Kemalist Secularism and Imam Hatip Schools

When the JDP attained power in 2002, there were three expectations relating to IHSs. First, the removal of restrictions on IHSs graduates wishing to attend university; second, the reopening of elementary IHSs that had closed after the February 28 coup; and third, the ending of negative and discriminatory discourse against IHSs, which defined them as at the centre of anti-secularism. Finding solutions to these three issues and propose a solution to them took the JDP almost a decade.

Indeed, the JDP began its reforms by taking baby steps to remove the bans and restrictions on religious education including IHS problems. One of the minor steps was intended in October 2003 by proposing a solution package for the removal of the co-efficient system, which had been the primary barrier preventing IHS graduates to study in the other departments of universities except Theology even if they fulfil all requirements.[92] However, it was dropped immediately from the parliament's agenda after receiving severe criticism from Kemalist seculars. When in 2004 another attempt was made on the same issue and this time, the chief of general staff reacted directly to oppose the amendment. Despite this, a law was passed in parliament, but then-President Sezer predictably vetoed the proposal stating that the law was not in line with the principles of secularism. Although the government had the right to bring it back, they preferred not to insist.[93]

Finally, the change in IHSs' situation in terms of the removal of the co-efficient system was made by the Council of Higher Education in 2009. However, the Council of State later cancelled this resolution as well. Later in the same year, the Council of Higher Education proposed a new arrangement, resulting in February 2010, in the Council of State suspended the execution of the resolution. Nonetheless, after a constitutional referendum in September 2010 altered several authoritarian controls and interpretations set by the 1982 Constitution (created by the military after the 1980 coup), the balance of political power to make decisions started to shift towards the JDP. In November 2011, the Council of Higher Education introduced a comprehensive change reopening universities' door to IHSs graduates after a period of 13 years. With this change, not only IHSs graduates but also all vocational high school graduates were entitled to enrol in whichever department they preferred to attend as long as they fulfilled the necessary conditions applied to all students. It should be noted that these changes did not provide any auxiliary advantages to IHSs graduates, but only provided equal conditions in response to their former disadvantaged position. With this development, the first and main problem encountered by the IHSs was solved.

The second issue concerned the closure of IHS's elementary section. The JDP resolved this problem in 2012 by passing a regulation stipulating that 12-year compulsory education could be dispensed with via a system called 4+4+4. The proposal jettisoned the 8-year uninterrupted education policy, which had been enacted after the February 28 coup d'état.[94] Under the new system, compulsory education was even longer than before, but it could take place in three separated parts as 4+4+4.[95] Additionally, according to Unal, "it was more flexible and offered more alternatives now."[96] Thus, secondary grades became available at IHSs again, after their closure in the aftermath of the 1997 coup d'état.[97]

While the rate of people being positive about this change was 56.4% according to Genar's survey,[98] the tensions in parliament concerning the discussions were quite high. During the debates in the Turkish Parliament with regard to this reform, the number of MPs raising concerns from a secularist point of view was very limited. RPP's MP Kamer Genç was one of those who found this change to be contrary to the secularism principle of the republic. Another RPP MP, Engin Altay established a direct link between this change and secularism stating, "secularism is the most basic feature of being a society and a state."[99] Similarly, Akif Hamzaçebi from the RPP described this change as a pragmatic move for the JDP, stating, "We witness how the JDP uses religion and Quran to get more vote."[100] Conversely, the Kurdish nationalist BDP (HDP now), were against this change believing there was a neo-liberal motivation behind this reform.[101] In addition, they identified other problems in the educational system, such as use of mother tongue by Kurdish citizens[102] (which had not been included in this regulation), which were also subsequently resolved. Although the nationalist MHP supported regulation, they nevertheless criticised the lack of discussion of it in the public sphere.[103] This proves that the reactions of politicians and parties have differed.

The last change in the status of IHSs was the removal of an aggressive state narrative towards IHS graduates. JDP's effort to change this situation started as soon as they came to power in 2002. Seemingly, since the beginning, the first and foremost subject of dispute had been about the approaches of the two sides to the IHSs. While Kemalist secularists considered IHSs as only suitable for educating future *imams*, conservatives viewed them as a sacred alternative space where their children can take religious education without being alienated and indoctrinated with Kemalist ideology. In this context, I contend that the IHSs became a battleground between the Kemalist centre and the conservative periphery since the very beginning. Finally, the graduates of IHSs, such as Erdoğan, began to emerge as political, intellectual, and economic forces, representing a looming threat to Kemalist seculars who had formerly wielded uncontested power. This of course triggered the tension between these two parties; and made Kemalists to take stricter stand day-by-day not only due to secularism concerns but also not to lose their privileges.

At this stage, one of the main issues that raised the tension was JDP's positive and promotive language towards IHSs. Although Erdoğan's idealised "religious generation" did not reflect Ministry of Education's position,[104] in the final instance, there had been a positive promotive language towards IHSs in the state level. It is clear that both the JDP and Erdoğan sympathised with these schools. The positive framing by President Erdoğan, especially during 2012, played a substantial role in this context. When participating in the IHSs' opening ceremonies[105] and graduate meetings,[106] Erdoğan often stated that his children had studied at IHSs and that he himself had graduated from an IHS, and as such he was very proud of his path.[107] On the 100th anniversary of the establishment of IHSs, Erdoğan stated: "I will carry this honour up to my very last breath. Four of my children studied and graduated from IHSs."[108] This reactionary narrative can be counted as an example of the sacralisation of IHSs as a battle between Kemalists and pious Muslims; however, the reason behind this reaction was indeed the criminalisation of religious education by the Kemalist elites.

Additionally, although opponents claimed the JDP was destroying the secular foundation of Turkey through IHS[109] the reforms only succeeded in alleviation of their disadvantaged situation and made society to reach a new normal according to Mahir Unal.[110] Erdoğan's positive language towards the IHSs was also similarly motivated; supporting a group of people who had been oppressed and humiliated under the state's authority can be understood as positive discrimination[111] rather than an effort of Islamisation. When we consider the ones oppressed by the state included were their wives, daughters, and even themselves, this approach is readily comprehended.

Thus, with the personal efforts of Erdoğan, state rhetoric towards the IHSs has changed. According to Özlem Zengin, the norm in Turkey was drinking alcohol, not wearing a headscarf, and being opposed to IHSs before; but "Erdoğan diversified what was "normal" in Turkey."[112] Indeed, the JDP tried to alter the image of IHSs in Turkey from the outset. Ravza Kavakcı, a JDP MP, examines this point stating, "in the past, Imam-Hatip students have always been despised, called 'dead washer', 'hodja', used with a negative meaning; this perception has suddenly changed. Now we have a group that stands upright and owns it."[113] Yusuf Tekin contributed to the same argument by saying, "There is a demand from citizens to provide their children with religious education. However, they want their children to learn the sciences, as well as religion. We are opening these schools to meet this request. This is the point where we diverge (from the RPP)."[114] Erdoğan highlighted this point several times in his speeches by stating that IHSs are not only institutes for religious education, noting that those who criticise these schools know nothing about the curriculum.[115]

These aforementioned reforms as well as the JDP's positive discourse with the state-society relations in the context of religion concluded with the rising popularity of growing image of the IHSs. After the changes were implemented, there was a major increase in the number of IHSs and students. The results of research into IHSs show that the number of students, who were 64,534 in 2002–2003, raised to 1,291,426 in 2016–2017. However, it should be remembered that this number was 511,502 in 1996–1997 (before the February 28, 1997 coup).[116] Yusuf Tekin says that the rate of students is almost the same as the rates before the February 28 coup. Statistically, before the 1997, the ratio of IHSs was 12 out of every 100 students, while today the ratio is 11 out of every 100 students.[117] He also states that the diversified option of IHSs provides different opportunities for students. According to Tekin, "in some cities, there is a growing demand for IHSs although the rate is up to 20 percent. In other cities, although IHSs have increased by up to 6–7 percent, there is no demand." He adds, "We establish (the schools) according to where the demands and preferences lead us."[118]

However, at the time several counter voices were raised to claim the opposite. The rise in the number of IHSs led to a discussion concerning the JDP's IHSs policies. At this stage, the public schools that had converted to IHSs offered enough evidence for opponents, who mostly rejected the arguments and revised data.[119] Indeed, most of the numbers applied claimed that the JDP was converting all high schools to IHSs, which can be falsified by applying the Ministry of Education's official data. While "82 general high schools were converted into IHS, 513 general high schools were converted into vocational high school"[120] during the 2011–2014 period.

Incidentally, criticisms raised were not solely due to secularist concerns; some Kemalists believed that the distribution of the state's financial support of education was unfair. When I asked this to Tekin, he stated that it was philanthropists who established the great majority of IHSs. He added: "IHSs and pre-school education are the fields that we receive the highest amount of philanthropic contribution. Therefore, the quality of the schools also depends on the contributions."[121] It should be high-lighted here that the public support for IHSs is not a novel phenomenon. Rather, it can be seen as the anonymous resistance of pious Muslims to the Kemalist establishment from the very beginning.[122]

162   P. KANDEMIR

The Former Minister of Education, Nabi Avcı also highlighted this phenomenon by revealing an anecdote in which he was exposed to many questions about whether or not IHSs were favoured during his Ministry:

> When I was the Minister of Education, I was asked a question from the opposition in the parliament: You give free lunch to students at IHSs in İstanbul, but you do not give it to the other schools. I was horrified, as I did not know there was such a practice. They (his fellows) immediately brought a note and it said: "Yes, it is true, in some IHSs, free lunch is provided, but not by us. Indeed, we discovered IHS Alumni provided this of their volition.[123]

He added,

> The IHS issue has long not been under the auspices of the State but rather embraced as a voluntary movement of people in Turkey. In other words, these are schools that were not supported but instead accepted for many years until the JDP's rule and operating in buildings completely through the voluntary donations of the people.[124]

Indeed, this phenomenon found a place for itself in the academic literature. In his doctoral dissertation, Tarhan explains this aspect in relation to field research conducted in 1996:

> Many people worked diligently for the survival and continuation of these schools, pooling their spiritual and financial resources over many years. From the very beginning, people have donated materials, land, and labour according to their financial capabilities. To a great extent, the IHSs system owes its survival to private efforts in the face of seemingly insurmountable obstacles.[125]

By providing a broad perspective on its historical context, Gökaçtı claims this is how the IHSs continued to exist with the moral and material support of society.[126] This was most probably one of the reasons behind the Kemalists' irritation with the IHSs; nevertheless, they were well aware that IHSs were a symbol of anonymous resistance from the periphery. Nevertheless, in spite of these justifications, JDP's secularism was also subject to motivational forces; "raising a religious generation" was one of the chief motivations present in JDP's rhetoric.[127] However, as for most of the JDP politicians highlights, Ömer Çelik states that the reason

5 THE JDP'S SECULARISM ... 163

behind the JDP's positive stance towards IHSs does not challenge "JDP's liberal secularism." He explains:

> IHSs should be evaluated from two aspects. First, they make a great contribution to Turkey's national security. With authentic religious education given by the IHSs, radical groups such as Taliban or Al Qaeda could not have found a base in Turkey. Second, due to the critical point of view given in IHSs, it has become difficult for any religious interpretation to exert pressure on society. This is also a guarantee for secularism.[128]

In addition to secularism discussions within the context of IHSs, we have to revisit another issue pertaining to IHSs; i.e. the reasons behind Kemalists' reactions against the IHSs in contemporary Turkey. According to Gökaçtı, another reason for Kemalist resistance is a new "pious Muslim prototype of citizen" rose in these schools. Gökçatı also claims this pious Muslim prototype also contributes to the development of conservative identity and creates a sophisticated infrastructure for this identity.[129] This brings about another problem for the Kemalists who equated conservatism to lower class, uneducated profiles. In fact, it has been emphasised in many academic studies that IHSs students tend to belong to underprivileged families.[130] However, the majority of these studies did not review the profile of IHSs after 2012. The reaction is getting louder because of the rising visibility of IHSs graduates in different sectors. At this stage, it is crucial to understand how they became more visible in contemporary Turkey. In the oppressive atmostphere of February 28 coup, thousands of youths had their educational rights violated by being prohibited from going to university or being forced to study for lesser degrees than they had been capable of because of restrictions, but there were some unintended positive consequences. Firstly, with the transformation of educational system, removal of the hard core Kemalist and militarist rhetoric from the schoolbooks and setting freedom for female students to wear headscarf in schools—in other words, with an end to the otherisation of religious education, pious Muslims have made peace with regular schooling. This has improved the level of education in Turkey.[131] In terms of female high school education, while the attendance percentage was 69.58% in 1997–1998, it increased to 90.54% in 2016–2017.[132] Most likely this has been due to conservative Muslims choosing to send their daughters to school after the lifting of the headscarf ban and the closure of IHSs at elementary school level.[133] Thus, the number of children from pious families increased and graduates began to be visible in sectors where they had never had a chance to exist before. Professional military service, police, judge, lawyer, and even acting can be given as examples.

Secondly, as mentioned before, those children from conservative families who graduated from IHSs, but could not enter Turkish universities due to the co-efficient system were sent to study in Western countries. The Association of Alumni and Sympathisers of the IHSs in Turkey (ONDER) provided scholarship opportunities for successful IHSs graduates at European universities with the support of conservative philanthropists.[134] This generation obtained their qualifications from outstanding universities, learned foreign languages, and increased their cultural awareness. Thus, this generation became counter force "preparing themselves for leading roles in Turkey when they can return."[135] Indeed, upon graduating and returning to Turkey, this generation was able to access good career opportunities. Notwithstanding, although visibility of these IHS graduates in the senior positions is criticised as favouritism by the opposition today,[136] in reality only 4% of all graduates in Turkey are from IHSs,[137] so any fears seem exaggerated.

As the demands of the most pious segment of society to higher education have increased with the normalisation of religious education, the number of educated, pious Muslims has also peaked during this period. While before it was necessary to uphold a secular lifestyle and defend Kemalist principles[138] to integrate into the upper class in Turkey, JDP's secularism policies have brought about change. Although there is still an inverse proportion between education level and conservatism,[139] my findings from interviews with the JDP's IHSs graduate politicians indicate that they and their families have a new sense of pride in being IHS graduates rather than being subject to the lameness imposed by the Kemalist regime for years.

In fact, what is happening in Turkey today is a move of power and influence from the centre to periphery. As suggested by Numan Kurtulmus, "those values that already exist in the periphery have begun to be move to the centre as a result of rising education level of the peripheral one and urbanisation."[140] He says, the Kemalists opposed improvements at IHSs due to "the fear of losing their privileges or sharing their cake with the ones coming from Anatolia."[141] The tension over IHSs and Kemalist reactions should be reconsidered within this context; to see these discussions solely as secularist concerns would only be superficial.

Conclusion

From the very beginning, as it established a relationship with modernity, the JDP did not reject its values but proposed a vision of modernity that feeds on history, cultural orientations, and local values. As a result, if "modern societies differ from each other",[142] the JDP's religious education policies should be considered within Turkey's own historical and sociological reality.

The most important repercussions of the reforms in the field of religious education are the end of tension between pious Muslims and the state. While this was happening, the role of IHSs in being the centre of anti-secularism in the eyes of Kemalists did not cease but decreased. Thus, in spite of the ongoing discussions on Quran Courses and pre-school religious education raised by Kemalists, IHSs and other religious institutions—formerly the biggest source of tension between the secular state and the devoted citizen, were finally no longer framed as a symbol of anti-secularism by the state. Although Kemalists and RPP continue to keep a similar position on religious education, no one can reject their rare positive steps towards conservative segment of the society. For instance, the leader of the RPP, Kemal Kılıçdaroğlu came together with IHSs students to ask their support in the upcoming election and this was indeed a surprising step for the RPP.[143] This shows the retrogressive symbolism of IHSs has slightly declined in Turkey.

As noted before, there are several public surveys that show religiosity type in Turkey is diversifying,[144] and individuals that define themselves as modern are rising dramatically. A veteran JDP politician and former Ministry of Education Nabi Avcı confirms this point by saying that "The forms of manifestation of religiousness were as diversified as the means and styles."[145] According to Konda's survey, individuals who define their lifestyle as modern increased from 34% in 2008[146] to 43% in 2018.[147] The same survey, conducted to evaluate the changing religiosity level in youths also showed that choosing to define oneself as pious or conservative fell from 28% in 2008[148] to 15% in 2018.[149] Expansion in education and modernity proves the JDP's Post-Kemalist secularism and its religion friendly approach has neither increased piety among youths nor declined the approval of secularism within this group. Then, this once again proves that opening a free space for religious education and removing the bans on it does not challenge with secularism; but, on contrary, it diversified the practices, which can be simply evaluated as pre-conditional approach for freedom of religious expression.

On the other hand, despite the discomfort experienced by Kemalists regarding the rising number of educated, modern, intellectual, and wealthy IHSs students and graduates, it is hard to claim the rising generation educated in these schools is becoming more religious; apparently, research reveals the opposite.[150] Indeed, when religious practices are evaluated, it has been asserted that IHSs' graduates perform fewer religious practices than before. In Turkey, the standard is to pray at least five times a day if one is to be considered a practising religious person. According to a study, only 52% high school students of IHSs pray regularly. Despite this, in a study conducted with IHSs students, 91.8% stated they enrolled at an IHS to develop their religious knowledge. Similarly, 83.9% of the surveyed students considered IHSs to bestow good moral values, 75.9% of them thought they produced respectable citizens, and 73.6% thought IHSs helped them become more religious.[151] In addition, pious families' preference to send their children public or private secular schools/institutions would have a consequence as liberalisation of the new generation belong to conservative segment of the society. Undoubtedly, financial improvement of the pious middle class as well as the impacts of social media in younger generation triggered the sociology of the young generation of Turkey.

Compulsory religion course still fears its importance as an important area of discussion on religious education. When we consider that 82.1% of society supports offering compulsory religious education in school as soon as its content is not monolithic,[152] we can understand that there is unlikely to be a move to prevent it. This means that it should be evaluated within the local dynamics and cultural underpinnings. In this regard, more important than what the JDP prefers, one should question whether it challenges with post-secularism or multiple modernities paradigm or not. By referring the religious education, Loobuyck notes that this can be an element that can help children understand each other and "learn how to live together." For him, "this kind of integrative religious education seems to be a promising and appropriate way to facilitate and establish complementary learning processes, wherein the secular student can learn from religious students, the religious student can learn from the secular one, and both can experience the right to disagree and develop an attitude of reciprocity."[153] In this regard, the JDP sees religious education as a natural sign of freedom of religion.

NOTES

1. Althusser, Louis. *On the Reproduction of Capitalism: Ideology and Ideological State Apparatuses.* Translated by G. M. Goshgarian, London: Verso, 2014, pp. 50–52.
2. Üstel, Füsun. *Makbul Vatandaşın Peşinde: II. Meşrutiyet'ten Bugüne Vatandşslık Eğitimi* [In Pursuit of Desirable Citizen: Education for Citizenship from Constitutionalism to Present Day]. İstanbul: İletişim Yayınları, 2004.
3. For a detailed comparative analysis of Kemalist education policies see Saleem, Raja M. Ali. *State, Nationalism, and Islamization: Historical Analysis of Turkey and Pakistan.* London: Palgrave, 2017.
4. Gökaçtı, Mehmet Ali. *Türkiye'de din eğitimi ve İmam Hatipler* [Religious Education in Turkey and Imam Hatips]. İstanbul: Iletisim, 2005.
5. For an example of this approach see: Ackerman, Xanthe and Calisir, Ekin. "Erdoğan's Assault on Education: The Closure of Secular Schools." *Foreign Affairs,* December 23, 2015. Also see Weise, Zia. "Turkey's New Curriculum: More Erdoğan, more Islam". *Politico,* February 13, 2017.
6. Loobuyck, Religious Education, 97.
7. Türk, Ercan. *Türk Eğitim Sistemi ve Ortaöğretim* [Turkish Education System and Secondary Education], 2015. Accessed February 2, 2019. http://ogm.meb.gov.tr/meb_iys_dosyalar/2017_06/13153013_TES_ve_ORTAYYRETYM_son10_2.pdf.
8. For an analysis of the content, see Zengin, Mahmut. "Türkiye'de Cumhuriyet Donemi Eğitim Politikalarinin Din Dersi Ogretim Programlarina Etkileri" [The Effects of Educational Policies on Religious Courses Curriculums in Republic Period in Turkey]. *Journal of Sakarya University Faculty of Theology* 19.36 (2017): 113–137, pp. 121–22.
9. Şimsek, Eyüp. "Çok Partili Dönemde Yeniden Din Eğitimi ve Öğretimine Dönüş Süreci (1946–1960)" [The Process of Return to Religious Education and Training in a Multi-Party Period (1946–1960)]. *Ankara Universitesi Türkiyat Araştırmaları Enstitüsü Dergisi* (2013): 391–414.
10. There were 29 IHSs with 2258 students in the academic year 1923–1924. Gokcacti, *İmam Hatipler,* 142.
11. Bozan, İrfan. *Devlet ile Toplum Arasında Bir Okul: İmam Hatip Liseleri... Bir Kurum: Diyanet İsleri Baskanlığı* [A School Between State and Community: Imam Hatip High Schools... An institution: Directorate of Religious Affairs] İstanbul: Tesev Yayınları, 2006, p. 4.
12. Saleem, *State, Nationalism, and Islamization,* 201.
13. Alasania, Giuli and Gelovani, Nani. "Islam and Religious Education in Turkey." *IBSU Scientific Journal,* 5.2 (2011): 35–50, p. 38.
14. Zengin, "Türkiye'de Cumhuriyet Donemi", 122.
15. Idem.

16. Feroze, Muhammad Rashid. *Islam and Secularism in Post-Kemalist Turkey*, Islamabad: NWC Books, 1976, pp. 23–40.
17. Gökaçtı, *İmam Hatipler*, 149.
18. Idem.
19. Mardin, *Türkiye'de din ve siyaset*, 99.
20. Zengin, "Türkiye'de Cumhuriyet Dönemi", 124.
21. In spite of this, the RPP group decided to open ten-month-long courses only. Simsek, "Cok Partili Donemde Yeniden Din Egitimi", 402.
22. Albayrak, Mustafa, *Türkiye Siyasi Tarihinde Demokrat Parti (1946–1960)* [Democrat Party in Turkish Political History (1946–1960)]. İstanbul: Phoenix Yayınevi, 2004, pp. 136–137.
23. Saleem, *State, Nationalism, and Islamization*, 205.
24. Jenkins, Richard. *Social Identity*. London and New York: Routledge, 2004, pp. 115–117.
25. Çakır, Ruşen, Bozan, Irfan and Talu, Balkan. *Imam Hatip okullari: Efsaneler ve Gercekler* [IHS: Myths and Facts]. İstanbul: Tesev Yayinlari, 2004, p. 15.
26. Simsek, "Cok Partili Donemde Yeniden Din Eğitimi", 391–414.
27. Akyüz,"Türkiye'de Uygulanan", 148.
28. See: Saleem, *State, Nationalism, and Islamization*, 205–207.
29. Öcal, Mustafa. *100. Yılında imam-Hatip liseleri (1913–2013)* [Imam-Hatip High Schools on Their Hundredth Year (1913–2013)]. İstanbul: Ensar Nesriyat, 2013, p. 169.
30. Akyüz, "Türkiye'de Uygulanan", 154–156.
31. "Constitution of the Republic of Turkey". *The Grand National Assembly of Turkey*, 2018, p. 17. Accessed February 7, 2019. https://global.tbmm.gov.tr/docs/constitution_en.pdf.
32. Önder, "Din Kültürü ve Ahlak Bilgisi", 28; Yürük, Tugrul. "İlk ve Orta Öğretimde Din Öğretimi Din Dersleri." In *Din Eğitimi El Kitabı*, edited by Recai Dogan and Remziye Ege, 105–120, Ankara: Grafiker Yayınları, 2012.
33. Çakır et al., *Imam Hatip okulları*, 15.
34. Bozan, *Devlet ile Toplum Arasında Bir Okul*, 17.
35. Öcal, Mustafa. "Cumhuriyet Doneminde Türkiye'de Din Eğitimi ve Ogretimi." *Uludag Universitesi Ilahiyat Fakultesi Dergisi* 7.7 (1998): 241–268, p. 265.
36. Kılavuz, M. Akif. "Adult Religious Education at the Qur'anic Courses in Modern Turkey." *The Journal of International Social Research* 2.6 (2009): 407–414, p. 410.
37. Akyüz, "Türkiye'de Uygulanan", 156.
38. Idem.

5 THE JDP'S SECULARISM ...   169

39. "Rakamlarla 28 Subat Raporu" [28 February Report with Numbers]. *Eğitim Bir Sen*, February 28, 2014, p. 29. Accessed March 23, 2018. https://www.ebs.org.tr/ebs_files/files/yayinlarimiz/28_subat_rapor_web.pdf.

40. "Askerin 20 Srtı" [Soldiers" 20 Condition]. *Hurriyet*, March 2, 1997. Print.

41. At this period, military's strategy to limit and even criminalise religious education was legitimised by the civilian branch of Kemalism. From the Association for Supporting Contemporary Life (CYDD, Cagdas Yasamı Destekleme Dernegi), to the Turkish Women's Union (Turk Kadınlar Birligi), many young Kemalist NGOs-mostly founded in the late 80s or early 90s voiced their support of the military decision. To illustrate the tactics and their strategy, one might consider the CYDD as an example. After its founding in 1989, the first panel that CYDD organised was "the importance of the transition into secular education in Turkey" and the first book they published was "the Transition to Secular Education in Turkey." The same year, they sent 3700 signed letters to the President "expressing concern that secularism was under threat." In the same period, they organised a march with the slogan "respect for secularism." This organisation played a significant role in the reformulation of Kemalist secularism in the educational system in 1990s. See: "ÇYDD From Past to Present." *Association for Supporting Contemporary Life (CYDD)*. Accessed March 23, 2018. https://www.cydd.org.tr/pages/from-past-to-present-cydd-8/.

42. Kılavuz, "Adult Religious Education", 410.

43. Özdemir, Esin. "Üniversiteye Girişte Katsayı Uygulamasına Ilişkin YÖK ve Danıştay Kararları Hakkında İnceleme ve Değerlendirme" [An Evaluation About YÖK and State Council Decisions on Coefficients Application at University Entrance]. *TOBB AB Muzakere ve Uyum Mudurlugu*, 2010. Accessed February 7, 2019. https://www.tobb.org.tr/AvrupaBirligiDairesi/Dokumanlar/RaporlarYayinlar/KATSAYI_SORUNU.pdf.

44. "Anadolu İmam Hatip Lisesi Haftalık Ders çizelgesi" [Anatolian IHS Weekly Curriculum]. *Milli Eğitim Bakanligi Din Öğretimi Genel Müdürlüğü* [Directorate of Religious Education at Ministry of National Education], 2017. Accessed February 7, 2019. https://dogm.meb.gov.tr/meb_iys_dosyalar/2017_06/15113722_AIHL_Fen_Sosyal_Bilimler_ProgramY_Cizelgesi1.pdf.

45. Aslamacı, Ibrahim. "Din Eğitimi Politika ve Uygulamalarinda Ak Parti'nin 15 yılı" [JDP's 15 Years in Politics and Application of Religious Education]. İn *Kurulusundan Bugune AK Parti: Toplum* [JDP Since İts Establishment: The Society], edited by İsmail Çaglar and Ali Aslan, 181–211. İstanbul: SETA Yayinlari, 2018, p. 192.

170   P. KANDEMIR

46. Akşit, Bahattin. "Islamic Education in Turkey: Medrese Reform in Late Ottoman Times and Imam-Hatip Schools in the Republic." In *Islam in Modern Turkey*, edited by IHSard L. Tapper, 145–170. London: IB Tauris, 1991.
47. Çakır et al., *Imam Hatip okulları*, 15.
48. Bozan, *Devlet ile Toplum Arasında Bir Okul*, 4.
49. AK Parti. *Adalet ve Kalkınma Parti Seçim Beyannamesi* [Election Manifests of the Justice and Development Party], 2003, pp. 79–82. Accessed July 29, 2019. https://acikerisim.tbmm.gov.tr/xmlui/bitstream/handle/11543/954/200304063.pdf?sequence=1&isAllowed=y.
50. "Millî Eğitim Bakanlığı bütçesini yaklaşık 11,4 kat artırdık" [We Increased the Budget of the Ministry of National Education Almost 11,4 times]. *AK Icraatler*, 2019. Accessed February 7, 2019. http://www.ililakicraatlar.com/Türkiye/icraat/milli-egitim-bakanligi-butcesini-yaklasik-114-kat-artirdik/30631.
51. Çayır, Kenan. "Citizenship, Nationality and Minorities in Turkey's Textbooks: From Politics of Non-recognition to "Difference Multiculturalism"." *Comparative Education* 51.4 (2015): 519–536.
52. World Bank. "Promoting Excellence in Turkey's Schools." *Human Development Sector Unit Europe and Central Asia Region*, March 1, 2013. Accessed June 13, 2019. http://documents.worldbank.org/curated/en/944721468110943381/pdf/777220REVISED00B00PUBLIC00Egitim0EN.pdf.
53. For a deep analysis on this issue, see Altınay, *The Myth of the Military Nation*.
54. "Milli Güvenlik Dersi Kaldırıldı" [National Security Course Has Been Lifted]. *Hurriyet*, January 25, 2012. Accessed July 27, 2019. http://www.hurriyet.com.tr/gundem/milli-guvenlik-dersi-kaldirildi-19765864.
55. JDP reached its aim in 2012. Indeed, for the first time, the President became more trusted than the army in public survey. "Türkiye Sosyal, Ekonomik ve Politik Analiz 6" [Turkey Social, Economic and Political Analysis 6]. İstanbul: GENAR, September 2012. Print.
56. "Bahçeli'den "andımız" açıklaması" [Bahceli's "Oath" Statement]. *Hurriyet*, October 20, 2018. Accessed July 27, 2019. http://www.hurriyet.com.tr/gundem/bahceliden-andimiz-aciklamasi-40993292.
57. "Cumhurbaskanı Erdoğan'dan cok sert "Ögrenci Andı" tepkisi" [Harsh Response by President Erdoğan on "Student Oath"]. *Hurriyet*, November 3, 2018. Accessed July 27, 2019. http://www.hurriyet.com.tr/gundem/cumhurbaskani-Erdoğan-mujdeyi-genclerimizle-paylasmis-olalim-41007383.
58. There are 23 elective courses in curriculum including a diverse range

from cultural to environmental issues, foreign languages to communication skills. See "2019–2020 Eğitim-Ogretim yılında okutulacak secmeli ders belirleme" [Designation of the Elective Courses for 2019–2020 Education Year]. *Milli Egemenlik Ortaokulu*, February 2, 2019. Accessed May 23, 2019. http://sme.meb.k12.tr/icerikler/128227-2019-2020-egitim-ogretim-yilinda-okutulacak-secmeli-ders-belirleme_6487373.html.

59. "Eğitim sistemine köklü çözüm: 4+4+4" [Substantial Solution for Education System: 4+4+4]. *AK Icraatler*, 2019. Accessed February 7, 2019. http://www.ililakicraatlar.com/Türkiye/icraat/egitim-sistem ine-koklu-cozum-444/30630.

60. Şen, "Müfredata Hâkimiyet Mücadelesi", 321–345.

61. "Tarihçe" [History]. *Eğitim Bir Sen*. Accessed July 24, 2019. https://www.ebs.org.tr/tarihce.

62. "2023'e Doğru Türk Eğitim Sistemi Bulma Konferansı ve Çalıştayı: Öneriler" [Towards 2023 Conference and Workshop on Turkish Education System: Suggestions]. *Eğitim Bir Sen*, p. 8, September 2018. Accessed June 29, 2019. https://www.ebs.org.tr/ebs_files/files/yayinl arimiz/2023TurkEgitimSistemiBulmaKonferansi_oneriler.pdf.

63. Tekin, Yusuf. "Eğitim Alanında Yaşanan Dönüşüm Bağlamında Ak Parti'nin 15 Yılı" [JDP's 15 Years in Regards of the Transformation in the Field of Education]. In *Kurulusundan Bugune AK Parti: Toplum* [JDP Since İts Establishment: The Society], edited by İsmail Çaglar and Ali Aslan, 139–157. İstanbul: SETA Yayinlari, 2018, p. 154.

64. Interview with Yusuf Tekin, the Undersecretary of National Education, Ankara, on May 12, 2018.

65. Under, Hasan, "Constructivism and the Curriculum Reform of the AKP." İn *Neoliberal Transformation of Education in Turkey*, edited by Kemal İnal and Guliz Akkaymak, 33–45. New York: Palgrave Macmillan, 2012, p. 43.

66. See the results of public survey: Konda, "Bilime İnanç ve Bilim Dışılık" [Belief on the Science and Nonscience]. *Konda Barometresi* January 2013, p. 4.

67. "Kuran Kursları Öğretici Kitabı: 4–6 Yaş Grubu" [Qur'an Courses Exercise Book: 4–6 Age Group]. *Diyanet İşleri Başkanlığı* [Directorate of Religious Affairs], 2014. Accessed January 5, 2019. http://www2.diyanet.gov.tr/EgitimHizmetleriGenelMudurlugu/Materyaller/4-6-yas-ogretici-kitabi.pdf.

68. "İstatistikler: Kuran Kursu" [Statistics: Quran Courses]. *T.C. Cumhurbaskanlığı Diyanet İsleri Baskanlığı Strateji Gelistirme Başkanlığı*, December 12, 2018. Accessed January 13, 2020. https://stratejigelisti rme.diyanet.gov.tr/sayfa/57/istatistikler.

172 P. KANDEMIR

69. "Kuran Kursları öğretici Kitabı: 4–6 Yaş Grubu", Diyanet *İşleri Başkanlığı*.
70. Idem.
71. "Diyanet İşleri Baskanlığı Çocuk Sayfası" [Children Page of Directorate of Religious Affairs]. Diyanet İsleri Baskanlığı [Directorate of Religious Affairs]. Accessed February 7, 2019. https://cocuk.diyanet.gov.tr/def ault.aspx.
72. See the comparison between 2007 and 2017. Konda, "Eğitim Sisteminin Yapısı ve Beklentiler" [The Structure of Education System and the Expectations]. *Konda Barometresi*, November 2017, p. 25.
73. One of the current example of this might be RPP's Ozgur Ozel's statement. By harshly criticising the pre-school religious education, RPP Group Deputy Chairman Özgür Özel stated in December 2021 that "While there is a possibility to raise children the way to whole world does, turning to medieval mentality and trying to institutionalise it is neither beneficial for the Republic, nor for this nation." CHP'li Ozgur Ozel din eğitimine "orta cag zihniyeti" dedi [RPP's Ozgur Ozel Called Religious Education 'Medieval Mentality']. *Yenisafak*, 29 December 2021, Accessed January 27, 2022. https://www.yenisafak. com/video-galeri/gundem/chpli-ozgur-ozel-din-egitimine-orta-cag-zih niyeti-dedi-2228798. Also see "Cemaat Yurtlari Kapatilsin" [Religious Community's Dormitories Should Be Closed]. *Cumhuriyet*, 11 January 2022, Accessed January 27, 2022. https://www.cumhuriyet.com.tr/tur kiye/tepkiler-buyuyor-cemaat-yurtlari-kapatilsin-1899438
74. Interview with Mahir Ünal, Ankara, on June 4, 2018.
75. For the website of the Syriac Ortodox Nursary, Accessed 27 January, 2022. http://www.suryanianaokulu.com/.
76. "Ilköğretim Din Kültürü ve ahlak bilgisi dersi (4,5,6,7, ve 8 sınıflar) öğretim programı ve kılavuzu" [The Programme and Guidebook for Course of Culture of Religion and Knowledge of Ethics (for 4,5,6,7 and 8th Grades]. *Diyanet İşleri Başkanlığı* [Directorate of Religious Affairs], 2010, p. 8. Accessed February 7, 2019. https://dogm.meb.gov.tr/meb_ iys_dosyalar/2017_08/17174424_DinKültürü_4-8.siniflar_2010.pdf.
77. "Ilköğretim Din Kültürü ve ahlak bilgisi dersi", 66–69.
78. For Kaymakcan's arguments see Kaymakcan, Recep. "Religious Education in Modern Turkey in The Context of Freedom of Religion or Belief." In *Teaching for Tolerance and Freedom of Religion or Belief*, edited by Lena Larsen and Ingvill T. Plesner. Oslo: Oslo Coalition on Freedom of Religion or Belief, 2002. Available online at http://folk.uio. no/leirvik/OsloCoalition/RecepKaymakcan.htm.
79. "Anayasaya Dair Tanım ve Beklentiler" [Expectations and Definitions on Constitution]. *Konda Araştırma ve Danışmanlık*, September, 2012, p. 52.

5 THE JDP'S SECULARISM ... 173

80. "Zorunlu din dersi anayasa hukumleri korunarak uygulamada degisecek" [Compulsory Religion Course Will Be Changed in Practice While Preserving the Constitutional Provisions]. *Hurriyet*, October 15, 2007. Accessed July 27, 2019. https://www.hurriyet.com.tr/egitim/zorunlu-din-dersi-anayasa-hukumleri-korunarak-uygulamada-degistirilecek-746 4146.
81. "Kuran ve Siyer secmeli ders" [Quran and Siyer became an Ellective Course]. Yenisafak, March 30, 2012. Accessed July 27, 2019. https://www.yenisafak.com/gundem/kuran-ve-siyer-secmeli-ders-375375.
82. Interview with Respondent 1.
83. Idem, 2–6.
84. Idem, 29–31.
85. Gurcan, Ayse Ezgi. *The Problems of Religious Education in Turkey: Alevi Citizen Action and the Limits of ECtHR*. İstanbul: İstanbul Policy Center, 2015, p. 7.
86. Interview with Bülent Arınç, Ankara, on April 12, 2019.
87. For the full document of Chamber Judgement see, ECHR. Accessed July 27, 2019. https://hudoc.echr.coe.int/app/conversion/pdf/?library=ECHR&id=003-4868983-5948734&filename=003-4868983-594 8734.pdf.
88. RPP's election declarations (2002 and onwards) are available online in the official website. "CHP Secim Bildirgeleri" [Election Manifesto Elections]. *CHP*, 2019. Accessed June 20, 2019. https://www.chp.org.tr/yayinlar/secim-bildirgeleri.
89. *HDP Official Website*. Accessed June 20, 2019. URL: hdp.org.tr.
90. Loobuyck, Religious Education, 100–101.
91. Idem, 102.
92. "Imamhatiplere din dişi alan" [Non-religious Area for Imamhatips], December 8, 2002. Accessed, 27 January 2022. https://www.hurriyet.com.tr/gundem/imam-hatiplere-din-disi-alan-38520007.
93. "Sezer YOK yasasini veto etti" [Sezer Vetoed YOK Law], May 28, 2004. Accessed 27 January 2022. https://www.hurriyet.com.tr/gundem/sezer-yok-yasasini-veto-etti-229186.
94. Interview with Mustafa Şen, Ankara, on August 24, 2015.
95. "Türkiye Büyük Millet Meclisi Tutanak Dergisi" [Minute Magazine of Turkish Grand National Assembly]. *TBMM*, March 27, 2012. Accessed February 8, 2019. https://www.tbmm.gov.tr/tutanak/donem24/yil2/bas/b083m.htm.
96. Interview with Mahir Ünal, Ankara, on June 4, 2018.
97. "İlkogretim ve Eğitim Kanunu ile Bazi Kanunlarda Değişiklik

174 P. KANDEMIR

Yapilmasına Dair Kanun" [Law on the Amendment of Some Laws Under Primary and Education Law]. *Resmi Gazete* [Official Gazette], 2012. Accessed February 2, 2019. http://www.resmigazete.gov.tr/esk iler/2012/04/20120411-8.htm.

98. "Türkiye Sosyal, Ekonomik ve Politik Analiz 4" [Turkey Social, Economic and Political Analysis 4]. İstanbul: GENAR, 2012.

99. "Türkiye Büyük Millet Meclisi Tutanak Dergisi" [Minute Magazine of Turkish Grand National Assembly]. *TBMM*, March 30, 2012. Accessed February 8, 2019. https://www.tbmm.gov.tr/tutanaklar/TUTANAK/TBMM/d24/c018/tbmm24018086.pdf.

100. Idem.

101. Idem.

102. Idem.

103. Idem.

104. Interview with Yusuf Tekin, Ankara, on May 12, 2018.

105. "Erdoğan İmam Hatip Lisesi açtı, ilk dersi kendisi verdi" [Erdoğan Launched an IHS, Gave the First Lecture]. *Türkiye Gazetesi*, September 29, 2017. Accessed February 2018. http://www.Türkiyegazetesi.com.tr/gundem/507410.aspx.

106. "Cumhurbaskanı Erdoğan İmam Hatip Gençlik Bulusması'nda" [President İs at the Imam Hatip Youth Convention]. *Aksam*, April 28, 2016. Accessed February 2018. http://www.aksam.com.tr/siyaset/cumhurbaskani-Erdoğan-imam-Hatip-genclik-bulusmasinda/haber-511523.

107. "Cumhurbaskanı Erdoğan imam Hatip lisesi öğrencilerine hitap etti" [President Erdoğan Addressed IHSs Students]. *Anadolu Ajansı* [Anadolu Agency], April 10, 2017. Accessed January 2018. https://aa.com.tr/tr/Türkiye/cumhurbaskani-Erdoğan-imam-Hatip-lisesi-ogrenc ilerine-hitap-etti/793729.

108. Erdoğan, Recep Tayyip. "Yüzyıllık hikaye İmam Hatip" [Imam Hatip: A Story of Hundred Years]. Recep Tayyip Erdoğan's speech at 100th anniversary of the foundation of IHS, İstanbul, January 17, 2014. Accessed January 2017. https://www.yenisafak.com/video-galeri/pol itika/Erdoğanin-imam-Hatiplilere-yaptigi-konusmanin-tamami-12877.

109. Butler, "With More Islamic Schooling, Erdoğan Aims to Reshape Turkey." *Reuters.*

110. Interview with Mahir Ünal, Ankara, on June 4, 2018.

111. Idem.

112. Interview with Özlem Zengin, Ankara, on August 25, 2015.

113. Interview with Ravza Kavakcı, Ankara, on February 24, 2015.

114. Interview with Yusuf Tekin, Ankara, on May 12, 2018 (emphasis added).

115. "Cumhurbaşkanı Erdoğan: İHL'leri elestirenlerin müfredattan bile haberi yok" [President Erdoğan: The Ones Who Criticise the IHSs Do Not Even Know the Curriculum]. *Karar*, September 29, 2017. Accessed

May 2018. http://www.karar.com/guncel-haberler/cumhurbaskani-Erd
oğan-ihlleri-elestirenlerin-mufredattan-bile-haberi-yok-612438#.
116. "Millî Eğitim İstatistikleri Örgün Eğitim (1. Donem)" [National Education Statistics Formal Education (First Semester)]. *T.C. Millî Eğitim Bakanligi Strateji Gelistirme Baskanligi* [Ministry of National Education Strategy Development Presidency], 2017. Accessed January 5, 2018. http://sgb.meb.gov.tr/meb_iys_dosyalar/2017_09/08151328_meb_istatistikleri_orgun_egitim_2016_2017.pdf.
117. Interview with Yusuf Tekin, Ankara, on May 12, 2018.
118. Idem.
119. Gur, Bekir S. "What Erdoğan Really Wants for Education in Turkey: Islamisation or Pluralisation?" *Al Jazeera Centre for Studies*, 17 March 2016. Accessed January 25, 2018. http://studies.aljazeera.net/en/reports/2016/03/160317094912447.html; For Kadri Gursel's arguments see Gürsel, Kadri. "Erdoğan Islamizes Education System to Raise 'Devout Youth'." *Al-Monitor*, December 9, 2014. Accessed June 23, 2019. http://www.al-monitor.com/pulse/originals/2014/12/Turkey-islamize-education-religion.html.
120. Idem.
121. Interview with Yusuf Tekin, Ankara, on May 12, 2018.
122. Interview with Mahir Ünal, Ankara, on June 4, 2018.
123. Interview with Nabi Avcı, Ankara, on December 14, 2018.
124. Idem.
125. Tarhan, Mehmet. *Religious Education in Turkey: A Socio-Historical Study of the Imam-Hatip Schools*. Philadelphia: Temple University, 1996, pp. 154–155.
126. Gökaçtı, *İmam Hatipler*, 19.
127. "Dindar genclik yetistirecegiz" [We Will Raise Pious Youth]. *Hurriyet*, February 2, 2012. Accessed June 23, 2019. https://www.hurriyet.com.tr/gundem/dindar-genclik-yetistirecegiz-19825231.
128. Interview with Ömer Çelik, Ankara, on May 3, 2018.
129. Gökaçtı, İmam Hatipler, 19.
130. Tarhan, *Religious Education in Turkey*, 154–155.
131. Uncu, "Secmen Kümeleri: Ak Parti Seçmenleri", 12.
132. "Okula gitmeyen kalmayacak" [There Will Be No One Who Does Not Go to School]. *AK Icraatler*, 2019. Accessed February 7, 2019. http://www.ililakicraatlar.com/Türkiye/icraat/okula-gitmeyen-kalmayacak/30632.
133. Diyanet's 2014 Public survey implicitly proves this. It states, 95% of uneducated girls wear a headscarf. See: "Türkiye'de Dini Hayat Araştırması." *Diyanet İsleri Baskanlığı*, Ankara, 2014, p. 104. Accessed March 20, 2020. https://dergi.diyanet.gov.tr/makaledetay.php?ID=6468.

176 P. KANDEMIR

134. Mustafa Şen was leading scholarship program then. Interview with Mustafa Sen, Ankara, on August 24, 2015.
135. Çaglar, İsmail. *From Symbolic Exile to Physical Exile: Turkey's IHS, the Emergence of a Conservative Counter-Elite, and İts Knowledge Migration to Europe.* Amsterdam: Amsterdam University Press, 2013, p. 21.
136. Interview with Tuncay Özkan, Ankara, on April 27, 2019. HDP MP Hişyar Özsoy stated a similar view. Interview with Hişyar Özsoy, Ankara, on April 13, 2019.
137. Konda, "Eğitim Sisteminin Yapısı ve Beklentiler" [The Structure of Education System and Expectations]. *Konda Barometresi,* November 2017, p. 25.
138. When the education rate decreases, the level of Kemalism declines. See: Konda, "Siyasal Kimlikler" [Political Identities]. *Konda Barometresi,* July 2010.
139. Idem.
140. Interview with Numan Kurtulmus, Ankara, on April 8, 2019.
141. Interview with Numan Kurtulmus, Ankara, on April 8, 2019.
142. Schmidt, Volker. "Modernity and diversity, p. 512.
143. "Kılıçdaroğlu, Genç İmam Hatipliler Dernegi uyeleriyle bir araya geldi: Partilerin dini olmaz" [Kılıçdaroğlu Met with the Members of Foundation of Young Imam Hatip Students: Parties Do Not Have Religion]. *Cumhuriyet,* June 1, 2019. Accessed June 23, 2019. http://www.cum huriyet.com.tr/haber/siyaset/1420656/Kılıçdaroğlu__Genc_imam_Hat ipliler_Dernegi_uyeleriyle_bir_araya_geldi__Partilerin_dini_olmaz.html.
144. Mahçupyan, *Türkiye'ye İçeriden bakış,* 3.
145. Interview with Nabi Avcı, Ankara, on December 14, 2018.
146. ""Biz Kimiz? Hayat Tarzları Araştırması" [Lifestyle Survey]. *Konda Araştırma ve Danışmanlık,* 2019.
147. "Hayat Tarzları Araştırması" [Lifestyle Survey]. *Konda Araştırma ve Danışmanlık,* March/April 2018. Print.
148. "Biz Kimiz? Hayat Tarzları Araştırması" [Lifestyle Survey]. *Konda Araştırma ve Danışmanlık,* April 2008.
149. "Hayat Tarzları Araştırması", *Konda Araştırma ve Danışmanlık,* 2018.
150. Ertit, "God Is Dying".
151. Idem.
152. Mahçupyan, *Türkiye'ye iceriden bakıs,* 18–19.
153. Loobuyck, "Religious Education", p. 98.

CHAPTER 6

JDP's Secularism and Turkey's Religious and Sectarian Minorities

Since the foundation of the Turkish Republic, minorities, whether ethnic, religious, or sectarian have suffered various forms of discrimination, ignorance, and prejudice. Thus, the JDP's relationship with Turkey's religious and sectarian minorities, and the steps taken during this period cannot be evaluated without a comprehensive understanding of Turkey's 150 years of modernisation and secularisation adventure. During the JDP era, social status of minorities has been reformed along with various changes in different fields including religious education, visibility in social life, and relation with state. Although these developments have mostly been evaluated with regard to discussions about European Union membership process,[1] in fact, the issue of minority rights is a subject of continual debate in Turkey; even as governments and ideologies have shifted, discussions have continued. Indeed, while earlier reforms were achieved under European Union guidelines, reforms continued even after 2007 when bilateral relations with the EU were deadlocked. Even the dialogue initiative of the *Alevi*s (Alevi Opening) began after this time. Thus, regarding Turkey-EU relations and by not rejecting its significance at the outset, I instead focus on the repercussions of the JDP's Post-Kemalist secularism on different religious and sectarian identities in Turkey, particularly those of non-Muslim minorities and *Alevi*s.

In this context, as might be understood from this framework, I oppose the argument that "only Sunnis benefited from the JDP's overhauling

© The Author(s), under exclusive license to Springer Nature Switzerland AG 2022
P. Kandemir, *The JDP and Making the Post-Kemalist Secularism in Turkey*, https://doi.org/10.1007/978-3-031-07605-3_6

177

reforms"[2] and religious or sectarian minorities did not receive their full rights in Turkey—simply because of growing Islamism. As this argument has been rejected since the beginning of this book, this chapter evaluates this discussion as a form of political tension; meaning religion is not merely the main factor. By way of example, these problems did not emerge during the JDP years; the problems identified by religious and sectarian minorities were backgrounded in either the final period of the Ottoman Empire or the early Republican years. In fact, the situation did not worsen for other religious or sectarian minority groups, in terms of either their legal rights or their social life under the JDP governments. On the contrary, as will be presented alongside tangible proof, conditions have been improving not only for non-Muslim minorities, but also for Alevis. This positive change takes its foundations from the JDP's post-secularism understanding, which does not reject the existence of religion in the public sphere and recognise its positive role there.

KEMALIST SECULARISM VERSUS RELIGIOUS AND SECTARIAN MINORITIES

After the collapse of the Ottoman Empire, the current geography of Turkey was saved through the National Resistance Movement under Atatürk's leadership. He and the other founding members of the Republic witnessed the First World War, and their ideological formation was completed with the dissolution of the Ottoman Empire.[3] While 1.2 billion kilometres of land was reduced to 866 thousand kilometres, the number of ethnicities and the scope of religious diversity were reduced to only a single identity glorified by the state: Muslim Turks. This situation proved to be of critical significance in the formation of Kemalist ideology. Indeed, when one examines the justification for the oppression of minorities in Turkey, two of the most fundamental pillars of Kemalism, nationalism, and secularism are the main factors.

Accordingly, these two pillars were applied to standardise all citizens under the same identity, i.e. Turk. The Kemalists aimed to construct palatable citizens, i.e. *makbul vatandas* in Turkish, as saliently named by the academic Fusun Ustel. While the principle of nationalism defines *makbul vatandas* as ethnically "Turk," the principle of secularism embeds an apparent contradiction within Kemalist secularism. According to this identification of the ideal citizen, the most important aspect of being a Turk is being a Muslim.[4]

In the following years, Greek-Christians, Armenian-Christians, Jewish-Turks, and even Alevi Kurds encountered considerable pressure for not fitting into this identification.[5] Defining the minority framework in the Lausanne Treaty, a peace treaty between Turkish military forces and several European powers signed on July 24, 1923, by referencing religious identity proved this argument. As previously mentioned, the Kurds and Alevis were not considered minorities in Lausanne, since both were classified under Islam, while Syriac Ortodoks(Assyrians), Chaldean, Yezidis, Nusayris, or Roman Catholic communities are also not counted as minority groups. Similarly, the Protestants, Baha'is, and Jehovah's Witnesses are also not recognised as minorities.[6]

However, although Islam was part of the Kemalist nationhood project from the beginning, it was removed from the Kemalist nationalism's citizenship definition in 1928, when it was eliminated from the constitution as the religion of the state. After the elimination, a re-imagined Islam appeared as a part of the Kemalist modernisation project, and only a certain interpretation of Islam was permitted in the public sphere.[7]

The radical practices of Kemalist nationalism, which peaked with the adoption of abhorrent racist components in their ideology[8],[8] coincided with the rise of fascism in the 1930s and 1940s, and the dynamics of Germany and Italy.[9] While evaluating the ethnic and sectarian policies of the Kemalist state in this period, it should be highlighted that as feelings of insecurity led the state to promote secularism to devout Muslims, it unexpectedly came to represent reformed or revised-Sunni/Hanafi Islam, in opposition to the religious minorities.[10]

The Alevis also suffered Kemalist oppression during this period. Following the laws that abolished all dervish lodges and zawiyas, including Alevi ones, the use of religious titles that are especially important in the Alevi faith, such as *Dede* and *Seyyid,* were also forbidden.[11] This reform directly affected Alevis' religious and social identities as well as those of other minorities. However, the Kemalist state's most severe oppression towards Alevis was performed during the Dersim massacre which created a traumatic experience in the Alevis' collective memory.[12] In 1937–38, under the order of state authorities, Alevi and Kurdish citizens living in Dersim (today's Tunceli) were shelled by air bombing under the guise of suppressing a rebellion. According to the historical records, around 13,000 civilians were killed by the state as part of this operation.

Following the early Republican years, the second period began with the transition to democracy and the multi-party era in 1946. In this

180   P. KANDEMIR

period, Kemalist nationalist debates were still at the centre of any discussion relating to non-Muslim minorities. Nevertheless, one of the groups that supported the DP, and which had succeeded in bringing together the different segments of society through the concepts of "national will and democracy," was a non-Muslim minority.[13] With the DP, not only did the leaders of minority communities become more visible, but also the voting rates of non-Muslims increased.[14]

During this period, Menderes' DP turned Kemalist nationalism into patriotism, removing strict ethnic references from it.[15] However, tragic events occurred in this period, too. The rising tension between Turkey and Greece in Cyprus resulted in the September 6–7 incidents in 1955 which the Turkish Greek minorities" houses were attacked.[16] Over the following years, the state continued to keep non-Muslim minorities under control. They never provided equal citizenship during this period, and their rights were either ignored or violated under the guidance of the Kemalist nationalism principle. As was effectively summarised by one of my interviewees, the then-Armenian Patriarch Ateşyan, "Normally Republics are beneficial for people, but Turkey's Republic has never been advantageous for minorities."[17] Obviously, as a constant positive reference by Toros Alcan to the Ottoman Empire's *millet system*, Ateşyan was also referring to the better conditions of non-Muslim minorities under the Ottoman Empire, which had been disrupted with secularisation in the Tanzimat years.[18] As might be gathered from this approach, the tension between the Kemalist state and non-Muslim minorities did not end until the early 2000s. Here, it should be noted that the atrocities committed by Greece against the Muslim minority sometimes constituted a justification and sometimes an excuse in determining Turkey's minority policies during the Republican history.

Alevis, who reacted negatively to the state as a consequence of the Dersim incident, became one of the groups that supported the DP during the transition to a multi-party era, as Dersim's election results (Tunceli) indicate.[19] However, this situation later changed not only as a result of this trauma, but also due to *Alevis*' sociological transformation. It should be highlighted that just after the Dersim incident, Kurds and Alevis were displaced by the state in order to reform the social structure of certain areas and control the more politically engaged citizens. However, as an unexpected result of this displacement, they changed their daily lifestyles, fearing they would again become targets. This migration produced more educated and urban elite *Alevis*.[20] In fact, it became possible with the emergence of this new educated class that *Alevi*s would be able to speak out against the discrimination they faced. There had been no serious debate over the rights and legal status of *Alevi*s prior to this date.

Unexpectedly and interestingly, those *Alevi*s became some of the key representatives and advocates of Kemalist secularism later on.[21] The secular citizenship model of Kemalism was welcomed by the *Alevi*s who experienced collective traumas under the dominance of the Ottoman Empire[22] as well as young Kemalist Republic. Koçan and Öncü noted,

> [I]n line with the nationalist ideology of the Turkish Republic, Alevis, especially the Turkish-speaking community, have characterized themselves as maintainers of true Turkish culture, religion, and folklore in the face of the influence of Sunni Islam. This view has been strengthened by the Kemalists who views Anatolian culture as the authentic source of Turkish national identity.[23]

Azak describes this period, which coincided with the post-1960s, as the formation of a pro-*Alevi* Kemalist discourse.[24] The *Alevi*s glorified Atatürk as a respectable and treasured figure, to the point that even a photograph of Atatürk was put next to Ali and his 12 caliphs in places of worship.

Thus, through this adoption, the Alevis became "good and true Muslims,"[25] as well as ideal citizens in the eyes of the state in the following years. The Alevis, who were seen as "egalitarians and progressivists" compared to Sunni Hanafi Muslims, even occasionally faced positive discrimination as "loyal citizens,"[26] which meant they were preferred for seats in the state bureaucracy. Their commitment to secularism made them valuable in the eyes of Kemalists, especially during the 1960s before they started to heterogenise in terms of their ideological preferences.[27]

After the 1960s, the political tendencies of the considered numbers of Alevis', who were living in the suburbs of the cities as a result of mass urbanisation of Turkey, have shifted, as a majority adopted a radical leftist ideological stance.[28] Therefore, Kemalism, which had been blended with socialism, was adopted as a political identity and incorporated into the narrative opposing centre-right conservative parties.[29] Another breaking point for Alevis' political identity took place after 1968. At this time, para-military radical leftist groups were founded and started to carry out their activities "in places densely populated by Alevi Kurds."[30] The result

182 P. KANDEMIR

being, Alevi identity became intertwined with the radical left in the eyes of Turkish society and the state.[31]

During these days, have scarred the Alevis' collective memory.[32] One such incident took place between 17 and 20 April 1978, in Malatya. During the violence in Malatya, leftists in general, and Alevis in particular, were targeted by right-wing Turkish nationalists. Similar events occurred in Kahramanmaras in the same year, between December 19 and 26, when Alevis and members of leftist groups were attacked by right-wingers. During seven days of violent clashes, more than a hundred people died; the majority being Alevis and over 200 houses and shops were vandalised.[33] In 1980, in Corum, similar tragic events happened and these incidents again resulted in the migration of Alevis from one city to another.[34]

Until this time, significantly, tension between the radical right and the radical left in the 1970s was the primary reason for these clashes, and Alevism was viewed as a marginal factor informing the motives of the radical right. However, the Sivas Massacre transformed this situation. In 1993, a group of radicals burned down a hotel earmarked for guests who arrived in the city for a festival to commemorate Pir Sultan Abdal, who holds great importance in the Alevi faith. Two days prior to the incident, locals had protested against the festival, because Aziz Nesin, an author known with his Atheist world view, was to be one of the guests. As Brussen writes, "the festival was protested by a large group of violent right-wing demonstrators, who clearly intended to kill Nesin."[35] In this incident, thirty-six Alevi singers and writers, and a Dutch female anthropology student, were burned to death.[36] This later became one of the main tragedies underlining the Dersim Massacre in the Alevi's collective memory.

Although the *Alevis*' integration into the state was interrupted by the 1980 coup, with the emergence of Turkish-Islam synthesis as the state ideology in the 1980s, the Kemalists succeeded in bringing the Turkish Alevis to the forefront of attention as part of their "attempt to mobilize a secularist oppositional bloc as a counterbalance to Islamic fundamentalism in 1990s."[37] Subsequently, as a result of this vision, state-sponsored Alevi associations became staunch defenders of Kemalist secularism. Thus, this period witnessed a sudden resurgence in Alevi identity.[38] The 1990s witnessed an increasing number of academic works detailing Alevism, and the Alevis' efforts to reformulate their political identity as an antidote to the growing popularity of the Welfare Party. While the rise of identity politics as a factor informing this resurgence cannot be denied, the Kemalist establishment also underhandedly supported Alevi NGOs as a counter political group when seeking to enrich and empower the Kemalist bloc. Indeed, political stance of the Alevi communities became one of the strongest opponents of NOM, and later the JDP.

The JDP's Post-Kemalist Secularism and Non-Muslim Minorities

Turkey's centre-right tradition, particularly DP and ANAP, has always been inconsistent with the Kemalism's ethnic nationalism principle. As a follower of this tradition, the JDP did not use the ethnic or religious identities of minorities to marginalise them in society but rather determined a position similar to other centre-right liberal parties. This approach explains why non-Muslim minorities were not antagonistic to the JDP, contrary to what happened between Kemalists and minorities during the entire Republican history.

When the JDP came to power in 2002, the reforms carried out to improve the situation for minorities started with the publication of reports prepared as a result of workshops held in 2003–2004. In this report prepared by the PM's Advisory Council for Human Rights,[39] a "democratic, liberal and a pluralist model" was proposed.[40] In this context, as a first step, the secondary commission, which was founded in 1962 and strengthened the idea of "minorities as a threat to national security" with representatives from the Turkish Intelligence Service, the General Staff, and the National Security Council, was closed. This step, which was taken prior to the introduction of legal regulations, had symbolic meaning.

Subsequently, the JDP initiated one of the most radical moves to construct a new formulation of citizenship, as an alternative to Kemalism's ideal citizens. When the components of being an ideal citizen, whether Turkish, Sunni Muslim, Kemalist, or laic, are considered, it becomes apparent that this new formulation clearly relates to the emergence of a Post-Kemalist approach. In this sense, by "constructing a new republican citizen model devoid of former prejudices,"[41] the JDP brought about a new concept to start a new discussion parallel to secularism: supra-identity. The supra-identity discussion proposed by the JDP was based on changes in the definition of citizenship, from "being Turk(Turkluk)" to "being from Turkey (Türkiyelilik)." The JDP's new citizenship proposal

184   P. KANDEMIR

was arguably more inclusive since it did not make any reference to ethnic or religious identity.

This discussion on identity created tensions in politics. Deniz Baykal, then the leader of the RPP, reacted to Erdoğan's a new citizenship proposal stating, "You cannot play with my Turkishness."[42] Therefore, due to the overwhelming reactions of the Kemalists and nationalist politicians, this discussion became a public sensation from 2007, when Erdoğan first mentioned it. The discussion relating to "being Turk" also found a place in the 27 April e-memorandum.[43] In this declaration, released as a warning against the JDP government by the Turkish military, it was noted "whoever is contradicting with " *Ne mutlu Türküm diyene*" (How happy is the one who says I am a Turk)[44] philosophy is the enemy of the Republic."[45] However, when the JDP was not shut down in 2008 in the Constitutional Court's closure case, this warning could no longer carry weight. With the 2013 Democratisation Package, the student oath, which had been read compulsorily in the mornings by students since 1932, starting with "I am a Turk, honest, and hardworking" and ending with "my existence shall be dedicated to the Turkish existence. How happy is the one who says; I am a Turk!" was removed by the JDP government. This step had a symbolic meaning for the Kurdish community. As the JDP's reforms to solve Kurdish issue under the name of Reconciliation Proccess (National Unity and Fraternity) in 2009 and later Democratisattion Package in 2013 is considered, it becomes more understandable why the RPP harshly reacted these changes.

Here one should not forget that while Kemalists reacted negatively to Erdoğan's new citizenship framework, the ethnic and religious minorities welcomed it,[46] allowing the JDP to strengthen "the ideological coalition of different forces and extended a hand of cooperation to the Armenian, Greek, and Jewish communities."[47] Although there are several indications that the non-Muslim minorities, mostly Armenians, had already tended to support the JDP during different periods, when one reconsiders the population of non-Muslim communities and their share of the vote, it becomes apparent that the JDP's main purpose was not to target the votes of religious minorities per se. Instead, the JDP has always been "more interested in constructing a symbolic alliance with marginalized communities."[48]

During the reform period, the JDP frequently faced criticism from oppositional voices, especially pro-Turkish MHP.[49] MHP's reactions show the perspective of nationalist voters on these reforms.[50] It is evident that the MHP considers settling the issue of the minorities as a bargaining chip for the party vis-à-vis foreign powers. Such an approach was historically adopted by the Kemalist state. The JDP, which did not pursue this policy, received criticism from the MHP.[51] When we consider the MHP had been the closest ally of the JDP, the slowdown in JDP reformative policies towards minorities, especially after 2015, becomes more understandable.

The following section evaluates the problems that the non-Muslim minorities faced in Turkey, and the JDP's response to them thematically without applying a chronological order.

Property Acquisition
One of the demands voiced by the non-Muslim minorities related to being able to acquire property. After the 1936 Declaration, which prevented minorities from acquiring new properties, a new arrangement was made in the nationalist atmosphere (due to the problem of Cyprus in 1974), to transfer all undocumented properties belonging to minority groups to the General Directorate of Foundations or the public purse.[52] According to a report that evaluates religious freedom in Turkey, this was because "Turkey cannot tolerate the notion of legal personality based solely on religious identity, as it would undermine the country's secular system."[53]

Regarding this problem, in 2003, the JDP initially enabled 160 community foundations to acquire properties to meet their needs and later lifted the bureaucratic difficulties on documenting current premises as a step in the accession process to the EU.[54] "As regards to property rights, out of 2,234 applications for registration of property in line with the January 2003 Regulation, 287 were approved."[55] In 2008, with a vital change, legal obstacles to the reinstatement of the properties of minorities were officially lifted. This alteration was vetoed and returned to the parliament by the President Sezer. He finally signed the law that re-circulated in parliament.[56] After that, either several properties were returned to minority foundations, or financial compensation was paid when return was not possible.[57] With another legal arrangement in 2011, it also became possible for minorities to register their names with acquired properties.[58] Thus, "more than 1,000 properties – valued at more than 2.5 billion Turkish Lira (1 billion U.S. Dollars) – had been returned or compensated for between 2003 and 2014 (...)."[59] When referring to the

186   P. KANDEMIR

rights bestowed by this regulation, the Armenian Patriarch Ateşyan identified it as an important step in ensuring freedom of religion. He says, "we could not even repair the churches then, but now we can."[60] Changing state policies towards places of worship not only for Sunni Muslims but also for non-Muslims exemplify the religion-friendly approach of post-Kemalist secularism. This state of affairs is one of the main differences between Kemalist and post-Kemalist secularisms.

Changing the Perspective Towards Non-Muslims
Laki Vingas, former elected representative of the Non-Muslim Foundations in Turkey and Council Member of the General Directorate of Foundations in Ankara, defines the transformation during the JDP era regarding minority rights as "the process of de-marginalisation of the non-Muslim minorities in Turkey and their return to the foreground of social life in the context of booming modern Turkish society."[61] Indeed, since the foundation of the Turkish Republic, the principal demand from non-Muslim minority groups has been equal citizenship.

By becoming aware that equal citizenship requires greater legal, technical, and practical changes, Ateşyan, and most minority representatives, highlight the priority and urgency of the removal of this form of discrimination in everyday practice.[62] In this regard, one of the first reforms demolishing the alienation of non-Muslim minorities was the removal of the religion section on national identity cards. People who belonged to religious communities other than Greek, Armenian, Christian, or Jewish were defined as other religions; a practice ended in 2006. Another reform was implemented during this period, as Ateşyan notes: "the freedom of changing the religion (on the identity card) was formerly ruled by the court. Now if you go to the registry office and ask them to change your religion, they do it."[63] He mentions individual resistance from some low-level bureaucrats to these reforms, stating that these issues were sorted out after being reported to the government; but slight discrimination and pressure remained in smaller cities.[64]

Another aspect worth mentioning here is that the curriculum was revised to transform perspectives; while previously it was picturing non-Muslim minorities as an internal enemy and a security threat, this language was totally removed from the curriculum. Additionally, during the rewriting of Religious culture and Ethics course, other religions and their history also added to the schoolbooks of this course. The course now covers references to various religions, which is regarded as a positive development by minorities.[65] One should understand this is a considerable improvement when the sacralisation of being ethnically Turk and religiously Muslim is considered.

Additionally, steps such as starting to broadcast in Armenian on a radio channel, Radio Voice of Turkey, for the public broadcaster TRT, and establishment of the first-ever Armenian TV channel founded with the support of TRT could also be seen as "efforts to integrate non-Muslim communities into the public sphere."[66] Comprehending this change is indeed important to understand the fundamental principles underpinning post-Kemalist Turkey.

To attendance of high-level state officials and politicians to the non-Muslim minorities events or high-level visits to minority institutions or places of worship have also been appreciated by the minorities due to their importance in declining the social tension. In this regard, the JDP was indeed very active making these kinds of visits. This also helped to trigger the change in the mindsets and decline in the preconceptions of both sides. The transformation at the level of state and society is recognised in the majority of international reports.[67]

In my interview with Kenan Gurdal, then head of Syriac Ortodox *Vakf*, he states that when he was a child he used to watch Turkish movies. Like his fellows, he applauded when someone from his own religious group was killed. Only later, when he grew older did he understand the ideology behind these films. He added that the underlying message that "Muslims are the only heroes" disturbed him.[68] Toros Alcan similarly states, "Although I am a Christian, I hated the Greeks when I was a child. They were always depicted in the movies as bad people who burn the villages. If you consider the 70 s, it was always like this."[69] Ateşyan, who is an Armenian from Diyarbakir, explains that in those days, "We did not speak in Armenian; the youth could not wear the cross, they could not show it. Back then, they were troubled days."[70] Additionally, Markar Esayan, another Armenian intellectual and JDP MP, highlights a similar concern in present-day Turkey. He expresses irritation towards the use of "non-Muslim" or "infidel" words, which are commonplace in daily life.[71]

Considering Kemalist policies, it is apparent that secularism, as well as nationalism, are equally responsible for this discriminatory approach. In this sense, when non-Muslim minorities examine the reasons for positive changes in their lives, some refer to the transformation of secularism:

188   P. KANDEMIR

Interreligious communication has started in the era of this government. We were not invited to *Iftaar*s in Ramadan. Now, we are attending these fast-breaking dinners every few days of the week. We are talking to each other. We were not invited even once before the rule of the JDP; we were despised; we did not exist.[72]

All this indicates that there is a remarkable change not only state's approach towards minorities but also Muslim citizens' approach to the "others" of the country.

Security and Vulnerability of the Minorities
Ensuring the safety of minorities is still a problem in Turkey.[73] One of the most tragic events in the history of the Turkish Republic was the 2007 assassination of Hrant Dink, the editor in chief of Agos, an Armenian newspaper. At the time he was facing trial for his alleged transgression of Article 301 of the Constitution.[74] Many intellectuals and public figures, including Nobel Prize winner and Turkish writer Orhan Pamuk, were tried due to the aforementioned article, which forbade degrading "Turkishness." The JDP amended the article in 2008,[75] as it had been used to oppressively to manipulate the opinion of the Turkish public towards minorities.

The years between 2006 and 2007 had witnessed several attacks on non-Muslim minorities. The majority of these attacks have been mentioned in international reports,[76] which also cite the government's long-term commitment to protect religious minorities, including the Armenians and Jews.[77] Although the murder of Hrant Dink, which was carried out by 17-year-old Ogun Samasti in January 2007, was first considered an ultra-nationalist attack, the investigation later connected the murder to an Ergenekon terrorist organisation and later the FETO/Gülenists.[78]

Ivo Molinas, the editor-in-chief of newspaper *Şalom*, a publication for the Jewish community in Turkey, observes that hate speeches towards the Jewish people presented on pro-government television channels deeply harm the community. Nevertheless, he also references Erdoğan's personal commitment to prevent far-right attacks on the Jewish community following incidents triggered by the Palestine and Israel conflict.[79]

The fact that no verbal or physical attacks have taken place against non-Muslim minorities in recent years is not only a sign of the depletion of the deep state's operational power in Turkey, it also proves that the prejudice against minorities is over. In this regard, one should remember that Hrant Dink's assassination generated a considerable reaction within society, and thousands of people demonstrated while carrying banners stating, "We are All Armenians." Arguably, this was the first time in Turkish history that people from different backgrounds united to oppose violent acts targeting *the other*. The demonstration became a solidarity drive in favour of minority groups,[80] providing clear evidence of a change in societal perspective. Stopping the ostracisation of non-Muslims in Turkey also indicates the end of the dominance of Kemalist nationalism and Kemalist secularism in Turkey.

Educational Demands

Although the Lausanne Treaty provides non-Muslim minorities with the right to establish schools, manage them, and teach their mother tongues and religions, multiple problems remain in terms of its implementation. When examining the systems at these schools, some remarkable characteristics emerge in the structure compared to public schools' system. First, the minority schools attached to the Ministry of National Education through the law on the unity of education have been kept under strict supervision. Second, minority schools are exempt from the religious culture and ethics course, which is compulsory in the curriculum of national education. Third, the medium of instruction in minority schools is Turkish.

During the JDP years, minority communities welcomed the abolition of the obligation to have a Turkish vice-principal,[81] a former state control mechanism.[82] While a vice-principal, authorised with greater power than the principal, was assigned by the MEB without input from the school, the obligation of engaging in a school's input was imposed with an amendment in 2010.[83] In 2015, the obligation of submitting school enrolment registers was abolished as requested by the minorities.[84] Additionally, authorising minority languages to be taught via language courses, and opening up professorships at universities to engage in research on the history of non-Muslim minority groups, is further JDP reforms.

With respect to opening up new schools, Alcan states that for Armenians there are now twelve primary and secondary schools, and five high schools, which are all remnants from the Ottoman Empire. He observes, "We do not need to increase this number now, but if we do, we can increase."[85] However, the situation is not the same for the Syriac Ortodox community. Despite being the second-largest non-Muslim

190   P. KANDEMIR

group in Turkey after Armenians, Syriac Ortodoxs have encountered many problems, as they were not officially granted minority status in the Lausanne Treaty. They do not have the right to open schools; as an option, they mostly prefer Armenian schools. However, due to sectarian differences, this is not an ideal solution for Syriac Ortodoxs. The first exception they encountered in the context of education was made during the JDP era. For the first time in Republican history, a kindergarten was opened in *Yeşilköy* in 2014. Syriac Ortodox children found a chance to receive Assyrian education at this school.[86]

Despite being on the JDP's agenda, the reopening of the Halki Seminary, another educational demand, has not yet occurred, although it was presented by the EU almost as a prerequisite for the accession process. In response to this demand, the government has frequently mentioned the issue of reciprocity. This has become a topic in publications that discuss the freedom of religion in Turkey: "The Armenian Orthodox community, which is Turkey's largest non-Muslim religious minority, also lacks a seminary in Turkey to educate its clerics and today only has 26 priests."[87] Although this issue does not reflect the JDP's secularism understanding due to its exceptional character as a politicised case, it still contradicts the JDP's minority policy, which rejects any kind of reciprocity in terms of human rights.

Worship Issues
One of the demands made by the Greek Orthodox Church was permission to use the title of ecumenical for the Fener Greek Patriarch.[88] During this period, some steps have been taken to improve the internal functioning of the Patriarchate. The rule requiring only Turkish bishops take up the Patriarchate in İstanbul has been disregarded. In 2004, the Patriarch's assignment of six non-Turkish metropolitans was unsanctioned. Other options have included providing the Turkish citizenship to the archbishop, and allowing Patriarchate personnel to receive an annual work permit without the stringent rules usually applied to entering and exiting the country.[89] Concerning the election of the Armenian Patriarch, in 2019, the Constitutional Court issued a historic decision ruling that the state or the bureaucracy cannot intervene in the Armenian Church's internal affairs[90]; this was also a first in Turkey's history.

In context of worship issues, many other symbolic steps have also been taken; the restoration of the Iron Church in İstanbul, the opening of which was attended by President Erdoğan and Prime Minister Binali

Yıldırım is considered one of those steps. Furthermore, the restoration and opening of the Grand Synagogue in Edirne, which is the biggest synagogue in Europe, holds further symbolic meaning. For the first time in forty-one years, a marriage ceremony was held in the Grand Synagogue in 2018.[91] Similarly, the Armenian Church Akdamar, located in the eastern part of Turkey in the city of Van, witnessed a remarkable moment upon opening its doors to hundreds of Armenian visitors.

Furthermore, in August 2019, Erdoğan attended the opening ceremony for the first Syriac Ortodox Church in Turkish history.[92] Yusuf Çetin, the Patriarchal Vicar of the Syriac Orthodox Church in Istanbul, Ankara and Izmir, explained the process as follows during my interview with him:

> We conveyed our request to build a church to Mr. Egemen Bağış, the then-Minister for EU Affairs during our mutual visits; then, he passed the matter to President Recep Tayyip Erdoğan, the then-Prime Minister. Upon the directive received from the President, Istanbul Metropolitan Municipality allocated us an empty plot of land in Istanbul Yeşilköy for the construction of the first church to be built from the ground up in the history of the Republic. Thus, it was the first time in the history of the Republic that an Syriac Ortodox Church was allowed to be built from the ground up.[93]

Lastly, although Erdoğan promised to return the Mor Gabriel Monastery, the oldest surviving Syriac Orthodox monastery in the world, to Syriac Ortodox, this decision has faced some legal obstacles. The European Human Rights court rejected the Assyrians' application to take ownership of it. When reviewing these developments within their historical context, the importance of each of these steps is apparent to understand the codes of Post-Kemalist secularism. These radical changes almost all of them are the first in Republican history, indicates that JDP's religion-friendly approach was not only applied for Muslim majority, but also for other religious groups. However, it is crucial to note that while Kemalists were trying to decline the power of religion in public sphere, today there is an efforts from the JDP side to increase power and prestige of religious institutions in the public sphere if not to increase religiosity within the society.

192   P. KANDEMIR

Demands for Representation in Politics and Bureaucracy
Following the 1960 coup d'état, while the political parties represented various spectrum of political view, few of the political parties had a non-Muslim MP in parliament. Prior to this time, they had been involved in politics as independent politicians until the multi-party era in 1946. They then began to participate in the political arena with the establishment of the DP after 1945. Between 1950 and 1960, while the Democrats had 10 MPs from Armenian, Christian, and Jewish minorities, the RPP had none.[94]

Later, another centre-right political party, Özal's ANAP, attempted to bring them back into politics. Although this attempt initially failed, after a long time, Cefi Josed Kamhi, the first Jewish MP, became deputy of another centre-right liberal party (DYP) between 1996 and 1999.[95] Subsequently, Syriac Ortodox MP Erol Dora was assigned from the HDP in the 24th, 25th, and 26th governments (2011–2018), Armenian deputy Markar Esayan was chosen by the JDP in the 25th, 26th, and 27th Terms of Parliament (2015–present), and Armenian Selina Dogan represented the RPP in the 25th, and 26th governments (2015–2018). Finally, Armenian Garo Paylan and Yezidi Feleknas Uca were selected as deputies from the HDP in the 25th, 26th, and 27th governments (2015–present). An initiative begun in 2015 enabled the assignment of more than one non-Muslim candidate for the first time since 1964.[96] It is noteworthy that, although the first Armenian MP entered parliament through the JDP in 2015, Erdoğan also invited other prominent Armenian intellectuals, including Hrant Dink, to join the party in 2002.[97] Lastly, it is important to note that as a first in Turkish Republican history, an Armenian who studied in one of the Armenian schools in Turkey was appointed a district governor by the state in October 2021.[98] There is no doubt, this is a breaking point and has a great symbolic meaning in state's relations with non-Muslim minorities.

As this development shows, the rising visibility of non-Muslims in politics is one of the biggest steps proving the emergence of Post-Kemalist secularism in Turkey. The increase in representation of non-Muslim in active politics shows while the integration of these communities to the social and political issues rising, their otherisation is also fading away in the new Turkey. These developments prove the success of the new citizenship proposal introduced by the JDP.

Public Apologies for Past Grievances

For the first time in the history of the Republic, a step was taken to address the events of 1915, shattering one of the most important taboos in Turkey. On April 24, 2014, Erdoğan published a letter of condolence to the Armenians, an act repeated in the following years. The letter was published in nine different languages in 2014 and had an impact inside and outside of the country. Also, at a ceremony held in the Armenian Patriarchate in 2018, Erdoğan's message was read aloud.[99] In his message, Erdoğan repeated a vow that he had made to minority groups since 2002, "No matter what, we will not allow a single citizen to be otherised, to be treated differently because of their beliefs, religion, and disposition."[100] Following this, several memorial ceremonies were organised in Turkey without any interference.[101] This was a radical development for Turkey, where even a conference on historical events pertaining to 1915 was harshly reacted to in 2005.[102] Since then, this conference has been held annually. These developments also represent an indication that tensions between the non-Muslim minorities and the post-Kemalist secular state have decreased which has found a chance to discuss historical issues without any oppression.

JDP's Post-Kemalist Secularism and the Alevis

Alevism is considered a heterodox sect[103] under Islam by the Turkish Sunni religious authorities; some even claims, "It is a specific interpretation of Islam —or even 'true Islam'."[104] On the other hand, there are additional approaches that define *Alevism* as a mixture of other beliefs, such as Christianity and Zoroastrianism, or even a "syncretic heterodox branch of Islam."[105] There are also those who argue that *Alevism* is not a religious belief, but rather a culture and philosophy specific to Anatolia.[106] Some consider it "a culture, a way of life characterised by critical-mindedness."[107] Another view is that it is a branch of Shi'ism.[108] As might be understood from the variety of different perspectives, it is challenging to find a mutually agreeable definition and framework for *Alevism*.[109]

As claimed by Koçan and Öncü, "while certain sets of traditions, rules and symbols shape the collective mind of *Alevi* communities, the social relations, feelings, thoughts and behaviour practised are multiple and complex."[110] That is, Turkey's Alevis' religious practices differ from Sunni ones. Unlike Sunni Muslims, they do not use mosques as a place of worship[111] and fulfil the five pillars of Islam.[112] The inherited title used by Alevi leaders is *Dede* for man and *Ana* for woman. Alevis, who mainly live in Syria, Iran, and Turkey, do not acknowledge the successor three Caliphs in Islam: Ebubekir, Ömer, and Osman. They believe Ali was the real heir of Prophet Muhammad, and was denied his right to become the Caliph. In this sense, there is one thing that everybody agrees on: Alevism means a follower and lover of Ali. Thus, the most important feature of Alevism is the glorification of, and devotion for the fourth Caliph, Ali, cousin and husband of the Prophet Muhammad's daughter.

Alevis are very fragmented, not only with regard to their approach towards the practising of their faith but also in terms of their ethnicity. According to a report conducted by Konda for Milliyet newspaper, 43% of Alevis are Turkish, 42% are Kurdish, 7% are Arab, and the rest are from other ethnic backgrounds.[113] It should be noted that of all the ethno-religious identities in Turkey, Alevi Kurds have always been the most excluded community among ethno-religious identities in Turkey. While one-third of Alevis live in İstanbul, the remaining two-thirds are mostly located in other cities in Anatolia such as Bingol, Maras, Tokat, Corum, Tunceli, Elazıg, and Malatya. Indeed, the study findings also prove that Alevis are more mobile than other groups living in Turkey. According to the actual ratio, six out of ten Alevis live away from their birthplace, indicating that Alevis are one of the communities in Anatolia that emigrates the most.[114] The total number of Alevis in Turkey is unclear because no census has tracked ethnic and religious identity in Turkey since 1965.[115] Nevertheless, according to a poll by Mazlumder in 2010, the number of people claiming to be Alevi-Shia is only 5.7%.[116] Two surveys conducted by Ali Çarkoğlu and Binnaz Toprak, and prepared for TESEV in 2000[117] and 2006,[118] achieved similar figures of 3.9 and 6.1%, respectively. The reason for the different figures appears to be that Alevis do not express their identity openly, and some in fact deliberately conceal their identity.[119] This is called *Taqiyya* (dissimulation) and has been referred to in many of the academic works relating to this issue.[120]

When we examine the state's legal ties with religious identities, it is apparent that the situation is different for non-Muslims and Alevis. While the Directorate of Religious Affairs is an institution that Sunni Muslims is associated with, the General Directorate for Foundations (Vakıflar Genel Müdürlüğü) regulates all activities engaged in by non-Muslim religious groups. Since the Alevis are considered a sect under Islam by the state authorities, they come under the auspices of the *Diyanet*, as do other

Muslim sects. No other religious groups in Turkey, including Sunni Muslims, hold a separate legal status. Under the strict secular system, there is no application of religious law, including within civil law, in Turkey. For example, it is forbidden for Muslim groups to have a religious marriage ceremony before their official state wedding or it was formerly not possible for Muslim communities-such as non-Muslim communities, to acquire properties; even if citizens build a mosque, the state owned the property. In addition, the sermons read by Imams after the Friday prayers in mosques are determined by the state's central system; Imams could not individually determine the content of the sermon, which is still survived.[121] Kemalist reforms also prohibited Muslims and minorities from wearing religious clothes outside of religious institutions. The only exceptions to this rule are the President of the Religious Affairs and leaders of religious minorities. These kinds of rules were likewise applied to *Alevis* during the Republican history.

Politically, while the Turkish *Alevis* mainly support the RPP, the Kurdish Alevis have either largely voted for the radical left or the pro-Kurdish HDP in recent years. When asked *Alevis* why they do not support the JDP, almost all mentioned the "RPP is their party since they were born."[122] It is apparent that the *Alevis*' religious identity and ideological preferences directly impact their voting behaviour. Research on the voting behaviour of *Alevis* and Sunni Zazas[123] reveals that while Sunni Zazas votes for the JDP, *Alevi* Zazas have not supported the JDP in any election or referendum. This indicates the main determinant of the voting behaviour of Alevis is not ethnic, but rather sectarian.[124] The JDP receives the lowest number of votes in every election in Tunceli, originally Dersim, in where the *Alevi* population is the majority. The RPP, on the other hand, i.e. the current political representatives of Kemalism in Turkey, receive a very high margin in every election there.[125]

Alevis have exemplified some of the harshest opposition against the JDP since the beginning.[126] According to Konda's survey conducted in 2017, only 5% of JDP votes come from Alevis.[127] The reason for their support of the left and Kemalism was discussed previously; here then, one should instead question the motivations behind their oppositional stance against the JDP. First of all, the *Alevis*' collective memory cautions them against trusting pious Sunni Muslims, especially those engaged in politics as part of a conservative or Islamist political party.[128] This is to say that the *Alevis* consider the rise of the JDP as an existential threat to their lifestyle.[129] Secondly, *Alevis* have very strong ties with Kemalism—having

196   P. KANDEMIR

been identified as one of the most loyal groups to the Kemalist secularism principle. Since the beginning, all the anti-Kemalist reforms made by the JDP were perceived negatively by the *Alevi* community, and defined as "desecularisation."[130] Due to this reason, there is a clearly recognisable standoff between the *Alevi* community and the JDP.[131] Finally, the start of Kemal Kılıçdaroğlu's leadership in RPP, who takes his family roots from a *Dede* family from Dersim, *Alevi*s became even closer to RPP. This change generated a de facto conclusion in terms of their political preferences.[132]

In spite of this tension since the beginning, the JDP government initiated first ever and the most comprehensive political dialogue process to solve the problems that the *Alevi*s face in 2007. It indeed represented the first attempt in the history of the Turkish Republic to discuss the Alevis' issues officially at the highest state level. Irrespective of the outcome, the simple fact that the problems of the *Alevi* community, which had accumulated over tens of years as a result of neglect, were officially handled at the highest level represents substantial progress. During this period, 63.3% of society supported the JDP's mandate to resolve the *Alevi* issue.[133] When one considers that in public surveys only 7.7% of Turkish society mentions "*Alevi*s" when asked who has been subjected to both state intervention and social pressure on various occasions,[134] it is clear that this issue was added to Turkish political agenda just after the JDP's initiative. While it was not an issue that concern the general public as might be understood from aforementioned public pool, it evolved into a public debate. However, it is crucial to understand that the fact that the society ignores this issue does not diminish the importance of it; this was what the JDP realised and decided to take a step.

JDP's initiation did not completed at the time; but it still gives signs for the new initiations. According to JDP's Mahir Unal, "the social crisis and interventions in this period have delayed some reforms that require a more stable (political) climate."[135] On the other hand, HDP MP Hişyar Özsoy claims that

> When factors such as the JDP's populist structure (indexing everything to elections and votes), resistance from the state (structures such as Ergenekon, Sledgehammer, Gülenists, nationalists, Eurasians), nationalist alliances established in the fight with the Gülen community, and the decline in relations with the European Union are combined; like the Kurdish Opening, the Alevi initiative was a dream.[136]

Additional to this point, both sides, who are already prejudiced against each other, were both negatively affected by the interventions of bias elements within themselves. Firstly, Alevis' latent mistrust and historical traumas not only under Ottoman Empire but also under young Turkish Republic did not allow them to develop a healthy relationship with the JDP or permit reconciliation with the Sunni conservative Muslims. This has been undermined the process of reconciliation and following efforts even after this time, making the considerable number of Alevi representatives reluctant to participate in negotiations. In other words, the political integration of considerable number of Alevi representatives with RPP and HDP had a negative effect to create a healthy process. In turn, casting doubt over the government's efforts and constantly inferring "malicious" intent took its toll on the motivations of the JDP.[137] An example of this-in the following years, might be the first attack on the then Deputy Prime Minister Bekir Bozdag at an event he attended in 2013. While the protestors unwelcomed him by saying, "Why did you come," they shouted, "We are the soldiers of Mustafa Kemal"—the famous slogan of Kemalists.[138] Years after, Erdogan spoke on a gathering where he met with minorities from different groups and expressed how disappointed he was by this attack.

Furthermore, the disagreements within the Alevi community regarding the Alevis' demands and changing proposals differed from one group to another. This further complicated negotiations between the Alevis and the state. One of the leading Alevi *dedes*, Prof Durmus Boztug, noted this point during my interview with him, claiming that fragmentation within the Alevi community sabotaged the process.[139] This was exacerbated because, contrary to other minority groups, mixed signals were sent by the Alevi community in terms of their demands, and their representatives further complicated things. Such diverging stances were noted in the United States Commission on International religious freedom report, as follows: "Since the Alevi community has varying views on its relation to Islam, ascertaining its collective goals is difficult. For example, some Alevis wish to have closer ties with the *Diyanet*, while others have indicated publicly that the *Diyanet* should be abolished."[140]

However, one should remember here that reconciliation process had faced serious governing issues. It was claimed that the JDP made very serious mistakes during this process.[141] First and foremost, the attempts of JDP politicians' initiatives to define Alevism frustrated the Alevis.[142] This deepened the existing crisis of mutual distrust, inhibiting dialogue

198   P. KANDEMIR

between the two parties. Additionally, the government invited former representatives of the *Diyanet* to the meetings, while some Alevi groups had already rejecting being represented under Islam. This also became one of the prominent discussions of the time in Alevi circles. According to public surveys, the general view of the Alevis towards the *Diyanet* was indeed negative.[143] This was then perceived as the JDP showing a tendency to guide discussion towards a predetermined route.[144] Bülent Arınç stated, during our interview, that he believes the social contract with Alevis should be strictly secular. He believes that involving theological discussions did not contribute to solutions, because for him, "there is no way that the JDP could negotiate with Alevis using any semblance of religious commonality, and that it would be the best to reach a political, not a religious, understanding."[145]

When I asked Bülent Arınç about the deadlock around the Alevi issue, he also cited the role of their piousness as a limitation. He said they were hesitant to talk about the Alevi issue in 2005, since they did not know what to say or how to solve the problem as Muslims.[146] On the other hand, Minister of Justice Abdulhamit Gül stated in my interview with him that JDP politicians' piousness had a positive influence on the formulation of the State's relationship with members of other religions and sects. Also, he refers JDP's secularism understanding as the foundation of freedom of religion for everyone in the country.

> Our President and religious politicians are the ones who know best the pain of being the *other* in this country due to their beliefs. Of course, our prerogative in politics and the policies we prefer are fueled by these past sufferings. Secondly, Mr. President defines secularism as the state's equal distance to all religions and beliefs, the freedom of people to be religious or not, and the peaceful coexistence of different beliefs. Thirdly, religious identity necessitates knowing that there is no coercion in religion and religious preference should be based on the free will of man[147]

In spite of reconciliation initiatives with Alevis since the outset, it seems like the Alevis turned into an opposition clique that would never open the door for JDP for dialogue; yet, for Alevis, the JDP is a destroyer of Kemalism and Kemalist secularism. At this stage, one should not forget that for Alevis in Turkey, secularism served to "restrain Sunni groups and prevent them from dominating the public sphere."[148] This is because their collective historical beliefs lead them to "consider the political expression of Sunni-Islam as a threat to their community's security."[149] Their sustained loyalty to Kemalism conceptualises it as a haven. There are several academic works that assess this alliance as contradictory.[150] For Mahir Unal "this stance is a form of retreat as a result of the ruthless attitude of RPP and Kemalism that started with the Dersim."[151]

By going one step further, labelling it as a love affair between the state and Alevis, Zurcher claims that Alevis were comfortable with the state's ignorance of their religious rights, as it "denies all forms of religions in the public sphere."[152] This dynamic, among others, will be elaborated upon in this chapter. In this part of the book, I defend the argument that the emergence of multiple secularism(s) within the post-Kemalist Turkey has created an environment benefitting the different religious identities.

While acknowledging JDP politicians' Sunni conservative identity and the *Diyanet*'s resistance as relevant to the deadlock, I believe the initial crisis between the JDP and the Alevis was political, rather than religious.[153] Although the tension did not prevent the JDP from taking certain steps towards Alevi problems, their initiatives could not be completed due to manipulation from both sides. As final words before discussing tangible examples, Bülent Arınç's words are helpful to understand how the JDP became mired in the Alevi question. According to Arınç, "service politics[154] has understandably never been enough for the Alevi community; in a world where identities are in revival, Alevi demands should have been responded to differently."[155] Speaker of the Grand National Assembly, Mustafa Şentop, confirmed this point by saying that the JDP could not come a long way regarding the Alevi issue. He said: "It is not enough. However, there are great difficulties in this regard. Are there any steps that all of our Alevi citizens can accept and find appropriate together?".[156]

Regarding this discussion, an example given by the former Minister of Education can be useful to understand the JDP's argument. It is interesting to hear that, during Nabi Avcı's tenure, he said they received a request from the Dosteli Alevi Association for a school including the Cemevi, where Alevi children would be educated, and Alevi Bektashi culture would be taught. He says that a place was found, the foundation was laid, and the protocol was signed.[157] But when it came to opening the school, newspaper reports show that both Alevis and the new administration of their ministry were reluctant. This news demonstrated that Alevis objected, saying that they will open the "Alevi Imam Hatips."[158] At this point, it is important to evaluate what were the Alevis' demands and the JDP's response? This will be discussed below thematically.

Recognition of Alevi Identity

In the long list of Alevi grievances, a major complaint is that the state has refused to acknowledge Alevis as a religious identity since the foundation of the Turkish Republic. Alevis are not recognised by official authorities and are not included in the minority groups defined by the Lausanne Treaty. Therefore, there is no institutional recognition in terms of minority laws or local legislation.

When the JDP came to power in 2002, as its first reform it removed the ban on "associations founded on the basis of racial (ethnic), religious, sectarian and regional differences with an intention to create minorities based on the same rights."[159] This legal reform gave Alevis the right to establish their own NGOs. Toktas and Soner claim, this led to the Federation of Alevi–Bektashi Association gaining legal recognition in April 2003, followed by various other associations, including the Cem Foundation and the Pir Sultan Abdal Cultural Association.[160]

As the most significant step regarding the recognition of Alevi identity, one should also revisit the formulation and announcement of the Alevi Opening. Although a formulation of a solution that would satisfy the Alevis has not been found during the JDP era thus far, the Alevi Opening nevertheless can be considered a first step, paving the way for "a gradual de-facto recognition of Alevis' collective identity."[161] As mentioned before this step carried Alevi issue to public sphere as a discussions that all segments of society mandatorily involved as well as the political parties.

The Alevis' Concerns About Compulsory Religious Instruction in Schools

The Religion and Ethics Course is among the compulsory courses taught in primary, secondary, and equivalent schools, which is based on the Sunni sect of Islam and Alevis who do not officially hold minority status have been taking these courses since the beginning. According to Alevis, compulsory religious instruction fails to acknowledge Alevi identity. All the reports published by the EU since 1998 have included criticism about compulsory religious instruction. After 2004, the EU specifically focused on this topic in Turkey's Progress Reports.[162] This problem, which is explained in detail in the education chapter, has been taken by Alevis to both the State Council and the European Court of Human Rights. While some cases ruled in favour of the Alevis, these verdicts did not succeed in altering the *status quo*.[163]

By taking decisions by the ECHR into account, the JDP did revise religious education programmes with three separate arrangements in 2005, 2006, and 2010. These included lectures primarily on Alevism and other interpretations of Islam than Sunnism. Following the period 2011–12, when the content of the Religious Culture and Ethics Knowledge course book was prepared, the views of Alevi, Bektashi, and Caferis were also consulted. In the new curriculum, Alevism is mentioned under the heading, "Mystic interpretations in Islamic thought." In this section, the definition of Alevism, Alevis' belief system, concepts, worship, and prayers are clarified.[164] Further additions have been made to the curriculum regarding references to *Ali* for Alevis. While some of the texts in the curriculum describe the courage and heroism of *Ali*, new chapters on Sufism and Bektashi were also included.[165] The public's support for these amends was limited at 59.6%, exhibiting a lack of consensus in Turkish society regarding the teaching of other religions in school textbooks.[166]

Although the government emphasised cooperating with Alevi associations when preparing textbooks, and even referred to Alevi foundations in the bibliography,some Alevi associations complained about the content.[167] Some express concerns about the insufficiency of changes made.[168]

Yusuf Tekin's response to this was as follows:

> [T]here is no reconciliation even on what has been requested in the cases. There is no single definition on Alevism, which even the Alevi associations have agreed on. The Alevis' representative groups are diverse and high in number. I was an academic during the Alevi dialogue. I have joined the workshops. I also know very well about the differences between views. There is no way to have a book that is reconciled on if we would say 'Write a course book about the Alevis for the Religious Culture and Ethics Knowledge course, and we will teach it in the class.[169]

Former Minister of Education Nabi Avcı also said: "It may be considered insufficient, but as I said, if our motivation was not to teach Sunni children the entire Sunni corpus through this lesson and to make each of them as knowledgeable about these subjects as a *hafiz* and a religious scholar, it was not possible to make such an addition about Alevism for Alevi children as well."[170]

202   P. KANDEMIR

This issue has turned into a crisis between the government and the Alevi representatives. While Alevi organisations initially complained about their lack of representation within religion and ethics course books, they escalated their demands steadily from demanding an option for Alevi children to not attend the course, to advocating for reforms in the curriculum, to finally backing the removal of compulsory religion courses altogether.[171] When one considers this course had been compulsory since the 1980s, made so by the military after 1980 coup for everyone including Alevis, the JDP's continuation cannot be judged Islamist. Furthermore, when one considers that public support for the existence of the course was 82.1%, it seems the Alevis demand did not reflect the demands of the majority of Turkish society.[172] Beyond, having a compulsory course on religion does not challenge the overall philosophy of Post-Kemalist secularism. Yet, the JDP does not represent the same secularism understanding defended by liberals, but rather it has its own stand towards anything related to the religion. It encourages rising visibility of religion in the public sphere and indeed, it does not stand in an equal distance to the religion or irreligion. Its secularism understanding is religion friendly and JDP believes the positive role of religion in the public sphere. Providing religion course in the public school rather than removing it from the curriculum or changing it into optional does not necessarily required by post-secularism understanding.

The Alevis' Request for Recognition of Cemevi as Places of Worship

Alevis have numerous expectations with regard to their places of worship. Some of these include the re-consideration of *Dede* as a spiritual guide, the employment of each *Dede* as a religious servant, and considering *Cemevi* as a place of worship.[173] The *Cemevis*, which is a place of worship, does not benefit from the many opportunities made available to mosques. With some exceptions, water and electricity services are not provided to the *Cemevis*, and while the salaries of *Imams* are paid by the state, Alevi religious leaders, *Dedes* are not. There is a different approach towards the solutions among Alevis as well.

Bülent Arınç highlighted that the JDP should open a dedicated department within the *Diyanet* to tackle Alevi problems, but he added that there are many Alevi groups do not want to be associated with Islam and would prefer to be recognised as a separate religion. Numan Kurtulmuş, Deputy Chairman of the JDP and former Minister of Culture, supported the recognition of Cemevis' status by the state as well. He stated, "The state is already late for this."[174] Another proposal consists of placing the Cemevi under the Ministry of Culture, but this proposal was similarly unacceptable for many Alevis.

On the other hand, there are different voices on this issue within the JDP. In 2012, the request by the RPP's Alevi deputy Hüseyin Aygün to open a *Cemevi* in parliament was rejected for a similar reason. Former Speaker of Turkish Grand Assembly, JDP MP Cemil Çiçek responded to the application by saying that "according to *Diyanet*, Alevism is not a separate religion, it is an Islamic formation and a wealth that emerged in the historical process."[175] He also added, "(...) The places of worship of Islam are the mosques."[176] This is one of the examples of the some of the JDP's politicians' perspective towards Alevism. However, one should remember that Çicek as a former JDP politician was not an Islamist politician and he was one of the strongest figures representing the centre-right in the JDP who previously worked closely with Özal as one of the founders of ANAP.

While some stalemates occurred at the supra-institutional level, there was considerable movement at the level of JDP-run municipalities. For example, the JDP Mayor of Pendik Municipality opened five *Cemevis* in his district. These were funded by the municipality from local budgets and were allocated to the Alevis free of charge.[177] The dramatic increase in the number of *Cemevis* during the JDP era also epitomises the change in situation. When the JDP came to power in 2002, the number of *Cemevis* was 106, and according to a statement by the President of Cem Foundation, the number was around 3500–4000 as of 2018.[178]

Recently, in 2018, Erdoğan pledged to grant legal status to *Cemevis*. In his declaration, Erdoğan made the following promises: "We will take the necessary steps on the basis of democratic consensus in dialogue with the Alevi opinion leaders on various issues such as information-sharing on *Cemevis*, health, education, and establishing research and application centres in universities. At this point, we will grant legal status to traditional knowledge centres and *Cemevis*."[179] Erdoğan's final promise shows the JDP's policy towards Alevis is expected to change in the future. At this stage, one should note that half the Turkish public (52%) supports the state's recognition of *Cemevis* as a place of worship. This indicates that Turkish public opinion is also transforming[180] under the Post-Kemalist secularism atmosphere.

Honouring the Memory of Alevi Victims

As one might recall from the initial discussion, the Dersim massacre (1937–8) had been legitimised by the Kemalists for a long time. Previously, it was even included as a subject of heroism in textbooks adhering to a very nationalist narrative. In 2011, Erdoğan apologised for the Dersim Massacre on behalf of the state.[181] Erdoğan was the first state official to make a public statement referring to this issue in Turkish Republican history, and he also included mention of it in parliament. This held significant symbolic meaning for all segments of society. A further symbolic step was later taken, i.e. transforming the Madımak Hotel, the location where the Sivas Massacre occurred, into a cultural centre. Nevertheless, this choose was not approved by the some *Alevis* since they wanted it to be turned into a Museum rather than a cultural centre.

CONCLUSION

The JDP argues that their secularism approach is not only compatible with democracy and minority rights, but has also made Turkey a place in which religious minority groups can live in dignity. From a critical perspective, this chapter tested the JDP's hypothesis by focusing on tangible reforms carried out since 2002. This in-depth discussion revolved around two separate reactions from two separate groups. While non-Muslim minorities proved relatively satisfied with the changes in their conditions, the other sectarian minority group, the Alevis expressed more displeasure with the change. In my view, two important points exemplify this dynamic.

Therefore, one of the outcomes of this discussion was that the road to reform pursued by the JDP led to the implementation of various positive initiatives for different religious groups, eliminating much of the toxicity that had been inherited during the hard-line Kemalist era. Although the Sunni interpretation of Islam continues to be favoured by the state during the JDP's rule, other religious groups have taken advantage of the JDP's interpretation of secularism, which encourages the right to practice one's religion and recognise positive role of religion in the public sphere. As a result, it is accurate to state that in contemporary Turkey, just as it is true that nobody can prevent Muslim majority to enjoy freedom of religion, it is also true that nobody can prevent non-Muslims or Alevis from practising their faith/religion either.

Another point noted in this chapter is that the JDP's motivation to improve the conditions of ethno-religious minorities was not simply a consequence of the EU accession process. The JDP wanted to realise the dream of a new and modern Turkey and the EU accession process has empowered the roadmap of the JDP to implement several reforms previously considered taboo by Kemalist elites. Accordingly, when the JDP's plans overlapped with the demands of the EU, it took the opportunity to convince Kemalist circles that some sweeping reforms needed to be implemented. Continuation of the reform steps even after the deadlock in EU accession process proves this argument as constantly referred during this chapter. Nevertheless, it is hard to claim that the EU and other international institutions are satisfied with the current conditions of non-Muslim and sectarian minorities in Turkey although they credit the previous reforms.[182]

Ultimately, with regard to the deadlock about the Alevi question, it seems like will be one of the limitations of the JDP's Post-Kemalist secularism that it is still unable to provide a full solution. Moreover, although the JDP was unable to institutionalise a solution to the Alevi problem, JDP's Post-Kemalist secularism allowed for practical solutions. For instance, when the İstanbul Buyuksehir municipality, which has been controlled by the RPP since 2019, can decide that Cemevis receive municipality services just like mosques and other places of worship places (by contradicting with general state policy on this), it is because of the environment that emerged with the post-Kemalist Turkey. If Cemevis can bring a proposal to the City Council to change their status to worship places, this also represents an indication of the emergence of multiple secularisms in Turkey.

In conclusion, as demonstrated by the results of public pools during this book, the JDP's post-Kemalism strategy did not bring less or more religiousness to Turkey. However, it resulted in the diversification of manifestations of religiousness in all sects and religions. Yet, while being anti-religion has been considered as modernism previously, today giving freedom to practice religion all the groups is considered as the genuine modernism. This is the most valuable addition to the modernism understanding by the multiple modernities paradigm since it does not deny religion's impact on society.[183]

NOTES

1. Yilmaz, Gozde. *Minority Rights in Turkey*. New York: Routledge, 2017; Toktas, Sule and Aras, Bülent. "The EU and Minority Rights in Turkey." *Political Science Quarterly* 124.4 (2009): 697–720; Bardakcı, Mehmet, Freyberg-Inan, Annette, Giesel, Christoph and Leisse, Olaf. *Religious Minorities in Turkey*. Basingstoke: Palgrave Macmillan, 2017.
2. Tombuş, H. Ertuğ, and Aygenç, Berfu. "(Post-)Kemalist Secularism in Turkey." *Journal of Balkan and Near Eastern Studies* 19:1(2017): 70–85, p. 78.
3. For a historical analysis of the foundation of the Republic of Turkey, see Ahmad, *The Making of Modern Turkey*.
4. Yıldız, *Ne Mutlu Turkum Diyebilene*, 115.
5. Ustel, *Makbul Vatandasın Peşinde*.
6. "United States Commission on International Religious Freedom (USCIRF) Annual Report 2011." *U.S. Commission on International Religious Freedom*, May 2011, p. 322. Accessed June 23, 2019. https://www.uscirf.gov/sites/default/files/resources/book%20with%20cover%20for%20web.pdf.
7. Idem.
8. For detailed work on conservative nationalism in the Turkish context, see Taskin, Yüksel. "Anti-Komünizm ve Türk Milliyetciliği: Endişe ve Pragmatizm" [Anti-communism and Turkish nationalism: Anxiety and Pragmatism] *Modern Türkiye'de Siyasî Duşunce: Milliyetcilik Vol: 4* [Political Thinking in Modern Turkey: Nationalism], edited by Tanıl Bora and Murat Gultekin, 618–622. İstanbul: İletişim, 2002.
9. See a detailed analysis on the emergence of "turkishness": Zurcher, *Turkey: A Modern History*.
10. Mahçupyan, Etyen. *Türkiye'de Gayrımüslim Cemaatlerin Sorunları ve Vatandaş Olamama Durumu Üzerine* [On the Problems of Non-Muslim Communities in Turkey and the Issue of Not Becoming a Citizen] İstanbul: TESEV Yayınları, 2004.
11. "Tekke ve Zaviyelerle Türbelerin Seddine ve Türbedarlıklar ile birtakım Unvanların Men ve İlgasına dair Kanun." [law on the Closure of Lodge and Islamic Monasteries and Abolition of Some titles and Tomb Keepernes]. *Mevzuat*, [The body of current law], November 11, 1925. Accessed July 27, 2018. http://www.mevzuat.gov.tr/MevzuatMetin/1.3.677.pdf.
12. Gezik, Erdal and Gultekin, Ahmet Kerim. *Kurdish Alevis and the Case of Dersim: Historical and Contemporary Insights*. New York: Lexington Books, 2019.
13. Sunar, "Demokrat Parti ve Populizm," 2082.

6 JDP'S SECULARISM AND TURKEY'S RELIGIOUS ... 207

14. Güven, Dilek. *Cumhuriyet öonemi Azınlık Politikaları Bağlamında 6 - 7 Eylul Olayları [6–7 September Incidents in the Context of Minority Politics in Republican Era]*. İstanbul: Tarih Vakfı Yurt Yayınları, 2005, p. 157.
15. For more details, see Karpat, Kemal. *Türk Demokrasi Tarihi [Turkish Democracy History]*. İstanbul: Afa Yayıncılık, 1996, p. 231.
16. Güven, *Cumhuriyet Donemi Azınlık Politikaları*, 147.
17. Interview with Aram Ateşyan, Acting Armenian Patriarch, İstanbul, on May 27, 2018.
18. See Umut Azak for a detailed discussion: Azak, *Islam*.
19. "1950 Genel Secim Sonucları" [1950 General Election Results]. *Yeni Safak*. Accessed June 23, 2019. https://www.yenisafak.com/secim-1950/secim-sonuclari.
20. Massicard, *Türkiye'den Avrupa'ya*, 52–53.
21. An in-depth analysis on this loyalty see Soner and Toktaş, "Alevis," 419–434; Dressler, Marcus. *Writing Religion: The Making of Turkish Alevi Islam*. New York: Oxford University Press, 2013.
22. Koçan, Gürcan and Öncü, Ahmet. "Citizen Alevi in Turkey: Beyond Confirmation and Denial." *Journal of Historical Sociology*, 17.4 (2004): 464–489.
23. Koçan, and Öncü, "Citizen Alevi in Turkey," 477.
24. Azak, *Islam*, 155.
25. Idem, 139.
26. Idem, 165.
27. Massicard, *Türkiye'den Avrupa'ya*, 60.
28. Idem. Also see Gezik and Gultekin, *Kurdish Alevis and the Case of Dersim*, 17–18.
29. For a detailed analysis on this, see Azak, *Islam*, 155.
30. Guler, Sabır. "The Relationship of Alevi Kurds with Election and Politics," 26.
31. Massicard, *Türkiye'den Avrupa'ya*, 60.
32. Solgun, Cafer. *Alevilerin Kemalizmle İmtihanı ["Alevis" Test with Kemalism]*. İstanbul: Timas Yayınları, 2011.
33. Mazlumder, "Türkiye'de Dini Ayrimcilik Raporu," 318.
34. Idem, 319.
35. van Bruinessen, Martin. "Kurds, Turks and the Alevi revival." *Middle East Reports* 200 (1996): 7–10. Accessed on June 19, 2018. https://www.academia.edu/707541/Kurds_Turks_and_the_Alevi_revival_in_Turkey.
36. Ahmad, *The Making of Modern Turkey*, 290.
37. Koçan and Öncü, "Citizen Alevi in Turkey," 478.
38. van Bruinessen, "Kurds, Turks and the Alevi Revival," 2018.

208 P. KANDEMIR

39. "Azınlık Hakları ve Kültürel Haklar çalısma Grubu Raporu" [Working Group Report on Minority Rights and Cultural Rights]. *Başbakanlık İnsan Hakları Danışma Kurulu [Prime Minister's Office of Advisory Board on Human Rights]* November 1, 2004. Accessed June 23, 2019. https://www.ab.gov.tr/p.php?e=33446.

40. Duran, Hazal. "AK Parti Dönemi Azınlık Politikaları" [Minority Politics During the JDP Era]. In *Ak Parti'nin 15 Yili: Siyaset, [JDP "s 15 years: Politics]*, edited by Nebi Mis and Ali Aslan, 361–378. İstanbul: Seta Yayınları, 2018, p. 362.

41. Ter-Matevosyan, "The Armenian Community and the JDP," 94.

42. "Kimlik atışması" [Identity Dispute]. *Hurriyet*, December 15, 2005. Accessed January 3, 2018. http://www.hurriyet.com.tr/gundem/kim lik-atismasi-3652511.

43. "Askerden Acıklama" [Announcement from the soldiers] *Cumhuriyet*, April 28, 2007. Print.

44. This pharase was first used by Atatürk in his speech for decennial of Republic, later it was added to the student oath, *Andimiz*. For the full transcript see: "Student Oath (Turkey)" Wikipedia, January 7, 2020. Accessed February 26, 2020. https://en.wikipedia.org/wiki/Student_O ath_(Turkey).

45. "Bir eşitlik arayışı: Türkiye'de azınlıklar" [A search for equality: Minorities in Turkey]. *Minority Rights Group International*, September 2007. Accessed July 27, 2018. https://minorityrights.org/wp-content/upl oads/2015/07/MRG_Rep_Turk2007_TURK.pdf.

46. Interview with Aram Ateşyan, İstanbul, on May 27, 2018.

47. Ter-Matevosyan, "The Armenian Community and the JDP," 98.

48. Ter-Matevosyan, "The Armenian Community and the JDP," 99.

49. One example can be Cemil Çiçek's speech in the Parliament on a conference held in Bogazici University on Ottoman Armenians, "Genel Kurul Tutanağı 22. Donem 3. Yasama Yılı 101. Birlesim" [Minutes of General Meeting 22nd Term 3rd Legislative Session 101st Sitting]. *Türkiye Buyuk Millet Meclisi [Grand National Assembly of Turkey]*, May 24, 2005. Accessed July 21, 2018. https://www.tbmm.gov.tr/develop/owa/Tutanak_B_SD.bir lesim_baslangic_yazici?P4=14565&P5=B&page1=18&page2=18.

50. "Genel Kurul Tutanağı 24. Dönem 2. Yasama Yılı 33. Birleşim" [Minutes of General Meeting 24th Term 2nd Legislative Session 33rd Sitting]. *Türkiye Buyuk Millet Meclisi [Grand National Assembly of Turkey]*, December 10, 2011. Accessed July 21, 2018. https://www.tbmm. gov.tr/develop/owa/tutanak_sd.birlesim_baslangic?P4=21065&P5=B& page1=52&page2=52&web_user_id=16563833.

51. Idem. For another example of this sort of stances; Erkan Akcay,

6 JDP'S SECULARISM AND TURKEY'S RELIGIOUS ... 209

MHP MP's speech in the parliament, "İnançlarımıza Yapılan Saldırılara İlişkin" [On the Attack Against Our Belief], *Türkiye Buyuk Millet Meclisi [Grand National Assembly of Turkey]*, July 16, 2014. Accessed July 21, 2018. https://www.tbmm.gov.tr/develop/owa/genel_kurul.cl_getir?pEid=32712.

52. For a detailed analysis of this issue, including perspectives from non-Muslim minorities in Turkey, see Kurban, Dilek and Hatemi, Kezban. *Bir Yabancılaştırma Hikayesi* [A Story of Othering]. İstanbul: TESEV Yayınları, 2009.

53. "USCIRF Annual Report 2007." *U.S. Commission on International Religious Freedom*, May 2007, p. 16. Accessed June 23, 2019. https://www.uscirf.gov/sites/default/files/resources/AR_2007/annualreport2007.pdf.

54. Duran, "AK Parti Dönemi Azınlık Politikaları", 365.

55. "2004 Regular Report on Turkey's Progress Towards Accession." *Commission of the European Communities*, October 6, 2004, p. 44. Accessed June 7, 2018. https://ec.europa.eu/neighbourhood-enl argement/sites/near/files/archives/pdf/key_documents/2004/rr_tr_2004_en.pdf.

56. "5555 sayili kanun" [The Law No. 5555]. *Türkiye Cumhuriyeti Cumhurbaskanlığı [Presidency of The Republic of Turkey]*, November 29, 2006. Accessed July 30, 2018. https://www.tccb.gov.tr/basin-aciklamal ari-ahmet-necdet-sezer/1720/7145/5555-sayili-kanun.

57. "USCIRF Annual Report 2012," p. 203.

58. "5737 sayili vakiflar kanunu" [Law of Foundations nN. 5737]. *Mevzuat [The Body of Current Law]*, February 27, 2008. Accessed July 27, 2018. http://www.mevzuat.gov.tr/MevzuatMetin/1.5.5737.pdf.

59. "USCIRF Annual Report 2016," April 2016, p. 202.

60. Interview with Aram Ateşyan, İstanbul, on May 27, 2018.

61. Vingas, "Non-Muslim Minorities in Modern Turkey." *HürriyetDaily News.*

62. Interview with Aram Ateşyan, İstanbul, on May 27, 2018.

63. Interview with Aram Ateşyan, İstanbul, on May 27, 2018.

64. Idem.

65. For a discussion on these changes see: Müftügil, Ayse. S. "Compulsory Religion Education and Religious Minorities in Turkey." *PhD thesis*, University of Amsterdam, 2011. Accessed July 28, 2018. https://pure.uva.nl/ws/files/1303731/96039_09.pdf.; Also see, "Religion and Schooling in Turkey: The Need for Reform." *Education Reform Initiative* (2005) Accessed July 28, 2018. http://en.egitimreformugiris imi.org/wp-content/uploads/2017/03/ERI.Religion-And-Schooling-In-Turkey_The-Need-For-Reform.pdf.

210   P. KANDEMIR

66. Interview with Ibrahim Eren, Director General of TRT, Ankara, on January 11, 2019.
67. The first report prepared by the European Commission in 1998. See all the reports online: "Turkey Reports Prepared by the European Commission." *Republic of Turkey Ministry of Foreign Affairs, Directorate for EU Affairs*, July 5, 2019. Accessed March 12, 2020. https://www.ab.gov.tr/regular-progress-reports_46224_en.html.
68. Interview with Kenan Gürdal, Deputy Chair of the İstanbul Syriac Ortodox Kadim Foundation, İstanbul, on May 27, 2018.
69. Interview with Toros Alcan, Former representative of Turkish Minority Foundations, İstanbul, on May 25, 2018.
70. Interview with Aram Ateşyan, İstanbul, on May 27, 2018.
71. Interview with Markar Esayan, Armenian intellectual and JDP MP, Ankara on July 15, 2018.
72. Interview with Aram Ateşyan, İstanbul, on May 27, 2018.
73. "Turkey 2016 Report," Brussels, 2016. Accessed February 2, 2021. https://ec.europa.eu/neighbourhood-enlargement/sites/near/files/pdf/key_documents/2016/20161109_report_turkey.pdf.
74. This article stipulates that any person who publicly denigrates the Turkish Nation, the State of the Turkish Republic, or the Grand National Assembly of Turkey and the judicial institutions of the State shall be punished by imprisonment from 6 months to 2 years.
75. "Türk Ceza Kanununda Değisiklik Yapılmasına Dair Kanun" [Law on the Amendment of Turkish Criminal Law]. *Resmi Gazete* [*Official Gazette*], May 8, 2008. Accessed February 2, 2019. www.resmigazete.gov.tr/eskiler/2008/05/20080508-5.htm.
76. "USCIRF Annual Report 2009," p. 208; "USCIRF Annual Report 2007," p. 18.
77. "USCIRF Annual Report 2011," p. 328.
78. "Hrant Dink davasında önemli gelişme! 99 yıl 6 ay hapis cezası" [Important Developments in Hrant Dink Case! Sentence for 99 Years and 6 Months]. *Hurriyet*, July 17, 2019. Accessed January 23, 2020. https://www.hurriyet.com.tr/gundem/hrant-dink-davasinda-one mli-gelisme-99-yil-6-ay-hapis-cezasi-41276763.
79. Interview with Ivo Molinas, editor in chief of Şalom Newspaper, the most reputable Jewish newspaper in Turkey, İstanbul, on May 9, 2018.
80. "Bir eşitlik arayışı: Türkiye'de azınlıklar" [A Search for Equality: Minorities in Turkey]. *Minority Rights Group International*, September 2007, Accessed July 27, 2018. https://minorityrights.org/wp-content/upl oads/2015/07/MRG_Rep_Turk2007_TURK.pdf.
81. Interview with Toros Alcan, İstanbul, on May 25, 2018.
82. "USCIRF Annual Report 2007," p. 18.
83. Duran, "AK Parti Donemi Azinlik Politikalari," 373–374.

6 JDP'S SECULARISM AND TURKEY'S RELIGIOUS ... 211

84. Duran, "AK Parti Donemi Azinlik Politikalari," 372–373.
85. Interview with Toros Alcan, İstanbul, on May 25, 2018.
86. "MEB'den Suryani anaokuluna onay" [Approval from Ministry of Education to Syriac Kindergarten]. *Hurriyet*, September 20, 2014. Accessed August 15, 2019. https://www.hurriyet.com.tr/egitim/meb den-suryani-anaokuluna-onay-27243103.
87. "USCIRF Annual Report 2010," p. 310.
88. Idem.
89. Duran, "AK Parti Donemi Azınlık Politikaları," 371–372.
90. "Türkiye Ermenileri Patrikligi Secimi Yapılması Talebinin Reddedilmesi Nedeniyle Din özgürlüğünün İhlal Edilmesi" [Violation of the Religious Freedom Due to Rejection of the Election Demand of Armenian Patriarchate of Turkey]. *Anayasa*, July 10, 2019. Accessed July 13, 2019. https://www.anayasa.gov.tr/tr/haberler/bireysel-basvuru-basin-duyurulari/Türkiye-ermenileri-patrikligi-secimi-yapilmasi-talebinin-red dedilmesi-nedeniyle-din-ozgurlugunun-ihlal-edilmesi/.
91. "Tarihi sinagogda 41 yıl sonra ilk düğün" [First Wedding in the Historical Synagogue After 41 Years]. *Hurriyet*, May 29, 2016. Accessed July 29, 2018. http://www.hurriyet.com.tr/tarihi-sinagogda-41-yil-sonra-ilk-dugun-37287821.
92. "Cumhurbaskanı Erdoğan Süryani Kilisesi temel atma töreninde konuştu" [President Erdoğan Gave a Speech During the Ground-Breaking Ceremony of Assyrian Church]. *Hurriyet*, August 3, 2019. Accessed August 15, 2019. http://www.hurriyet.com.tr/gundem/cum hurbaskani-Erdoğan-suryani-kilisesi-temel-atma-toreninde-konusuyor-41292483.
93. Interview with Yusuf Çetin, the Patriarchal Vicar of the Syriac Orthodox Church in Istanbul, Ankara and Izmir, Istanbul, May 27, 2018.
94. Onuş, Sinan. "80 yilda 24 gayrimuslim milletvekili" [24 Non-Muslim MP in 80 Years]. *BBC Turkce*, April 20, 2015. Accessed on July 29, 2018. https://www.bbc.com/turkce/haberler/2015/04/150420_secim_gayrimuslim_adaylar.
95. Bali, Rifat N. "Cumhuriyet Doneminde Azinlik Milletvekilleri" [Members of Parliaments from Minority Groups in Republican Era]. *Toplumsal Tarih* 186 (2009): 60–64. Accessed July 29, 2018. http://www.rifatbali.com/images/stories/dokumanlar/cumhuriyet_d oneminde_azinlik_milletvekilleri.pdf.
96. Onus, "80 yilda 24 gayrimuslim milletvekili." *BBC Turkce*.
97. Ter-Matevosyan, "The Armenian Community and the JDP," 99.

212 P. KANDEMIR

98. "Turkiye Ermeni toplumundan bir kisi kaymakam olmaya hak kazandi" [One Person from the Armenian Community of Turkey Was Entitled to Become the District Governor]. AGOS, October 28, 2021. Accessed, January 27, 2022. http://www.agos.com.tr/tr/yazi/26345/turkiye-ermeni-toplumundan-bir-kisi-kaymakam-olmaya-hak-kazandi.

99. For the news, see Armenian newspaper, AGOS: "Erdoğan'dan 1915 icin taziye mesaji" [Condolence from Erdoğan About 1915]. *AGOS*, April 24, 2018. Accessed July 29, 2018. http://www.agos.com.tr/tr/yazi/20539/Erdoğan-dan-1915-icin-taziye-mesaji.

100. "Erdoğan'dan Ermeni Patrikhanesi'nde duzenlenen torene mesaj" [A Massage from Erdoğan to the Ceremony at the Armenian Patriarchate]. *Hurriyet*, April 24, 2018. Accessed July 29, 2018. http://www.hurriyet.com.tr/gundem/Erdoğandan-ermeni-patrik hanesinde-duzenlenen-torene-mesaj-40815152.

101. "24 Nisan'da Sultanahmet ve Şishane'de anma" [Commemoration on April 24 at Sultanahmet and Sishane]. *AGOS*, April 23, 2019. Accessed February 20, 2020. http://www.agos.com.tr/tr/yazi/22349/24-nisan-da-sultanahmet-ve-sishane-de-anma.

102. "Ermeni konferansı Bilgi Üniversitesi'nde başladı" [Armenian Conference Has Started at Bilgi University]. Hurriyet, September 24, 2005. Accessed February 20, 2020. https://www.hurriyet.com.tr/gundem/ermeni-konferansi-bilgi-universitesinde-basladi-352577.

103. An article examines "how the widespread denomination of the Alevi tradition as heterodox Islam was introduced in the academic field in the late nineteenth century" see Karolewski, Janina. "What Is Heterodox About Alevism? The Development of Anti-Alevi Discrimination and Resentment." *Die Welt des Islams*, 48 (2008): 434–456.

104. Massicard, Elise. "Democratisation in Turkey? Insights from the Alevi Issue." In *Turkey's Democratization Process*, edited by C. Rodriguez, A. Avalos, H. Yılmaz, A. I. Planet, 376–390. London: Routledge, 2013.

105. Azak, *Islam;* Shankland, David. *The Alevis in Turkey: The Emergence of a Secular Islamic Tradition*. London: Routledge, 2003.

106. Ecevitoglu, Pınar. "Aleviligi Tanimlamanin Dayanilmaz Siyasal Cazibesi" [Irresistible Political Lure of Identification of Alevism] *Ankara Universitesi SBF Dergisi* 66.3 (2011): 137–156.

107. Massicard, "Democratisation in Turkey?."

108. Oran, *Türkiye'de Azınlıklar*, 54–55.

109. Koçan and Öncü, "Citizen Alevi in Turkey," 464-489; Olson, Tord, Ozdalga, Elizabeth and Raudvere, Catherina. *Alevi Identity: Cultural, Religious and Social Perspectives*. İstanbul: Swedish Research Institute in İstanbul, 1998; Shankland, *The Alevis in Turkey*, 13–33.

110. Koçan and Öncu, "Citizen Alevi in Turkey," 473.

6 JDP'S SECULARISM AND TURKEY'S RELIGIOUS ... 213

111. For a historical background of the emergence of *Cemevi* as the alternative places of worship for Alevis, see Rençber, Fevzi. "Alevi Geleneğinde 'Cem Evinin' Tarihsel Kökeni" [Historical Roots of "Cem Evi" in Alevi Tradition]. *Dinbilimleri Akademik Araştırma Dergisi* 12.3 (2012): 73–86.

112. Five pillars of Islam: Shahadah (reciting the Muslim profession of faith), salat (performing in a prescribed manner five times each day), zakat (paying the alms tax levied to benefit the poor and the needy), sawn (fasting during the month of Ramadan), hajj (pilgrimage to Mecca, if financial and physical conditions permit). See "Pillars of Islam." *Encyclopaedia Britannica* March 13, 2020. Accessed March 20, 2020. https://www.britannica.com/topic/Pillars-of-Islam.

113. Konda and Milliyet. *Toplumsal Yapı Araştırması [Research on Social Structure]*. İstanbul: 2006, p. 27. Available online.

114. For a detailed report on this see Mazlumder, "Türkiye'de Dini Ayrimcilik Raporu," 43.

115. Kaçer, Murat and Yılmaz Bingöl. "AK Parti dönemi Sünni ve Alevi Zazaların seçmen davranışları" [Voter Behaviour of Sunni and Alevi Zazas During the JDP Era]. *Bingol Universitesi Sosyal Bilimler Enstitüsü Dergisi*, 8.15 (2018): 65–87.

116. For a detailed report on this see Mazlumder, "Türkiye'de Dini Ayrımcılık Raporu," 43.

117. Çarkoğlu and Toprak, *Religion, Society and Politics in a Changing Turkey*.

118. Idem.

119. Malumder, "Türkiye'de Dini Ayrimcilik Raporu," 43.

120. Massicard, "Democratisation in Turkey?"; Koçan and Öncü, "Citizen Alevi in Turkey," 474.; Zurcher et al., *The European Union, Turkey and Islam*, 124.

121. "USCIRF Annual Report 2011," p. 317.

122. Gölbaşı, Haydar. "16 Nisan 2017 Referandum Sonuçlarına göre Alevilerin tercihi (Sivas ili örneği)" [The Preference of Alevis according to The Results of the Referendum on 16th April 2017 (The Example of Sivas Province)] *Alevilik-Bektaşilik Araştırmaları Dergisi* 17 (2018): 75–96, pp. 85–86.

123. Zazas are largely located in the eastern part of Turkey, speak the language Zaza and define themselves as ethnic Kurds. Their population is around 3 million.

124. Kacer and Bingol, "AK Parti dönemi Sünni ve Alevi Zazaların seçmen davranışları," 65–87.

125. See the all election results in Tunceli in Turkish Republican history: "Tunceli Secim Sonucları" [Tunceli Election Results] *Yeni*

214   P. KANDEMIR

Safak. Accessed June 23, 2019. https://www.yenisafak.com/yerel-secim-2019/tunceli-ili-secim-sonuclari.
126. "78 percent of Gezi Park protest detainees were Alevis: Report." *HürriyetDaily*, November 25 2013, Accessed on June 23, 2019. https://www.hurriyetdailynews.com/78-percent-of-gezi-park-protest-detainees-were-alevis-report--58496 Also see, Interview with Erdal Dogru in Cafer Solgun's book: Solgun, *Alevilerin Kemalizmle İmtihanı*.
127. See "7 Haziran Sandık ve Secmen Analizi" [7 June: Ballot and Voter Analysis] *Konda Araştırma ve Danışmanlık*, June 18, 2015.
128. Interview with Durmus Boztug, *Alevi Dede* and Former Rector of Munzur University in Tunceli, Ankara, April 12, 2019.
129. Konda's 2017 survey provides tangible results that enrich this discussion, Çelik, Ayşe Betul, Balta, Evren and Paker, Murat. "Yeni Türkiye'nin Yurttaşları: 15 Temmuz Darbe Girişimi Sonrası Siyasi Tutumlar, Değerler ve Duygular" [Citizens of New Turkey: Attitudes, Morals and Emotions after July 15 Coup Attempt]. *Konda Araştırma ve Danışmanlık*, May 2017, p. 48.
130. Çelik et al., "Yeni Türkiye'nin Yurttaşları", 43.
131. Interview with Bülent Arınç, Ankara, on April 12, 2019.
132. This part prepared as an outcome of my interviews on this topic.
133. "Alevi Açılımı" [Alevi Openning]. *Türkiye Gündem Araştırması 2*, İstanbul: GENAR, 2009.
134. Konda, "İnsan Hakları Algısı". [Human Rights Perception] *Konda Barometresi* June 2012.
135. Interview with Mahir Ünal, Ankara, on June 4, 2018.
136. Interiew with Hişyar Özsoy, Ankara, on April 13, 2019.
137. Tugsuz, Nigar "Alevi Açılımı'nın Neresindeyiz" [Where Are We at the Alewi Openning]. *SETA Perspektif 81*, November, 2014.
138. "Basbakan Yardimcisi Bekir Bozdag'a once protesto sonra yumruklu saldiri" [Protest and Then Fist Attack on Deputy PM Bekir Bozdag]. Hurriyet. Accessed June 23, 2019. https://www.hurriyet.com.tr/gundem/basbakan-yardimcisi-bekir-bozdaga-once-protesto-sonra-yumruklu-saldiri-24530724.
139. Interview with Durmus Boztuğ, Ankara, April 12, 2019.
140. "USCIRF Annual Report 2016," p. 203.
141. Interview with Durmus Boztuğ, Ankara, April 12, 2019.
142. Tugsuz, "Alevi Açılımı'nın Neresindeyiz."
143. "Diyanet İşleri Başkanlığı Araştırması," *Konda Araştırma ve Danışmanlık*, p. 5.
144. Bülent Arınç also engages in self-criticism by referring this issue. Interview with Bülent Arınç, Ankara, on April 12, 2019.
145. Interview with Bülent Arınç, Ankara, on April 12, 2019.
146. Idem.

147. Interview with Abdulhamit Gül, Ankara, on April 9, 2019.
148. Soner, Bayram Ali and Toktaş, Şule. "Alevis and Alevism in the Changing Context of Turkish Politics: The Justice and Development Party's Alevi Opening." *Turkish Studies* 12.3 (2011): 419–434, p. 421.
149. Idem, 422.
150. For one example, see, Massicard, Elise. *Türkiye'den Avrupa'ya Alevi Hareketinin Siyasallaşması.* [Politisation of Alevi Movement from Turkey to Europe] translated by Ali Berktay, İstanbul: İletisim Yayınları, 2007. pp. 42–48.
151. Interview with Mahir Ünal, Ankara, on June 4, 2018.
152. Zurcher, Erik Jan. and van der Linden, Hans and Netherlands Scientific Council for Government Policy. *The European Union, Turkey and Islam.* Amsterdam: Amsterdam University Press. 2004, p. 128.
153. There are academic works focusing on the emergence of Alevi identity as an opposition to the JDP, see Yilmaz, Nail and Bayram, Ahmet Kemal. "Taksim Gezi Parkı Olayları ve Bir Muhalefet Ögesi Olarak Aleviler" [Taksim Gezi Park Issues and Alevis as an Element of Opposition]. *Marmara Üniversitesi Siyasal Bilimler Dergisi* 4.1 (2016): 1–21.
154. He means devoloping infrastructure in their villages or opening a university, etc.
155. Interview with Bülent Arınç, Ankara, on April 12, 2019.
156. Interview with Mustafa Şentop, Ankara, on April 19, 2019.
157. Interview with Nabi Avcı, Ankara, on December 14, 2018.
158. "Türkiye'nin ilk 'Alevi lisesine' yönelik tepkiler farklı: Asimilasyon mu kazanım mı?" [Different Reactions to Turkey's First Alewite High School: Asimilation or a Gain?]. *Euronews*, August 9, 2019. Accessed January 15, 2021. Available at: https://tr.euronews.com/2019/08/06/turkiyenin-ilk-alevi-lisesine-yonelik-tepkiler-farkli-asimilasyon-mu-kaz anim-mi.
159. Soner and Toktaş, "Alevis," 422.
160. Idem.
161. Soner and Toktaş, "Alevis," 422–423.
162. "Turkey 2011 Progress Report: Accompanying the Document Communication from the Commission to the European Parliament and the Council Enlargement Strategy and Main Challenges 2011–2012." *Commission Staff Working Paper.* Brussels: Commission of the European Communities, October 12, 2011. Accessed June 7, 2018. https://www.ab.gov.tr/files/AB_Iliskileri/AdaylikSureci/Ilerle meRaporlari/tr_rapport_2011_en.pdf
163. Massicard, "Democratisation in Turkey?."

216   P. KANDEMIR

164. To browse the textbooks for Education on Religious Culture and Moral, see http://www.eba.gov.tr/ekitap?icerik-id=6500 For the sections related with Alevism, see "Alevilik-Bektaşilik" [Alewism-Bektashism]. *Ortaokul Din Kültürü ve Ahlak Bilgisi 7. Sınıf Kitabı*, pp. 135–142. Accessed August 20,2019. http://img.eba.gov.tr/517/762/b9b/7e6/74f/0c4/802/856/b25/634/2ad/67e/3c7/9a0/008/517762b9b7e674f0c4802856b256342ad67e3c79a0008.pdf; "Alevilik-Bektaşilik" [Alewism-Bektashism]. *Ortaokul Din Kültürü ve Ahlak Bilgisi 12. Sınıf Kitabı*, pp. 79–85. Accessed August 20, 2019. http://img.eba.gov.tr/269/462/e76/af0/686/144/214/b1b/dc3/2af/2c5/7d6/fae/392/018/269462e76af0686144214b1bdc32af2c57d6fae392018.pdf.

165. "Ilköğretim Din Kültürü ve ahlak bilgisi dersi," 79–83.

166. Mahçupyan, *Türkiye'ye içeriden bakış*, 18–19.

167. "Turkey 2014 Progress Report: Accompanying the Document Communication from the Commission to the European Parliament, the Council, the European Economic and Social Committee and the Committee of the Regions—Enlargement Strategy and Main Challenges 2014–2015." *Commission Staff Working Paper*, Brussels: Commission of the European Communities, October 8, 2014. Accessed June 7, 2018. https://www.ab.gov.tr/files/IlerlemeRaporlari/2014_progress_report.pdf

168. Gurcan, *The Problems of Religious Education in Turkey*, 9.

169. Interview with Yusuf Tekin, Ankara, on May 12, 2018.

170. Interview with Nabi Avcı, December 14, 2018.

171. "Turkey 2019 Report: Accompanying the document Communication from the Commission to the European Parliament, the Council, the European Economic and Social Committee and the Committee of the Regions—2019 Communication on EU Enlargement Policy" *Commission Staff Working Paper*, Brussels: Commission of the European Communities, May 29, 2019. Accessed June 17, 2019. https://ec.europa.eu/neighbourhood-enlargement/sites/near/files/20190529-Turkey-report.pdf.

172. Mahçupyan, *Türkiye'ye iceriden bakıs*, 18–19.

173. Subası, Necdet. "AKP ve Aleviler, Yol ve Yordam arayısı" [AKP and Alevis, Search for the Right Way Do]. *Finans Politik & Ekonomik Yorumlar* 45.516 (2008): 8–15.

174. Interview with Numan Kurtulmus, Ankara, on April 8, 2019. For his speech on this issue when he was the Minister of Culture see "Bakan Kurtulmus: Aleviler icin Vaatler Bizim icin Sozdur" [A Word for Alevis Is a Promise for Us]. *TC Kultur ve Turizm Bakanlıgı*, June 2018. Accessed June 23, 2019. https://basin.ktb.gov.tr/TR-210811/bakan-kurtulmus-aleviler-icin-vaatler-bizim-icin-sozdur.html.

175. For the details of this discussion see the Parliament website, see "CHP'nin Cemevi sistemine ret" [Rejection to SHP's *Cemevi* System].

TBMM, July 10, 2012. Accessed January 14, 2020. https://www.tbmm.gov.tr/develop/owa/GazeteHaberBaskan.haber_detay?pkayit_no=1423417.

176. Idem.
177. "Ak Partili Belediye 5. Cemevini Açtı" [Municipality that run by JDP opened its fifth Cemevi] *Sabah*, July 7, 2018. Accessed June 23, 2019. https://www.sabah.com.tr/gundem/2018/07/06/ak-partili-belediye-5inci-cemevini-acti.
178. "Cem Vakfı Genel Başkanı Erdoğan Döner: Bizim Alevi sorunumuz ülkemizin beka sorunundan once gelmez" [Erdoğan Doner, The president of Cem Vakfı: Our Alewi issue does no come before the survival problem of our country]. *Anadolu Ajansı*, June 17, 2018. Accessed June 23, 2019. https://www.aa.com.tr/tr/Türkiye/cem-vakfi-genel-baskani-Erdoğan-doner-bizim-alevi-sorunumuz-ulkemizin-beka-sorunundan-once-gelmez/1176981; Oral Calıslar's book on Alevis gives a similar number. Calislar, Oral. *Aleviler. [Alewis]*. İstanbul: Everest Yayınları, 2015.
179. "Cumhurbaşkanlığı Seçimleri ve Genel Secimler Secim Beyannamesi 2018" [Election Manifesto for Presidential Elections and General Elections of 2018] *Ak Parti*, 2018. Accessed June 20, 2019. http://www.akparti.org.tr/media/271931/secim-beyannamesi-2018.pdf.
180. "Diyanet İşleri Başkanlığı Araştırması," *Konda Araştırma ve Danışmanlık*, 7.
181. "Dersim Özrü" [Apology for Dersim]. *Hürriyet*, November 24, 2011 Accessed June 23, 2019. https://www.hurriyet.com.tr/gundem/dersim-ozru-19314519.
182. "Turkey 2019 Report," Brussels, May 29, 2019. Accessed June 17, 2019. https://ec.europa.eu/neighbourhood-enlargement/sites/near/files/20190529-Turkey-report.pdf.
183. Eisenstadt, *Comparative Civilizations*.

CONCLUSION

In spite of the myriad potential designations, this study does affirm that the JDP is a secular political movement comprising economically liberal, culturally conservative, politically pragmatic, democratic, rationalist, and socially moralist aspects. The JDP's relationships with religion and secularism have been shaped and are still being informed by the multiple historical variables and contemporary trends which appear to have successfully been integrated into its identity. From this vantage point, one can argue that the JDP has no single, static, and fixed identity, but rather that its leadership is open and able to absorb contemporary mainstream social demands and cultural values, while also drawing on the glorious past. Due to the multi-layered and multidimensional connections, the JDP has established with both religion and secularism, the Party defines itself as a conservative democrat, centre-right political party, noting that it emerged in a Muslim majority country that had been ruled by oppressive secular elites since its foundation in 1923.

By locating the main criticisms directed towards Kemalist secularism, ethnic nationalism, statist economy, and the civil-military relationship at the centre of its narrative, the JDP represented a new political approach. Once this approach had attracted a broad diverse coalition, the JDP came to power, becoming the founding force in a new Post-Kemalist Turkey. One of the most important aspects of the JDP is that it demolished and transformed many taboos formerly perpetuated by the ruling elites.

© The Editor(s) (if applicable) and The Author(s), under exclusive license to Springer Nature Switzerland AG 2022
P. Kandemir, *The JDP and Making the Post-Kemalist Secularism in Turkey*, https://doi.org/10.1007/978-3-031-07605-3

220 CONCLUSION

Consequently, it has built an almost new social and political environment since 2002.

Thus, despite being subjected to constant attack from secular Kemalist elites on the basis of the socially conservative norms and pious lifestyles of its founders and the majority of its politicians, the JDP has managed to win every successive election since the foundation. By becoming a dominant party and changing the power balance within the state, it has transformed a previously restrictive style of secularism to a moderate form at state level. The JDP offers a new iteration of modernity that does not exclude tradition and history, reinterpreting secularism within the framework of that modernity, thereby successfully legitimising it as an another form to Kemalist modernism and secularism project. Today, there are multiple competing and coexisting secularisms within contemporary Turkey, however, one has maintained power, while the remainder have been in opposition at the mainstream level.

However, one should admit that this transformation has been a long and contentious process for Turkey. During the JDP's first decade in governance, removing some of the most prominent and aggressive aspects of secularism became the most significant point of friction. The JDP, which consistently reiterated its attachment to secularism, but nevertheless was still accused of being anti-secularist by Kemalists from the outset, promised to create "real secularism" from the beginning. My general finding in this study is that it has succeeded in formulating and legitimising its new approach to secularism in Post-Kemalist Turkey. Despite differences in practice, the coexistence of different and competing concepts of secularism in contemporary society showcases that Turkey is still a secular and democratic country in where politically capable parties can apply their secular policies.

In this regard, this book indicates that JDP policymakers consider their reforms vis-à-vis secularism affairs as an improvement of secularism. They believe in self-corrected modernism[1] one that has made Turkey more modern and democratic than ever. However, it also claims that the inaccurate and limiting definitions of secularism as simply "irreligiousness" were corrected by the JDP to include an improved and modern understanding of secularism within the context of freedom of religion.

Therefore, since Turkey's modernisation experience has not resulted in the homogenization of the Turkish society and ended with changing forms of piety, I simply claim that everyone is modern in Turkey today to varying degrees; all political movements are modern, they are just not modern in an identical way.[2] One should not forget the fact that diversification also in modernisation does not necessarily bring clashing interests with it.[3] While this separation is taking place, there may certainly be conflicts—which had been in the Turkish case as well—but this can also facilitate a suitable environment in which different modes of secularism(s), in discourse and practice will ultimately coexist together.

While no political party had previously been able to institutionalise a different understanding of secularism, the JDP both managed to accomplish this and did so without the eradication of prior conceptions of secularism. For instance, while the JDP has been in power and implementing Post-Kemalist secularism in the relevant areas, the RPP has begun to implement its own secularism practices (it is moderate Kemalist secularism today), especially following its victory in the big cities (İstanbul, Ankara, Antalya etc.) in the last local election. Therefore, different approaches to secularism that have existed as discursive distinctions are now also present in practice. This shows us that Eisenstadt's multiple modernities can be realised with the same country simultaneously. Here, it is worth remembering that, "the multiple modernities approach insists on the indespensability of the concept of modernity, but without persisting in its one-sided orientation to a seemingly univesalistic Western model."[4] As a repercussion of this new condition, the emergence of different secularisms in discourse and practice did not result in a decline in religiosity, but rather a broadening of the manifestations of religiosity.[5] Indeed, this is the main argument of those who oppose classical modernisation and those who support Eisenstadt's multiple modernities paradigm. This reality exhibits that contemporary Turkey may be one of the best test cases for the multiple modernities paradigm and an example of how multiple understandings of secularism can coexist within the same country.

Based on this general framework and to provide a theoretical context to the secularism discussion within Turkey, the historical background chapter of this book discussed secularism as the core value of Kemalism. As a modest contribution to the Post-Kemalist literature, a critical approach was applied towards Kemalist reforms by centralising the secularism issue here. In this regard, and inspired by Berna Turam's relevant approach, my first finding is that Kemalist secularism has been the most significant element alienating the religious citizen from the state throughout the history of the republic. While the state's elite became the main followers of secularism, citizens were oppressed and compelled to become

222 CONCLUSION

similarly secularised or westernised. Consequently, while the centre was secular, the periphery was pious; a fact even oppression could not alter. All it achieved was to reinforce barriers between the secular state and its conservative citizens. The second finding of this chapter is that it is only possible to examine religion-state relations in Turkey by not creating a secularism-Islam dichotomy. Studies that position secularism and Islam as opposites of each another will remain inadequate in terms of explaining religion-state relations in Turkey. In fact, academic studies attempting to explain the JDP's relationship with secularism from this perspective have failed to extend beyond one-sided, superficial, and misleading debate. In turn, what I criticise in this chapter is the existence of a false dichotomy between pious citizens and secularism, or Islam and secularism in Turkish case. Instead, what I suggest is the necessity for an empirically grounded discussion based on the political, social, and historical realities of the country.

Moreover, to expand the discussion on the tense relations between the Kemalist state and citizen, or the *centre* and the *periphery*, this chapter analysed the effects of aggressive Kemalist secularism on its own citizens, ranging from devout Sunnis to Alevis and non-Muslims. To discontinue aforementioned dichotomy, this chapter proposed the creation of a new discussion embracing the centre-right DP and ANAP as the ideological roots of the JDP along with the NOM. The findings of this research substantiated the view that the JDP's secularism approach was initially envisioned by Menderes and Özal; it was implemented by Erdoğan reflecting his long-term struggle and strategic victory against the Kemalist regime.

From this vantage point, the third chapter of this book explored the foundation of the JDP, its politicians' profiles, the party programme, its secularism approach, and its delineation of Post-Kemalist secularism. When one evaluates this information, it is conspicuous that the new Turkey, or Post-Kemalist Turkey, is built upon different values than Kemalist Turkey. The New Turkey's most defining feature is its promotion of reconciliation with cultural and historical values, instead of solely Western values. It also promotes freedom of religious expression, as well as the fostering of traditional values. While some modernist literature criticises this approach and views on tradition and historical roots as antithetical to modernity, the case of New Turkey demonstrates that history and modernity are not antithetical. This combination of findings provides some support for the conceptual premise that local secularism is possible in a Muslim country, reconciled with its local culture, history, and religious values; the JDP is a salient example of this.

Furthermore, by outlining each of my findings, I can confidently claim that JDP's approach to secularism impacted the way that the pious Muslim sees the secularism. There is no doubt, Erdogan and his JDP see their version as the most suitable to Turkey's social fabric. Especially, following Erdoğan's recommendation of secularism to Egypt in 2011, and other Muslim countries after the Arab uprisings that spiralled through North Africa and the Middle East, one could realise that he views his version of secularism as an endpoint.[6] One should not forget that during his visit to Egypt in 2011, Erdoğan encouraged the Egyptians to not "be afraid of secularism." At that time, he promoted secularism understanding to the whole world, saying that "secularism does not mean being against religion."[7] Similar quotations from JDP politicians and policymakers in several recorded and unofficial speeches also lead to this conclusion. While formulating the content of Post-Kemalist secularism during this period, the JDP voluntarily adapted it and successfully integrated it into its own political identity. This changed the position of individuals to political groups towards secularism. Now, secularism is a principle that even the *Saadet* Party—the current representative of Islamism in Turkey, no longer disputes. The more pious Muslims integrate into the modern system and way of life, the closer the relationship they establish with secularism, albeit in different forms and content.

Chapter 4 examines the evolution of the headscarf issue during the JDP years in the context of secularism. The headscarf issue holds a symbolic meaning with respect to secularism. The lifting of the headscarf bans in universities and various other sectors was undoubtedly a critical turning point for Turkey. The ban violated human rights despite coming under the banner of protecting a secular lifestyle. Indeed, the main finding of this chapter was that, contrary to the dominant argument, the headscarf controversy is not solely related to the Kemalist concerns of secularism in Turkey. It was more about Kemalists' resistance to the possible emergence of a counter elite to threaten their privileged position within the state. By using the headscarf as a buffer, the Kemalist establishment sought to justify their authoritarian secularist policies to continue to exclusively dominate the *centre*.

While headscarf freedom liberalised pious Muslim women socially, it also reintegrated them into the public sphere, took them out from

224 CONCLUSION

their ghettos, ending their alienation. The politicising of the head-scarf was ended with its removal from the political parties' agendas. In contemporary Turkey, three of the four political parties in Parliament currently have deputies wearing headscarves, and the fact that a significant number of headscarf-wearing intellectuals, academics, and ordinary citizens supported parties with secular discourses, such as the RPP or the HDP in recent elections indicates that the politicisation of headscarf came to an end point under the new secularism proposal of the JDP.

This finding may help us to understand why headscarf freedom would be considered a step along Turkey's democratisation path rather than Islamisation. Indeed, when the ban was lifted, Turkey did not become an Islamic country as had been claimed by several Kemalists as well as respected experts. By referring the classical and even *clishe* assumption(rise in veiled women) applied to prove that Turkey had been Islamised by the JDP, the percentage of veiled women did not rise[8], instead the percentage of girls receiving education increased[9] when they were permitted to enter universities and schools. Consequently, pious Muslims have finally been reconciled with the state and its education system.

Chapter 5 evaluates the JDP's educational policies in the context of secularism. The re-liberation of religious education in the pre-school period, the reopening of secondary IHSs as well as the removal of the co-efficient system, and the continuation of compulsory religious courses in public schools are some of the instances presented as evidence that the JDP is de-secularising Turkey. Although, the rise in number of IHSs, and the JDP's positive language towards them, have been heavily criticised by the opposition, as constituting steps to Islamise society, my findings, however, indicate that the JDP's educational reforms do not contradict its religion-friendly secularism approach and socially conservative policies. Rather, revising the curriculum of an already-existing compulsory religion and ethics course to a more pluralistic format, including additional courses on the life of Prophet Muhammed and the Quran as elective options instead of compulsory, re-liberating pre-school religious education not only for Muslims but also for other religious groups, and using positive discrimination towards the previously oppressed and alienated IHSs are compatible with JDP's secularism understanding, which propounds religiosity as an option. When we consider that Erdoğan is more pious than the average ordinary citizen in Turkey, his tendency to encourage religious education is not in a controversy in his party's secularism proposal. Beyond, despite this encouragement, liberalisation, and improvements to religious education, as discussed in the chapter by applying the field researches, Turkish youths have not become more religious during the JDP era, rather their manifestations of religiosity have diversified. This hyberdisation in the ways of performing religious practices and lifestyle of the pious Muslims cannot be counted as an indicator of rising religiosity in Turkey, nor is it an indicator of rising secularisation. Instead, removal of the uniformity is an evidence of the democratisation of the public sphere.

Final chapter focuses on the relationship between the JDP and other religious identities in the context of secularism by putting non-Muslim minorities and Alevis at the centre of the discussion. The most obvious finding to emerge from the analysis is that the religion friendly approach of the JDP was not only benefited by the pious Sunni Muslims of Turkey, but the conditions of the non-Muslim minorities and other sectarian groups also improved during this process. However contrary to expectations, while the JDP's relationship with non-Muslim minorities has been constructive under the auspices of Post-Kemalist secularism, it has been less so in the relationship with the Alevis. Briefly stated, while the reforms made by the JDP have been welcomed by non-Muslim minorities, the Alevis' reaction has been relatively more complex. In spite of the fact that the JDP has broken new ground in Turkish history by becoming the first ruling party to address the problems experienced by Alevis by bringing together the representatives of Alevi organisations and highest-level state officials for the first time ever in Turkish political history, the JDP's Alevi opening has not been successful so far. Neither constructive recognition of Alevi problems and traumas officially and at the public level nor changing the content of the religion course curriculum by adding Alevi faith or apologising on behalf of the state for the Dersim massacre, among other steps, have restored relations between the JDP and Alevis. While, the JDP's policies to address the questions of the Alevi community have been seen as insufficient and Alevi's historical traumas and the mooed of being alienated and ignored by Sunni majority played a major role in this, the rising integration of Alevis with the Kilicdaroglu's RPP and their strong links with mass opposition has largely effected to the intractability of the situation. These findings will doubtless be much scrutinised, but there are immediately dependable conclusions for limits of JDP's Post-Kemalist secularism here.

After these analyses, I can claim that in this new form, in which centre-periphery integration occurred, at least in decision-making processes, secularism is no longer the main source of tension in Turkish politics.

226 CONCLUSION

With the neutralisation of secularism as a flashpoint, the RPP is no longer a party for which pious people would never vote, and the JDP is no longer a party that pious people would vote for under any circumstances. This means that one's position relative to secularism is no longer adequate to create a narrative in Turkey; leading to the conclusion that secularism is no longer a reflection of identity, but merely a component of identity. While secularism used to be associated with the political identity and positioning of Kemalist elites, it is now a principle around which all the nation's political parties offer different proposals, tone, and rhetoric in a democratic culture. Ultimately, these discussions can be summarised in one sentence: There is no longer one single Kemalist secular model approved by the Turkish state, sacred and untouchable, and different and more flexible models of secularism have emerged. With Kemalist secularism no longer under the protection of the state, the conditions for competing secularisms to emerge have been granted. These secularisms, which mainly have tonal differences, now face competition in contemporary Turkey.

Within this context, the 2019 local elections can be considered the most significant confirmation that secularism is no longer a make-or-break subject. In these elections, the *Saadet* Party, representing Islamism in Turkey, entered into a coalition with the RPP, and in Ankara and İstanbul, the RPP mayor candidates succeeded in get the votes from the pious Muslims of Turkey. Certainly, it was not the first time the RPP had made such a radical coalition after an election to form a government; but it was a first in a pre-election period. Even so, the voters of both parties were mindful that they were voting for ultra-secularists (RPP) or Islamists (Saadet) in this case. This kind of changes had some surprising repercussions to prove diversification of secularism understanding and practices. For instance, while *Cemevi*s are not recognised as a place of worship by the state, Maltepe Municipality under RPP Mayor officially recognised them as houses of worship with the votes of the local municipality which signs a different implementation of state's policy. Another example was RPP Mayoral candidate Ekrem İmamoğlu's İstanbul Rally before the local election, which started with a Quran Recitation. These moves, undoubtedly, radically challenge with RPP's Kemalist secularism perspective. Today, the RPP's transformed secularism mode, which continues to evolve for pragmatic and rational reasons, is currently the biggest rival to the JDP's Post-Kemalist secularism. This shows that Kemalist secularism is now lacklustre, not even being retained by the RPP, yet the original version of it continues to exist as an ideological choice representing the political identity of different cliques within the RPP. Of course, it has the potential to be applied at the first opportunity if the RPP were to ascend to power.

Ultimately, in spite of the positive repercussions of secularism discussions within the political sphere, there still remains Kemalist resentment towards the pious people of Turkey. Since the victory of the RPP in the 2019 local elections in İstanbul and Ankara, there has been evidence of rising aggression towards religious Muslims within society. There are video footages showing that veiled women continue to be attacked in the streets by Kemalists not only verbally but also physically. Headscarf still symbolises backwardness and ignorance for most of the Kemalists. While members if the younger generation from wealthy secular families have had their luxurious lifestyles criticised, Kemalist newspapers constantly disparage veiled women who drive expensive cars, eat at fashionable restaurants, and wear expensive brands. They are underhandedly attacked by the Kemalists, with the claim that they are corrupt and taken advantage of the "religious government." This shows that a class conflict exists between Kemalists, who have dominated the state since the beginning of the Republic, and non-Kemalists, who have long been alienated and oppressed by Kemalist state elites having been accused of not being sufficiently secular.

Although this conclusion indicates the necessity of further research into the repercussions of the JDP's Post-Kemalist secularism approach on the different segments of society, it also presents one of the main limitations of my work. Since my research has mostly concentrated on defining the nature of transformation and the new shape of secularism and its difference from the Kemalist form, to discuss its sociological effects would also be a beneficial topic for additional academic work. Nevertheless, the effect of the JDP's new secularism on Turkish society, namely on how religiously practicing people and Kemalists have changed during this process, has been discussed to the extent possible within the limitations of this work.

Above several repercussions, there is one very important conclusion of change in secularism issue in Turkey, the growing sympathy towards this term. The JDP's role in this change cannot be ignored. Its eclectic centre-right identity, which has provided an umbrella for multiple diverse identities at different times, has enabled the JDP to sway disparate segments of society towards acceptance of a new, revamped secularism. As a result, conservative, Islamist, and liberal ideologies, as much as non-Muslim minorities and Kurds, who had previously stayed critical and

228   CONCLUSION

unwilling towards the secularism practices performed by Kemalist establishment, have largely reconciled with the state. Therefore, beyond ending the conflict between the secular state and the religious citizen by establishing relations with various social and political segments of society under a flexible identity, and by embracing diverse identities since 2001, the JDP has mobilised "others" from the periphery to the centre. My usage of "others" in this case connotes veiled woman, pious Muslims, non-Muslim religious groups, Alevis, Kurds, and even Islamists. This judgement, while arguably subjective, can also be crosschecked with the number of non-Muslim MPs, veiled woman in different sectors, and the visibility of the Alevi identity in politics and public sphere. Despite some failures in Turkey's democracy in recent years, it remains true that Post-Kemalist Turkey provides greater room for distinct identities than Kemalist Turkey, and the emergence of multiple secularism(s) within Turkey can be seen as one of the main dynamics behind this change.

NOTES

1. Göle, *The Forbidden Modern*.
2. There is an indirect reference to Eisenstadt and Wagner here. See Wagner, *Modernity as Experience*.
3. Kaya, İbrahim. *Social Theory and Later Modernities*. Liverpool: Liverpool University Press, 2004, pp. 142–143.
4. Burchardt and Wohlrab-Sahr. "Multiple Secularities", 605–611.
5. "Konda'nın 10 yıllık raporu", *Cumhuriyet*.
6. Interview with Hüseyin Besli, İstanbul, May 3, 2019.
7. "Brotherhood angry at Erdoğan call for secular Egypt." *Jerusalem Post*, September 14, 2011. Accessed January 3, 2019. https://www.jpost.com/Middle-East/Brotherhood-angry-at-Erdoğan-call-for-secular-Egypt-237916.
8. "Konda'nın 10 yıllık raporu: Ateist oranı arttı" [Konda's 10-Year Research: The Proportion of the Atheist İncreased]. *Cumhuriyet*, January 3, 2019. Accessed January 23, 2020. http://www.cumhuriyet.com.tr/haber/Türkiye/1189902/kondanin-10-yillik-raporu-ateist-orani-artti.html.
9. "Gündelik yaşamda din, laiklik ve türban araştırması." *Konda Araştırma ve Danışmanlık*, p. 4.

Bibliography

Personal Interviews

Aktay, Yasin. Former Siirt MP, Deputy chairman and Spokesperson of the JDP. Interview by author. Personal Interview. Ankara, December 12, 2018.

Alcan, Toros. Former representative of Turkish Minority Foundations. Interview by author. Personal Interview. Istanbul, May 25, 2018.

Arınç, Bülent. Former Minister, Former Deputy Prime Minister, Former Parliament Speaker to and one of the main founders of the JDP. Interview by author. Personal Interview. Ankara, April 12, 2019.

Ateşyan, Aram. Former Armenian Patriarch. Interview by author. Personal Interview. Istanbul, May 27, 2018.

Avcı, Nabi. Former Minister of Education (2013–2016), Former Minister of Culture and Tourism (2016–2017), Former chief advisor to the Turkish Prime Minister Recep Tayyip Erdoğan, Interview by author. Personal Interview. Ankara, December 14, 2018.

Aydın, Ertan. Former Ankara MP and Political Scientist. Interview by author. Personal Interview. Ankara, April 29, 2019.

Benli, Fatma. Benli, JDP MP for 25–26th terms and woman rights activist. Interview by author. Personal Interview. Ankara, May 8, 2018.

Besli, Hüseyin. Former Istanbul MP of JDP, Former Chief advisor to Prime Minister. Interview by author. Personal Interview. Ankara, May 3, 2019.

Bilgin, Vedat. MP of JDP. Interview by author. Personal Interview. Ankara, March 27, 2019.

Bostancı, Naci. Deputy Chief of JDP and Ankara MP. Interview by author. Personal Interview. Ankara, April 28, 2019.

© The Editor(s) (if applicable) and The Author(s), under exclusive license to Springer Nature Switzerland AG 2022
P. Kandemir, *The JDP and Making the Post-Kemalist Secularism in Turkey*, https://doi.org/10.1007/978-3-031-07605-3

229

230 BIBLIOGRAPHY

Boynukalın, Abdurrahim. United Kingdom Representative of JDP and former MP and Head of the Youth Branch of the JDP, Interview by author. Personal Interview. Ankara, May 27, 2019.

Boztuğ, Durmuş. Alevi Dede and Former Rector of Munzur University in Tunceli. Interview by author. Personal Interview. Ankara, April 12, 2019.

Çelik, Ömer. Former Minister of European Union Affairs and Former Minister of Culture and Tourism(2013–2015). Interview by author. Personal Interview. Ankara, May 3, 2018.

Çetin, Yusuf. the Patriarchal Vicar of the Syriac Orthodox Church in Istanbul, Ankara and Izmir. Interview by author. Personal Interview. Istanbul, May 27, 2018.

Çiçek, Cemil. Former Deputy Prime Minister. Interview by author. Personal Interview. Ankara, May 28, 2019.

Dağ, Hamza. Deputy Chairman of JDP, İzmir MP. Interview by author. Personal Interview. Ankara, January 3, 2019.

Duran, Burhanettin. Professor at Ibn Haldun University and General Coordinator of SETA Foundation. Interview by author. Personal Interview. Ankara, May 25, 2018.

Durdu, Erkan. Deputy General Manager at TRT and Former Chief Media Advisor to Bülent Arınç and Abdüllatif Şener. Interview by author. Personal Interview. Ankara, May 28, 2018

Ecertaş, Melih. Former Head of the Youth Branch of the JDP. Interview by author. Personal Interview. Ankara, January 25, 2019.

Eren, İbrahim. Director General of TRT. Interview by author. Personal Interview. Ankara, January 11, 2019.

Esayan, Markar. Armenian intellectual and JDP MP. Interview by author. Personal Interview. Ankara, July 15, 2018.

Gider, Ayhan. Former Çanakkale MP. Interview by author. Personal Interview. Ankara, June 8, 2018.

Gül, Abdulhamit. Minister of Justice of the Republic of Turkey. Interview by author. Personal Interview. Ankara, April 9, 2019.

Gürdal, Kenan. Deputy Chair of the İstanbul Syriac Ortodox Kadim Foundation. Interview by author. Personal Interview. Istanbul, May 27, 2018.

Haşimi, Cemalettin. Former Director of Public Diplomacy Office (2014–2016). Interview by author. Personal Interview. Ankara, January 25, 2019.

Hamzaçebi, Akif. Istanbul MP of RPP. Interview by author. Personal Interview. Ankara, May 28, 2019.

Kadak, Rümeysa. Istanbul MP of JDP. Interview by author. Personal Interview. Ankara, May 28, 2019.

Karagöz, Serdar. Editor in Chief of Daily Sabah. Interview by author. Personal Interview. Istanbul, July 14, 2018.

BIBLIOGRAPHY 231

Kavakçı Kan, Ravza. MP of JDP, Former Deputy Chairperson of the JDP. Interview by author. Personal Interview. Ankara, February 24, 2015.

Kesici, İlhan. RPP MP. Interview by author. Personal Interview. Ankara, April 7, 2020.

Küçükcan, Talip. Former Adana MP of JDP and Professor of sociology at Marmara University. Interview by author. Personal Interview. Ankara, February 6, 2019.

Kurtulmuş, Numan. Deputy Chairman of the JDP and Former Minister of Culture. Interview by author. Personal Interview. Ankara, April 8, 2019.

Molinas, Ivo. The editor-in-chief of newspaper Şalom. Interview by author. Personal Interview. Istanbul, May 9, 2018.

Özkan, Tuncay. RPP MP and former journalist for the Cumhuriyet newspaper and the head organizer of Republican Rallies. Interview by author. Personal Interview. Ankara, April 27, 2019.

Özsoy, Hişyar. HDP MP. Interview by author. Personal Interview. Ankara, April 13, 2019.

Respondent 1, senior JDP Politician, Interview by author. Personal Interview. Ankara. June 5, 2018.

Respondent 2, senior RPP Politician, Interview by author. Personal Interview. Ankara, June 4, 2018.

Respondent 3, Former Minister, Interview by author. Personal Interview. December 25 2018.

Respondent 4, senior bureaucrat, Interview by author. Personal Interview. Ankara, January 25, 2019.

Safi, İsmail. Turkish Presidency Security and Foreign Policy Board Member and Former JDP MP. Interview by author. Personal Interview. Ankara, February 23, 2015.

Şahin, Fatih. General Secretary of the JDP, Ankara MP. Interview by author. Personal Interview. Ankara, April 13, 2019.

Şahin Usta, Leyla. Konya MP of JDP. Interview by author. Personal Interview. Ankara, December 14, 2018

Şahin, Mustafa. Former Speechwriter of President Recep Tayyip Erdogan. Interview by author. Personal Interview. Ankra, April 19, 2019.

Şen, Mustafa. Director of GENAR, Head Advisor to Former Prime Minister. Interview by author. Personal Interview. Ankara, August 24, 2015.

Şentop, Mustafa. Speaker of The Grand National Assembly of Turkey and Tekirdağ MP for JDP. Interview by author. Personal Interview. Ankara, on April 19, 2019.

Sözen, Edibe. Professor and Former JDP Deputy. Interview by author. Personal Interview. Ankara, December 24, 2018.

Tekin, Yusuf. Former Undersecretary of National Education. Interview by author. Personal Interview. Ankara, May 12, 2018.

232 BIBLIOGRAPHY

Ünal, Mahir. Deputy Chairperson of the JDP, Maraş MP, Former Spokesperson and Former Minister. Interview by author. Personal Interview. Ankara, June 4, 2018.

Zengin, Özlem. JDP MP, Head Advisor to President Erdoğan and Former Head of Women Branch in JDP Istanbul Branch. Interview by author. Personal Interview. Ankara, August 25, 2015.

PRIMARY SOURCES

Archival Sources

Anayasa. "Anayasa Mahkemesi Karar Sayısı: 1989/12" [Consitutional Court Decision No: 1989/12], 1989. http://kararlaryeni.anayasa.gov.tr/Karar/ Content/152e95a6-8e5c-4e9e-ae1a-197acdaefe66?higllightText=başörtü% 3Bbaşörtü&excludeGerekce=False&wordsOnly=False

Anayasa. "Anayasa Mahkemesi Karar Sayısı: 2008/2" [Consitutional Court Decision No: 2008/2], July 30, 2008. http://kararlaryeni.anayasa.gov.tr/ Karar/Content/5664600f-6ce5-4b3b-885f-6a936d14abe2?higllightText=baş örtü%3Bbaşörtü&excludeGerekce=False&wordsOnly=False

ECHR. "Information Note on the Court's case-law 80- Leyla Sahin v. Turkey [GC] - 44774/98." *European Court of Human Rights*, 2005. https://hudoc.echr.coe.int/app/conversion/pdf/?library=ECHR&id= 002-3628&filename=002-3628.pdf&TID=thkbhnilzk

Mevzuat. "Tekke ve Zaviyelerle Türbelerin Seddine ve Türbedarlıklar ile birtakım Ünvanların Men ve Ilgasına dair Kanun" [Law on the Closure of Lodge and Islamic Monasteries and Abolition of Some Titles and Tomb Keepernes], November 11, 1925. http://www.mevzuat.gov.tr/MevzuatMetin/1.3.677. pdf

Resmi Gazete. "Anayasa Mahkemesi Kararı No: 2007/54" [The Decision of the Constitutional Court Nr: 2008/2], June 27, 2007. https://www.resmigazete. gov.tr/eskiler/2007/06/20070627-17.htm

Resmi Gazete. "Anayasa Mahkemesi Kararı No: 2008/2" [The Decision of the Constitutional Court Nr: 2008/2], October 24, 2008. http://www.resmig azete.gov.tr/eskiler/2008/10/20081024-10.htm

Resmi Gazete. "Anayasa Mahkemesi Kararı sayı: 27032" [Constitutional Court's Decision No: 27032], October 22, 2008. http://www.resmigazete.gov.tr/esk iler/2008/10/20081022-15.htm

Resmi Gazete. "Anayasa Mahkemesinde Sözlü Savunma" [Verbal Self-Defense at the Constitutional Court], October 24, 2008. http://www.resmigazete.gov. tr/eskiler/2008/10/20081024-10.htm

Resmi Gazete. "Bazı kanunlar ile 375 sayılı kanun hükmünde kararnamede değişiklik yapılması hakkında kanun", June 11, 2013. https://www.resmig azete.gov.tr/eskiler/2013/06/20130611.pdf

BIBLIOGRAPHY 233

Resmi Gazete. "İlköğretim ve Eğitim Kanunu ile Bazı Kanunlarda Değişiklik Yapılmasına Dair Kanun" [Law on the Amendment of Some Laws Under Primary and Education Law], April 11, 2012. http://www.resmigazete.gov.tr/eskiler/2012/04/20120411-8.htm

Resmi Gazete. "Temel hak ve hürriyetlerin geliştirilmesi amacıyla çeşitli kanunlarda değişiklik yapılmasına dair kanun" [Law on Making Changes at Some of the Laws to Improve the Fundamental Rights and Liberities], March 13, 2014. https://www.resmigazete.gov.tr/eskiler/2014/03/20140313-15.htm

Resmi Gazete. "Türk Ceza Kanununda Değişiklik Yapılmasına Dair Kanun" [Law on the Amendment of Turkish Criminal Law], May 8, 2008. http://www.resmigazete.gov.tr/eskiler/2008/05/20080508-5.htm

Resmi Gazete. "Türkiye Cumhuriyeti Anayasasının Bazı Maddelerinde Değişiklik Yapılması Hakkında Kanun" [Law on Making Changes at Some of the Articles of the Constitution of Turkish Republic], June 16, 2007. https://www.resmigazete.gov.tr/eskiler/2007/06/20070616-1.htm

Resmi Gazete. "Türkiye Cumhuriyeti Anayasasının Bazı Maddelerinde Değişiklik Yapılması Hakkında Kanun" [Law on Making Changes at Some of the Articles of the Constitution of Turkish Republic], May 13, 2010. https://www.resmigazete.gov.tr/eskiler/2010/05/20100513-1.htm

TBMM. "Darbeleri Araştırma Komisyonu Raporu" [Report on Commission for the Investigation of Coups]. TBMM 24.1 (2012). http://www.tbmm.gov.tr/sirasayi/donem24/yil01/ss376_Cilt1.pdf

TBMM. "Meclis Araştırma Komisyonu Raporu Cilt 2" [Assembly Investigation Commission Vol. 2], November 2012. https://www.tbmm.gov.tr/sirasayi/donem24/yil01/ss376_Cilt2.pdf

TBMM. "Refah Partisine Kapatma Davası" [Closure Case Against the Welfare Party], 1997. https://www.tbmm.gov.tr/eyayin/GAZETELER/WEB/MEC LIS%20BULTENI/2469_1997_1998_0059_0000/0004.pdf

TCCB. "5555 sayılı kanun" [The Law No. 5555]. *Türkiye Cumhuriyeti Cumhurbaşkanlığı* [Presidency of the Republic of Turkey], November 29, 2006. https://www.tccb.gov.tr/basin-aciklamalari-ahmet-necdet-sezer/1720/7145/5555-sayili-kanun

Government Publications and Private Reports (Turkey)

"Alevi Çalıştayları Nihai Rapor" [Final Report of Alevites Workshops]. *Türkiye Cumhuriyeti Devlet Bakanlığı* [Ministry of Turkish Republic], 2010. https://serdargunes.files.wordpress.com/2013/08/alevi-c3a7alc4b1c5 9ftaylarc4b1-nihai-rapor-2010.pdf

Avrupa Birliği Başkanlığı. "Turkey Reports Prepared by the European Commission". *Republic of Turkey Ministry of Foreign Affairs, Directorate for EU Affairs*, July 5, 2019. https://www.ab.gov.tr/regular-progress-reports_4 6224_en.html

234 BIBLIOGRAPHY

Diyanet. "Diyanet İşleri Başkanlığı Çocuk Sayfası" [Children Page of Directorate of Religious Affairs]. *Diyanet İşleri Başkanlığı* [Directorate of Religious Affairs]. https://cocuk.diyanet.gov.tr/default.aspx

Diyanet. "İstatistikler: Cami" [Statistics: Mosque]. *T.C. Cumhurbaşkanlığı Diyanet İşleri BaşkanlığıStrateji Geliştirme Başkanlığı*, December 12, 2018. https://stratejigelistirme.diyanet.gov.tr/sayfa/57/istatistikler

Diyanet. "İstatistikler: Kuran Kursu" [Statistics: Quran Courses]. *T.C. Cumhurbaşkanlığı Diyanet İşleri BaşkanlığıStrateji Geliştirme Başkanlığı*, December 12, 2018. https://stratejigelistirme.diyanet.gov.tr/sayfa/57/istatistikler

Diyanet. "Kuran Kursları Öğretici Kitabı: 4–6 Yaş Grubu" [Qur'an Courses Exercise Book: 4–6 Age Group]. *Diyanet İşleri Başkanlığı* [Directorate of Religious Affairs], 2014. http://www2.diyanet.gov.tr/EgitimHizmetleriGenelMudurlugu/Materyaller/4-6-yas-ogretici-kitabi.pdf

Diyanet. "Türkiye'de Dini Hayat Araştırması." 2014, https://dergi.diyanet.gov.tr/makaledetay.php?ID=6468

Eğitim Bir Sen. "2023'e Doğru Türk Eğitim Sistemi Bulma Konferansı ve Çalıştayı: Öneriler" [Towards 2023 Conference and Workshop on Turkish Education System: Suggestions], September 2018. https://www.ebs.org.tr/ebs_files/files/yayinlarimiz/2023TurkEgitimSistemiBulmaKonferansi_oneriler.pdf

Eğitim Bir Sen. "Bir daha asla, 17 yıl sonra 28 Şubat" [Never Again, 28 February After 17 Years], February 28, 2014. https://www.ebs.org.tr/ebs_files/files/yayinlarimiz/28_subat_rapor_web.pdf

Eğitim Bir Sen. "Gecikmiş Bir Reform: Müfredatın Demokratikleştirilmesi" [A Delayed Reform: Democratization of the Curriculum], January 1, 2017. https://www.ebs.org.tr/ebs_files/files/yayinlarimiz/gecikmis_bir_reform_mufredatin_demokratiklestirilmesi.pdf

Egitim Bir Sen. "Rakamlarla 28 Şubat Raporu" [28 February Report with Numbers], February 28, 2014. https://www.ebs.org.tr/ebs_files/files/yayinlarimiz/28_subat_rapor_web.pdf

Kültür ve Turizm Bakanlığı. "Bakan Kurtulmuş: 'Aleviler için Vaatler Bizim için Sözdür'" [A Word for Alewis Is a Promise for Us], June 2018. https://basin.ktb.gov.tr/TR-210811/bakan-kurtulmus-aleviler-icin-vaatler-bizim-icin-sozdur.html

Mazlumder. "Türkiye'de Dini Ayrımcılık Raporu", 2010. http://İstanbul.mazlumder.org/fotograf/yayinresimleri/dokuman/turkiyede_dini_eyrimcilik_raporu.pdf

MEB. "2019–2020 Eğitim-Öğretim yılında okutulacak seçmeli ders belirleme" [Designation of the Elective Courses for 2019–2020 Education Year]. *Milli*

BIBLIOGRAPHY   235

Egemenlik Ortaokulu, February 2, 2019. http://sme.meb.k12.tr/icerik
ler/128227-2019-2020-egitim-ogretim-yilinda-okutulacak-secmeli-ders-belirl
eme_6487373.html

MEB. "Anadolu İmam Hatip Lisesi Haftalık Ders Çizelgesi" [Anatolian
Imam Hatip High school Weekly Curriculum]. *Millî Eğitim Bakanlığı Din
Öğretimi Genel Müdürlüğü* [Directorate of Religious Education at Ministry
of National Education], 2017. https://dogm.meb.gov.tr/meb_iys_dosyalar/
2017_06/15113722_AIHL_Fen_Sosyal_Bilimler_ProgramY_Cizelgesi1.pdf

MEB. "İlköğretim Din Kültürü ve Ahlak Bilgisi dersi (4,5,6,7, ve 8 sini-
flar) öğretim programı ve kılavuzu" [The Programme and Guidebook for
Course of Culture of Religion and Knowledge of Ethics (for 4,5,6,7
and 8 th Grades]. *Diyanet İşleri Başkanlığı* [Directorate of Religious
Affairs], 2010. https://dogm.meb.gov.tr/meb_iys_dosyalar/2017_08/171
74424_DinKulturu_4-8.siniflar_2010.pdf

MEB. "Millî Eğitim İstatistikleri Örgün Eğitim (1. Dönem)" [National Education Statistics Formal Education (1st Semester)]. *T.C. Millî Eğitim Bakanlığı
Strateji Geliştirme Başkanlığı* [Ministry of National Education Strategy
Development Presidency], 2017. http://sgb.meb.gov.tr/meb_iys_dosyalar/
2017_09/08151328_meb_istatistikleri_orgun_egitim_2016_2017.pdf

MEB. "Syllabus Diversity in Anatolian IHSs (Project Schools)." *Directorate
General for Religious Teaching.* Accessed on July 20, 2019. http://dogm.
meb.gov.tr/pdf/ProjeKitapEN.pdf

YÖK. "History of the Council of Higher Education." *Council of Higher Education.* Accessed on June 23, 2019. https://www.yok.gov.tr/en/institutional/
history

Party Documents (JDP)

AK Party. "Adalet ve Kalkınma Partisi 2023 Vizyonu" [2013 Political Vision of
the Justice and Development Party], 2012. http://www.akparti.org.tr/eng
lish/akparti/2023-political-vision

AK Party. *Adalet Ve Kalkınma Partisi Acil Eylem Planı* [Immediate Action Plan].
Ankara: AK Party, 2003a. Available online at: www.akparti.org.tr

AK Party. *Adalet ve Kalkınma Partisi Seçim Beyannamesi* [Election Manifests of
the Justice and Development Party], 2003b. Available online at: http://www.
akparti.org.tr/beyanname2011.pdf

AK Party. *Adalet ve Kalkınma Partisi İcraatlar* [Reforms of the AK Party].
Available online at: http://www.akparti.org.tr/english/icraatlar

AK Party. *Adalet ve Kalkınma Partisi Programı* [The Political Program of the
Justice and Development Party], 2003c. Available online at: http://www.akp
arti.org.tr/site/akparti/parti-programi

236 BIBLIOGRAPHY

AK Party. *Adalet ve Kalkınma Partisi Tüzüğü* [By-Law of the Justice and Development Party], 2003d. Available online at: http://www.akparti.org.tr/eng lish/akparti/parti-tuzugu

AK Party. *Adalet Ve Kalkınma Partisi Kalkınma ve Demokratikleşme Programı* [Justice and Development Party Development and Democratisation Programme]. Ankara: AK Party, 2004a. Available online at: www.akparti. org.tr

AK Party. *Uluslararası Muhafazakarlık ve Demokrasi Sempozyumu* [International Symposium on Conservatism and Democracy], İstanbul: January 10–11, 2004b.

"Demokratikleşme Paketi" [Democratisation Package]. *Ak Parti Halkla İlişkiler Başkanlığı*, November 7, 2013. Accessed January 20, 2020. https://docpla yer.biz.tr/35489780-Demokratiklesme-paketi.html

İl İl Ak İcraatler. "Eğitim sistemine köklü çözüm: 4+4+4" [Substantial Solution for Education System: 4+4+4], 2019. http://www.ililakicraatlar.com/tur kiye/icraat/egitim-sistemine-koklu-cozum-444/30630

İl İl Ak İcraatler. "Millî Eğitim Bakanlığı bütçesini yaklaşık 11,4 kat artırdık" [We Increased the Budget of the Ministry of National Education Almost 11,4 times], 2019. http://www.ililakicraatlar.com/turkiye/icraat/milli-egitim-bak anligi-butcesini-yaklasik-114-kat-artirdik/30631

İl İl Ak İcraatler. "Okula gitmeyen kalmayacak" [There Will Be No One Who Does Not Go to School], 2019. http://www.ililakicraatlar.com/turkiye/icr aat/okula-gitmeyen-kalmayacak/30632

International Reports and Documents

EUROPA. "2004 Regular Report on Turkey's Progress Towards Accession." *Commission of the European Communities*, October 6, 2004. https://ec.eur opa.eu/neighbourhood-enlargement/sites/near/files/archives/pdf/key_doc uments/2004/rr_tr_2004_en.pdf

EUROPA. "Joint Answer Given by Mr Füle on Behalf of the Commission." *European Parliament*, November 4, 2013. Accessed June 23, 2019. http://www.europarl.europa.eu/sides/getAllAnswers.do?reference=E-2013-011262&language=EN

EUROPA. "Turkey 2016 Report: Accompanying the Document Communication from the Commission to the European Parliament, the Council, the European Economic and Social Committee and the Committee of the Regions-2016 Communication on EU Enlargement Policy." Commission Staff Working Paper, Brussels: Commission of the European Communities, November 9, 2016. https://ec.europa.eu/neighbourhood-enlargement/sites/near/files/pdf/key_documents/2016/20161109_report_turkey.pdf

EUROPA. "Turkey 2018 Report: Accompanying the Document Communication from the Commission to the European Parliament, the Council, the European

BIBLIOGRAPHY 237

Economic and Social Committee and the Committee of the Regions-2018 Communication on EU Enlargement Policy." Commission Staff Working Paper, Brussels: Commission of the European Communities, April 17, 2018. https://eeas.europa.eu/sites/eeas/files/20180417-turkey-report1_0.pdf

EUROPA. "Turkey 2019 Report: Accompanying the Document Communication from the Commission to the European Parliament, the Council, the European Economic and Social Committee and the Committee of the Regions-2019 Communication on EU Enlargement Policy." Commission Staff Working Paper, Brussels: Commission of the European Communities, May 29, 2019. https://ec.europa.eu/neighbourhood-enlargement/sites/near/files/20190529-turkey-report.pdf

EUROPA. "Turkey 2020 Report: Accompanying the Document Communication from the Commission to the European Parliament, the Council, the European Economic and Social Committee and the Committee of the Regions-2020 Communication on EU Enlargement Policy." Commission Staff Working Paper, Brussels: Commission of the European Communities, October, 10, 2020. https://ec.europa.eu/neighbourhood-enlargement/sites/near/files/turkey_report_2020.pdf

Minority Rights Group International. "Bir eşitlik arayışı: Türkiye'de azınlıklar" [A Search for Equality: Minorities in Turkey], September 2007. https://minorityrights.org/wp-content/uploads/2015/07/MRG_Rep_Turk2007_TURK.pdf

Parliament UK. "The UK's relations with Turkey." *House of Commons Foreign Affairs Committee*, pp. 37–38. March 21, 2017. https://publications.parliament.uk/pa/cm201617/cmselect/cmfaff/615/615.pdf

U.S. Commission on International Religious Freedom. "TURKEY Annual Reports." https://www.uscirf.gov/countries/turkey

World Bank. "Promoting Excellence in Turkey's Schools." *Human Development Sector Unit Europe and Central Asia Region*, March 1, 2013. Accessed June 13, 2019. http://documents.worldbank.org/curated/en/944721468110943381/pdf/777220REVISED00B00PUBLIC00Egitim0EN.pdf

Speeches

Akcay, Erkan. MHP MP's speech in the parliament, "İnançlarımıza Yapılan Saldırılara İlişkin" [On the Attack Against Our Belief], Türkiye Büyük Millet Meclisi [Grand National Assembly of Turkey], July 16, 2014. Accessed July 21, 2018. https://www.tbmm.gov.tr/develop/owa/genel_kurul.cl_getir?pEid=32712

AK Party, *Recep Tayyip Erdoğan'ın konuşmalarından tematik seçmeler* [Thematic Selections from the Speeches of Recep Tayyip Erdogan], edited by Abdurrahman Tığ, İsak Baydaroğlu, Sakiye Erdem. Ankara: AK Party Publicity and Media Chairmanship, 2010.

238 BIBLIOGRAPHY

Dengir, Mir Mehmet Fırat. speech at "Uluslararası Muhafazakarlık ve Demokrasi Sempozyumu" [International Symposium on Conservatism and Democracy] (İstanbul, January 15, 2004), Ak Parti. Accessed January 23, 2019. http://www.akparti.org.tr/media/272223/uluslararasi-muhafazak arlik-ve-demokrasi-sempozyumu.pdf

Erdoğan, Mustafa. Speech at "Uluslararası Muhafazakarlık ve Demokrasi Sempozyumu"[International Symposium on Conservatism and Democracy] (İstanbul, January 15, 2004), *Ak Parti*. Accessed: January 23, 2019. http://www.akparti.org.tr/media/272223/uluslararasi-muhafazak arlik-ve-demokrasi-sempozyumu.pdf

Erdoğan, Recep Tayyip. *Grup Konuşmaları 1, 2* [Group Speeches]. Ankara: AK Party Advertising and Media Chairmanship, 2003–2007a.

Erdoğan, Recep Tayyip. *Konuşmalar: 22. Yasama Dönemi 1. Yıl AK Parti grup konuşmaları, 10 Kasım 2002–28* [Speeches: AK Party Group's Speeches of 22nd Executive Year First Year]. Ankara: AK Party Advertising and Media Chairmanship, 2003.

Erdoğan, Recep Tayyip. *Küresel Barış Vizyonu* [Global Peace Vision]. Edited by Bekir Karlıağa. İstanbul: Meydan, 2012.

Erdoğan, Recep Tayyip. Speech at 1st Ordinary Grand Congress of the Justice and Development Party held in Ankara, on October 12, 2003. Accessed January 2017. https://acikerisim.tbmm.gov.tr/xmlui/bitstream/ handle/11543/964/200403930.pdf?sequence=1&isAllowed=y

Erdoğan, Recep Tayyip. Speech at "Uluslararası Muhafazakarlık ve Demokrasi Sempozyumu" [International Symposium on Conservatism and Democracy] (İstanbul, January 15, 2004), *Ak Parti*. Accessed: January 23, 2019. http://www.akparti.org.tr/media/272223/uluslararasi-muhafazak arlik-ve-demokrasi-sempozyumu.pdf

Erdoğan, Recep Tayyip. *Ulusa Sesleniş Konuşmaları* [Calling out to Nation]. Ankara: AK Party Advertising and Media Chairmanship, 2003–2007a.

Erdoğan, Recep Tayyip. *Uluslararası Konuşmaları 1, 2* [International Speeches]. Ankara: AK Party Advertising and Media Chairmanship, 2003–2007b.

Erdoğan, Recep Tayyip. *Ülke Konuşmaları 1, 2,3,4* [National Speeches]. Ankara : AK Party Advertising and Media Chairmanship, 2003–2007c.

Erdoğan, Recep Tayyip. "Yüz yıllık hikaye İmam Hatip" [Imam Hatip: A Story of Hundred Years]. Recep Tayyip Erdogan's Speech at 100th Anniversary of the Foundation of Imam Hatip Schools, İstanbul, January 17, 2014. Accessed January 2017. https://www.yenisafak.com/video-galeri/politika/erdoganin- imam-hatiplilere-yaptigi-konusmanin-tamami-12877

TBMM. "CHP'nin Cemevi sistemine ret" [Rejection to SHP's *Cemevi* System], July 10, 2012. https://www.tbmm.gov.tr/develop/owa/Gazete HaberBaskan.haber_detay?pkayit_no=1423417

BIBLIOGRAPHY 239

TBMM. "Constitution of the Republic of Turkey." *The Grand National Assembly of Turkey*, 2018. https://global.tbmm.gov.tr/docs/constitution_en.pdf
TBMM. "Genel Kurul Tutanağı 22. Dönem 3. Yasama Yılı 101. Birleşim" [Minutes of General Meeting 22nd Term 3rd Legislative Session 101st Sitting]. *Türkiye Büyük Millet Meclisi* [Grand National Assembly of Turkey], May 24, 2005. https://www.tbmm.gov.tr/develop/owa/Tutanak_B_SD.bir lesim_baslangic_yazici?P4=14565&P5=B&page1=18&page2=18
TBMM. "Genel Kurul Tutanağı 24. Dönem 2. Yasama Yılı 33. Birleşim" [Minutes of General Meeting 24th Term 2nd Legislative Session 33rd Sitting]. *Türkiye Büyük Millet Meclisi*, [Grand National Assembly of Turkey], December 10, 2011. https://www.tbmm.gov.tr/develop/owa/tutanak_sd. birlesim_baslangic?P4=21065&P5=B&page1=52&page2=52&web_user_id= 16563833
TBMM. "Türkiye Büyük Millet Meclisi Tutanak Dergisi" [Minute Magazine of Turkish Grand National Assembly], March 27, 2012. https://www.tbmm. gov.tr/tutanak/donem24/yil2/bas/b083m.htm
TBMM. "Türkiye Büyük Millet Meclisi Tutanak Dergisi" [Minute Magazine of Turkish Grand National Assembly], March 30, 2012. https://www.tbmm. gov.tr/tutanaklar/TUTANAK/TBMM/d24/c018/tbmm24018086.pdf
TBMM. "Türkiye Büyük Millet Meclisi Tutanak Dergisi" [Minute Magazine of Turkish Grand National Assembly], October 31, 2012. https://www.tbmm. gov.tr/tutanak/donem24/yil2/bas/b085m.htm
TBMM. *Türkiye Bülteni* [Turkey Bulletin] 2:19 Ankara: AK Party, 2004.
TBMM. *Türkiye Bülteni* [Turkey Bulletin] 3:27 Ankara: AK Party, 2005.

Surveys
Çelik, Ayşe Betul, Balta, Evren and Paker, Murat. "Yeni Turkiye'nin Yurttaşları: 15 Temmuz Darbe Girişimi Sonrası Siyasi Tutumlar, Degerler ve Duygular" [Citizens of New Turkey: Attitudes, Morals and Emotions after July 15 Coup Attempt]. *Konda Araştırma ve Danışmanlık*, May 2017. https://konda.com.tr/wp-content/uploads/2017/05/KONDA_ Yeni_Turkiyenin_Yurttaslari_Mayis2017.pdf
Erdem, Tarhan. "Yeni Türkiye'yi Anlamak" [Understanding New Turkey], November 3, 2007. https://konda.com.tr/wp-content/uploads/2017/02/ 2007_11_KONDA_Yeni_Turkiye.pdf
GENAR. "3 Kasım 2002'den 3 Kasım 2003'e Türkiye'nin Bir Yılı Araştırması" [Research on Turkey's One Year Since November 2002 to November 2003], 2003, print.
GENAR. "Alevi Açılımı" [Alevi Openning]. *Türkiye Gündem Araştırması 2*, 2009, print.
GENAR. "Partiler 22 Temmuz yarışına nereden başlıyor?" [Where Do Parties Start July 22 Race?], 2007, print.

240 BIBLIOGRAPHY

GENAR. "Simgesel Kültürel Sınıflar Analizi" [Analysis of Symbolic Cultural Classes], 2009, print.

GENAR. "Türkiye Gündem Araştırması: Demokratik Açılım" [Research on Turkey's Agenda: Democratic Initiative], 2009, print.

GENAR. "Türkiye Sosyal, Ekonomik ve Politik Analiz 4" [Turkey Social, Economic and Politic Analysis 4], April 2012, print.

GENAR. "Türkiye Sosyal, Ekonomik ve Politik Analiz 6" [Turkey Social, Economic and Politic Analysis 6], October 2012, print.

GENAR. "Türkiye Sosyal, Ekonomik ve Politik Analiz 7" [Turkey Social, Economic and Politic Analysis 7]. İstanbul: GENAR, January 2013.

GENAR. "Türkiye Sosyal, Ekonomik ve Politik Analiz 8" [Turkey Social, Economic and Political Analysis 8], 2013, print.

GENAR. "Türkiye Sosyal, Ekonomik ve Politik Analiz 9" [Turkey Social, Economic and Politic Analysis 9], June 2013, print.

GENAR. "Türkiye Toplum ve Siyaset Araştırması 1. Çeyrek" [Research on Turkey, Society and Politics, First Quarter], April 2009, print.

GENAR. "Türkiye Toplum ve Siyaset Araştırması 2. Çeyrek" [Research on Turkey, Society and Politics, Second Quarter], July 2009, print.

GENAR. "Türkiye Toplum ve Siyaset Araştırması: 3. Çeyrek" [Research on Turkey, Society and Politics: Third Quarter], 2009, print.

GENAR. "Türkiye Toplum ve Siyaset Araştırması" [Research on Turkey, Society and Politics], 2011, print.

GENAR. "Türkiye Toplum Siyaset Araştırması" [Research on Turkey, Society and Politics], 2012, print.

HAZAR. *Türkiye'nin Örtülü Gerçeği; Başörtüsü Yasağı Alan Araştırması* [The Vailed Truth of Turkey: Field Research on Headscarf Ban]. İstanbul: Hazar Eğitim Kültür ve Araştırma Derneği, 2007.

Konda, "Anayasaya Dair Tanım ve Beklentiler" [Expectations and Definitions on Constitution], September 2012. https://konda.com.tr/wp-content/upl oads/2017/02/2012_11_KONDA_Anayasa_Anket.pdf

Konda, "Başını örtme ve türban araştırması" [Survey on Wearing Headscarf and Veil]. *Konda Barometresi*, November 2010. https://konda.com.tr/wp-con tent/uploads/2017/03/KONDA_1011_BASINI_ORTME_VE_TURBAN. pdf

Konda, "Bilime İnanç ve Bilim Dışılık" [Belief on the Science and Nonscience]. *Konda Barometresi*, January 2013. https://konda.com.tr/wp-content/upl oads/2017/03/KONDA_1301_BILIME_INANC_VE_BILIM_DISILIK. pdf

Konda. "Diyanet İşleri Başkanlığı Araştırması: Algılar, Memnuniyet, Beklen-tiler" [Research on Directorate of Religious Affairs: Perseptions, Satisfaction and Expectations], November 2014. https://konda.com.tr/wp-content/upl oads/2017/02/HYD_DIBArastirmasiRapor_Kasim2014.pdf

BIBLIOGRAPHY 241

Konda, "Eğitim Sisteminin Yapısı ve Beklentiler" [The Structure of Education System and the Expectations]. *Konda Barometresi*, November 2017. https://konda.com.tr/wp-content/uploads/2019/06/TR1711_Barometre81_Egitim_Sisteminin_Yapisi_ve_Beklentiler.pdf

Konda. "Gündelik yaşamda din, laiklik ve türban araştırması" [Survey on Religion, Secularism and Headscarf in Daily Life], September 9, 2007. https://konda.com.tr/wp-content/uploads/2017/02/2007_09GündelikHayattaDinLaiklikTürban.pdf

Konda. "7 Haziran Sandık ve Seçmen Analizi" [7 June: Ballot and Voter Analysis], June 18, 2015. https://konda.com.tr/wp-content/uploads/2017/03/KONDA_7HaziranSandıkveSeçmenAnaliziRaporu.pdf

Konda, "İnsan Hakları Algısı" [Human Rights Perception]. *Konda Barometresi*, June 2012. https://konda.com.tr/wp-content/uploads/2017/03/KONDA_1206_INSAN_HAKLARI_ALGISI.pdf

Konda, "Ramazan Pratikleri" [Ramadan Practices]. *Konda Barometresi*, June 2017. https://konda.com.tr/wp-content/uploads/2019/05/TR1706_Barometre77_Ramazan_Pratikleri.pdf

Konda, "Siyasal Kimlikler" [Political Identities]. *Konda Barometresi*, July 2010. https://konda.com.tr/wp-content/uploads/2017/03/KONDA_1007_SIYASAL_KIMLIKLER.pdf

Konda, "Toplumdaki Ayıp, Günah ve Suç Algı ve Tanımları" [Definitions of Shame, Sin and Crime Within the Society]. *Konda Barometresi*, May 2012. https://konda.com.tr/wp-content/uploads/2017/03/KONDA_1205_TOPLUMDAKI_AYIP_GUNAH_VE_SUC_ALGISI.pdf

Konda, "Toplumsal Kutuplaşma" [Social Polarisation]. *Konda Barometresi*, April 2010. https://konda.com.tr/wp-content/uploads/2017/03/KONDA_1004_TOPLUMSAL_KUTUPLASMA.pdf

Konda. "Vatandaşlık Araştırması 3–6 Mart" [Citizen Survey 3–6 March], March, 2016. https://konda.com.tr/wp-content/uploads/2017/02/2016_03_VatandaslikArastirmasi.pdf

Konda and Milliyet. *Toplumsal Yapı Araştırması* [Research on Social Structure]. İstanbul, 2006. http://konda.com.tr/wp-content/uploads/2017/02/2006_09_KONDA_Toplumsal_Yapi.pdf

Özensel, Ertan and Mehmet Ali Aydemir. "Türkiye İmam Hatip Lisesi Öğrenci Profili Araştırması (Temel Sorunlar, Beklentiler ve Değer Yapıları)" [Research on the Profile of the Imam Hatip School Students in Turkey]. *Türkiye İmam Hatipliler Vakfı* (2012). http://timav.org.tr/raporlar/turkiye-imam-hatip-lisesi-ogrenci-profili-arastirmasi/

Uncu, Baran Alp. "Seçmen Kümeleri: Ak Parti Seçmenleri" [Voter Groups: Ak Parti Voters]. *Konda Araştırma ve Danışmanlık*, May 2018. Accessed July

242 BIBLIOGRAPHY

24, 2019. https://konda.com.tr/wp-content/uploads/2018/05/KONDA_ SecmenKumeleri_AkParti_Secmenleri_Mayis2018.pdf

Official Websites/Archives
Directorate of Religious Affairs https://www.diyanet.gov.tr/
Official Speeches of Prime Minister Erdogan. Available online: http://www.bbm. gov.tr
Official Website of the AK Party http://www.akparti.org.tr/
Official Website of the CHP https://www.chp.org.tr
Official Website of the MHP http://www.mhp.org.tr/
Republic of Turkey, Ministry of Educational Affairs http://www.meb.gov.tr
Republic of Turkey, Ministry of Foreign Affairs http://www.mfa.gov.tr/default. en.mfa
The Grand National Assembly of Turkey https://www.tbmm.gov.tr/

Local and International Media Sources
"24 Nisan'da Sultanahmet ve Şişhane'de anma" [Commemoration on April 24 at Sultanahmet and Şişhane]. *AGOS*, April 23, 2019. http://www.agos.com. tr/tr/yazi/22349/24-nisan-da-sultanahmet-ve-sishane-de-anma
"28 Şubat, MÜSİAD'a Anadolu Kaplanları'na yapıldı!" [28 February Was for MUSIAD, Anatolian Tigers., *Habertürk*, April 28, 2012. https://www.hab erturk.com/ekonomi/makro-ekonomi/haber/737930-28-subat-musiada-
"78 Percent of Gezi Park Protest Detainees Were Alevis: Report." *Hurriyet Daily News*, November 25, 2013. https://www.hurriyetdailynews.com/78-percent-of-gezi-park-protest-detainees-were-alevis-report--58496
"411 el kaosa kalktı" [411 Hands for the Caos]. *Hürriyet*, February 10, 2008. Printed
"Adalet ve Kalkınma Partisi kuruldu" [Justice and Development Party Is Established]. *Hürriyet*, August 14, 2001. http://www.hurriyet.com.tr/gundem/ adalet-ve-kalkinma-partisi-kuruldu-10017
"Ak Partili Belediye 5. Cemevini Açtı" [Municipality That Run by AK Party Opened Its fifth Cemevi]. *Sabah*, July 7, 2018. https://www.sabah.com.tr/ gundem/2018/07/06/ak-partili-belediye-5inci-cemevini-acti
"AKP Kapatılmadı" [JDP Is Not Closed]. *Hürriyet*, July 30, 2008. https:// www.hurriyet.com.tr/gundem/akp-kapatilmadi-9546038
"AKP Lideri Erdoğan: DP'nin devamıyız" [AKP Leader Erdogan: We Are the Successor of DP]. *Hürriyet*, May 16, 2003. http://hurarsiv.hurriyet.com.tr/ goster/ShowNew.aspx?id=147213
"Anayasa Mahkemesi 367 şart dedi" [Constitutional Court Stated That 367 Is Necessary]. *Hürriyet*, May 2, 2007. http://www.hurriyet.com.tr/gundem/ anayasa-mahkemesi-367-sart-dedi-6436574

BIBLIOGRAPHY 243

"Askerden Açıklama" [Announcement from the Soldiers]. *Cumhuriyet*, April 28, 2007. Print.

"Bahçeli'den 'andımız' açıklaması" [Bahceli's "Oath" Statement]. *Hürriyet*, October 20, 2018. Accessed July 27, 2019. http://www.hurriyet.com.tr/gun dem/bahceliden-andimiz-aciklamasi-40993292

"Brotherhood Angry at Erdogan Call for Secular Egypt." *Jerusalem Post*, September 14, 2011. https://www.jpost.com/Middle-East/Brotherhood-angry-at-Erdogan-call-for-secular-Egypt-237916

"Bu ne rezalet" [What a Disgrace]. *Sabah*, February 2, 1997. Print.

"Cem Vakfı Genel Başkanı Erdoğan Döner: Bizim Alevi sorunumuz ülkemizin beka sorunundan önce gelmez" [Erdogan Döner, the President of Cem Vakfı: Our Alewi Issue Does No Come Before the survival Problem of Our Country]. *Anadolu Ajansı*, June 17, 2018. https://www.aa.com.tr/tr/tur kiye/cem-vakfi-genel-baskani-erdogan-doner-bizim-alevi-sorunumuz-ulkemi zin-beka-sorunundan-once-gelmez/1176981

"Cemevinin elektrik faturasını Diyanet ödeyecek" [The Electricity Bill of the Cemevi Will Be Covered by Diyanet]. *Hürriyet*, December 12, 2018. http://www.hurriyet.com.tr/gundem/cemevinin-elektrik-faturasini-diy anet-odeyecek-41049229

"Cumhurbaşkanı Erdoğan İmam Hatip Gençlik Buluşmasında" [President Is at the Imam Hatip Youth Convention]. *Akşam*, April 28, 2016. http://www. aksam.com.tr/siyaset/cumhurbaskani-erdogan-imam-hatip-genclik-bulusmasi nda/haber-511523

"Cumhurbaşkanı Erdoğan imam hatip lisesi öğrencilerine hitap etti" [President Erdogan Addressed Imam Hatip High School Students]. *Anadolu Ajansı*, April 10, 2017. https://aa.com.tr/tr/turkiye/cumhurbaskani-erd ogan-imam-hatip-lisesi-ogrencilerine-hitap-etti/793729

"Cumhurbaşkanı Erdoğan Süryani Kilisesi temel atma töreninde konuştu" [President Erdogan Gave a Speech During the Groundbreaking Ceremony of Assyrian Church]. *Hürriyet*, August 3, 2019. http://www.hurriyet.com.tr/ gundem/cumhurbaskani-erdogan-suryani-kilisesi-temel-atma-toreninde-kon usuyor-41292483

"Cumhurbaşkanı Erdoğan'dan çok sert 'Öğrenci Andı' tepkisi" [Harsh Response by President Erdogan on "Student Oath"]. *Hürriyet*, November 3, 2018. http://www.hurriyet.com.tr/gundem/cumhurbaskani-erdogan-muj deyi-genclerimizle-paylasmis-olalim-41007383

"ÇYDD From Past to Present." *Association for Supporting Contemporary Life (CYDD)*. https://www.cydd.org.tr/pages/from-past-to-present-cydd-8/

"Dersim Özrü" [Apology for Dersim]. *Hürriyet*, November 24, 2011. https:// www.hurriyet.com.tr/gundem/dersim-ozru-19314519

244 BIBLIOGRAPHY

"Dindar gençlik yetiştireceğiz" [We Will Raise Pious Youth]. *Hürriyet*, February 2, 2012. https://www.hurriyet.com.tr/gundem/dindar-genclik-yet istirecegiz-19825231

"Duygulandıran Pinarhisar mektupları" [Emotional Letters from Pinarhisar]. *Yenişafak*, September 3, 2013. http://yenisafak.com.tr/politika-haber/duy gulandiran-pinarhisar-mektuplari-03.09.2013-560650

"Ecevit: Kavakcı'nın TBMM'de yeri yok" [Ecevit: Kavakcı Has No Place in the Parliament]. *Hürriyet*, May 8, 1999. https://www.hurriyet.com.tr/gundem/ ecevit-kavakcinin-tbmmde-yeri-yok-39078219

"Erbakan'ın MGK'daki zor anları" [Hard Times of Erbakan During National Security Council]. *Milliyet*, August 12, 1997. http://www.milliyet.com.tr/ 1997/08/12/siyaset/erbakan.html

"Erdoğan 'laiklik' ile ilgili ne demişti?" [What Did Erdogan Say About Secularism]. *CNN Türk*, April 27, 2016. https://www.cnnturk.com/video/ yasam/erdogan-laiklik-ile-ilgili-ne-demisti

"Erdoğan'dan anayasa çıkışı: İslam vurgusuna ihtiyaç yok" [Erdogan's Statement on Constitution: No Need for Emphasis on Islam]. *Hürriyet*, April 28, 2016. http://www.hurriyet.com.tr/gundem/laiklik-ladinilik-olursa-itiraz-gelir-40095714

"Erdoğan'dan Ermeni Patrikhanesi'nde düzenlenen törene mesaj" [A Massage from Erdogan to the Ceremony at the Armenian Patriarchate]. *Hürriyet*, April 24, 2018. http://www.hurriyet.com.tr/gundem/erdogandan-ermeni-patrikhanesinde-duzenlenen-torene-mesaj-40815152

"Erdoğan'dan 1915 için taziye mesajı" [Condolence from Erdogan About 1915]. *AGOS*, April 24, 2018. http://www.agos.com.tr/tr/yazi/20539/erdogan-dan-1915-icin-taziye-mesaji

"Ermeni konferansı Bilgi Üniversitesi'nde başladı" [Armenian Conference Has Started at Bilgi University]. *Hürriyet*, September 24, 2005. https://www.hur riyet.com.tr/gundem/ermeni-konferansi-bilgi-universitesinde-basladi-352577

"Genç Subaylar Tedirgin" [Young Soldiers Are Anxious]. *Cumhuriyet*, May 23, 2003. Print.

"Gerekirse silah bile kullanırız" [If It Is Necessary, We Can Even Use Gun]. *Hürriyet*, July 12, 1997. Print.

"Hrant Dink davasında önemli gelişme! 99 yıl 6 ay hapis cezası" [Important Developments in Hrant Dink Case! Sentence for 99 Years and 6 Months]. *Hürriyet*, July 17, 2019. https://www.hurriyet.com.tr/gundem/hrant-dink-davasinda-onemli-gelisme-99-yil-6-ay-hapis-cezasi-41276763

"Huge Rally for Turkish Secularism." *BBC News*, April 29, 2007. http://news. bbc.co.uk/2/hi/6604643.stm

"Hükümet genelkurmay açıklamasını değerlendirdi" [The Government Assessed General Staff's Statement]. *Hürriyet*, April 28, 2007. https://www.hurriyet. com.tr/gundem/hukumet-genelkurmay-aciklamasini-degerlendirdi-6424353

BIBLIOGRAPHY   245

"İşte 'Demokratikleşme Paketi'nin tam metni" [Here Is the Full Script of the Democratization Package]. *Yenişafak*, September 30, 2013. https://www.yen isafak.com/gundem/iste-demokratiklesme-paketinin-tam-metni-569627

"Kılıçdaroğlu: Başörtüsü sorunu vardı biz çözdük" [Kılıçdaroğlu: There Was a Headscarf Issue, We Solved It]. *İhlas Haber Ajansı*, March 6, 2014. http://www.iha.com.tr/haber-kemal-kilicdaroglu-basortusu-sorunu-vardi-biz-cozduk-338040/

"Kimlik atışması" [Identity Dispute]. *Hürriyet*, December 15, 2005. http://www.hurriyet.com.tr/gundem/kimlik-atismasi-3652511

"Kişi laik olmaz, devlet laik olur" [Persons Cannot Be Secular, States Can]. *Cumhuriyet*, September 16, 2011. http://www.cumhuriyet.com.tr/haber/diger/282650/_Kisi_laik_olmaz__devlet_laik_olur_.html

"Kılıçdaroğlu radyo yayınına katıldı" [Kılıçdaroğlu Joined the Radio Broadcast]. *Anadolu Ajansı*, June 18, 2018. https://www.aa.com.tr/tr/politika/kilicd aroglu-radyo-yayinina-katildi/1178221

"Kılıçdaroğlu, Genç İmam Hatipliler Derneği üyeleriyle bir araya geldi: Partilerin dini olmaz" [Kılıcdaroglu met with the Members of Foundation of Young Imam Hatip Students: Parties Do Not Have Religion]. *Cumhuriyet*, June 1, 2019. http://www.cumhuriyet.com.tr/haber/siyaset/1420656/Kilicdaro glu__Genc_imam_Hatipliler_Dernegi_uyeleriyle_bir_araya_geldi__Partilerin_d ini_olmaz.html

"Konda'nın 10 yıllık raporu: Ateist oranı arttı" [Konda's 10-Year Research: The Proportion of the Atheist Increased]. *Cumhuriyet* January 3, 2019. http://www.cumhuriyet.com.tr/haber/turkiye/1189902/kondanin-10-yil lik-raporu-ateist-orani-artti.html

"Köşk'ten 'kırmızı halı' açıklaması" ["Red Carpet" Announcement from the Presidential House]. *Hürriyet*, October 21, 2010. http://www.hurriyet.com. tr/gundem/koskten-kirmizi-hali-aciklamasi-16102964

"Laiklik her dine eşit mesafede" [Secularism Is Distant to Each Religion Equally]. *Hürriyet*, September 15, 2011. http://www.hurriyet.com.tr/gundem/laiklik-her-dine-esit-mesafede-18735423

"Milli Güvenlik Dersi Kaldırıldı" [National Security Course Has Been Lifted]. *Hürriyet*, January 25, 2012. http://www.hurriyet.com.tr/gundem/milli-guv enlik-dersi-kaldirildi-19765864

"Muharrem İnce: Endüstri 4,0 diyen bir cumhurbaşkanı olacak" [Muharrem İnce: There Will Be a President Who Says Industry 4.0]. *Hürriyet*, May 11, 2018. http://www.hurriyet.com.tr/gundem/muharrem-ince-erdoganin-selamini-iletiyorum-40833468

"Muhtıra gibi tavsiye" [Advice Like a Memorandum]. *Cumhuriyet*, March 1, 1997. Print.

246 BIBLIOGRAPHY

"Protokole reis ayarı" [Chief Adjustment in the Protocol]. *Sabah*, May 14, 2012. https://www.sabah.com.tr/gundem/2012/05/14/devlet-protok olunde-sivillesme-donemi

"Rektörler Endişeli' [Rectors Are Concerned]. *Sabah*, December 10, 1996. Print.

"RPP'den türbanlı milletvekili kararı" [Hijabi Parliament Member Decision from RPP]. *Hürriyet*, October 28, 2013. http://www.hurriyet.com.tr/gundem/ RPPden-turbanli-milletvekili-karari-24997255

"Seçim 2007: Türkiye Geneli Seçim Sonuçları" [Election 2007: General Turkey Results]. *Hürriyet*, July 22, 2007. http://secim2007.hurriyet.com.tr/partid etay.aspx?pid=8

"Sezer'in Sınır Aşan Başörtüsü Yasağı" [Sezer's Borderless Headscarf Ban]. *Yenişafak*, January 7, 2006. https://www.yenisafak.com/gundem/sezerin-sinir-asan-basortu-yasagi-2718691

"Siyasi Hayatı Bitti" [His Political Life Is Over]. *Hürriyet*, November 1, 1998. http://www.hurriyet.com.tr/gundem/siyasi-hayati-bitti-39045560

"Taksim Camii'nin Temelleri Atıldı" [Taksim Camii's Foundations Are Found]. *Hürriyet*, February 17, 2017. https://www.hurriyet.com.tr/gundem/taksim-camiinin-temeli-atildi-40368952

"Tarihi sinagogda 41 yıl sonra ilk düğün" [First Wedding in the Historical Synagogue After 41 Years]. *Hürriyet*, May 29, 2016. http://www.hurriyet.com. tr/tarihi-sinagogda-41-yil-sonra-ilk-dugun-37287821

"Timeline: Turkey's 'Ergenekon' Trial." *Al Jazeera*, August 5, 2013. https:// www.aljazeera.com/news/europe/2013/08/20138512358195978.html

"Tunceli Seçim Sonuçları" [Tunceli Election Results]. *Yenişafak*. https://www. yenisafak.com/yerel-secim-2019/tunceli-ili-secim-sonuclari

"Türbanlı milletvekilleri Genel Kurul'da" [Hijabi Parliament Members Are in General Assembly]. *Hürriyet*, November 1, 2013. http://www.hurriyet.com. tr/gundem/turbanli-milletvekilleri-genel-kurulda-25017264

"Türk Toplumu mesajımı aldı" [Turkish Society Received my Message]. *Hürriyet*, April 20, 2007. http://www.hurriyet.com.tr/gundem/turk-top lumu-mesajimi-aldi-6366872

"Türkiye'de kaç cami var?" [How Many Mosques in Turkey?]. *İhlas Haber Ajansı*, July 12, 2013. https://www.iha.com.tr/haber-turkiyede-kac-cami-var-285986/

"Turkey's Islamists and Secularists Join Forces in Bid to Unseat Erdoğan." *The Guardian*, June 18, 2018. https://www.theguardian.com/world/2018/jun/ 18/turkey-islamists-and-secularists-join-forces-in-bid-to-unseat-erdogan

"Turkey's Minority Leaders Sign Joint Declaration Denying 'Pressure' on Communities." *Daily Sabah*, July 31, 2018. https://www.dailysabah.com/ minorities/2018/07/31/turkeys-minority-leaders-sign-joint-declaration-den ying-pressure-on-communities

BIBLIOGRAPHY 247

"TÜSİAD: Refah Türkiye'nin partisi olmayı başaramadı" [TUSIAD: Refah Couldn't Manage to Become a Party of Turkey]. *Hürriyet*, January 23, 1998. http://www.hurriyet.com.tr/ekonomi/tusiad-refah-turkiyenin-partisi-olmayi-basaramadi-39003540

"Yarınlar ülkemiz için bu noktadan çok daha iyi olacak" [Tomorrow Is Going to be Much Better for Our Country Than Today]. *Yenişafak*, April 29, 2017. https://www.yenisafak.com/gundem/yarinlar-ulkemiz-icin-bu-noktadan-cok-daha-iyi-olacak-2650890

Yenişafak. "Utanç görüntüleri: Bülent Ecevit meclisten Merve Kavakcı'yı böyle kovdu" [Images of Shame: This Is How Bulent Ecevit Dismiss from the Parliament]. *YouTube*, February 28, 2017. https://www.youtube.com/watch?v=gvT2QMpjQeQ&feature=youtu.be

Media Sources with Authors

Ackerman, Xanthe and Ekin Çalışır. "Erdogan's Assault on Education: The Closure of Secular Schools." *Foreign Affairs*, December 23, 2015. https://www.foreignaffairs.com/articles/turkey/2015-12-23/erdogans-assault-education

Akdoğan, Yalçın. "İslamcılık ve AK Parti" [Islamism and Ak Party]. *Star*, May 28, 2013. http://haber.stargazete.com/yazar/islamcilik-ve-ak-parti/yazi-757689

Arsu, Şebnem. "Ex-Chief of Turkish Army Is Arrested in Widening Case Alleging Coup Plot." *The New York Times*, January 5, 2012. https://www.nytimes.com/2012/01/06/world/europe/turkey-arrests-ex-chief-of-military-gen-ilker-basbug.html

Bali, Aslı U. "Turkey's Referendum: Creating Constitutional Checks and Balances." *Foreign Policy*, September 15, 2010. https://foreignpolicy.com/2010/09/15/turkeys-referendum-creating-constitutional-checks-and-balances/

Bila, Fikret. "Resepsiyon sorunu 10 yaşına bastı" [Reception Problem Exists for 10 Years]. *Milliyet*, October 29, 2012. http://www.milliyet.com.tr/yazarlar/fikret-bila/resepsiyon-sorunu-10-yasina-basti-1618500

Butler, Daren. "With More Islamic Schooling, Erdogan Aims to Reshape Turkey." *Reuters*, January 25, 2018. https://www.reuters.com/investigates/special-report/turkey-erdogan-education/

Eliaçık, İhsan. "Yeni İslamcılık" [New Islamism]. *Tempo*, December 13, 2006. http://www.ihsaneliacik.com/2006/12/soylesi-tempo.html

Ergin, Sedat. "Tarikat İftarı Bardağı Taşırdı" [Iftaar with Religious Cults Was the Limit]. *Hürriyet*, August 23, 1997. https://www.hurriyet.com.tr/tarikat-iftari-bardagi-tasirdi-39260952

Filkins, Dexter. "The Deep State: The Prime Minister Is Revered as a Moderate, but How Far Will He Go to Stay in Power?" *New Yorker*, March 5, 2012. https://www.newyorker.com/magazine/2012/03/12/the-deep-state

248 BIBLIOGRAPHY

Gürsel, Kadri. "Erdogan Islamizes Education System to Raise 'Devout Youth.'" *Al-Monitor*, December 9, 2014. http://www.al-monitor.com/pulse/origin als/2014/12/turkey-islamize-education-religion.html

Hamsici, Mahmut. "2010 referandumu: 'Evet', 'Hayır' ve 'Boykot' cepheleri ne demişti?" [2010 Referandum: What Did "Yes", "No" and "Boycot" Parties Say?]. *BBC Türkçe*, April 5, 2017. https://www.bbc.com/turkce/haberler-turkiye-39462061

Karaalioğlu, Mustafa. "Başbakan Referanduma gider mi?" [Will the Prime Minister Hold a Referendum?]. *Yenişafak*, June 7, 2005. https://www.yen isafak.com/arsiv/2005/haziran/07/mkaraalioglu.html

Onuş, Sinan. "80 yılda 24 gayrimüslim milletvekili" [24 Non-Muslim MP in 80 Years]. *BBC Türkçe*, April 20, 2015. https://www.bbc.com/turkce/hab erler/2015/04/150420_secim_gayrimuslim_adaylar

Özkök, Ertuğrul. "İmam Hatiplere arka bahçemiz diyenlerle biz yolumuzu ayırdık" [We Break Up with the Ones Who Called Imam Hatips' Their Back-yard]. *Hürriyet*, July 7, 2005. http://www.hurriyet.com.tr/gundem/imam-hatiplere-arka-bahcemiz-diyenlerle-biz-yolumuzu-ayirdik-38746336

Özkok, Ertuğrul. "Cumhuriyet mitingleri dosyasını açıyorum" [I Open the Files of Demonstrations for the Republic]. *Hürriyet*, April 2, 2009. http://www.hurriyet.com.tr/cumhuriyet-mitingleri-dosyasini-aciyorum-11345082

Shaheen, Kareem and Gökçe Saraçoğlu. "Turkey's Islamists and Secular-ists Join Forces in Bid to Unseat Erdoğan." *The Guardian*, June 18, 2018. https://www.theguardian.com/world/2018/jun/18/turkey-islamists-and-secularists-join-forces-in-bid-to-unseat-erdogan

Vingas, Laki. "Non-Muslim Minorities in Modern Turkey." *Hurriyet Daily News*, July 14, 2014. http://www.hurriyetdailynews.com/non-muslim-minorities-in-modern-turkey-69065

Waldman, Simon A. "Elections in Turkey: The Waning Charisma of Recep Tayyip Erdogan." *Simon A. Waldman*, June 19, 2018. http://www.simonwaldman.org/blog/elections-in-turkey-the-waning-charisma-of-recep-tayyip-erdogan

Weise, Zia. "Turkey's New Curriculum: More Erdoğan, More Islam." *Politico*, February 13, 2017. https://www.politico.eu/article/erdogan-turkey-educat ion-news-coup-analysis-curriculum-history-İstanbul/

Yıldız, Güney. "Ergenekon: The Court Case That Changed Turkey." *BBC*, August 5, 2013. https://www.bbc.com/news/world-europe-23581891

SECONDARY SOURCES

Ağaoğlu, Ahmet. *İki Parti Arasındaki Farklar* [Differences Between Two Parties]. Ankara: Arbas Matbaası, 1947.

Ahmad, Feroz. *The Making of Modern Turkey*. London: Routledge, 2003.

BIBLIOGRAPHY 249

Akdoğan, Yalçın. *AK Parti ve Muhafazakâr Demokrasi* [AK Party and Conservative Democracy]. İstanbul: Alfa, 2004a.

Akdoğan, Yalçın. *Muhafazakar Demokrasi* [Conservative Democracy]. İstanbul: Alfa, 2004c.

Akdoğan, Yalçın. "Adalet ve Kalkınma Partisi" [Justice and Development Party]. In *Modern Türkiye'de Siyasi Düşünce: İslamcılık Vol. 6* [Political Thinking in Modern Turkey: Islamism Vol. 6], edited by Yasin Aktay, Murat Gültekingil and Tanıl Bora. İstanbul: İletisim Yayınları, 2005.

Akdoğan, Yalçın. *Asker-Sivil İlişkileri ve Kumpastan Darbeye FETÖ* [Military-Civilian Relationship and FETO from Conspiracy to Coup]. İstanbul: Alfa Yayınları, 2016.

Akdoğan, Ali and Erol Sungur. "Post-Modern Ortamda dindarın değişen giyim anlayışı: Başörtüsü ve Tesettür örneği üzerinden kimlik tartışması" [Changing Dressing Style of Pious People in Postmodern Atmospheric: Debates on Identity on the Basis of Headscarf and Modest Dress]. *Erzincan Üniversitesi Sosyal Bilimler Enstitüsü Dergisi* 9, no. 1 (2016): 67–78.

Akşit, Bahattin. "Islamic Education in Turkey: Medrese Reform in Late Ottoman Times and Imam-Hatip Schools in the Republic." In *Islam in Modern Turkey*, edited by Richard L. Tapper, 145–170. London: IB Tauris, 1991.

Aksu, Abdulkadir. *Yeni Siyaset Paradigması üzerine yazıla* [Essays on the Paradigm of the New Politics]. Ankara: Orient, 2012.

Aktar, Ayhan. *Varlık Vergisi ve Türkleştirme Politikaları* [The Property Tax and Policies of 'Turkification']. İstanbul: İletişim Yayınları, 2000.

Aktar, Ayhan. "Homogenising the Nation, Turkifying the Economy." In *Crossing the Aegean: An Appraisal of the 1923 Compulsory Population Exchange Between Greece and Turkey*, edited by Renée Hirschon, 79–97. New York: Berghahn Books, 2003.

Aktay, Yasin. *Karizma Zamanları: Türkiye Siyasetine Karizma Sosyolojisi Açısından Bir Yaklaşım* [Time of Charisma: An Approach to Turkish Politics with Charisma Sociology]. İstanbul: Tezkire, 2015.

Akyasan, Pınar. "Muhalefet Yıllarında DP ve Kemalizm" [Democrat Party and Kemalism During the Opposition Period (1946–50)]. Master Diss., Yıldız Teknik University, 2011.

Akyüz, İsmail. "Türkiye'de Uygulanan Din Politikaları İçin Bir Tipoloji Denemesi" [A Typology Essay for Religious Policies Applied in Turkey]. *Research Journal of Politics, Economics and Management* 5, no. 1 (2017): 144–164.

Alasania, Giuli and Nani Gelovani. "Islam and Religious Education in Turkey". *IBSU Scientific Journal* 5, no. 2 (2011): 35–50.

Albayrak, Mustafa, *Türkiye Siyasi Tarihinde Demokrat Parti (1946–1960)* [Democrat Party in Turkish Political History (1946–1960)]. İstanbul: Phoenix Yayınevi, 2004.

250 BIBLIOGRAPHY

Altınay, Ayşe Gül. *The Myth of the Military Nation: Militarism, Gender, and Education in Turkey*. New York: Palgrave Macmillan, 2004.

Altunışık, Meliha Benli and Özlem Tür. *Turkey: Challenges of Continuity and Change*. London and New York: Routledge Curzon, 2005.

An-Na'im, Abdullahi Ahmed. "Islam and Secularism." In *Comparative Secularism in a Global Age*, edited by Linell E. Cady and Elizabeth Shakman Hurd, 217–228. New York: Palgrave Macmillan, 2010.

Aras, Bülent. *Turkey and the Greater Middle East*. İstanbul: Tasam Publications, 2004.

Arat, Yeşim. "The Project of Modernity and Women in Turkey." In *Rethinking Modernity and National Identity in Turkey*, edited by Sibel Bozdoğan and Reşat Kasaba. Seattle: University of Washington Press, 1997.

Arat, Yeşim. *Rethinking Islam and Liberal Democracy: Islamist Women in Turkish Politics*. Albany: State University of New York Press, 2005.

Arık, Hülya. "Speaking of Women? Exploring Violence against Women through Political Discourses: A Case Study of Headscarf Debates in Turkey." *e-cadernos ces* 16 (2012): 10–31. June 1, 2012. http://eces.revues.org/1009

Arslan, Zühtü. *Başörtüsü, Ak Parti ve Laiklik: Anayasa Mahkemesinden İki Karar Bir Gerekçe* [Headscarf, Ak Party and Secularism: Two Decisions and a Justification from Constitutional Court]. İstanbul: Seta Analiz, 2009.

Asad, Talal. *Formations of the Secular: Christianity, Islam, Modernity*. California: Stanford University Press, 2003.

Aslamacı, İbrahim. "Din Kültürü ve Ahlak Bilgisi Derslerinin Çoğulculuk Açısından Değerlendirilmesi" [Evaluation of Religious Culture and Ethics Knowledge Courses in Terms of Pluralism]. *Hikmet Yurdu* 6, no. 12 (2013): 267–282.

Aslamacı, İbrahim. "Din Eğitimi Politika ve Uygulamalarında Ak Parti'nin 15 yılı" [Ak Party's 15 Years in Politics and Application of Religious Education]. In *Kuruluşundan Bugüne AK Parti: Toplum* [Ak Party since its Establishment: The Society], edited by İsmail Çağlar and Ali Aslan, 181–211. İstanbul: SETA Yayınları, 2018.

Aslan, Ali. "Post Kemalist Türkiye'de Siyaset" [Politics in Post-Kemalist Turkey]. In *Ak Parti'nin 15 Yılı: Siyaset* [Ak Party's 15 Years: The Politics], edited by Nebi Miş and Ali Aslan, 13–46. İstanbul: SETA Yayınları, 2018.

Ataman, Muhittin. "Özal Leadership and Restructuring of Turkish Ethnic Policy in the 1980s." *Middle Eastern Studies* 38, no. 4 (2002): 123–142.

Atasoy, Yıldız. *Turkey, Islamists and Democracy: Transitions and Globalization in a Muslim State*. London and New York: I. B. Tauris, 2005.

Atay, Tayfun. "Cumhuriyet Türkiyesi'nde bir sorun olarak dine bakış" [Perspectives on Religion as a Problem in Republican Turkey]. *Birikim*, no. 105–106 (1998): 100–106.

BIBLIOGRAPHY 251

Axiarlis, Evangelia. *Political Islam and the Secular state in Turkey.* New York: I. B. Tauris, 2014.

Aydın, Ertan and İbrahim Dalmış, "The Social Bases of the Justice and Development Party." In *Secular and Islamic Politics in Turkey: The making of the Justice and Development Party,* edited by Ümit Cizre, 201–223. New York: Routledge, 2008.

Ayoob, Mohammed. "The Future of Political Islam: The Importance of External Variables." *International Affairs* 81, no. 5 (2005): 951–961.

Azak, Umut. *Islam and Secularism in Turkey: Kemalism, Religion and the Nation State.* New York: I. B. Tauris, 2010.

Bali, Asli U. "Turkey's Referendum: Creating Constitutional Checks and Balances." *Foreign Policy,* September 15, 2010.

Bali, Rıfat. "Cumhuriyet Döneminde Azınlık Milletvekilleri" [Members of Parliaments from Minority Groups in Republican Era]. *Toplumsal Tarih* 186 (2009): 60–64.

Bardakçı, Mehmet, Annette Freyberg-Inan, Christoph Giesel and Olaf Leisse. *Religious Minorities in Turkey.* Basingstoke: Palgrave Macmillan, 2017.

Baser, Bahar and Ahmet Erdi Öztürk. *Authoritarian Politics in Turkey: Elections, Resistance and the AKP.* New York: I. B. Tauris, 2017.

Bayar, Celal. *Başvekilim Adnan Menderes* [My Prime Minister Adnan Menderes]. İstanbul: Baha Matbaasi, 1969.

Bayat, Asef. "What Is Post-Islamism?" *ISIM Review*16 (2005): 5. https://openaccess.leidenuniv.nl/bitstream/handle/1887/17030/ISIM_16_What_is_Post?sequence=1

Bayat, Asef. *Post-Islamism: The Changing Faces of Political Islam.* Oxford: Oxford University Press, 2013.

Bayramoglu, Ali. *28 Şubat: Bir Müdahalenin Güncesi* [28 February: A Diary of an Intervention]. İstanbul: İletişim Yayınları, 2007.

Bekaroğlu, Edip Asaf. "Post-Laik Türkiye? AK Parti İktidarları ve Güncellenen Laiklik Sözleşmesi" [Post-Secular Turkey? Justice and Development Party Governments and Updating the Secular Contract]. *İnsan ve Toplum* 5, no. 9 (2015): 103–122.

Benli, Fatma. "1964–2011 Türkiye ve Dünyada Başörtüsü Yasağı Kronolojisi" [Chronology of Headscarf Ban in Turkey and World: 1964–2011]. *Mazlumder* 2011. http://www.mazlumder.org/fotograf/yayinresimleri/dokuman/turkiyede-dunyada-basortusu-yasagi-kronolojisi.pdf

Beris, Hamit Emrah. *Tek Parti Döneminde Devletçilik* [Statism in the Single Party Era]. İstanbul: Liberte, 2009.

Berger, Peter. *Social Reality of Religion.* London: Faber & Faber, 1969.

Berger, Peter. *The Desecularization of the World: Resurgent Religion and World Politics.* Michigan: Eerdmans, 1999.

252 BIBLIOGRAPHY

Berger, Peter. "Secularisation Falsied." *First Things*, February 2008. https://www.firstthings.com/article/2008/02/secularization-falsified

Berger, Peter, Grace Davie and Effie Fokas, *Religious America, Secular Europe? A Theme and Variations*. London: Ashgate Publishing Limited, 2008.

Berkes, Niyazi. *The Development of Secularism in Turkey*. New York: Routledge, 1998.

Berkes, Niyazi. *Türkiye'de Çağdaşlaşma* [Modernisation in Turkey]. İstanbul: Yapı Kredi Yayınları, 2002.

Berkes, Niyazi. *Teokrasi ve Laiklik* [Theocracy and Secularism]. İstanbul: Yapı Kredi Yayınları, 2016.

Berktay, Halil and Kandemir, Pınar. *History and Memory: TRT World in the Face of the July 15 Coup*. İstanbul: TRT World Research Centre, 2017.

Besli, Hüseyin and Özbay, Ömer. *Bir liderin doğuşu: Recep Tayyip Erdoğan* [The Birth of a Leader]. İstanbul: Yeni Türkiye Yayınları, 2014.

Bilgin, Pınar. "The Securityness of Secularism: The Case of Turkey." *Security Dialogue* 39, no. 6 (2008): 593–614.

Bilgrami, Akeel. *Beyond the Secular West*. New York: Columbia University Press, 2016.

Birand, Mehmet Ali. *Son Darbe 28 Şubat* [The Last Coup 28 February]. İstanbul: Doğan Kitap, 2012.

Bora, Tanıl. *Türk Sağının Üç Hali: Milliyetçilik, Muhafazakarlık, İslamcılık* [Three Ways of Turkish Right: Nationalism, Conservatism, Islamism]. İstanbul: Birikim Yayınları, 1998.

Bora, Tanıl and Murat Gültekingil. *Modern Türkiye'de Siyasi Düşünce: Milliyetçilik* [Political Thought in Modern Turkey: Nationalism]. İstanbul: İletişim Yayınları, 2005.

Bora, Tanıl and Yüksel Taşkın. "Sağ Kemalizm" [Right Kemalism]. In *Modern Türkiye'de Siyasi Düşünce: Kemalizm* [Political Thought in Modern Turkey: Kemalism], edited by Murat Gültekingil and Tanıl Bora, 529–554. İstanbul: İletişim Yayınları, 2002.

Bozan, İrfan. *Devlet ile Toplum Arasında Bir Okul: İmam Hatip Liseleri... Bir Kurum: Diyanet İşleri Başkanlığı* [A School Between the State and the Society]. İstanbul: TESEV Yayınları, 2006.

Bozkurt, Gülnihal. *Batı Hukukunun Türkiye'de Benimsenmesi: Osmanlı Devleti'nden Türkiye Cumhuriyeti'ne Resepsiyon Süreci (1839–1939)* [The Familirisation of Western Law in Turkey: Reception Process from Ottoman State to Turkish Republic]. Ankara: Türk Tarih Kurumu Yayınları, 1996.

Byrd, Dustin J. *Islam in a Post-Secular Society: Religion, Secularity and the Antagonism of Recalcitrant Faith*. Leiden: Brill, 2017.

Bulaç, Ali. *Modern Kavramlar ve Düzenler* [Modern Terms and Systems]. İstanbul: Pınar Yayıncılık, 1987.

BIBLIOGRAPHY 253

Burchardt, Marian and Monika Wohlrab-Sahr. "Multiple Secularities: Religion and Modernity in the Global Age." *International Sociology* 28, no. 6 (2015): 605–611.

Burke, Edmund. *Reflections on the Revolution in France.* New York: Liberal Arts Press, 1955.

Cady, Linel E. and Elizabeth S. Hurd. *Comparative Secularism in a Global Age.* New York: Palgrave Macmillan, 2010.

Çağlar, İsmail. *From Symbolic Exile to Physical Exile: Turkey's Imam Hatip Schools, the Emergence of a Conservative Counter-Elite, and Its Knowledge Migration to Europe.* Amsterdam: Amsterdam University Press, 2013.

Çakır, Ruşen. *Ayet ve Slogan: Türkiye'de İslami Oluşumlar* [Verse and Slogan: Islamic Formations in Turkey]. İstanbul: Metis, 1990.

Çakır, Ruşen, İrfan Bozan and Balkan Talu. *İmamhatip okulları: Efsaneler ve Gerçekler* [Imam Hatip Schools: Myths and Facts]. İstanbul: Tesev Yayinlari, 2004.

Calhoun, Craig, Mark Juergensmeyer and Jonathan Van Antwerpen. *Rethinking Secularism.* Oxford, Oxford University Press, 2011.

Çalışlar, Oral. *Aleviler* [Alewis]. İstanbul: Everest Yayınları, 2015.

Çamuroglu, Reha. "Alevi Revival in Turkey." In *Alevi Identity: Cultural, Religious and Social Perspectives,* edited by Tord Olson, Elizabeth Özdalga and Catherina Raudvere, 112–116. İstanbul: Swedish Research Institute in İstanbul, 1998.

Çarkoğlu, Ali and Binnaz Toprak. *Değişen Türkiye'de Din, Toplum ve Siyaset* [Religion, Society and Politics in Changing Turkey]. İstanbul: Tesev Yayınları, 2006.

Çarkoğlu, Ali and Ersin Kalaycıoğlu. *The Rising Tide of Conservatism in Turkey.* New York: Palgrave Macmillan, 2009a.

Çarkoğlu, Ali and Ersin Kalaycıoğlu. *Türkiye'de dindarlık: Uluslararası bir karşılaştırma* [Religiousness in Turkey: An International Comparison]. İstanbul: İstanbul Policy Center, 2009b.

Çarkoğlu, Ali. "Turkey's 2011 General Elections: Towards a Dominant Party System?" *Insight Turkey* 13, no. 3 (2011): 43–62.

Çarkoğlu, Ali. "Ak Parti seçmen tabanının değişimi" [The Change of Ak Party's Voter Base]. In *Ak Parti'nin 15 Yılı: Siyaset* [Ak Party's 15 years: The Politics], edited by Nebi Miş and Ali Aslan, 115–128. İstanbul: SETA Yayınları, 2018.

Casanova, Jose. *Public Religions in the Modern World.* Chicago: University of Chicago Press, 1994.

Casanova, Jose. "Civil Society and Religion: Retrospective Reflections on Catholicism and Prospective Reflections on Islam." *Social Research: An International Quarterly* 68, no. 4 (2001): 1064–1965.

254 BIBLIOGRAPHY

Casanova, Jose. "Rethinking Secularization: A Global Comparative Perspective." *The Hedgehog Review* 8, no. 1/2 (2006): 7–22. https://www.uef.fi/doc uments/661547/931509/03_Casanova_Secularization.pdf/c30fd487-a56c-4478-9eb3-5d336626bc0b

Çayır, Kenan. "The Emergence of Turkey's Contemporary 'Muslim Democrats'." In *Secular and Islamic Politics in Turkey: The Making of the Justice and Development Party*, edited by Ümit Cizre, 62–80. New York: Routledge, 2008.

Çayır, Kenan. "Citizenship, Nationality and Minorities in Turkey's Textbooks: From Politics of Non-recognition to 'Difference Multiculturalism'." *Comparative Education* 51, no. 4 (2015): 519–536.

Çelik, Nur Betül. "Kemalizm: Hegemonik Bir Söylem" [Kemalism: A Hegemonic Discourse]. In *Modern Türkiye'de Siyasi Düşünce: Kemalism Vol: 2* [Political Thinking in Modern Turkey: Kemalism], edited by Ahmet İnsel, 75–80. İstanbul: İletişim Yayınları, 2001.

Celik, Zafer. "Yeni Türkiye'nin Eğitimi, Eğitimin Yeni Türkiyesi" [Education at the New Turkey, New Turkey of Education]. *Yeni Türkiye Özel Sayısı* 56, no. 10 (2014): 653–657.

Çiçek, Cemil. *Demokrasi Savunması* [Defending for Decmoracy]. Ankara: AK Party, 2012.

Çigdem, Ahmet. "Muhafazakarlık Uzerine" [On Conservatism]. *Toplum ve Bilim Dergisi* 74 (1997): 32–51.

Çınar, Alev. "Bodies, Places and Time: Islamic Visibilities in the Public Sphere and the Contestations of Secular Modernity in Turkey." PhD diss., University of Pennsylvania, 1998.

Çınar, Alev. *Modernity, Islam, and Secularism in Turkey: Bodies, Places and Times.* Minneapolis: University of Minnesota Press, 2005.

Çınar, Alev. "Subversion and Subjugation in the Public Sphere: Secularism and the Islamic headscarf." *Signs* 33, no. 4 (Summer 2008): 891–913.

Çınar, Menderes. "The Justice and Development Party and the Kemalist Establishment." In *Secular and Islamic Politics in Turkey: The Making of the Justice and Development Party*, edited by Ümit Cizre, 109–131. New York: Routledge, 2008.

Çınar, Menderes. "The Militarization of Secular Opposition in Turkey." *Insight Turkey* 12, no. 2 (2010): 109–123.

Çınar, Menderes and Burhanettin Duran. "The Specific Evaluation of Contemporary Political Islam in Turkey and Its Difference." In *Secular and Islamic Politics in Turkey: The Making of the Justice and Development Party*, edited by Ümit Cizre, 17–41. New York: Routledge, 2008.

Cizre, Ümit. "Ideology, Context and Interest: The Turkish Military." In *Turkey.* edited by Resat Kasaba, 301–332. Cambridge: Cambridge University Press, 2008a.

BIBLIOGRAPHY 255

Cizre, Ümit. *Secular and Islamic Politics in Turkey: The Making of the Justice and Development Party.* New York: Routledge, 2008b.

Cizre, Ümit and Joshua Walker. "Conceiving the NEW Turkey After Ergenekon." *The International Spectator* 45, no. 1 (2010): 89–98.

Cohen, Louis, Lawrance Manion and Keith Morison. *Research Methods in Education.* 6th ed. London: Routledge, 2007.

Çolak, Mustafa. *Bülent Ecevit-Karaoğlan.* İstanbul: İletişim Yayınları, 2010.

Connolly, William. E. *Why I Am Not a Secularist.* Minnesota: Minnesota University Press, 2010.

Dağı, İhsan. "The Justice and Development Party: Identity, Politics, and Human Rights Discourse in the Search for Security and Legitimacy." In *The Emergence of a new Turkey: Democracy and the Ak Party*, edited by Hakan Yavuz, 88–106. Salt Lake City: The University of Utah Press, 2006.

Dağı, İhsan. "Post Islamism a la Turca." In *Post-Islamism: The Changing Faces of Political Islam*, edited by Asef Bayat, 71–108. Oxford: Oxford University Press, 2013.

Dalacoura, Katerina. "The Secular in Non-Western Societies." *Social Science Research Council*, February 11, 2014. https://tif.ssrc.org/2014/02/11/the-secular-in-non-western-societies/

Davie, Grace. "Europe: The Exception That Proves the Rule?" In *The Desecularization of the World: Resurgent Religion in World Politics*, edited by Peter L. Berger, 65–83. Washington: Ethics and Public Policy Center, 1999.

Davison, Andrew. *Secularism and Revivalism in Turkey: A Hermeneutic Reconsideration.* New Haven, Connecticut: Yale University Press, 1998.

Davison, Andrew. "Turkey, a 'Secular' State? The Challenge of Description." *The South Atlantic Quarterly* 102, no. 2–3 (2003): 333–350.

Davison, Andrew. *Türkiye'de Sekülarizm ve Modernlik* [Secularism and Revivalism in Turkey]. Translated by Tuncay Birkan. İstanbul: İletişim Yayınları, 2006.

Davutoğlu, Ahmet. *Stratejik Derinlik* [Strategic Depth]. İstanbul: Küre, 2001.

Demir, Ömer, Mustafa Acar and Metin Toprak. "Anatolian Tigers or Islamic Capital: Prospects and Challenges." *Middle Eastern Studies* 40, no. 6 (2004): 159.

Demirel, Ahmet. "İsmet İnönü." In *Modern Türkiye'de Siyasi Düşünce: Kemalizm Vol. 2* [Political thinking in Modern Turkey: Kemalism Vol. 2], edited by Tanıl Bora and Murat Gültekin 124–137. İstanbul: İletişim Yayınları, 2002.

Demirel, Tanel. "Demokrat Parti ve Liberalizm." In *Modern Türkiye'de Siyasi Düşünce: Liberalizm vol. 7* [Political Thinking in Modern Turkey: Liberalism Vol. 7], edited by Murat Yılmaz, 480–529. İstanbul: İletişim Yayınları, 2005.

Demirkol, Gülşen. *Psikolojik bir işkence metodu olarak: İkna Odaları* [Persuasion Room: A Pyschological Torture Method]. İstanbul: Beyan Yayınları, 2005.

256 BIBLIOGRAPHY

Denoeux, Guilain. "The Forgotten Swamp: Navigating Political Islam." *Middle East Policy* 9, no. 2 (2002): 56–81.

Dobbelaere, Karel. *Secularization: A Multidimensional Concept*. London: Sage, 1981.

Dornyei, Zoltan. *Research Methods in Applied Linguistics: Quantitative Qualitative, and Mixed Methodologies*. Oxford: Oxford University Press: 2007.

Dressler, Marcus. *Writing Religion: The Making of Turkish Alevi Islam*. New York: Oxford University Press, 2013.

Duran, Burhanettin. "The Justice and Development Party's 'New Politics': Steering Toward Conservative Democracy, a Revised Islamic Agenda or Management of New Crises?" In *Secular and Islamic Politics in Turkey: The making of the Justice and Development Party*, edited by Ümit Cizre, 80–107. New York: Routledge, 2008.

Duran, Burhanettin. "AK Parti'nin İdeolojik Dönüşümünün Kodları" [The Codes of AK Party's Ideological Transformation]. In *AK Parti'nin 15 Yılı: Siyaset* [AK Party's 15 Years: Politics], edited by Nebi Miş and Ali Aslan, 47–74. İstanbul: SETA, 2018.

Duran, Hazal. "AK Parti Dönemi Azınlık Politikaları" [Minority Politics During the AK Party Era]. In *Ak Parti'nin 15 Yılı: Siyaset* [Ak Party's 15 Years: Politics], edited by Nebi Miş and Ali Aslan, 361–378. İstanbul: Seta Yayınları, 2018.

Ecevit, Bülent. *Bu Düzen Değişmelidir* [This Order Should Change]. Ankara: Tekin Yayınevi, 1973.

Eisenstadt, Shmuel N. *Modernization: Protest and Change*.New Jersey: Prentice-Hall, 1966.

Eisenstadt, Shmuel N. *Multiple Modernities*. New Jersey: Transaction Publishers, 2002a.

Eisenstadt, Shmuel N. "Concluding Remarks: Public Sphere, Civil Society, and Political Dynamics in Islamic Societies." In *The Public Sphere in Muslim Societies*, edited by Miriam Hoexter et al. New York: State University of New York Press, 2002b.

Eisenstadt, Shmuel N. *Comparative Civilizations and Multiple Modernities*. Netherlands: Brill, 2003.

Eisenstadt, Shmuel N. *Modernity and Modernization*. Israel: The Hebrew University of Jerusalem and Van Leer Jerusalem Institute, 2010.

Erbakan, Necmettin. *Milli Görüş* [National Vision]. İstanbul: Dergah Yayınları, 1975.

Eroğul, Cem. *Demokrat Parti* [Democract Party]. Ankara: İmge, 1998.

Ertit, Volkan. "God Is Dying in Turkey as Well: Application of Secularization Theory to a Non-Christian Society." *Open Theology* 4, no. 1 (2018): 192–211.

Ertit, Volkan. *Sekülerleşme Teorisi: Sekülerleşen Türkiye'nin Analizi* [Theory of Secularisation: Analysis of Secularising Turkey]. İstanbul: Liberte, 2020.

BIBLIOGRAPHY 257

Ete, Hatem. "Turkey's Constitutional Referendum of 2010." *SETAV*, February 15, 2011. https://www.setav.org/en/turkeys-constitutional-referendum-of-2010/

Fenn, Richard K. "The Secularization of Values: An Analytical Framework for the Study of Secularization." *Journal for the Scientific Study of Religion* 8, no. 1 (1969): 112–124.

Feroze, Muhammad Rashid. *Islam and Secularism in Post-Kemalist Turkey*. Islamabad: NWC Books, 1976.

Foucault, Michel. *Discipline and Punish: The Birth of the Prison*. Vintage, 2012.

Fourie, Elsje, "Does Modernity Still Matter? Evaluating the Concept of Multiple Modernities and Its Alternatives." *Bath Papers in International Development and Wellbeing* No. 10 (2010).

Fourie, Elsje. "A Future for the Theory of Multiple Modernities: Insights from the New Modernization Theory." *Social Science Information* 51, no. 1 (2012): 52–69.

Fukuyama, Francis. *The End of History and the Last Man*. New York: Free Press, 1992.

Fuller, Graham E. "The Future of Political Islam." *Foreign Affairs* 81, no. 2 (2002): 48–60.

Fuller, Graham E. "Freedom and Security: Necessary Conditions for Moderation." *The American Journal of Islamic Social Sciences* 22 (2005): 21–28.

Gellner, Ernest. *Muslim Society*. Cambridge: Cambridge University Press, 1981.

Genç, Özge and Ebru İlhan. *Başörtüsü Yasağına İlişkin Değerlendirme ve Öneriler* [Evaluations and Suggestions in regard to Headscarf Ban]. İstanbul: Tesev Yayınları, 2012.

Gezik, Erdal and Ahmet Kerim Gültekin. *Kurdish Alevis and the Case of Dersim: Historical and Contemporary Insights*. New York: Lexington Books, 2019.

Gökaçtı, Mehmet Ali. *Türkiye'de din eğitimi ve İmam Hatipler* [Religious Education in Turkey and Imam Hatips]. İstanbul: İletişim Yayınları, 2005.

Gökarıksel, Banu and Katharyne Mitchell. "Veiling, Secularism, and the Neoliberal Subject: National Narratives and Supranational Desires in Turkey and France." *Global Networks* 5, no. 2 (2005): 147–165.

Göksel, Oğuzhan. "Assessing the Turkish Model as a Guide to the Emerging Democracies in the Middle East." *Ortadoğu Etütleri* 4, no. 1 (2012): 99–120.

Göksel, Oğuzhan. "Assessing the Turkish Model: The Modernisation Trajectory of Turkey Through The Lens of the Multiple Modernities Paradigm." PhD diss., Durham University, 2015.

Gölbaşı, Haydar. "16 Nisan 2017 Referandum Sonuçlarına göre Alevilerin tercihi (Sivas ili örneği)" [The Preference of Alevis According to the Results of the Referendum on 16th April 2017 (The Example of Sivas Province)]. *Alevilik-Bektaşilik Araştırmaları Dergisi* 17 (2018): 75–96.

258 BIBLIOGRAPHY

Göle, Nilüfer. *The Forbidden Modern: Civilization and Veiling*. Ann Arbor: University of Michigan Press, 1996.

Göle, Nilüfer. "Secularism and Islamism in Turkey: The Making of Elites and Counter-Elites." *Middle East Journal* 51, no. 1 (1997): 46–58.

Göle, Nilüfer. "Batı Dışı Modernlik: Kavram Üzerine" [Non-Western Modernism: On the Concept]. In *Modern Türkiye'de Siyasî Düşünce: Modernleşme ve Batıcılık Vol:3* [Political Thinking in Modern Turkey: Modernisation and Westernisation], edited by Uygur Kocabaşoğlu, 56–68. İstanbul: İletişim Yayınları, 2002a.

Göle, Nilüfer. *İslam ve Modernlik Üzerine Melez Desenler* [Hybrid Patterns: On Islam and Modernism]. İstanbul: Metis Yayınları, 2000b.

Göle, Nilüfer. "Post-secular Turkey." *New Perspectives Quarterly* 29, no. 1 (2012): 7–11.

Göle, Nilüfer. *Islam and Secularity: The Future of Europe's Public Sphere*. Durham: Duke University Press, 2015.

Gramsci, Antonio. *Selections from the Prison Notebooks*. Edited by Quintin Hoare and Geoffrey Nowell Smith, London: International Publishers Co, 1989.

Grigoriadis, Ioannis. *Trials of Europenization: Turkish Political Culture and the European Union*. Basingstoke: Palgrave Macmillan, 2009.

Gülalp, Haldun. "Islamist Party Poised for National Power in Turkey." *Middle East Report* 194/195 (1995): 54–56.

Gülalp, Haldun. "Using Islam as Political Ideology Turkey in Historical Perspective." *Cultural Dynamics* 14, no. 1 (2002): 23.

Gülalp, Haldun. "Enlightenment by Fiat: Secularization and Democracy in Turkey." *Middle Eastern Studies* 41, no. 3 (2005): 351–372.

Gülalp, Haldun. "Islam and Democracy: Is Turkey an Exception or a Role Model?" In *The Sage Handbook of Islamic Studies*, edited by Akbar Ahmed and Tamara Sonn, 240–262. London: Sage, 2010.

Gümüşçü, Şebnem. "The Emerging Predominant Party System in Turkey." *Government and Opposition* 48, no. 2 (2013): 223–244.

Gusfield, Joseph R. "Tradition and Modernity: Misplaced Polarities in the Study of Social Change." *American Journal of Sociology* 72, no. 4 (1967): 351–362.

Gür, Bekir S. "What Erdogan Really Wants for education in Turkey: Islamisation or Pluralisation?" *Al Jazeera Centre for Studies*, March 17, 2016.

Güven, Dilek. *Cumhuriyet Dönemi Azınlık Politikaları Bağlamında 6 - 7 Eylül Olayları* [6–7 September Incidents in the context of Minority Politics in Republican Era]. İstanbul: Tarih Vakfı Yurt Yayınları, 2005.

Habermas, Jürgen. "Notes on Post-Secular Societies." *New Perspectives Quarterly* 25, no. 4 (2008): 17–29.

Habermas, Jürgen. *Europe: The Faltering Project*. Malden, MA: Polity Press, 2009.

BIBLIOGRAPHY   259

Hadden, Jeffrey K. "Toward Desacralizing Secularization Theory." *Social Forces* 65, no. 3 (1987): 587–611.

Hale, William. *Turkish Politics and the Military.* London: Routledge, 1993.

Hale, William and Ergun Ozbudun. *Islamism, Democracy, and Liberalism in Turkey: The Case of the AKP.* New York: Routledge, 2009.

Harvey, William S. "Strategies for Conducting Elite Interviews." *Qualitative Research* 11, no. 4 (2011): 431–441.

Haynes, Jeffrey, ed. *Religion and Politics in Europe, the Middle East and North Africa.* Vol. 64. Routledge, 2009.

Haynes, Jeffrey. "Politics, Identity and Religious Nationalism in Turkey: From Ataturk to the AKP." *Australian Journal of International Affairs* 64, no. 3 (2010): 312–327.

Haynes, Jeffrey. "Politics and Religion in a Global Age." In *Religion and Politics: European and Global Perspectives,* edited by Johann P. Arnason and Ireneusz Paweł Karolewski. Edinburgh: Edinburgh University Press, 2014.

Heper, Metin. "Islam, Polity and Society in Turkey: A Middle Eastern Perspective." *Middle East Journal* 35, no. 3 (1981): 345–363.

Heper, Metin and Sabri Sayarı. *Political Leaders and Democracy in Turkey.* London: Lexington Books, 2002.

Heater, Derek. B. *A History of Education for Citizenship.* London: Routledge, 2004.

Hesse-Biber, Sharlene N. and Leavy Patricia. *The Practice of Qualitative Research.* London: Sage, 2006.

Hoexter, Miriam, Shmuel N. Eisenstadt, and Nehemia Levtzion. *Public Sphere in Muslim Societies.* Albany: State University of New York Press, 2002.

Holyoake, George Jacob. *Principles of Secularism.* London: Book Store, 1871.

Huntington, Samuel P. "Conservatism as an Ideology." *The American Political Science Review* 51, no. 2 (1975): 454–473.

Huntington, Samuel P. *The Clash of Civilizations and the Remaking of World Order.* New York: Simon & Schuster, 1996.

İnal, Kemal and Guliz Akkaymak. *Neoliberal Transformation of Education in Turkey: Political and Ideological Analysis of Educational Reforms in the Age of the AKP.* New York: Palgrave Macmillan, 2012.

İnce, Basak. "Citizenship Education in Turkey: Inclusive or Exclusive." *Oxford Review of Education* 38, no. 2 (2012): 115–131.

İnsel, Ahmet. "Cumhuriyet Döneminde Otoritarizmin Sürekliliği." *Birikim* 125–126 (1999): 143–166.

İnsel, Ahmet. "The AKP and Normalizing Democracy in Turkey." *The South Atlantic Quarterly* 102, no. 2–3 (2003): 293–308.

Jacoby, Tim "A Historical Perspective on the July 2016 Coup Attempt in Turkey." *Insight Turkey* 18, no. 3 (2016): 119–138.

260 BIBLIOGRAPHY

Jenkins, Gareth H. *Between Fact and Fantasy: Turkey's Ergenekon Investigation*. Washington: The Central Asia-Caucasus Institute, 2009.

Jenkins, Richard. *Social Identity*. London and New York: Routledge, 2004.

Kaçer, Murat and Yılmaz Bingöl. "AK Parti dönemi Sünni ve Alevi Zazaların seçmen davranışları" [Voter Behaviour of Sunni and Alevi Zazas During the Ak Party Era]. *Bingöl Üniversitesi Sosyal Bilimler Enstitüsü Dergisi* 8, no. 15 (2018): 65–87.

Kadıoğlu, Ayşe. "Women's Subordination in Turkey: Is Islam Really the Villain?" *Middle East Journal* 48, no. 4 (1994): 645–660.

Kahraman, Hasan B. "Bir zihniyet, kurum ve kimlik kurucusu olarak Batılılaşma" [Westernisation as a Founder of Mentality, Institute and Identity] In *Modern Türkiye'de Siyasi Düşünce: Modernleşme ve Batıcılık Vol: 3* [Political Thinking in Modern Turkey: Modernisation and Westernisation], edited by Uygur Kocabaşoğlu. İstanbul: İletişim, 2002.

Kandiyoti, Deniz. "Identity and Its Discontents: Woman and the Nation." *American Journal of Political Science* 20, no. 3 (1991): 429–443.

Kandiyoti, Deniz. "Gendering the Modern: On Missing Dimensions in the Study of Turkish Modernity." In *Rethinking Modernity and National Identity in Turkey*, edited by Sibel Bozdoğan and Reşat Kasaba. Washington: University of Washington Press, 1997.

Karasipahi, Sena. *Muslims in Modern Turkey: Kemalism, Modernism, and the Revolt of the Islamic Intellectuals*. New York: I. B.Tauris, 2009.

Karolewski, Janina. "What Is Heterodox About Alevism? The Development of Anti-Alevi Discrimination and Resentment." *Die Welt des Islams* 48 (2008): 434–456.

Karpat, Kemal. *Türk Demokrasi Tarihi* [Turkish Democracy History]. İstanbul: Alfa Yayıncılık, 1996.

Karpat, Kemal. *The Politicization of Islam: Reconstructing Identity, State, Faith, and Community in the Late Ottoman State*. New York: Oxford University Press, 2001.

Kasaba, Reşat. "Kemalist Certainties and Modern Ambiguities." In *Rethinking Modernity and National Identity in Turkey*, edited by Sibel Bozdoğan and Reşat Kasaba, 15–36. Seattle and London: University of Washington Press, 1997.

Kavakcı, Merve. "Questioning Turkey's Role Model Status: A Critical Examination of the Social and Political Implications of the Headscarf Ban in Turkey." PhD diss., Howard University, 2007.

Kavakcı Islam, Merve. *Headscarf Politics in Turkey: A Postcolonial Reading*. New York: Palgrave Macmillan, 2010.

Kaya, Ayhan. "Multiple Modernities and Turkish Modernity." In *Europeanization and Tolerance in Turkey. Identities and Modernities in Europe*, edited by Ayhan Kaya, 28–71. Palgrave Macmillan, London, 2013.

BIBLIOGRAPHY 261

Kaya, İbrahim. *Social Theory and Later Modernities*. Liverpool: Liverpool University Press, 2004.

Kaya, Serdar. "The Rise and Decline of the Turkish 'Deep State': The Ergenekon Case." *Insight Turkey* 11, no. 4 (2009): 99–113.

Kaymakcan, Recep. "Religious Education in Modern Turkey in the Context of Freedom of Religion or Belief." In *Teaching for Tolerance and Freedom of Religion or Belief*, edited by Lena Larsen and Ingvill T. Plesner. Oslo: Oslo Coalition on Freedom of Religion or Belief, 2002. http://folk.uio.no/lei rvik/OsloCoalition/RecepKaymakcan.htm

Keddie, Nikki R. "Secularism and Its Discontents." *On Secularism and Religion* 132, no. 3 (2003): 14–30.

Keyder, Çağlar. *State and Class in Turkey: A Study in Capitalist Development*. London and New York: Verso, 1987.

Keyman, E. Fuat. *Türkiye'de Sivil Toplumun Serüveni: İmkansızlıklar içinde bir vaha* [The Adventure of Civil Society in Turkey: An Oasis in the Impossibilities]. Ankara: Sivil Toplum Geliştirme Merkezi Yayını, 2006.

Keyman, E. Fuat. "Modernity, Secularism and Islam: The Case of Turkey." *Theory, Culture & Society* 24, no. 2 (2007): 215–234.

Keyman, E. Fuat. "Assertive Secularism in Crises: Modernity, Democracy, and Islam in Turkey." In *Comparative Secularism in a Global Age*, edited by Linell E. Cady and Elizabeth Shakman Hurd, 143–158. New York: Palgrave Macmillan, 2010.

Keyman, E. Fuat. "The AK Party: Dominant Party, New Turkey and Polarization." *Insight Turkey* 16, no. 2 (2014): 19–31.

Khan, Mujeeb R. "The July 15th Coup: A Critical Institutional Framework for Analysis." In *Turkey's July 15th Coup: What Happened and Why*, edited by M. Hakan Yavuz and Bayram Balci, 46–77. Chicago: University of Utah Press, 2018.

Kılavuz, M. Akif. "Adult Religious Education at the Qur'anic COURSES in modern Turkey." *The Journal of International Social Research* 2, no. 6 (2009): 407–414.

Koçan, Gürcan and Ahmet Öncü. "Citizen Alevi in Turkey: Beyond Confirmation and Denial." *Journal of Historical Sociology* 17, no. 4 (2004): 464–489.

Köker, Levent. *Modernleşme, Kemalizm ve Demokrasi*. [Modernisation, Kemalism and Democracy] İstanbul: İletişim Yayınları, 2016.

Kömeçoğlu, Uğur. "New Sociabilities: Islamic Cafes in İstanbul." In *Islam in Public: Turkey, Iran and Europe*, edited by Nilüfer Göle and Ludwig Amman, 163–188. İstanbul: İstanbul Bilgi University Press, 2006.

Kösebalaban, Hasan. "The Impact of Globalization on Islamic Political Identity: The Case of Turkey." *World Affairs* 168 (2005): 27–37.

262 BIBLIOGRAPHY

Küçükcan, Talip. "Sacralisation of the State and Secular Nationalism: Foundation of Civil Religion in Turkey." *The George Washington International Law Review* 41, no. 4 (2011): 963–983.

Küçükcan, Talip. "Are Muslim Democrats a Threat to Secularism and Freedom of Religion?" In *The Future of Religious Freedom: Global Challenges*, edited by Allen D. Hertzke, 269–288. Oxford: Oxford University Press, 2013.

Kurban, Dilek and Kezban Hatemi. *Bir Yabancılaştırma Hikayesi* [A Story of Othering]. İstanbul: Tesev Yayınları, 2009.

Kuru, Ahmet T. *Secularism and State Policies Toward Religion: The United States, France, and Turkey.* Cambridge: Cambridge University Press, 2009.

Laclau, Ernesto. *On Populist Reason.* London: Verso, 2005.

Lewis, Bernard. *Emergence of Modern Turkey.* Oxford: Oxford University Press, 1961.

Loobuyck, Patrick. "Religious Education in Habermasian Post-Secular Societies." In *Global Secularisms in a Post-Secular Age*, edited by Michael Rectenwald, Rochelle Almeida,= and George Levine, 91–109. Berlin: De Gruyter, 2015.

Lukes, Steven. *Power: A Radical View.* Vol. 1. London: Macmillan, 1974.

Mackenzie, Kenneth. "Turkey in Transition." *The World Today* 42, no. 6 (1986): 101–104.

Mahçupyan, Etyen. *Türkiye'ye içeriden bakış: Yükselen İslami Orta Sınıf* [An Insider Gaze to Turkey: Rising Islamist Middle Class]. İstanbul: Tesev Yayınları, 2014.

Mardin, Şerif. "Centre-Periphery Relations: A Key to Turkish Politics." *Daedalus* 102, no. 1 (Winter 1973): 169–190.

Mardin, Şerif. "Religion and Secularism in Turkey." In *Atatürk: Founder of a Nation State*, edited by Ali Kazancıgil & Ergun Özbudun, 347–363. Hamden, CT: Archon, 1981.

Mardin, Şerif. *Türkiye'de Toplum ve Siyaset* [Society and Politics in Turkey]. İstanbul: İletişim Yayınları, 1990.

Mardin, Şerif. *Türkiye'de Din ve Siyaset* [Religion and Politics in Turkey]. İstanbul: İletişim Yayınları, 1997.

Mardin, Şerif. *Din ve İdeoloji* [Religion and Ideology]. İstanbul: İletişim Yayınları, 2002a.

Mardin, Şerif. *Türk Modernleşmesi* [Turkish Modernisation]. İstanbul: İletişim Yayınları, 2002b.

Mardin, Şerif. "Turkish Islamic Exceptionalism Yesterday and Today: Continuity, Rupture and Reconstruction in Operational Codes." *Turkish Studies* 6 (2005): 145–165.

Martin, David. "The Denomination." In *Sociology of Religion Vol. 2*, edited by Steve Bruce. London: Edward Elgar Publishing Limited, 1995.

BIBLIOGRAPHY 263

Massicard, Elise. *Turkiye'den Avrupa'ya Alevi Hareketinin Siyasallasması* [Politisation of Alevi Movement from Turkey to Europe], translated by Ali Berktay. İstanbul: İletişim Yayınları, 2007.

Massicard, Elise. "Democratisation in Turkey? Insights from the Alevi Issue." In *Turkey's Democratization Process*, edited by C. Rodriguez, A. Avalos, H. Yılmaz and A. I. Planet, 376–390. London: Routledge, 2013.

Massicard, Elise. *The Alevis in Turkey and Europe: Identity and Managing Territorial Diversity*. London: Routledge, 2017.

McDowell, Linda. "Elites in the City of London: Some Methodological Considerations." *Environment and Planning* 30, no. 12 (1998): 2133–2146.

Meral, Ziya. *Compulsory Religious Education in Turkey—A Survey and Assessment of Textbooks*. Washington: United States Commission on International Religious Freedom, 2015.

Müftügil, Ayşe. S. "Compulsory Religion Education and Religious Minorities in Turkey." PhD thesis, University of Amsterdam, 2011

Navaro-Yashin, Yael. *Faces of the State: Secularism and Public Life in Turkey*. Princeton: Princeton University Press, 2002.

Öcal, Mustafa. "Cumhuriyet Döneminde Türkiye'de Din Eğitimi ve Öğretimi." *Uludağ Üniversitesi İlahiyat Fakültesi Dergisi* 7, no. 7 (1998): 241–268.

Öcal, Mustafa. *100. Yılında imam-hatip liseleri (1913–2013)* [Imam-Hatip High Schools on their Hundredth Year (1913–2013)]. İstanbul: Ensar Neşriyat, 2013.

Öktem, Niyazi. "Religion in Turkey." *Brigham Young University Law Review* 2, no. 2 (2002): 371–403.

Olson, Tord. Elizabeth Özdalga and Catherina Raudvere. *Alevi Identity: Cultural, Religious and Social Perspectives*. İstanbul: Swedish Research Institute in İstanbul, 1998.

Öniş, Ziya. "Turgut Özal and His Economic Legacy: Turkish Neo-Liberalism in Critical Perspective." *Middle Eastern Studies* 40, no. 4 (2004): 113–134.

Öniş, Ziya. "The Political Economy of Islam and Democracy in Turkey: From the Welfare Party to the AKP." In *Democratization and Development*, edited by Dietrich Jung, 103–128. New York: Palgrave Macmillan, 2006.

Oran, Baskın. *Türkiye'de Azınlıklar: Kavramlar, Teori, Lozan, İç Mevzuat, İçtihat, Uygulama* [Minorities in Turkey: Concepts, Theory, Lausanne, Local Rules, Case Law, Implementation]. İstanbul: İletişim Yayınları, 2004.

Özbudun, Sibel. Kadınlar, İslam, AKP ve Ötesi [Women, Islam, AKP and Beyond]. Ankara: Utopya Yayınevi, 2016.

Özipek, Bekir Berat. *Muhafazakârlık -Akıl, Toplum, Siyaset* [Conservativism-Mind, Society, Politics]. Ankara: Liberte, 2004.

Özkok, Ertuğrul. *Bir Beyaz Türk'ün Hafıza Defteri* [A Memory Book of a White Turk]. İstanbul: Doğan Kitap, 2014.

264 BIBLIOGRAPHY

Özyürek, Esra. *Nostaljia for the Modern*. Durham and London: Duke University Press, 2006.

Pamuk, Şevket. "Globalization, Industrialization and Changing Politics in Turkey." *New Perspectives on Turkey* 38 (2008): 267–273.

Parla, Taha. *Kemalist Tek Parti İdeolojisi ve CHP'nin Altı Oku* [Kemalist Single-Party Ideology and CHP's Six Arrows]. İstanbul: İletişimYayınları, 1992.

Preyer, Gerhard and Sussman, Michael. "Introduction on Shmuel N. Eisenstadt's Sociology: The Path to Multiple Modernities." In *Varieties of Multiple Modernities*, edited by Gerhard Preyer and Michael Sussman, 1–29. Netherlands: Brill, 2015.

Ramadan, Tariq. *Islam, the West and the Challenges of Modernity*. Leicester: The Islamic Foundation, 2009.

Ramadan, Tariq. *The Arab Awakening: Islam and the New Middle East*. London: Penguin, 2012

Rosati, Massimo. *The Making of a Postsecular Society: A Durkheimian Approach to Memory, Pluralism and Religion in Turkey*. New York: Routledge, 2016.

Roy, Olivier. *Globalised Islam: The Search for a New Ummah*. London: Hurst Co, 2002.

Roy, Olivier. *Secularism Confronts Islam*. translated by George Holoch. New York: Columbia University Press, 2007.

Safi, İsmail. "Türkiye'de Muhafazakarlığın düşünsel-siyasal temelleri ve Muhafazakar Demokrat Kimlik arayışları" [The Ideologic and Political Foundations of Conservatism in Turkey and the Search for Conservative Democract Identity]. PhD diss., Ankara Üniversitesi, 2005.

Saktanber, Ayşe. *Living Islam. Women, Religion and Politicization of Culture in Turkey*. London: I. B. Tauris, 2002.

Saktanber, Ayse and Gül Çorbacıoğlu. "Veiling and Headscarf-Skepticism in Turkey." *Social Politics: International Studies in Gender, State & Society* 15, no. 4 (2008): 514–538.

Saleem, Raja M. Ali. *State, Nationalism, and Islamization: Historical Analysis of Turkey and Pakistan*. London: Palgrave, 2017.

Sandıkçı, Özlem and Güliz Ger. "Veiling in Style: How Does a Stigmatized Practice Become Fashionable?" *Journal of Consumer Research* 37, no. 1 (2010): 15–36.

Sarıbay, Ali. Y. *Türkiye'de Demokrasi ve Politik Partiler* [Democracy in Turkey and Political Parties]. İstanbul: Alfa, 2001.

Sayyid, Bobby S. *A Fundamental Fear: Eurocentrism and the Emergence of Islamism*. London and New York: Zed Books, 2004.

Schmidt, Volker. "Modernity and Diversity: Reflections on the Controversy Between Modernization Theory and Multiple Modernists." *Social Science Information* 49, no. 4 (2010): 511–538.

BIBLIOGRAPHY 265

Shankland, David. *The Alevis in Turkey: The Emergence of a Secular Islamic Tradition.* London: Routledge, 2003.

Shils, Edward. "Centre-Periphery." In *The Logic of Personal Knowledge: Essays Presented to M. Polanyi on His Seventieth Birthday, 11th March, 1961,* edited by Polanyi Festschrift Committee. New York: Routledge, 2016.

Shiner, Larry. "The Concept of Secularization in Empirical Research." *Journal for the Scientific Study of Religion* 6, no. 2 (1967): 207–220.

Shively, Kim. "Religious Bodies and the Secular State: The Merve Kavakci Affair." *Journal of Middle East Women's Studies* 1, no. 3 (2005): 46–72.

Subaşı, Necdet. "AKP ve Aleviler, 'Yol' ve 'Yordam' arayışı" [AKP and Alewis, Search for the Right Way Do]. *Finans Politik & Ekonomik Yorumlar* 45, no. 516 (2008b): 8–15.

Suvanto, Pekka. *Conservatism from the French Revolution to the 1990s.* Translated by Roderick Fletcher, Ipswich: The Ipswich Book Company Ltd., 1997.

Soner, Bayram Ali and Şule Toktaş. "Alevis and Alevism in the Changing Context of Turkish Politics: The Justice and Development Party's Alevi Opening." *Turkish Studies* 12, no. 3 (2011): 419–434.

Solgun, Cafer. *Alevilerin Kemalizmle İmtihanı.* [Alevis' test with Kemalism]. İstanbul: Timaş Yayınları, 2011.

Şen, Abdulkerim. "Müfredata Hâkimiyet Mücadelesi: Seküler-Milliyetçiliğe Karşı Muhafazakâr-Milliyetçilik" [Struggle to Control the Curriculum: Secular Nationalism Versus Religious Nationalism]. *Mülkiye Dergisi* 42, no. 3 (2018): 321–345.

Tarhan, Mehmet. *Religious Education in Turkey: A Socio-Historical Study of the Imam-Hatip Schools.* Philadelphia: Temple University Press, 1996.

Taşkın, Yüksel. "Anti-Komünizm ve Türk Milliyetçiliği: Endişe ve Pragmatizm" [Anti-communism and Turkish nationalism: Anxiety and Pragmatism]. In *Modern Türkiye'de Siyasî Düşünce: Milliyetçilik Vol: 4* [Political Thinking in Modern Turkey: Nationalism], edited by Tanıl Bora, 618–622. İstanbul: İletişim Yayınları, 2002.

Taşkın, Yüksel. *AKP Devri: Türkiye Siyaseti, İslamcılık ve Arap Baharı* [The Era of AKP: Turkish Politics, Islamism and Arab Spring]. Ankara: Birikim Yayınları, 2013.

Taşpınar, Ömer. "Turkey: The New Model?" *Brookings,* April 25, 2012. https://www.brookings.edu/research/turkey-the-new-model/

Taylor, Charles. "Modes of Secularism." In *Secularism and Its Critics,* edited by Rajeev Bhargava, 31–53. Delhi: Oxford University Press, 1999.

Taylor, Charles. *A Secular Age.* Cambridge, MA: Belknap Press of Harvard University Press, 2007.

Ter-Matevosyan, Vahram. "The Armenian Community and the AK Party: Finding Trust Under the Crescent." *Insight Turkey* 12, no. 4 (2010): 93–111.

266 BIBLIOGRAPHY

Tok, Gül Ceylan. "The securitization of the headscarf Issue in Turkey: 'The Good and Bad Daughters' of the Republic." *The International Studies Association of Ritsumeikan University: Ritsumeikan Annual Review of International Studies* 8 (2009): 113–137.

Toktaş, Şule and Bülent Aras. "The EU and minority rights in Turkey." *Political Science Quarterly* 124, no. 4 (2009): 697–720.

Toprak, Binnaz. *Islam and Political Development in Turkey*. Leiden: Brill, 1981.

Toprak, Zafer. "Halk Fırkası'ndan Önce Kurulan Parti: Kadınlar Halk Fırkası" [The Party Founded Before the Populist Party: Populist Party of Women]. *Tarih ve Toplum* 9, no. 51 (1988): 30–31.

Toruk, İbrahim. "Türkiye'de Başörtüsü Sorunu ve Yazılı Medyada Sunumu" [The Headscarf Problem in Turkey and Its Presentation in the Press]. *Türkiyat Araştırmaları Dergisi* 30 (2011): 483–514. https://dergipark.org.tr/tr/download/article-file/257725

Tuğal, Cihan. *Passive Revolution: Absorbing the Islamic Challenge to Capitalism*. San Francisco: Stanford University Press, 2009.

Tuğsuz, Nigar. "Alevi Açılımı'nın Neresindeyiz" [Where Are We at the Alewi Opening]. *SETA Perspektif 81*, November 2014.

Tunaya, Tarık Zafer. *Türkiye'de Siyasi Partiler (1859–1952)* [Political Parties in Turkey (2859–1952)]. İstanbul: Arba yayınları, 1952.

Tunaya, Tarık Zafer. *Türkiye'nin Siyasi Hayatında Batılılaşma Hareketleri.* [Westernisation Movements in Turkish Political Life]. İstanbul: Yenigün Matbaası, 1960.

Tuncay, Mete. *Türkiye Cumhuriyetinde Tek Parti Yönetiminin Kurulması 1923–1931* [The Foundation of Single Party Rule in Turkish Republic 1923–1931]. 3th ed. İstanbul: Türkiye Ekonomik ve Toplumsal Tarih Vakfı. 1999.

Turam, Berna. *Secular State and Religious Society: Two Forces in Play in Turkey.* NewYork: Palgrave Macmillan, 2012.

Ünder, Hasan. "Constructivism and the Curriculum Reform of the AKP." In *Neoliberal Transformation of Education in Turkey*edited, by Kemal İnal and Guliz Akkaymak, 33–45. New York: Palgrave Macmillan, 2012.

Üstel, Füsun. *Makbul Vatandaşın Peşinde* [In Pursuit of Desirable Citizen]. İstanbul: İletişim Yayınları, 2004.

Usul, Ali Resul. "The Justice and Development Party and the European Union: From Euro-Skepticism to Euro-Enthusiasm and Euro-Fatigue." In *Secular and Islamic Politics in Turkey: The Making of the Justice and Development Party*, edited by Ümit Cizre, 175–197. London: Routledge: 2007.

Uzun, Hakan. "İktidarını Sürdürmek İsteyen Bir Partinin Kimlik Arayışı: Cumhuriyet Halk Parti'sinin 1947 Olağan Kurultayı" [Identity Search of a Party Wishing to Maintain Its Power: 1947 Ordinary General Assembly of the Republican People's Party]. *Çağdaş Türkiye Tarihi Araştırmaları Dergisi* 12, no. 25 (2012): 101–139.

BIBLIOGRAPHY 267

Van Bruinessen, Martin. "Kurds, Turks and the Alevi revival." *Middle East Reports* 200 (1996): 7–10. https://www.academia.edu/707541/Kurds_Turks_and_the_Alevi_revival_in_Turkey

Wagner, Peter. *Modernity as Experience and Interpretation.* Cambridge: Polity Press, 2008.

Walzer, Michael. "Yeni Kabile Varlığı" [Existence of New Clan]. *Birikim* 45/46 (1993): 60–66.

Watmough, Simon and Ahmet Erdi Öztürk. "The Future of the Gülen Movement in Transnational Political Exile: Introduction to the Special Issue." *Politics, Religion & Ideology* 19, no. 1 (2018): 1–10.

Weiss, John. *Conservatism in Europe 1770–1945: Traditionalism, Reaction and Counter-Revolution.* London: Thames and Hudson, 1977

Wilson, Bryan, R. *Religion in Secular Society: Fifty Years On.* Oxford: Oxford University Press, 2016.

White, Jenny B. "Islam and Politics in Contemporary Turkey." In *Turkey*, edited by Reşat Kasaba, 357–380. Cambridge: Cambridge University Press, 2008.

Yavuz, M. Hakan. "Political Islam and the Welfare Party in Turkey." *Comparative Politics* 30, no. 1 (1997): 63–82.

Yavuz, M. Hakan. *The Emergence of a New Turkey: Democracy and the Ak Party.* Salt Lake City: The University of Utah Press, 2006.

Yavuz, M. Hakan. *Secularism and Muslim Democracy in Turkey.* Cambridge: Cambridge University Press, 2009.

Yavuz, M. Hakan. *Erbakan'dan Erdoğan'a Laiklik, Demokrasi, Kürt Sorunu ve İslam* [Secularism, Democracy, Kurdish Issue and Islam from Erbakan to Erdogan]. Translated by Leman Adal. İstanbul: Kitap, 2011.

Yavuz, M. Hakan. "The Three Stages of the Gülen Movement: From Pietistic Weeping Movement to Power-Obsessed Structure." In *Turkey's July 15th Coup: What Happened and Why*, edited by M. Hakan Yavuz and Bayram Balci, 20–45. Chicago: University of Utah Press, 2018.

Yavuz, M. Hakan. "Understanding Turkish Secularism in the 21 Century: A Contextual Roadmap." *Southeast European and Black Sea Studies* 19, no. 1 (2019): 1–24.

Yavuz, M. Hakan and Ahmet Erdi Öztürk. "Turkish Secularism and Islam Under the Reign of Erdoğan." *Southeast European and Black Sea Studies* 19, no. 1 (2019): 1–9.

Yavuz, M. Hakan and Bayram Balcı. *Turkey's July 15th Coup: What Happened and Why.* Chicago: University of Utah Press, 2018.

Yavuz, M. Hakan and Rasim Koç. "The Turkish Coup Attempt: The Gülen Movement vs. the State." *Middle East Policy* 23, no. 4 (2016): 136–148.

Yıldız, Ahmet. *Ne Mutlu Türküm Diyebilene: Türk Ulusal Kimliğinin Etno-Seküler Sınırları (1919–1938)* [How Happy Is the One Who Calls Himself

268 BIBLIOGRAPHY

a Turk: Ethno-Secular Boundaries of Turkish National Identity]. İstanbul: İletişim Yayınları, 2001.

Yıldız, Ahmet. "Kemalist Milliyetçilik" [Kemalist Nationalism]. In *Modern Türkiye'de Siyasî Düşünce: Kemalism Vol: 2* [Political Thinking in Modern Turkey: Kemalism], edited by Ahmet Insel, 210–214. İstanbul: İletişim Yayınları, 2002.

Yıldız, Ahmet. "Politico-Religious Discourse of Political Islam in Turkey: The Parties of National Outlook." *The Muslim World* 93, no. 2 (2003): 187–209.

Yıldız, Ahmet. "AK Partinin 'Yeni Muhafazakâr Demokratlığı': Türkiye Siyasetinde Adlandırma Problemi" [AK Party as New Conservative Democrat: The Problem of Naming in Turkish Politics]. *Liberal Düşünce* 9, no. 34 (2004a): 5–12.

Yıldız, Ahmet. "Muhafazakârlığın Yerlileştirilmesi ya da AKP'nin 'Yeni Muhafazakâr Demokratlığı'" [Localising Conservatism or AK Party's New Conservative Democratism]. *Karizma* 5, no. 17 (2004b): 53–54.

Yıldız, Ahmet. "Problematizing the Intellectual and Political Vestiges: From 'Welfare' to 'Justice and Development'." In *Secular and Islamic Politics in Turkey: The Making of the Justice and Development Party*, edited by Ümit Cizre, 41–62. New York: Routledge, 2008.

Yıldız, Ahmet. "Muhafazakarlık-Liberalizm Sarkacında 'İnformel' Bir Demokrat: Turgut Özal'dan kalan" [An "Informal" Democrat on a Pendulum of Liberalism and Conservatism: The Legacy of Turgut Ozal]. *Muhafazakar Düşünce*, no. 55 (2018): 39–57.

Yılmaz, Nail and Bayram, Ahmet Kemal. "Taksim Gezi Parkı Olayları ve Bir Muhalefet Ögesi Olarak Aleviler" [Taksim Gezi Park Issues and Alevis as an Element of Opposition]. *Marmara Üniversitesi Siyasal Bilimler Dergisi* 4, no. 1 (2016): 1–21.

Yılmaz, Nuh. "İslamcılık, AKP ve Siyaset" [Islamism, AKP and Politics]. In *Modern Türkiye'de Siyasi Düşünce: İslamcılık Vol. 6* [Political Thinking in Modern Turkey: Islamism Vol. 6], edited by Yasin Aktay, Murat Gültekingil and Tanıl Bora, 604–620. İstanbul: Iletisim Yayinlari, 2005.

Zakariyya, Fouad. *Myth and Reality in the Contemporary Islamist Movement.* London: Pluto Press, 2005.

Zengin, Mahmut. "Türkiye'de Cumhuriyet Dönemi Eğitim Politikalarinin Din Dersi Öğretim Programlarina Etkileri" [The Effects of Educational Policies on Religious Courses Curriculums in Republic Period in Turkey]. *Journal of Sakarya University Faculty of Theology* 19, no. 36 (2017): 121–122.

Zuckerman, Harriet. "Interviewing an Ultra-Elite." *Public Opinion Quarterly* 36, no. 2 (1972): 159–175.

Zürcher, Erik Jan. *Political Opposition in the Early Turkish Republic: The Progressive Republican Party 1924–1925.* Leiden: Brill, 1991.

Zürcher, Erik Jan. *Turkey: A Modern History.* London: I.B. Tauris, 1998a.

Zürcher, Erik Jan. "Kemalist Düşüncenin Osmanlı Kaynakları" [The Ottoman Sources of the Kemalist Thinking]. In *Modern Türkiye'de Siyasî Düşünce: Kemalizm Vol: 2* [Political Thinking in Modern Turkey: Kemalism], edited by Ahmet Insel, 44–56. İstanbul: İletişim Yayınları, 2001.

Zürcher, Erik Jan, Hans van der Linden and Netherlands Scientific Council for Government Policy. *The European Union, Turkey and Islam*. Amsterdam: Amsterdam University Press, 2004.

INDEX

0–9

1960 coup, 38, 114, 192
1980 coup, 38, 45, 56, 88, 114, 115, 144, 147, 155, 158, 182, 202.
  See also September 12, 1980
July 15 coup attempt, 78, 108
27 April e-memorandum, 80, 81, 184
February 28 coup, 49, 57, 59, 116, 150, 153, 157, 158, 161, 163.
  See also post-modern coup
4+4+4 educational reform, 151, 158
2002 elections, 63, 67, 68, 120, 150
1971 military declaration, 80, 147.
  See also March 12, 1971

A

Adil Düzen (Just Order), 44, 70
Adnan Menderes, 35, 37, 42
Advisory Council for Human Rights, 183
Akinci Air Base, 90
Alevis
  Alevi communities, 183, 193, 196, 197, 199, 225

Alevi issue, 196, 198–200
Alevism, 182, 193, 194, 197, 201, 203, 212, 215
Alevi Zazas, 195, 213
alternative, 2, 5–7, 36, 39, 41, 44, 48, 50, 68, 71, 96, 142, 152, 153, 156, 158, 159, 183, 213
  alternative political stand, 2, 39
  alternative proposal, 6, 34, 44
alternative modernities, 14, 15
An-Naim, Abdullahi, 7
anti-capitalist Muslims, 58
anti-Kemalist, 6, 29, 54, 60, 79, 111, 196
anti-secular, 7, 34, 37, 47, 62, 63, 93, 105, 132
anti-secularism, 120, 124, 132, 154, 157, 165
anti-secularist, 9, 83, 132, 220
Arab uprising, 72, 102, 223
Arınç, Bülent, 18, 19, 63, 79, 80, 82, 83, 99, 100, 104, 105, 137, 156, 173, 198, 199, 202, 214, 215
Armenian issue, 190

© The Editor(s) (if applicable) and The Author(s), under exclusive
license to Springer Nature Switzerland AG 2022
P. Kandemir, *The JDP and Making the Post-Kemalist Secularism in Turkey*, https://doi.org/10.1007/978-3-031-07605-3

271

272 INDEX

Ataturk, Mustafa Kemal
  Ataturkism, 35
  Atatürk's Mausoleum, 60, 113
  Commendar in Chief, 35
  Eternal Chief, 35
  Kemalism, 35
  National Chief, 35
  Teacher in Chief, 35
atheism, 72, 182, 228
authoritarianism, 2, 34, 46, 48, 53,
    66, 74, 77, 113, 158, 223

B
Batmaz, Kemal, 90
Bayar, Celal, 35, 36, 54
Bayat, Asef, 8, 9
Baykal, Deniz, 184
bourgeoisie, 30, 95, 129

C
Caliphate, 33, 34
Casanova, Jose, 4, 5, 21, 22
cemaat, 85
Cemevi, 199, 202, 203
centre-periphery, 225
  centre-periphery polarity, 5
  Kemalist centre, 29, 70, 159
centre-right, 1, 2, 18, 20, 29, 30, 34,
    37, 39, 42, 43, 49–51, 60, 64,
    68, 70, 96, 112, 148, 154, 181,
    183, 192, 203, 219, 222, 227
changing forms of piety, 6, 129, 220
Christian Democrats, 192
Cinar, Alev, 140
civil initiatives, 41
civil-military relations, 2, 7, 38, 48,
    79, 81, 85, 88, 94, 96, 151
civil religion, 33, 53
civil society, 41, 66, 80, 129, 150
classical Modernisation theory, 12

coalition, 2, 20, 30, 40, 44–46, 48,
    60, 63, 64, 71, 86, 87, 92, 96,
    147, 184, 219, 226
co-efficient system, 151, 224
cold war, 9, 38
Colonialism, 50
competing secularism(s), 2, 226
compulsory religion course, 5
conservatism, 65, 67, 68, 92, 151,
    163, 164
conservative democracy, 9, 59, 64–68,
    71, 99
constitution
  constitutional change, 11, 88, 126
  Constitutional Court, 5, 22, 44–46,
    48, 63, 64, 81–83, 95, 115,
    119, 124, 125, 138, 184, 190
  constitutional referendum, 2, 6, 16,
    78, 87, 88, 96, 107, 150, 158
Constructivist, 152
contemporary Turkey, 2, 10, 11, 73,
    78, 132, 133, 144, 163, 204,
    220, 221, 224, 226
Copenhagen criteria(s), 67
Council of Higher Education (YÖK),
    115, 123, 149, 158
coup, 5, 7, 11, 20, 37–39, 44–49, 80,
    85, 86, 88, 90–92, 98, 103, 108,
    116, 119, 124, 144, 147, 151.
    See also military intervention
culture
  cultural hegemony, 4, 31, 41
  cultural orientations, 12, 165
  cultural values, 219
Cumhuriyet Gazetesi, 19, 47
curriculum, 5, 36, 76, 143, 145,
    150–152, 155–157, 161, 170,
    174, 186, 189, 201, 202, 224,
    225

D
Daesh, 91

INDEX 273

Davison, Andrew, 21
Davutoğlu, Ahmet, 19, 63
Decision of 367, 81, 84
decline in religiosity, 11, 221. *See also*
    decline in spirituality
decline in spirituality, 4
decline of religion, 12, 14
Dede, 179, 194, 196, 197, 202
Demirel, Süleyman, 43
democracy
    democratic, 2, 4, 9, 10, 22, 29, 31,
        36–38, 44, 48, 49, 63, 65, 70,
        77–79, 81, 83, 85–88, 90–92,
        95, 97, 119, 125, 152, 183,
        203, 219, 220, 226
    democratisation, 2, 7, 10, 64, 79,
        86, 88–90, 92, 224, 225
    non-democratic, 31, 84
    semi-democratic, 31
democratic elections, 1, 2, 10, 29,
    36–38, 48, 63
Democratic Opening, 90
Democratisation Package, 87–89,
    111, 112, 126, 151, 184
Democratic Party (DP), 2, 30, 35–37,
    50, 51, 54, 70, 96, 112, 114,
    146, 147, 180, 183, 192, 222
Dersim massacre, 179, 182, 204, 225
desecularisation, 12, 13, 196
developmentalism, 69
Development and Democracy
    Programme, 66
dichotomy, 8, 50, 51, 112, 148, 152
    Islam-secularism dichotomy, 7, 15,
    222
different form(s) of secularism, 13,
    223
different segments of society, 60, 62,
    89, 180, 227
diversification of religiosity, 14. *See*
    also changing forms of piety

diversification of secularism, 10, 97,
    226
diversity, 66, 178
Diyanet İsleri BaskanlııDiyanet İşleri
    BaşkanlııDiyanet İşleri Başkanlığı
    (Directorate of Religious Affairs),
    5, 33, 73, 153, 154, 194
dominant party, 63, 220
Dressler, Marcus, 207

E
early Republican period, 1, 29, 31,
    74, 111–114, 143, 144, 178, 179
early Republican years, 1, 29, 31, 74,
    111–114, 143, 144, 178, 179
İnönü, Ismet, 31
Ecevit, Bülent, 29, 38, 44, 51, 117
economic liberalisation, 6, 10, 39
education, 5, 10, 17, 20, 32, 33, 40,
    43, 50, 67, 76, 86, 89, 114, 117,
    119, 124, 125, 128, 129, 136,
    143–161, 163–167, 169, 172,
    177, 189, 190, 200, 201, 203,
    224, 225
Eğitim-Birsen, 152
Eğitim-sen, 152
Egypt, 47, 72, 92, 223
eight years of uninterrupted
    education, 148
Eisenstadt, S.N., 3, 7, 12, 13, 16, 21,
    23, 25, 65, 101, 130, 133, 142,
    217, 221
election results, 46, 63, 180, 213
election(s), 1, 2, 10, 29, 36–39,
    44–46, 48, 50, 55, 61–63, 66,
    68, 75, 79–82, 92, 93, 96, 98,
    101, 103, 115–117, 120, 122,
    123, 125–128, 146, 148, 150,
    157, 165, 173, 190, 195, 196,
    220, 221, 224, 226, 227. *See also*
    democratic elections
elite(s)

274 INDEX

hybrid elite, 18
political elite, 18, 73
ultra-elite, 18
Enlightenment, 12
Erbakan, Necmettin, 30, 42–48, 51,
  56, 59, 63, 92, 147
Erdoğan, Recep Tayyip, 9, 18, 42, 43,
  48, 51, 59–63, 65, 68, 70–72,
  79, 80, 83, 87–89, 91–94,
  96–99, 101, 102, 118–121, 123,
  124, 131, 137, 159, 160, 170,
  174, 184, 188, 190–193, 197,
  203, 204, 222–224
  Erdoğan's charisma, 92, 93
  Erdoğan's leadership, 63, 92, 93
Ergenekon, 84, 86, 96, 106, 188, 196
EU membership, 7, 151, 177
Eurocentric, 12
European Court of Human Right
  (ECHR), 173
European Court of Human Rights
  (ECHR), 119, 130, 156, 200,
  201
European cultural norms, 31
European Union (EU), 7, 10, 19, 67,
  68, 73, 78, 79, 88, 127, 150,
  151, 177, 185, 190, 191, 196,
  200, 205
EU accession, 10, 79, 140, 185,
  205. See also EU membership
Evren, Kenan, 38, 115, 147
Ezan (call to prayer)
  Arabic call to prayer, 33, 36

F
feminist, 113
five pillars of Islam, 194, 213
formative years, 3. See also early
  Republican period
freedom of religion/religious
  expression, 42, 71, 72, 87, 95,

133, 154, 155, 166, 186, 190,
  198, 204, 220, 222
French Revolution, 32

G
Genar, 19, 128, 159
gender-segregated school, 116
General Directorate for Foundations
  (Vakıflar Genel Müdürlüğü), 194
Gezi Protests, 78, 90
ghetto, 122, 131, 224
Gökalp, Ziya, 62
Gole, Nilufer, 133, 135
Green capital, 49, 58
guardianship of Kemalist
  establishment on secularism, 11
guardians of the regime, 30
Gül, Abdullah, 63, 79–81, 83, 84, 93
Gülen, Fethullah
  FETO, 85, 86, 90, 188
  Gulenist, 90
Gül, Hayrunnisa, 121, 123
Günaltay, Şemsettin, 146

H
Habermas, Jurgen, 13, 16, 26, 27,
  89, 101, 108, 134, 142
Hajj (Pilgrimage), 39, 126, 213
Halk Evleri (People's Houses), 36
Halki Seminary, 190
Head of General Staff, 80
headscarf, 17, 20, 67, 69, 79, 82, 89,
  93, 94, 111–129, 131–134, 147,
  150, 160, 163, 223, 224, 227
headscarf ban, 7, 89, 111, 112, 115,
  116, 118–123, 126–128, 130,
  137, 139, 144, 163, 223
headscarf, Islamic, 67, 93. See also veil
headscarved woman, 114
hegemonic discourse, 5

INDEX 275

hegemonic ideology, 5, 30, 97. *See also* Kemalism
historical experience(s), 3, 12, 130
historical realities, 3, 10, 144, 222
Holyoake, Jacob, 3, 21
homogenisation of society, 4
human rights, 9, 11, 49, 66, 67, 88, 94, 112, 120, 127, 133, 134, 140, 190, 223
Hürriyet (Gazetesi), 19, 47

I
ideal citizen, 143, 151, 178, 181, 183. *See also* loyal citizen; respected citizen
ideology, 1, 5, 6, 8, 12, 15, 20, 31, 32, 35, 37–39, 42–44, 59, 64, 67, 71, 78, 92, 124, 143, 151, 159, 177–179, 181, 182, 187, 227
İhsanoglu, Ekmelettin, 93
illegal implementations, 133
Imam Hatip Schools (IHSs), 20, 36, 45, 61, 82, 94, 144, 146–151, 157–167, 174, 224
İmamoğlu, Ekrem, 48, 93, 226
İnce, Muharrem, 127
Independent Industrialists and Businessmen Association (MUSIAD), 41, 49, 58
İnönü, Ismet, 31
Iranian revolution, 45, 61
Reza Shah, 50
irreligiousness, 220
Islam
Islamic morality, 9. *See also* Islamic ethical norms
Prophet Muhammad, 156, 194, 224
Sharia law, 8, 32, 76
Islamic
Islamic agenda, 47, 99

Islamic movement, 40, 45
Islamic reactionary activities, 118
Islamic *tariqas*, 47
Islamic ethical norms, 44
Islamism, 6, 7–9, 38, 43, 45–47, 49–51, 56, 64, 66–68, 93, 111, 144, 148, 152, 178, 223, 226. *See also* political Islamism
Islamisation, 7, 10, 23, 95, 129, 144, 145, 152, 156, 157, 160, 224
Islamist
Islamist intentions, 47
Islam-sympathetic, 8, 64
moderate Islamist, 8
new Islamist, 8, 9, 64
post-Islamist, 8, 9, 64
pro-Islamist, 43, 56
reactionary Islamist, 34
transformed Islamist, 8, 9
Istanbul Municipality, 191
Istanbul University, 116

J
Jacobin, 5, 33, 124
JDP's secularism, 17, 20, 73, 164, 190, 198, 222, 224
Jerusalem Night, 47
Justice and Development Party (JDP)
2002 election victory, 120, 150
closure case, 11, 78, 82–84, 120, 125, 131, 184
conservative democracy, 9, 59, 64–68, 71, 99
Erdoğan, Recep Tayyip, 9, 18, 43, 48, 59–61, 63, 65, 68, 70, 71, 80, 83, 87–89, 91–94, 96, 118–121, 123, 131, 159, 160, 184, 191, 192, 197, 203, 222–224

276 INDEX

K

Kavakcı, Merve, 113, 117, 118, 126
Kılıçdaroğlu, Kemal, 127, 165, 176, 196
Kemalism, 1, 2, 5–7, 15, 31–37, 40, 41, 45–49, 51, 59, 68, 81, 82, 89, 96, 112, 114, 124, 128, 135, 154, 169, 176, 178, 181, 183, 195, 198, 199, 221
  sacralisation of Kemalism, 3
  six arrows of Kemalism, 31
Kemalist
  anti-Kemalist, 6, 29, 54, 60, 79, 111, 196
  Kemalist bloc, 41, 49, 82, 183
  Kemalist civilians, 90
  Kemalist elites, 4, 6, 29, 33, 34, 36, 37, 41, 97, 114, 129, 144, 160, 205, 220, 226
  Kemalist establishment, 1, 2, 5, 6, 11, 29, 41, 42, 44, 46, 48, 64, 68, 81, 82, 87, 94, 112, 120, 123, 124, 128, 148, 150, 153, 161, 183, 223, 228
  Kemalist hegemony, 2, 120
  Kemalist modernisation, 14, 15, 32, 33, 112, 179
  Kemalist order, 87
  Kemalist reforms, 1, 34, 36, 112, 195, 221
  Kemalist secularism, 2–5, 7, 10, 11, 14, 16, 19, 20, 29–39, 45, 51, 60, 72, 73, 76, 78, 89, 97, 111–113, 115, 125, 143, 145, 149, 150, 152, 169, 178, 181, 182, 189, 196, 198, 219, 221, 222, 226
  non-Kemalist, 2, 5, 16, 17, 19, 29, 30, 37, 40, 47, 50, 51, 59, 60, 71, 84–86, 94, 96, 111, 112, 114, 115, 133, 227
  Kemalist-owned media, 121

Keyman, Fuat, 20, 22, 27, 55, 98
Konda, 19, 69, 75, 77, 100, 103, 135, 140, 141, 165, 171, 172, 176, 194, 195, 214
Köy Enstituleri (Village Institutes), 36
Kubilay, 34
Kurdish Opening, 196
Kurdish Separatism, 38
Kurds, 5, 62, 89, 90, 96, 179–181, 194, 227, 228

L

Law on Protection of Atatürk, 37
leftist, 130, 147, 181, 182
liberalism, 42
  economic liberalism, 2, 41, 59, 66, 219. *See also* open market
  liberal economic policies, 10. *See also* economic liberalisation
  liberalisation, 2, 6, 7, 10, 39, 40, 42, 49, 129, 151, 154, 166, 224
  liberal secularism, 75, 163
  political liberalism, 39
Libya, 47, 72
life of Prophet Muhammad, 156, 224
limited state, 39
loyal citizen, 181

M

March 12, 1971, 38
Mardin, Serif, 5, 14, 15, 22, 26, 29, 32, 36, 51, 52, 54, 70, 146, 168
mass party, 45, 65
medrese (religious school), 33, 145
Menemen Incident, 34
middle class, 10, 95, 129, 166
military, 1, 5, 6, 10, 11, 31, 34, 37–39, 44, 45, 47–49, 79–81, 84–86, 88, 91, 94, 115, 118–120, 125, 132, 144,

147–149, 151, 158, 164, 169, 179, 184, 202, 219
military intervention, 6, 38, 120
military pressure, 48
millet system, 4, 180
Milli Görüş (National outlook Movement), 43
Milli irade (popular will), 35
Ministry of National Education, 116, 146, 150, 156, 189
minority/minorities
  ethnic minorities, 177, 184
  religious minorities, 177, 184
  sectarian minorities, 17, 20, 177, 178, 204, 205
moderate, 8, 11, 44, 105, 128, 134, 220, 221
Moderate Kemalist secularism, 10, 16
modern, 4, 9, 12, 13, 26, 30, 31, 45, 77, 111, 113, 114, 118, 128, 129, 131, 144, 165, 166, 186, 205, 220, 221, 223
modernisation, 3, 7, 11, 12, 14, 15, 20, 26, 32, 50, 71, 113, 148, 177, 179
  in European style, 31
  modernisation in non-western societies, 14
modernism
  alternative modernities, 14, 15
  classical modernism, 11
  in non-western form, 15
  multiple modernities, 3, 8, 12, 15, 16, 19, 65, 71, 130, 133, 134, 142, 166, 205, 221
  self-corrected modernism, 220
modernities
  alternative modernities, 14, 15
  extra modernity, 15
  local modernities, 14, 15
monopoly, 33
  (in) monopoly of Kemalist(s), 40

(in) state monopoly, 40, 41, 75, 86, 94
multi-party democracy, 2, 29, 34, 35, 43, 54. *See also* multi-party era; multi-party system
multi-party era, 144, 179, 180, 192
multi-party system, 59, 146
multiple modernities, 3, 8, 11, 12, 15, 16, 19, 65, 71, 130, 133, 134, 166, 205, 221
multiple secularism, 11, 13, 16, 130, 132, 199, 205, 228
Muslim
  Muslim democrat, 9, 64
  Muslim Turks, 178
  Muslim world, 9, 44, 45, 50, 72

N
national curriculum, 5
nationalism, 1, 6, 8, 31, 68, 143, 151, 178–180, 183, 187, 189, 219
  Kurdish nationalism, 64, 96, 124, 159
  Turkish nationalism, 2, 15, 33, 64, 96
National Resistance Movement, 178
National Security Council, 48, 116, 148, 183
National Security Course, 151
National Unity and Brotherhood Project, 87
New Age spirituality, 14
New Islamism, 8, 9, 58
new right, 39
New Turkey, 1, 6, 60, 71, 88, 192, 222
Non-Kemalism, 2, 16, 19, 29, 37, 51, 71, 84, 86, 94, 111, 133, 27
Non-Muslim minorities
  Armenian-Christians, 179
  Greek-Christians, 179
  Jewish-Turks, 179

278 INDEX

non-religious, 13, 76, 145
non-Western, 11, 13, 15, 50
normalisation, 10, 133, 164

O
Oksuz, Adil, 91
Olcok, Erol, 91, 97
old regime, 1
open market, 42
opinion pools, 73
Orientalism, 7
Ottoman Empire
  collapse of the Ottoman Empire, 30
  Ottoman Caliphate, 33
  Ottoman-Islamic tradition, 32
  Ottoman reformists, 31, 32. *See also*
    Young Turks
Özal, Semra, 40
Özal, Turgut
  ANAP, 30, 39, 40, 42, 51, 59,
    192, 203
  liberal economy, 59
  limited state, 39
  neo-liberal policies, 41, 49
  open market, 42
  privatisation and private sector, 40
  tripod of values, 42
  Turkey's transition to a capitalist
    system, 41

P
patriotism, 68, 91, 92, 180
periphery, 5, 7, 19, 30, 36, 41, 43,
    48, 69, 70, 114, 118, 127, 134,
    162, 164, 222, 228
  non-Kemalist periphery, 5
  peripheral force, 70
persuasion rooms, 116, 117
piety, 5, 6, 11, 129, 165, 220
pious, 13, 39, 40, 42, 49, 67, 68, 71,
    77–79, 93, 94, 106, 111, 114,

115, 129, 147, 148, 160, 161,
    163–166, 195, 222–228
pious lifestyles, 220, 225
PKK, 91
pluralism, 66, 71
political ban, 48, 68, 83
political battlefield, 111, 133
political Islamism, 8, 43
political parties
  Adalet Partisi (AP), 43
  Adalet ve Kalkinma Partisi (JDP),
    1–3, 6–11, 15, 17–20, 23, 30,
    37, 41, 44, 45, 47, 49–51,
    55–57, 59, 60, 63–98,
    100–102, 105, 106, 108, 111,
    112, 117, 119–128, 130–133,
    135, 140, 141, 144, 150–162,
    164–166, 170, 177, 178,
    183–192, 195–205, 217,
    219–228
  Anavatan Partisi (ANAP), 2, 30,
    39, 40, 42, 51, 59, 64, 70, 96,
    112, 148, 183, 192, 203, 222
  Democrat Parti (DP), 2, 30, 35–37,
    39, 40, 50, 51, 54, 70, 96,
    112, 114, 146, 147, 180, 183,
    192, 219, 222
  Dogru Yol Partisi (DYP), 42, 46,
    192
  Fazilet Partisi, 44, 62, 63, 98
  Halklarin Demokratik Partisi
    (HDP), 19, 75, 90–92, 124,
    132, 138, 157, 159, 192,
    195–197, 224
  Millet Partisi, 37
  Milli Nizam Partisi (MNP), 43
  Milli Selamet Partisi, 44
  Milliyetci Hareket Partisi (MHP),
    81, 91, 92, 123, 124, 127,
    132, 141, 151, 157, 159, 184,
    185, 209

Refah Partisi (RP), 23, 47, 48, 58, 62, 64, 115, 117
Saadet Partisi (SP), 44, 49, 223, 226
political system, 9, 12, 29, 54, 59
political transformation, 2, 95
populism, 1, 31, 39, 66
positivism, 32, 83, 152
post-Enlightenment world, 13
post-Islamism, 8, 9, 24, 49, 58, 98, 100, 101
post-Kemalism, 14, 16, 20, 205
Post-Kemalist literature, 3, 15, 19, 221
Post-Kemalist secularism, 10, 11, 15–17, 59, 72, 76, 77, 111, 132, 145, 152, 165, 177, 186, 191, 192, 202, 203, 205, 221–223, 225–227
post-modern, 48, 144
post-modern coup, 48, 144
post-secularism
    Habermasian post-secular societies, 16
    post-secular, 14, 71, 73, 134, 145, 157
    post-secular condition, 14
    post-secular society, 13, 89, 93
power balance within the state, 85, 96, 220
power sharing, 37, 41, 84, 144
presidential elections, 63, 81, 93, 98, 123
private sphere, 111, 114
privileged minority, 84
Prophet Muhammad, 156, 194, 224
pro-Western, 4, 9
psychological pressure, 116
public sphere, 10, 29, 60, 73, 91, 102, 112, 117, 128, 129, 134, 151, 159, 178, 179, 187, 191, 198–200, 202, 204, 223, 225, 228

Q
Quran Courses, 39, 145, 146, 148, 150, 151, 153, 154, 156, 165, 224

R
radical, 5–7, 9, 10, 16, 33, 65, 66, 85, 87, 89, 93, 121, 127, 163, 179, 183, 191, 193, 226
radical left, 38, 182, 195
raproachment, 93
rationalism, 32
    rationalist, 219
reactionary Islamist, 34
referandum, 97
reformist, 7, 32, 63, 90
refugee, 91
re-imagined Islam, 179
religion, 2, 3–5, 7, 10–17, 32, 33, 36, 38–40, 42, 49, 60, 65–67, 71–77, 83, 87, 92, 96, 103, 111, 112, 124, 133, 134, 144–146, 151, 153–157, 159–161, 165, 166, 178, 179, 181, 186, 189, 191, 193, 198, 199, 201–205, 219, 222–225. See also spirituality
Christian, 72, 84, 127, 186, 187
Jewish, 72, 184, 186, 188
Muslim, 4, 5, 7–9, 12, 20, 31, 38, 40, 44–46, 49, 50, 62, 64, 67, 72, 74, 76–79, 89, 93, 94, 96, 97, 115, 121, 129–131, 143, 145, 147, 155, 160, 161, 163–165, 178–180, 183, 184, 186–189, 191, 194, 195, 197, 198, 204, 213, 219, 223–228
religion-friendly, 202, 224
religion-state, 222

280 INDEX

religiosity, 11, 12, 14, 67, 68, 96,
143, 144, 154, 155, 165, 191,
221, 224, 225
religious, 1, 3, 4, 7, 8, 10, 13, 14,
16–20, 30–34, 36, 38–40, 43,
47, 49, 50, 61, 62, 67, 71–79,
86, 89, 93–96, 111, 114, 120,
122, 124, 125, 127, 132, 133,
143–155, 157, 159, 160,
163–166
non-religious, 13, 76, 145, 173
religious communities, 186
religious education, 10, 76, 143–146,
148, 150, 151, 153, 154, 157,
161, 165, 166, 169, 172, 177,
201, 224
religious marriage ceremony, 195
religious muslims, 227. *See also* pious
Republicanism, 1, 31
Republican People's Party (RPP)
Kılıçdaroğlu, Kemal, 127, 165, 196
RPP's 1931 convention, 30
RPP's 1948 Congress, 146
Republican Rallies, 78–80, 82, 103,
122
respected citizen, 77, 166
respect for religious belief, 29, 38
resurgence of religion, 14, 36, 43,
183. *See also* revival of religion
revival of religion, 11–13
routinisation of charisma, 93
ruling elites, 5, 219. *See also* Kemalist,
Kemalist elites; secular elites,
secular elite class

S
sacralisation of Atatürk image, 42
sacralisation of Kemalism, 3. *See also*
sacralisation of Atatürk image
sacralisation of secularism, 34
Savas, Vural, 48
sectarianism

sectarian minorities, 17, 20, 177,
178, 204, 205
secular
secular political movement, 219
semi-secular (state), 4
ultra-secular, 4
secular elites, 219
secular elite class, 4
secularisation
macro-secularisation, 12
meso-secularisation, 12
micro-secularisation, 12
secularism
Assertive secularism, 22
liberal secularism, 75, 163
multiple secularism, 11, 13, 16,
130, 132, 199, 205, 228
Post-Kemalist secularism, 10, 11,
15–17, 59, 72, 76, 77, 87,
111, 125, 132, 145, 152, 153,
155, 157, 165, 177, 186, 191,
192, 202, 203, 205, 221–223,
225–227. *See also* JDP's
secularism
post-secularism, 13, 73, 76, 166
real secularism, 220
secularism proposal, 7, 224
secularity, 13
securityness of secularity, 48
self-corrected
self-corrected modernism, 220
semi-secular state, 4
separation of state and religion, 4. *See
also* secularism
September 12, 1980, 38
Serbest Cumhuriyet Fırkası, 34
seyyid, 179
Sezer, Ahmet Necdet, 82, 121
Sharia, 77
Sharia law, 8, 32, 76
Sheik Said Rebellion, 34

INDEX   281

single party, 5, 46, 52. *See also* single-party era, single-party regime
single-party era, 29, 53, 144, 149
single-party regime, 29, 35
six arrows of Kemalism, 31
Siyer, 173. *See also* life of Prophet Muhammad
social actions, 12
social contract, 2, 10, 198
social democrat, 39, 40
socially moralist, 219
social structure, 12, 180
spirituality, 4, 14
state agenda, 4
state control, 31, 40, 153, 189
  over economy, 10
  over religion, 4, 36, 38
State of Emergency, 91
state-religion, 3, 7, 20, 29, 33
  state-religion relations, 4, 12
statism, 1, 2, 6, 31, 114. *See also* statist economy
statist economy, 219
status quo, 30, 78, 79, 81, 82, 84, 86, 92, 143, 201
student oath, 151, 184, 208
Sultan Abdulhamid, 32
Sunni Islam, 4, 38, 46, 76, 154, 181
  Hanafi, 179
Sunni Zazas, 195. *See also* Alevi Zazas
supra-identity, 183
supra-sectarian, 156
Suvanto, Pekka, 65, 99
Syriac Ortodox, 154, 187, 189–192
Syrian Civil War, 78, 90, 92

T
Taksim Mosque, 48
tariqas, 47
Taylor, Charles, 4, 21, 25, 72, 101

tekke (dervish lodges), 33, 36, 179
Terakki Perver Cumhuriyet Fırkası, 34
terrorist attacks, 91
Tesev, 19, 77, 98, 103, 194
Tevhid-i Tedrisat, 145
The Association of Alumni and Sympathisers of the IHSs in Turkey (ONDER), 164
tolerance, 66, 94, 128
top-down reforms, 5, 29, 35, 50
Toprak, Binnaz, 4, 21, 194
tradition, 3, 8, 10, 12, 13, 38, 39, 42, 44, 51, 64–67, 75, 79, 117, 133, 134, 183, 193, 212, 220, 222
tradition and modernity, 12
transformation of secularism, 17, 20, 30, 187
Tunisia, 9, 50, 72
türban, 115, 125, 126, 135. *See also* headscarf
turbe (religious shrines), 33
Turkey's transition to capitalist system, 41
Turkish army, 5, 38, 118, 119
Turkish bureaucracy, 5
Turkish Industry and Business Association (TUSIAD), 41, 49
Turkish Intelligence Service (MIT), 183
Turkish-Islam synthesis, 38, 147, 182
Turkish military, 38, 80, 179, 184. *See also* Turkish army
Turkish modernisation, 32
Turkishness, 38, 184, 188, 206
Turkish Parliament (TBMM), 22, 91, 123, 159
Turkish politics, 1, 2, 9, 35, 37–39, 41–44, 48, 50, 66, 69, 70, 78, 80, 81, 96, 97, 126, 225
Turkish secularism, 3, 14, 16, 20–22, 106. *See also* Kemalist, Kemalist secularism

282 INDEX

tutelage, 48, 75, 81, 82, 84, 86, 87
twenty-first century, 2

U
Ulama, 31
university entrance exam, 82, 116, 149

V
veil, 111, 123, 131, 134, 135, 140. *See also* headscarf; türban
veiled woman, 121, 130, 133, 228. *See also* headscarved woman

W
War of Liberation, 30, 31
Weber, Marx, 11, 92, 93
West, 9, 14, 15, 44, 71, 154

Western, 3, 6, 8, 9, 12, 15, 30, 31, 33, 34, 44, 46, 50, 65, 67, 68, 88, 113, 150, 164, 221, 222
Westernisation, 7, 11, 14, 22, 32, 67, 113
Western civilisation, 31
Western Colonialism, 50
Western experience, 50
Western model, 3, 221
Western secularism, 3
Western-style clothing, 33, 112, 113
Western values, 15, 44, 222
World is bigger than five, 70

Y
Yalçınkaya, Abdurrahman, 82
Yavaş, Mansur, 93, 127
Yenisafak Gazetesi, 19
Yıldırım, Binali, 128, 140, 191
Yılmaz, Mesut, 42
Young Turks, 31, 32

Printed in the United States
by Baker & Taylor Publisher Services